Electoral Rules and Democracy in Latin America

Electoral Rules and Democracy in Latin America

CYNTHIA MCCLINTOCK

OXFORD
UNIVERSITY PRESS

Oxford University Press is a department of the University of Oxford. It furthers
the University's objective of excellence in research, scholarship, and education
by publishing worldwide. Oxford is a registered trade mark of Oxford University
Press in the UK and certain other countries.

Published in the United States of America by Oxford University Press
198 Madison Avenue, New York, NY 10016, United States of America.

© Oxford University Press 2018

All rights reserved. No part of this publication may be reproduced, stored in
a retrieval system, or transmitted, in any form or by any means, without the
prior permission in writing of Oxford University Press, or as expressly permitted
by law, by license, or under terms agreed with the appropriate reproduction
rights organization. Inquiries concerning reproduction outside the scope of the
above should be sent to the Rights Department, Oxford University Press, at the
address above.

You must not circulate this work in any other form
and you must impose this same condition on any acquirer.

Library of Congress Cataloging-in-Publication Data
ISBN 978–0–19–087976–1 (pbk.)
ISBN 978–0–19–087975–4 (hbk.)

For My Family, in All Its Iterations

CONTENTS

Acknowledgments   ix

1. Introduction   1

2. Research Design and Quantitative Analysis   12

3. Why Was Runoff Superior? Theory and Cross-National Evidence   29

4. Plurality: Problems in Honduras, Mexico, Nicaragua, Paraguay, and Venezuela (and the Panama Exception)   65

5. Runoff: Success in Brazil, Chile, the Dominican Republic, El Salvador, and Uruguay   106

6. Runoff Amid a Plethora of Political Parties: Colombia, Ecuador, Guatemala, and Peru   139

7. Runoff: Is a Reduced Threshold Better? Argentina and Costa Rica   175

8. Conclusion and the Future of Presidential-Election Rules   192

Appendices   209
Notes   263
Bibliography   273
Index   295

ACKNOWLEDGMENTS

The road to the completion of this book took many unexpected turns. My colleagues' guidance, my friends' encouragement, and my family's love helped me find my way.

The original inspiration for this book came from a conversation with Arturo Valenzuela about Chile's 1970 election at a conference on presidentialism at Georgetown University in 1989. My interest was reignited during a trip to Venezuela in 2004; to my surprise, the problems of Venezuela's fraught 1993 election were repeatedly raised in interviews. At the same time, my colleague Jim Lebovic and I were co-authoring an article on the correlates of democracy in Latin America and we found that a larger number of political parties was not significant to inferior levels of democracy. The question of presidential-election rules and political parties has also been very salient in Peru, and I gained many insights from stimulating exchanges with wonderful Peruvian and Peruvianist scholars.

At the start, I had expected that the book would be based on statistical analysis worldwide and on four Latin American country cases. However, statistical analysis worldwide was impossible because of the paucity of plurality rules and, as I assessed the trajectory of democracy in countries under plurality and runoff, I realized that, to understand statistical trends, it would be necessary to incorporate virtually all Latin American countries. Also, each country added a unique insight. The project became more ambitious as the "N" for the statistical analysis decreased and the "N" for the country cases increased.

I did not anticipate that the statistical analysis for the book would be as challenging as it was. The statistical skills of my research assistants at George Washington University (GWU) were a *sine qua non*. I am very grateful to Kelly Bauer, Barnett Koven, and Josiah Augustine for their patient responses to my queries and assiduous collection and analysis of data. They all achieved major breakthroughs in the analysis. My GWU colleagues Eric Lawrence and Michael Miller provided expert guidance to us all.

It was a joy to work on the statistical analysis and other parts of this project with Barnett. He was invariably thoughtful and rigorous, providing innumerable data updates and calculations with astounding efficiency and precision. He deserves much more credit than I can provide in this acknowledgment.

I also owe a special thank-you to Aldo F. Ponce. In the summer of 2011, Aldo was at GWU in our Minerva Program for PhD students completing their doctoral dissertations. Aldo was the first to provide a statistical breakthrough—and the last, resolving a perplexing problem in July 2017. Aldo is now a professor at CIDE and I am looking forward to future collaboration with him on electoral rules and political parties in Latin America.

In addition, GWU PhD students made tremendous contributions to various datasets. The collection of the data on pre-election opinion polls was a major effort, and Barnett Koven and Julian Waller were tremendously helpful. Barnett tracked down some of the hardest-to-find poll numbers and Julian gathered data for European countries. The collection of the data on old-timers was also challenging and Julian provided the information for old-timers in European countries. In addition, in the early stages of the project, Amanda Alcorn provided very useful overviews of key issues in elections in numerous countries.

I am also very appreciative of the research assistance of other students. Francisco Hernández, Shana Montrose, Abigail Poe, Adam Schaffer, and Sayre Weir all contributed significantly. Among their many important endeavors, they checked candidates' backgrounds for the data on outsiders and researched smaller parties' endorsements or lack thereof between first rounds and runoffs.

For insights into political dynamics in countries for which my knowledge was limited, I benefited greatly from the help of numerous colleagues who responded to my queries and commented on my drafts. I would especially like to thank Diego Abente (for insights about Paraguay), Paula Alonso (Argentina), Michael Coppedge (Venezuela), David Fleischer (Brazil), Jonathan Hartlyn (Dominican Republic), Adam Isacson (Colombia), Jennifer McCoy (Venezuela), Kevin Middlebrook (Mexico), Stephen B. Kaplan (Argentina), Nazih Richani (Colombia), and Geoff Thale (El Salvador).

Numerous colleagues were also very helpful. Richard Webb provided me with a wonderful office for several months at the Universidad San Martín de Porres, where I greatly benefited from many conversations. The survey on legislators' preferences for runoff versus plurality was only possible through the good graces of Diego Abente (Paraguay), Rafael Fernández de Castro (Mexico), Claudio Fuentes and Gonzalo Alvarez (Chile), and the late Henry Pease (Peru). For data about the number of political parties in particular countries prior to the third wave, information from Fabrice Lehoucq, Mark P. Jones, and Martin Needler was indispensable. Alejandro Moreno aided in the collection of survey data from Mexico. Scott Mainwaring and Aníbal Pérez-Liñán kindly made datasets from their research available to me.

I am grateful for valuable comments about my research from various scholarly venues. My colleagues at the GWU Comparative Politics Workshop in 2011 provided outstanding recommendations. Feedback from colleagues at the American Political Science Association (APSA) in 2006, 2007, 2013, and 2016 was also very helpful. The insights of Michelle Taylor-Robinson and Juan Pablo Luna at an APSA panel in 2016 were particularly valuable.

All of this was made possible by the generous support of a Woodrow Wilson International Center for Scholars Fellowship in 2006–2007 and from the Department of Political Science at George Washington University during the summers of 2008 through 2017. The Director of the Latin America Program at the Center, Cynthia Arnson, was not only a wonderful colleague but became a good friend. The Assistant Director, José Raúl Perales, was a joy to work with—exceptionally generous with his time and insights.

This book project was the longest and, in numerous respects, the most challenging of my career. In some difficult moments, the interest and enthusiasm for the project expressed by friends, such as my Harvard College classmate John Endicott and my high-school classmate Devie Meade, were vital. Throughout, I was very fortunate to have enjoyed the love and support of my family. My daughter, Alicia, is not only bright, beautiful, talented, and vibrant, but—time and again—gets me out of technology crises. Throughout my life, my sister Jeannette and my brother Kelly have been there for me, providing warmth and wisdom. My cousin Marion inspires me to ask the biggest questions about the world and about life. My great friend Gary Wright grounds me, guides me, and reminds me what is most important. My *comadre* (mother of one's godchild) Lee Evans has been my best friend since fifth grade; she is passionate and compassionate, and we share the details of our lives, good and bad. By the age of twenty-one, my godson James Evans was providing excellent life counsel and insights. Lee's lovely, kind daughter Daphne lives in Washington and I enjoy nothing more than a dinner with Daphne and Alicia. My *comadre* Justina Bedón is the model of Peruvian *cariño* (affection) and I am forever happy that she risked naming me, a *gringa* (foreigner), as the godmother to her wonderful sons, Toño and Arturo. And, with the extraordinarily thoughtful, capable, fun, and level-headed Arturo has come his marvelous family, including Heli, Elizabeth, and Erich. I am very fortunate indeed.

Electoral Rules and Democracy in Latin America

1

Introduction

The Puzzle

In 1973, a savage military coup overthrew the elected president of Chile, Salvador Allende. Founded in 1833 and undergoing only two brief interruptions, Chile's democracy had been one of the oldest in the world. The military coup took almost three thousand lives and initiated more than sixteen years of dictatorial rule. Among the explanations for the coup was that the Allende government had "started out with a serious birth defect" (Smith, 2005: 159). In Chile's 1970 election, there were three major political blocs—one at the left, a second at the center, and a third at the right; Allende, the candidate at the left, was elected with only 36.6% of the vote. Allende's margin was narrow; the candidate at the right tallied 35.3% and the candidate at the center, 28.1%. The "birth defect" of the Allende government was election through plurality (or, first-past-the-post—in other words, victory to the candidate with the most votes, even if not a majority of the votes). Although Chile's constitution provided that, if no candidate won a majority, the president would be chosen between the top two vote-getters by the legislature, the tradition was that the candidate with the most votes would be approved, and this tradition was maintained in 1970.

Election with a small plurality was a factor in military coups elsewhere in Latin America. In Brazil in 1955, the winner secured only 36% of the vote; prominent rightists called the election invalid and the winner was inaugurated only after a coup against an acting rightist president by pro-democratic military leaders. In Peru in 1962, three candidates tallied more than 25% but not the 33.33% required to avoid the selection of the president by the congress; the subsequent politicking was unscrupulous and a military coup ensued. In Argentina in 1963, the winner had only 32%; in Ecuador in 1968, only 33%; and in Uruguay in 1971, the winner's party had 41%, less than one point more than the runner-up's party. Although these three elections were problematic in numerous respects and military coups were not immediate, the presidents' dubious legitimacy worried political leaders.

Accordingly, when Latin American countries were returning to democracy in the 1970s and 1980s in what is called the third democratic wave, political leaders were considering alternatives to plurality—namely, runoff (a second popular vote between the two leading candidates after the first round). In Latin America prior to the 1970s, runoff was in place only in Costa Rica, but it seemed possible that the rule was one factor in Costa Rica's favorable democratic record. Also, a runoff had been adopted in France in 1958 and its effect appeared positive (Alexander, 2004: 217).

As of 2016, runoff was in use by twelve of the eighteen Latin American countries that held elections.[1] Since 1970, every Latin American nation save Nicaragua in 1987 and Venezuela in 1999 that adopted a new constitution chose runoff.[2] Most (Brazil, Chile, Colombia, the Dominican Republic, Ecuador, El Salvador, Guatemala, Peru, and Uruguay) chose a threshold for victory of 50% plus one vote while others (Argentina and Bolivia, as of 2009) chose a threshold below 50% but above 40%, often depending on the margin of the first-round winner's lead over the runner-up. Five Latin American countries—Honduras, Mexico, Panama, Paraguay, and Venezuela—continued to use plurality. The rule has changed frequently in Nicaragua; between 2000 and 2013, Nicaragua applied a threshold below 40%, and I classify this rule as "qualified plurality" (see Chapter 2).

Indeed, runoff rules are now predominant across the globe. During the 1950s, plurality was used in more than 50% of presidential elections but, during 2000–2011, in less than 30%; concomitantly, during the 1950s, runoff was used in less than 10% but, during 2000–2011, in about 60% (Bormann and Golder, 2013: 360–369). Indeed, the rarity of plurality in other regions of the world is a major reason for the circumscription of this study to Latin America. In 2016, among the countries with presidential systems classified by Freedom House as "electoral democracies," 75% in Latin America, 88% in sub-Saharan Africa, 86% in Europe, and 63% in the Asia-Pacific region used runoff.[3]

As Gabriel Negretto (2013: 2–8) points out, Latin American leaders changed their presidential-election rule in part because of partisan interests and in part because of beliefs that the new rule would work better. To explore these beliefs, I carried out surveys among legislators in several Latin American countries, primarily Chile, Mexico, and Peru (see Appendix 1). In Chile and Peru—two runoff countries—runoff was favored overwhelmingly. But runoff was also favored in Mexico, a plurality country; of the seventy-one Mexican legislators who responded, 44% favored runoff, versus 41% plurality. This result was very similar to a survey of 280 legislators by the Mexican newspaper *Reforma*; in this survey, 53% favored runoff versus 47% plurality.[4] Whereas criticism of runoff was rare in runoff countries, criticism of plurality was common in plurality countries. In Mexico, plurality was criticized by two former presidents—Vicente Fox and Felipe Calderón—and by former presidential candidate Andrés Manuel López Obrador.[5] Criticism of plurality has also been made by former presidents or presidential candidates in Nicaragua, Paraguay, and Venezuela.[6] In Panama, the winner of the 1994 election did not tally 40%; in 1994, a legislative proposal for runoff gained attention and, in

1996, the president included it in a constitutional-reform package.[7] Amid concerns about the 2013 election in Honduras, legislators' debate about adoption of runoff was considerable.[8]

Despite Latin American leaders' enthusiasm about runoff, the vast majority of scholars are skeptical. Their primary argument is that plurality inhibits the proliferation of political parties and, concomitantly, decreases the risks of "outsiders" and executive-legislative gridlock—which can provoke democratic breakdown.

One of the foremost scholars of political institutions, Juan Linz (1994: 21–22), declared that "a number of dysfunctional consequences derive from this method of election [the runoff]" and elaborated on them. Arturo Valenzuela (1993: 8) commented, "The second round does not resolve the problem [of lack of majority support for the president] . . . . What is more, the second ballot may have a counterproductive effect." Jorge I. Domínguez (2003: 371) stated that runoff rules "enhance the unpredictability of presidential elections and encourage divided government." Matthew S. Shugart and John Carey (1992: 213) concurred: "We find the plurality rule appealing because it is more likely than majority runoff to give voters an efficient choice between the candidates of two broad coalitions." Aníbal Pérez-Liñán (2006: 129) argued, "The empirical evidence suggests that both the necessity and convenience of this institution [runoff] can be questioned." After an in-depth study, Mark Jones (1995: 14) concluded, "Unfortunately, despite the superiority of the plurality formula an overwhelming majority of emerging presidential systems have selected the majority runoff formula." Other scholars favoring plurality include John Carey (2003: 14–15), Jonathan Hartlyn (1994b: 46–49), Martín Tanaka (2005: 126–127), and Scott Mainwaring (with Matthew S. Shugart) (1997b: 467–468).

Are these scholars right? Have Latin American leaders made a bad choice? My study is the most rigorous test of the implications of runoff versus plurality for democracy to date.

The Argument

In this book, I argue that runoff is superior for democracy in Latin America. Runoff opens the political arena to newcomers; it lowers barriers to entry into effective competition in the presidential election. But, at the same time, it assures that (a) the president has majority support and, accordingly, legitimacy and (b) the president is not at an ideological extreme. Each of these points and the concepts of legitimacy and ideological moderation are briefly discussed in this chapter and elaborated further in subsequent chapters. The statistical evidence for the superiority of runoff is provided in Chapter 2.

In addition, in Latin America during the third wave, a virtuous circle emerged among the lower barriers to entry, the requirement for majority support, and ideological moderation. During the Cold War, polarization between left and right was intense in many Latin American countries; Marxist parties were common and, amid the Latin American debt crisis in the 1980s and early 1990s, they did not lose their appeal. During the third wave, a key challenge was the incorporation of leftist political leaders into the democratic political arena. By lowering barriers of entry, the democratic process was more respected by parties that were formerly excluded and, with this new respect, parties that were formerly excluded and possibly at ideological extremes were more likely to moderate. For their part, although formerly dominant parties would have preferred higher barriers to entry, they knew that, by definition, an extremist party could not win 50%; they were less likely to panic at the prospect of a victory by a leftist party or another new party and less likely to resort to ugly tactics—again, gaining the respect of the leftist party or other new party. By contrast, in most plurality countries, fraud was more likely to be suspected by leftist parties and was more likely to have been a resort by elites.[9] It is relevant here that scholars such as Ahmed (2013) and Acemoglu and Robinson (2006) have highlighted that elites' fears often influence the adoption of particular electoral rules during transitions to democracy.

Electoral Rules and the Openness of the Political Arena

Runoff opens a presidential election to new parties. The reasons are various. Runoff elections are not one "single-payoff game" but a "two-level game"; they are more complex and uncertain with more opportunities for new parties (Schedler, 2002). A new party is not a "spoiler" party; rather, in the first round, voters can vote sincerely (for the candidate in the entire field whom they prefer), rather than strategically (for the candidate that they think has a good chance to win whom they prefer). This is especially important in Latin America, where pre-election opinion polls are frequently inaccurate and strategic voting can be difficult; whereas plurality requires strategic coordination among opposition parties before the election, runoff allows the first round to be a test of their strength. Further, a new party has a second opportunity in the runoff—if it is the runner-up, to win, but otherwise to have its voice heard, usually through its power of endorsement.

Indeed, as Chapter 3 elaborates, in Latin American presidential elections between 1978 and 2012, a "new party" became a "significant contender" considerably more often under runoff than under plurality. A "new party" was also considerably more likely to become one of the two leading parties in the legislature.

But are lower barriers to entry actually advantageous? Aren't new parties disturbing the party system? Aren't they destabilizing? The answer to the second two questions is: yes. Put slightly differently, "runoff gives greater power to the opposition."[10] By definition, new parties lead to uncertainty and change, which can be "destabilization"—or, "adaptation."

Often, a new party is channeling voters' current concerns and demands. Even if a new party never wins, it can represent sectors of voters who feel excluded. Said public-opinion analyst Marta Lagos, "There is a demand for diversity.... 60% of the people in Chile say that none of the candidates represent their ideas well. There is a real questioning here of what is democracy."[11] Voters have an option by which they can "reject the status quo and still remain within the system" (Morgan, 2011: 258).

In Latin America at the start of the third wave, voters' demands were focused on economic growth and equality. In the 1990s and early 2000s most incumbent parties faced a severe challenge: what is called the "debt crisis." The crisis is dated from 1982, when Mexico announced that it could not service its debt. The International Monetary Fund (IMF) stepped in and demanded that countries shift to market economic policies; the costs were steep. Most Latin American governments tried to negotiate with the IMF but considered the agency hostile and its demands draconian. The result was the "lost decade" of the 1980s and, in some countries as well, "the lost half-decade" of 1998–2002. Many countries, in particular major oil exporters such as Ecuador and Venezuela, were wracked by unemployment and hyperinflation. Between 1980 and 1990, real wages in Latin American urban areas fell by at least 20% (Felix, 1990: 742). For most incumbent parties that had advocated statist intervention, the shift to neoliberalism exacted a huge toll (Lupu, 2014).

In the twenty-first century, voters' concerns were often focused on corruption. Newcomers who emphasized integrity and concern about the environment, such as Marina Silva in Brazil, Marco Enríquez Ominami in Chile, Antanas Mockus in Colombia, and Ottón Solís in Costa Rica, won surprisingly large tallies.

New parties may also be advantageous because, unfortunately, many long-standing parties in Latin America were either never very democratic or gradually became undemocratic. In Latin America, as in other regions where authoritarian regimes were common in the past, some long-standing parties harbor significant "authoritarian legacies" (Hicken and Martínez Kuhonta, 2011: 588). Also, some entrenched parties are "cartel" parties; intertwined with the state, they gain power over electoral laws and machinery and, when there are two long-standing parties, collude to ensure that at least one of them wins (Katz and Mair, 2009). Parties are not bridges between state and society but castles with vast moats that protect their lords from the masses. Further, the phenomenon of *"caudillismo (strongmen)"* continues; incumbents and former presidents want to "die with their boots on" and refuse to retire (Corrales, 2008).

Yet, these entrenched parties and leaders have significant advantages. This is the case by definition for cartel parties; also, by implication, parties harboring authoritarian legacies are more likely to skew electoral institutions in their favor. Old-timer leaders also enjoy advantages merely as a result of their longevity. They have loyal campaign donors and friends in important places such as the courts and the media. They have name recognition. There may be a cultural bias in favor of known quantities; a common Latin American saying about politicians is "Better the bad one we know than the good one we don't."

Further, under plurality, an entrenched party is unlikely to be defeated unless opposition parties achieve strategic coordination—usually, unless they ally. However, strategic coordination is often very difficult. Among the well-known obstacles are leaders' ambition and rivalry, ideological differences, and other political cleavages in the country. An obstacle that has not been previously highlighted but is very evident in Latin America during the third wave is inaccurate opinion polls.

None of this, however, is to suggest that a new party is not also problematic. By definition, a new party is not institutionalized. Almost always, it lacks organization and deep roots in society. Usually, leadership is key; in other words, the "party" is personalistic. The "party" is the candidates' friends. When personalistic parties win, they lack both a team of experienced professional politicians and a network of militants with ties to the grassroots. Further, leaders without institutionalized parties are prone to making dramatic, abrupt policy shifts that alienate their supporters.

These concerns are significant—and worsened when more than one new party emerges and the effective number of political parties becomes very large. Just as it is clear that runoff facilitates the entry of new parties, it is clear that, for the same reasons, runoff enables an increase in the number of political parties. Although the number of parties did not invariably increase in Latin America under runoff and a large number was not invariably dangerous (see Chapters 2 and 3), the number did increase in several countries and a very large number was worrisome.

As plurality advocates fear, the president is less likely to have a legislative majority after runoff elections, usually with a larger number of parties, than after plurality elections. When the number of parties is very large, most parties are personalistic and volatile—which can lead to presidents who are not accountable to a political base and try to govern amid legislative turmoil. The problems of a very large number of parties were especially evident in Ecuador between 1990 and 2009. Numerous presidents' parties held less than 30% of the legislative seats and executive–legislative conflict was severe. Without institutionalized parties, successive presidents shifted their policy positions and, with neither a political base nor legislative majorities, were ousted.

Another relevant concern is that, in a field of many presidential candidates, the two who reach the runoff may not include the "Condorcet winner"—the candidate who, if he or she exists, defeats all other candidates in pair-wise contests (Shugart and Taagepera, 1994: 329; Wright and Riker, 1989: 167–171). Indeed, in a field with many candidates, it may be difficult to know if there was a Condorcet winner and, if so, which candidate it might have been (Greene, 2007b). Put more simply, as under plurality, the two candidates who reach the runoff may win due to their strong political bases; the vote at the most popular space in the political spectrum may be split among several candidates. Also, a candidate who is everyone's second choice—who would win under ranked-choice voting (see Chapter 8)—may not reach the runoff.

In sum, the greater openness of the political arena under runoff is an important advantage. As a Chilean senator said, "Democracy requires a good number of candidates and real choice among them."[12]

Still, plurality advocates are correct that runoff enables a large number of parties and that, when the number rises to six, seven, or more, the plethora is dangerous. Are there measures by which a "sweet spot" between openness to new parties and a plethora of parties can be achieved?[13] Although evidence is limited, Chapter 7 suggests that a reduced 40%-of-the-vote threshold for a runoff is not advantageous. Chapter 8 proposes alternatives, including higher thresholds for parties' entry into the legislature and the scheduling of the legislative election after the runoff.

Electoral Rules and Presidential Legitimacy

Runoff assures that the winner is the candidate preferred by a majority of voters. In the view of Latin American leaders and many analysts, majority support in the election is key to presidential legitimacy. The classic definition of legitimacy and the definition in this book is "the consent of the people; ... legitimate government rests on the consent of the governed" (Plattner, 2009: 60).

However, legitimacy remains a complex concept that is notoriously difficult to measure. Traditionally, the concept of legitimacy has been applied to the state, rather than to the president. Controversies endure about the criteria for legitimacy, including the justifiability for the arrangements for the determination of consent, accommodation for the degrees of intensity of preferences, and for the protection for minorities. Responding to questions about presidential legitimacy, a top Peruvian political scientist said, "Legitimacy comes from acceptance of the rules of the game."[14] A leading Mexican political scientist suggested, "Legitimacy comes first and foremost from the national election commission."[15] An additional relevant issue is whether or not a president who wins only after a runoff—a president who was not the first choice of most voters—also suffers a legitimacy deficit (Thompson, 2010).

Still, it is clear what presidential legitimacy is not: it is not a president elected by a minority of voters and opposed by the majority. As Georgetown University Professor Michael Kazin (2017) noted about the four U.S. presidents before 2016 who finished second in the popular vote, "Each battled the perception that his victory was undemocratic and *illegitimate* [italics mine]; each soon lost the confidence of his own partisans in Congress and led an administration that historians regard as a failure. Each faced an uphill struggle to keep his base happy and mobilized while also reaching out to the majority, which preferred policies his voters detested."

I contend that Latin American presidents who were uncertain or unlikely to have won a majority of votes, or virtually certain not to have won a majority of votes, suffered a legitimacy deficit. As Chapter 3 elaborates, for the twenty-four elections under plurality between 1978 and 2012, I found the result of a runoff was uncertain in 33% and that a reversal of the first-round result was likely or virtually certain in 29% and that some of the legitimacy deficits were grave. The deficit after Mexico's 2006 election was a factor in increased violence; the deficit after Paraguay's 1993 election was a factor in a coup attempt and after its 2008 election a factor in the president's impeachment; and, the deficit after Venezuela's 1993 election was a factor in the subsequent election of Hugo Chávez.

Further, for the forty-two first-round elections under runoff plus the twenty-four elections under plurality, I found that a runoff victory by the first-round winner was (or would have been) uncertain in 56% and a reversal of the first-round result was likely or virtually certain in 17% (see Table 3.3). Even when a candidate's first-round tally is 45%, or indeed even 49.9%, the candidate may not be virtually certain to win a majority in a runoff (see Appendix 6). The first-round winner may have been opposed by two or more candidates who, for whatever variety of reasons, did not coordinate in the first round but are more similar to each other than to the first-round winner. Further, most Latin American presidential campaigns are volatile and poorly predicted by opinion polls; especially when the winner or runner-up is a surprise, voters may only be beginning to make their assessment.

Electoral Rules and Ideological Moderation

Runoff reduces the possibility that a president will be at an ideological extreme. By definition, a candidate cannot appeal only to the 30% or 40% of voters who are his or her "base" but outside mainstream opinion in the country. Usually in Latin America during the third wave, moderation did not spurt briefly between the first round and the runoff but evolved over the span of several elections as a candidate became fully aware that, if he or she were to win, an appeal to the center would be necessary.

As mentioned previously, in many Latin American countries during the third wave, it was necessary that a long-standing authoritarian right accommodate a left with various degrees of Marxist pasts. During the Cold War, Marxist parties had grown in many countries; but, for the most part, there was a "veto against the left" (Reid, 2007: 280). Still, despite military coups and repression, at the start of the third wave Marxist parties endured. After the collapse of the Soviet Union in the early 1990s, Marxist ideology was in retreat, but the debt crisis continued and in most Latin American countries economic growth was low and inequality severe. For some voters who wanted change, Marxist political perspectives were compelling. The lower barriers to entry under runoff persuaded Marxist parties that their country's democracy was "real"—inclusive, not exclusive; and Marxist parties gained respect for the democratic process. In turn, rightist parties were less frightened by their rise. In short, a virtuous circle emerged: leftist parties did not have as hard a time entering the political arena; leftist parties gained respect for the democratic process; and elites did not resort to undemocratic tactics to exclude them.

By contrast, a vicious circle emerged in some plurality countries. Especially in Honduras, Paraguay, and Venezuela, plurality was one factor blocking the emergence of leftist parties. In Mexico and Venezuela, leftist leaders believed that they lost at least one election due to plurality and fraud. Angry leftist leaders were subsequently more likely to play to their electoral bases. Concomitantly, long-standing parties were more fearful and yet more inclined to abuse their political advantages. It is noteworthy that the only plurality country that has sustained high levels of democracy since 2000 is Panama—and that no leftist party was trying to emerge in the country (see Chapter 5).

Of course, at the same time, an ideological shift is not exactly favorable. A candidate may lose credibility with both the left and the right. A candidate is likely to be perceived as opportunistic by party militants—and, in fact, probably is somewhat opportunistic. Still, this book shows that democracy weathers presidents' ideological shifts better than their ideological extremes.

As Chapter 3 elaborates, although "left" and "right" are complex, contested concepts, classifications for left and right are common. I use in particular the left-right assessments of political leaders' ideologies by Latin American countries' legislators in the surveys of the Proyecto Elites Parlamentarias de América Latina (Parliamentary Elites of Latin American Project, PELA).

PELA data provide robust evidence of the link between runoff and ideological moderation (see Chapter 3). Between 2000 and 2012, a president or top presidential candidate was classified at the extreme left in four of the six plurality countries but only one of the eleven runoff countries; presidents at the moderate left were rare in the plurality countries but common in runoff countries. Similarly, a president classified at the extreme right was elected in 50% of the plurality countries but only 27% of the runoff countries.

Often, runoff pulled presidential candidates toward the center. In runoff countries, some of the presidents and presidential candidates classified at the moderate left by PELA were classified at the extreme left in previous elections, or would have been likely to have been classified at the extreme left if they had been included in a survey (see Chapters 5 and 6). Among the presidents shifting toward the center over the course of one or more elections were: Brazil's Luiz Inácio (Lula) da Silva; Guatemala's Álvaro Colom; Peru's Ollanta Humala; and Uruguay's Tabaré Vázquez. Also, although El Salvador's Mauricio Funes was placed at the extreme left in PELA surveys, the more conventional view was that, in 2009, El Salvador's major political party, the Frente Farabundo Martí de Liberación Nacional (Farabundo Martí National Liberation Front, FMLN), was not itself moderating significantly but yet nominated a moderate, Funes, who won. In addition, during periods prior to consistent PELA surveys, Ecuador's Jaime Roldós moved toward the mainstream in 1978–1979 and the Dominican Republic's Leonel Fernández shifted the Partido de la Liberación Dominicana (Party of Dominican Liberation, PLD) toward the mainstream in the 1990s. The only president whose move to the center was so precipitous and drastic that it alienated a majority of citizens was Ecuador's Lucio Gutiérrez.

The more effective incorporation of the left in runoff countries was evident in the trends in levels of democracy under leftist presidents (see Chapters 4, 5, 6, and 7). Between 2000 and 2012, a candidate at some point on the left was elected in eight of eleven runoff countries (all but Colombia, Costa Rica, and the Dominican Republic); levels of democracy did not decline during the president's term in any of the eight. This was not the case for plurality countries. After the elections of Daniel Ortega and Hugo Chávez, levels of democracy in Nicaragua and Venezuela plummeted. Amid intensely nervous elites, President Manuel Zelaya was overthrown in Honduras and President Fernando Lugo was impeached in Paraguay; levels of democracy fell in both countries. After a very close 2006 election result, protested for months by Andrés Manuel López Obrador (AMLO), levels of democracy declined in Mexico, too.

The Structure of the Book

Chapter 2, "Research Design and Quantitative Analysis," first describes the measurement of my independent variable—plurality or runoff—and my dependent variable, levels of democracy between 1990 and 2016. The level of democracy is measured first by Freedom House scores; second, by Varieties of Democracy (V-Dem) scores; and, third, by voter turnout. Next, I graph trends over time and then report my regression analysis: runoff was statistically significant to superior Freedom House and V-Dem scores.

Chapter 3, "Why Was Runoff Superior? Theory and Cross-National Evidence," elaborates the scholarly arguments about plurality and runoff and presents the cross-national evidence for and against these arguments. I elaborate on my preceding assessment that many long-standing parties were either never very democratic or became undemocratic. I also highlight barriers to entry that, to date, have received minimal scholarly attention: the difficulties under plurality for opposition parties to make alliances and coordinate strategically, especially in the Latin American context of inaccurate opinion polls. Most of the cross-national data are for the period 1978 (or the first democratic election) through 2012; at times, however, due to the limits of data availability, the start year is later. Of a total of 110 presidential elections in Latin America in the dataset between 1978 and 2012, forty-five (41%) were under plurality and sixty-five (59%) under runoff.

Subsequent chapters turn to analysis of each Latin American country under plurality and runoff. I indicate trends in levels of democracy from the first democratic election through 2016 and, for each election, describe presidential legitimacy, long-standing and new parties, and parties' ideological positions.

Although the end date of my descriptions is 2016, various averages were calculated through 2014, and, commensurate with my cross-national data, I emphasize the elections through 2012.

Chapter 4, "Plurality: Problems in Honduras, Mexico, Nicaragua, Paraguay, and Venezuela (and the Panama Exception)," explores the effects of plurality in these six countries. As the title of the chapter implies, the level of democracy or the trend in the level of democracy was inferior in all countries except Panama. The records under plurality of the countries that adopted runoff after their third-wave starts (Argentina, Colombia, the Dominican Republic, and Uruguay) are discussed in the chapters about runoff so that their records under plurality and runoff can be easily compared.

Chapter 5, "Runoff: Success in Brazil, Chile, the Dominican Republic, El Salvador, and Uruguay," examines the five nations where levels of democracy improved and runoff worked well (especially, in the cases of the Dominican Republic and Uruguay, relative to plurality). Runoff opened the political arena to new parties, enhanced presidential legitimacy, and/or enticed parties at extremes toward the center. The number of parties did not increase in the Dominican Republic, El Salvador, or Uruguay and, although the number of parties was large in Brazil and Chile, two broad coalitions formed for presidential elections.

Chapter 6, "Runoff Amid a Plethora of Political Parties: Colombia, Ecuador, Guatemala, and Peru," explores the impact of runoff in the four nations where the number of parties was large. Between 1990 and 2014, the number of parties averaged above 3.75 in all four countries. The large number was a factor in Ecuador's declining levels of democracy of my description and, to a lesser degree, Peru's uneven levels. However, to date, the large number has not been problematic in Colombia or Guatemala, where levels of democracy improved (although they were still below regional averages). In all four countries, runoff helped to increase the legitimacy of presidents and to incorporate the left into the democratic arena.

Amid the goal of a "sweet spot" between openness to new parties and a plethora of parties, Chapter 7, "Runoff: Is a Reduced Threshold Better? Argentina and Costa Rica," explores the impact of a threshold between 40% and 50%. Unfortunately, Argentina since 1995 and Costa Rica were only two countries with reduced thresholds for extended periods and a rigorous test is not possible. (More recently—since 2002—a reduced threshold was also in place in Ecuador; these elections are described with the country's previous elections in Chapter 6.) Overall, a reduced threshold appeared risky for presidents' legitimacy and likely to raise barriers to entry too high.

The concluding chapter reviews my argument for the superiority of runoff and considers additional measures for the amelioration of the problem of a plethora of parties. The chapter also explores the potential for the advantages of runoff to travel beyond Latin America to the United States. It also briefly considers the potential for a second alternative to plurality, ranked-choice voting, in the United States.

2

Research Design and Quantitative Analysis

This chapter provides quantitative tests of my argument that runoff is superior to plurality. The first section explains the elaboration of the dataset. The second section shows trends in levels of democracy between 1990 and 2016 for nations under plurality versus runoff. The third section reports my regression analysis and key findings. The final section indicates the sources for other data and information frequently cited in subsequent text.

Research Design and Measurement

This section describes the measurement of the key dependent variable, level of democracy, and the key independent variable, presidential-election rule. Next, I discuss my decisions about elections that met standards for freedom and fairness and, concomitantly, the years in the dataset.

The Dependent Variable: Level of Democracy

Democracy is a disputed concept. Through the twentieth century, there was little consensus on its definition or measurement. However, in the twenty-first century, scholars have developed expert, objective, worldwide indices.

As of 2015, Freedom House indices, measuring political rights and civil liberties (www.freedomhouse.org), were widely considered the best available (Mainwaring and Pérez-Liñán, 2013: 246–249; Munck and Verkuilen, 2002: 31; Brinks and Coppedge, 2006: 468–469). Beginning in 1972, Freedom House indices at first had serious flaws. Scores for many countries were relatively generous in the 1970s and early 1980s relative to the 1990s, in particular for Brazil, Colombia, and Mexico; also, "scores for leftist governments were tainted by political considerations" (Mainwaring, Brinks, and Pérez-Liñán, 2001: 53–54). By the 1990s, however, Freedom House indices were deemed "very good"—considerably superior to the major rival index, Polity (Mainwaring and Pérez-Liñán, 2013: 63 and 246).

As is conventional practice (Mainwaring and Pérez-Liñán, 2013: 246), I add Freedom House scores for political rights and civil liberties, so that the best possible score is 2 and the worst possible score 14. In the quantitative analysis in this chapter, the scores are normalized so that 100 is the best score and 0 the worst.

In January 2016, new indices became available at the Varieties of Democracy (V-Dem) project at www.v-dem.net; the data were updated in early 2017 (V-Dem Dataset 7.1) and these are the data here. V-Dem's innovations and rigor are described by the project's key leaders in Lindberg, Coppedge, Gerring, and Teorell (2014). Due to the newness of the data, as of the writing of this book they have not been incorporated into many publications, but it is evident that they will be soon.[1] The project incorporates approximately fifteen researchers at more than ten universities not only in the United States and Europe but also in Latin America, as well as at least thirty regional managers and more than two thousand country experts. The V-Dem project considers five varieties of democracy: Liberal, Electoral, Participatory, Deliberative, and Egalitarian. Liberal democracy is "constitutionally protected civil liberties, strong rule of law, and effective checks and balances that limit the use of executive power" (Lindberg et al., 2014: 160). It is the classic variety and the variety in my analysis. A perfect score is 1.00 and the nadir 0.

Another indicator of level of democracy is voter turnout. As Lindberg et al. (2014: 162–163) suggest, the participatory dimension of democracy is important but insufficiently assessed by Freedom House; and the V-Dem index for the participatory dimension embraces civil society and mechanisms of direct democracy that are beyond the scope of this study. Voter turnout is a reflection of citizens' engagement in elections—their perceptions that elections matter and are reasonably fair—and also of national electoral commissions' concern for their engagement (Barnes, 1997). Further, as noted previously, turnout has been salient in the discussion of the impact of plurality versus runoff.

Although for these reasons voter turnout is included as a dependent variable in my cross-national analysis, analysis of trends over time within one country is the most telling because of variation in countries' rules about compulsory voting. In most Latin American countries, the vote is compulsory, and, unless otherwise mentioned in my analysis, this is the case. However, in a few countries—Colombia, Guatemala after 1985, Nicaragua, and Venezuela after 1994—the vote is voluntary. Further, in countries where the vote is compulsory, the degree of enforcement varies greatly and is sometimes minimal to none. Unfortunately, as Power (2009: 100) indicates, information on the degree of enforcement is "rudimentary" and "impressionistic"; there are major discrepancies in the data provided by Payne, Zovatto G., and Mateo Díaz (2007: 241–270). However, changes in enforcement after democratic transitions have been rare and, accordingly, analysis of turnout over time within a country is rarely problematic.

Turnout data from 1978 through 2006 are available from Payne, Zovatto G., and Mateo Díaz (2007: Appendix 2) and subsequently from International IDEA at www.idea.net and also at www.electionguide.org. As is customary (Dettrey and Schwindt-Bayer, 2009: 1328), for an election with a first round and a runoff, the turnout rate for the two was averaged. There are two common measures: as a percentage of registered voters and as a percentage of voting-age population. Each measure has advantages and disadvantages. However, although consistent data for both measures were available for the years 1978 through 2006 in the compilation by Payne, Zovatto G., and Mateo Díaz, subsequent consistent data were available only for the percentage of registered voters. Accordingly, this is the measure used here.

As indicated previously, executive-legislative conflict is a key concern for plurality advocates. Several scholars, in particular Pérez-Liñán, Lodola, Castagnola, Su, Polga-Hecimovich, Negri, and Quebral (2011) are compiling data about executive-legislative conflict, but the task is difficult; the executive's party or coalition undergoes membership shifts almost annually in many countries and the significance of these shifts is difficult to interpret. Further, executive-legislative conflict is not invariably nefarious for democracy; an executive may be challenged by the legislature for good reason. Nor is the interruption of a presidency invariably nefarious; as in the case of the flight of Alberto Fujimori from Peru in 2000, the interruption of a presidency can signify a recovery of democracy. In short, the level of democracy is better indicated by Freedom House scores or V-Dem scores than by executive-legislative conflict or the interruption of presidencies.

The Independent Variable: Presidential-Election Rule

Scholars concur that rules in which a runoff is mandated if no candidate wins 50% plus one vote should be classified as runoff and rules in which there is no runoff provision should be classified as plurality.

There is also scholarly agreement about classification of certain anomalies. In Argentina until 1994, an electoral college was stipulated, but scholars concur that in practice elections operated under plurality (Payne, Zovatto G., and Mateo Díaz, 2007: 19–25; Negretto, 2004: 110–112). And, until 2009, Bolivia's rule was anomalous: if no candidate tallied 50%, the president was selected by the legislature from among the top two or three finishers. (Before 1990, it was the top three, but after citizens' dismay at the previous selection of the third-place finisher, it was changed to the top two.) René Mayorga (1997: 79) highlighted the vast difference in the impact of Bolivia's rule and conventional plurality or runoff: "Bolivian parties strive to maximize their vote shares, but they do not expect popular balloting to be the last stage of the arbitration. Rather, they focus on post-electoral bargaining and it is this that will determine who actually ends up in the congressional majority and with executive power." Daniel Chasquetti (2001),

Josep Colomer (1994: 39), Mark Jones (1999: 173), Charles Kenney (1998: 2), and other scholars concur that Bolivia should be omitted from cross-national studies of plurality and runoff.

However, there is no consensus about the classification of rules where the threshold for victory without a runoff is below 50%. Until the mid-1990s, Costa Rica was the only nation with a threshold lower than 50% and it was usually classified as plurality (Jones, 1995: 204; Mainwaring and Shugart, 1997a: 409; Shugart and Carey, 1992: 209). However, in 1994 Argentina adopted 45% or 40% with a ten-point lead; in 1998, Ecuador adopted 40% with a ten-point lead; in 2009, Bolivia adopted 40% with a ten-point lead; and for its 1996 election Nicaragua had 45%. Further, in 2000 Nicaragua adopted a threshold of 35% with a 5% margin or 40%. Accordingly, most scholars opted for a separate classification for these reduced thresholds but used different labels, including "runoff with reduced threshold" (Payne, Zovatto G., and Mateo Díaz, 2007: 24–27); "threshold two-round system" (Martínez, 2004: 541); and "plurality runoff" (Kenney, 1998: 24).

In Table 2.1, I have classified countries where the threshold for first-round victory is between 40% and 50% as "qualified runoff" (or, in Chapter 7, as "runoff with a reduced threshold") and countries where the threshold is below 40% as "qualified plurality." This is because 40% is the figure below which a president is considered to be vulnerable to charges that he or she was not the choice of a majority and not legitimate even among most plurality advocates (Diamond, 2006; Shugart and Carey, 1992: 217).[2] As Jones (1995: 217) elaborates, "The choice of 40% as the threshold for below which a mandate is deemed to be precariously low and above which it is considered acceptable is somewhat arbitrary. However, ... it does represent a rough dividing line."

The only country that used qualified plurality for more than one election was Nicaragua. Nicaragua's threshold was introduced in 2000 as a component of a pact between two Nicaraguan caudillos (see Chapter 4). At the time, a former president, Daniel Ortega, was seeking re-election but doubted that he could win more than 40% in a first round or win a subsequent runoff. Ortega "coveted" plurality (Dye with Spence and Vickers, 2000: 18).

The new qualified plurality rule was widely criticized as permitting the election of a candidate, like Ortega, who was unlikely to achieve a majority (Aizenman, 2006: A20; DeShazo, 2006: 1–3; Lacey, 2006: A5; Ortega, 2007: 19). Elaborated Kenneth Morris (2010: 187), "Another change, important to Ortega, was lowering the threshold ... to 35%. Ortega realized that he was not likely to attract over 45% of the vote in a general election, or over 50% of a runoff election ... so he needed the threshold lowered to a percentage that he could foreseeably attain." Added Nidya Sarria (2009), "Ortega came up with the devious scheme to devote his efforts to lowering the minimum percentage of votes required to win an election. He created a new paradigm that would reflect his normal harvest of ballots."

In the statistical analysis below, majority runoff and qualified runoff are combined and plurality and qualified plurality are combined. Although interest in majority runoff versus qualified runoff is considerable, the number of elections is small (see Chapter 7). Interest in plurality versus qualified plurality is negligible.

Table 2.1 **Runoff and Plurality Rules in Latin America as of 2013**

Country	Minimum Threshold	Year Adopted
MAJORITY RUNOFF		
Brazil	50%	1988
Chile	50%	1980
Colombia	50%	1991
Dominican Republic	50%	1995
El Salvador	50%	1983
Guatemala	50%	1985
Peru*	50%	1979
Uruguay	50%	1997
QUALIFIED RUNOFF		
Argentina	45% or 40% plus 10-point lead	1994
Bolivia	40% plus 10-point lead	2009
Costa Rica	40%	1936
Ecuador**	40% plus 10-point lead	1998
PLURALITY		
Honduras	Plurality	1957
Mexico	Plurality	1917
Panama	Plurality	1946
Paraguay	Plurality	1992
Venezuela	Plurality	1947
QUALIFIED PLURALITY		
Nicaragua***	40% or 35% plus 5-point lead	2000

*Majority runoff was adopted in 1979 but, for the 1980 election, qualified plurality was used. See Chapter 6.

**Prior to the adoption of qualified runoff in 1998 (not used until 2002), Ecuador adopted majority runoff in 1978.

***Prior to the adoption of qualified plurality in 2000, Nicaragua adopted plurality in 1987 and qualified runoff (with a 45% threshold) in 1995. In 2014, thresholds were eliminated and plurality again became the rule.

Sources: Payne, Zovatto G., and Mateo Díaz (2007: 23–25); www.pdba.georgetown.edu/Constitutions.constudies.html.

Table 2.1 shows the classification of Latin American countries according to their presidential-election rule as of 2013. Eight nations—Brazil, Chile, Colombia, the Dominican Republic, El Salvador, Guatemala, Peru, and Uruguay—used majority runoff while five—Honduras, Mexico, Panama, Paraguay, and Venezuela—used plurality. Three—Argentina, Costa Rica, and Ecuador—used qualified runoff. Nicaragua used qualified plurality.

Free and Fair Elections and Years in the Dataset

To establish the start year for my statistical and qualitative analysis of a country, I made decisions about whether or not an election was free and fair and, accordingly, whether or not the election marked the start year for third-wave democracy. These decisions are very unlikely to affect my statistical results because my statistical analysis begins in 1990 (see the last paragraph in this section) and, with the exception of the 1994 election in Mexico, these decisions are about elections prior to 1990.

I set a relatively high bar for the freedom and fairness of an election and the inclusion of that election and subsequent years of the president's term. Electoral rules such as plurality versus runoff are unlikely to matter in non-democratic elections (Mylonas and Roussias, 2008: 1466–1491). Accordingly, it makes little sense to include such elections in the dataset. Other scholars agree; exploring the effect of plurality and runoff rules, Pérez-Liñán (2006: 134) excludes numerous elections due to "the lack of minimum democratic conditions."

Still, I concur with the year stipulated for most Latin American countries by Payne, Zovatto G., and Mateo Díaz (2007: xi): 1983 in Argentina, 1990 in Chile, 1978 in the Dominican Republic, 1979 in Ecuador, 1985 in Guatemala, 1982 in Honduras, 1990 in Nicaragua, 1980 in Peru, and 1985 in Uruguay. I also concur that elections in Colombia, Costa Rica, and Venezuela were already free and fair in 1978 and begin analysis as of 1978. However, I set a higher bar than Payne, Zovatto G., and Mateo Díaz (2007: xi) for the year of transition in five countries: Brazil, El Salvador, Mexico, Panama, and Paraguay. For Brazil, the bar is set at 1989 rather than 1985; for El Salvador, at 1994 rather than 1984; for Mexico, at 2000 rather than 1982; for Panama, at 1994 rather than 1989; and, for Paraguay, at 1993 rather than 1989.

These various elections fell seriously short. The 1985 election in Brazil was an indirect election by the legislature and is excluded by Corrales (2008: 26) and Pérez-Liñán (2006: 134). In Panama, the vote count for the 1989 election was suspended and the election annulled by the incumbent government; the likely winners were installed only seven months later after a U.S. military invasion. This election is also excluded by Pérez-Liñán (2006: 134).

The year of transition to democracy in El Salvador is controversial. The year 1989 is specified by Corrales (2008: 26) but the year 1984 by Pérez-Liñán (2006: 134).

However, due to the ongoing civil war and continuing human rights violations, the 1984 and 1989 elections were not deemed free and fair by most country specialists (Booth, Wade, and Walker, 2010: 126; Lehoucq, 2012: 70). El Salvador's 1984 election was the only election without voter registration that was included in the data compiled by Payne, Zovatto G., and Mateo Díaz (2007). By contrast, the 1994 elections were held after peace accords had been signed in 1992; they were the first in which the former insurgents participated as a political party. As Fen Osler Hampson (1996: 129) reported, the 1994 elections were "conducted in an atmosphere free of violence and intimidation" and were dramatically superior.

Nor are scholars unanimous about the year of transition to democracy in Mexico. Both Corrales (2008: 27) and Pérez-Liñán (2006: 134) include Mexico's 1988 and 1994 elections. However, most country specialists, including Eisenstadt (2004: 8), Lawson (2004: 1), and Levy and Bruhn (2006: 3), specify the 2000 elections as the first that were free and fair. Prior to 2000, Mexico's hegemonic party, the Partido Revolucionario Institucional (Institutional Revolutionary Party, PRI), ruled Mexico for seventy-one years without interruption. And, "the executive branch of government [i.e., the PRI] controlled the institutions that organized elections and certified their results" (Haber et al., 2008: 125). Only in 1996 did Mexico's election commission become independent of the PRI. Concluded Lawson (2004: 1), "On July 2, 2000, Mexican voters brought to a definitive end the world's oldest one-party regime."

Paraguay's 1989 election is excluded also by Corrales (2008: 28). It was a snap election held only three months after a coup against ruling General Alfredo Stroessner and was won by the interim president (who was also the mastermind of the coup). Commented Darren McKewen (1989: 1):

> Opposition parties agreed to participate in the May election as a way to develop their organizations and push for a genuine democratic opening, not in hopes of winning. After years of persecution, they had only a few weeks in which to select nominees and campaign. The elections were held under the existent electoral law, which had been designed to facilitate Stroessner's sham elections. The May election was not a fair, democratic contest....

Similar assessments were made by Marcial Riquelme (1994) and Paul Sondrol (2007: 333).

Although I set a high bar for the freedom and fairness of the start election, I set a low bar for the freedom and fairness of elections subsequently. That is because, although I am analyzing electoral rule as an independent variable, I am also analyzing the level of democracy as a dependent variable, and declines in the level of democracy matter. Accordingly, after the start year for each country, only the two elections that were not deemed free and fair by the Organization of American States—the election in the Dominican Republic in 1994 (and the year 1995 with a new election in 1996) and the election in Peru in 2000 (with a new election in 2001) were excluded (see Chapters 5 and 6).

The year 1990 is selected as the start year. One reason is that it is at this time that, as previously noted, Freedom House scores became "very good." A second reason is that, prior to 1990, five countries (El Salvador, Mexico, Panama, Paraguay, and Nicaragua) were still not considered to have transitioned to democracy, and three of these countries consistently used plurality. On the one hand, a later start year would have been advantageous because, through the 1990s, a number of countries adopted runoff (Argentina in 1995, Colombia in 1994, the Dominican Republic in 1996, and Uruguay in 1999) and the statistical result is affected by whether or not a country adopting the rule had a higher or lower level of democracy at the time. On the other hand, in the case of a later start year, the number of years in the dataset is reduced. In any case, it is after 1998 that scores began to markedly diverge and, with the exception of Uruguay in 1999, all rule changes were complete by this year.

Trends in Levels of Democracy Under Plurality and Runoff

Given that the key question of this book is the effect of presidential-election rules on levels of democracy over time, it is important to examine these trends. This section shows the trajectories of Freedom House scores, V-Dem scores, and voter turnout for plurality and runoff.

Figure 2.1 graphs the trajectory of Freedom House scores with runoff versus plurality between 1990 and 2016. The graph shows that average Freedom House scores were similar between 1990 and 1998 but subsequently improved with runoff and plummeted with plurality. Between 2011 and 2016, the difference was approximately thirty percentage points. For 1990–2014, the average non-normalized Freedom House score across the dataset was 5.29.

Figure 2.2 shows the trajectory of V-Dem Liberal Democracy scores. The trajectory parallels that by Freedom House: scores for runoff and plurality are similar through 1998 but then improve with runoff and plummet with plurality. However, there are slight variations. The scores for runoff do not improve after 1998 as much for V-Dem as for Freedom House, and the scores for runoff more clearly dip after 2014. (This dip was a change from the V-Dem data released in January 2016; amid the corruption scandal in Brazil in particular, scores were retroactively downgraded.) Between 2011 and 2016, the difference between scores for runoff and plurality is smaller—a little more than twenty points. For 1990–2014, the average Liberal Democracy score across the dataset was .545.

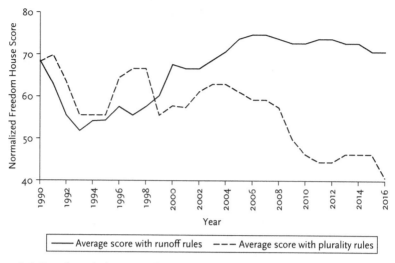

Figure 2.1 Presidential-Election Rules and Freedom House Scores, 1990–2016

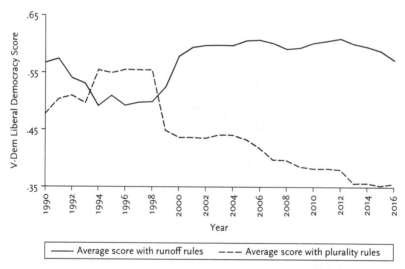

Figure 2.2 Presidential-Election Rules and V-Dem Liberal Democracy Index (LDI) Scores, 1900–2016

Why was 1998 a turning point in both the Freedom House and V-Dem datasets? Changes in two countries were important: first, in Venezuela, Hugo Chávez was elected, and this plurality country's scores fell; second, in Peru, Alberto Fujimori fled, and this runoff country's scores recovered. Scores for the plurality countries Honduras and Nicaragua also declined after 1998 whereas scores for the runoff countries Brazil, Chile, the Dominican Republic, El Salvador, and Uruguay rose.

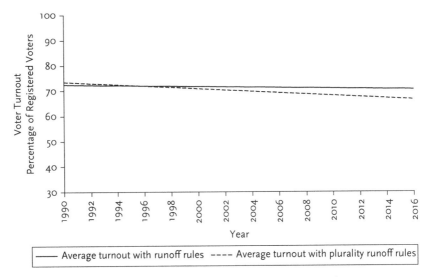

Figure 2.3 Presidential-Election Rules and Voter Turnout, 1990–2016

Figure 2.3 shows the trajectory of voter turnout with runoff versus plurality between 1990 and 2016: turnout was steady with runoff but dipped slightly with plurality. In part because the problems with cross-national comparison of turnout are considerable and in part because variations were usually slight, I do not elaborate at length about turnout in most country analyses. I do, however, when variations were considerable. For example, in Honduras and in Venezuela between 1978 and 2000 with plurality, turnout plummeted. Also, in El Salvador and Guatemala with runoff, turnout increased markedly. In the context of a change in rules for registration and mandatory voting in Chile, turnout for its 2013 election declined. For 1990–2014, across the dataset average voter turnout was 71%.

Statistical Analysis and Results

Is it presidential-election rules that affect levels of democracy, or are other independent variables at work? To answer this question, my research team, including in particular Josiah Augustine, Barnett S. Koven, and Aldo Ponce, and I conducted regression analysis. We considered the effects of both socioeconomic and institutional factors. Replication materials for the dataset and analysis are available at the Harvard Dataverse at https://dataverse.harvard.edu/dataverse.cmcclintock.

To explore the impact of socioeconomic factors, we incorporated the variables GDP per capita (in constant 2010 U.S. dollars), the Gini coefficient of inequality, and education (percentage completion of primary school). As Mainwaring and Pérez-Liñán (2013: 98–101) explain, these variables comprise the key facets of what is widely known as modernization theory and are very common in analyses of explanations for levels of democracy. Also, as a measure of regime performance, we include the annual percentage change in GDP growth. Our data were drawn from the World Bank at https://databank.worldbank.org/data-catalog/world-development-indicators. Data for the Gini coefficient for 2015 were drawn from SEDLAC (Socio-Economic Database for Latin America and the Caribbean) at http://cedlas.econo.unlp.edu/ar/wp/en/esadisticas/sedlac/estadisticas.

When data were missing for one year (which was particularly common for the Gini coefficient and for completion of primary school), we assigned values that averaged the previous number and the next number, or, for missing values for 2016, we calculated the slope from the previous two years and continued that trend. Missing values were replaced only for up to two years from the last entry.

To explore the impact of institutional factors, we included the variables that are almost universally considered the most important in studies of levels of democracy: the age of the democratic regime and the effective number of political parties (ENPP) (Mainwaring and Pérez-Liñán, 2013: 102–104). The age of the democratic regime was the number of years that the current democratic regime had been in place (in other words, for Chile in 1990, 1 year; for Venezuela in 1990, 23 years).

The effective number of parties was calculated through the index developed by Murkku Laakso and Rein Taagepera (1979). When the legislature is seated after July 1 of the year, the variable is lagged by one year. For 1978–2006, data are drawn from Payne, Zovatto G., and Mateo Díaz (2007: Appendix 3); for 2007–2011, from the Nils-Christian Bormann and Matt Golder dataset available at www.v-dem.net; and for 2011–2016 from Election Resources at www.electionresources.org. In addition, because the relationship between ENPP and levels of democracy might be non-linear (see Figure 3.2 in Chapter 3), we introduced a quadratic (squared) term of ENPP (ENPPq in the tables that follow) to control for this problem.

Several institutional variables are common in studies of levels of democracy worldwide but not in studies in Latin America because there is little to no variation among the Latin American countries. In particular, presidentialism is the rule throughout Latin America. Similarly, proportional representation is almost ubiquitous. Those countries that do not have proportional representation, such as Mexico and Chile, have unique sets of rules.

For our regression analysis, we used a random effects model to account for potential unobserved heterogeneity. A random effects linear model better accounts for the two types of variation in our dataset: within-country variation over time (specifically, years) and between-country. A Hausman statistical test confirmed that a random effects model would be superior to a fixed effects model. To help account for ceiling effects, we included among our control variables Freedom House and V-Dem variables lagged by the standard one year. Runoff is coded as 1, plurality as

0, and accordingly a positive relationship indicates that runoff predicts higher levels of democracy or turnout. Our regression results for presidential-election rule are shown in Tables 2.2 and 2.3. Table 2.2 shows the relationship between rule (runoff versus plurality) and levels of democracy between 1990 and 2016. Runoff is significant to both the Freedom House index and the V-Dem index at the .05 level.

Among the control variables, several are statistically significant. GDP growth is positively related to Freedom House scores, with significance at the .10 level. Unexpectedly, the Gini coefficient (in other words, more severe inequality) is positively related to V-Dem scores at the .01 level. Not surprisingly, the control variables for the lag of Freedom House scores and for the lag of turnout are positively related to both dependent variables and statistically significant at the .01 level. Despite the overall scant effect of control variables in the statistical analysis, they are widely considered relevant and are often mentioned in the country analyses below.

Table 2.3 shows the relationship between presidential-election rule (either runoff or plurality) and voter turnout between 1990 and 2016. Rule was not significant to turnout. In other words, in contrast to plurality advocates' expectations but in accord with Figure 2.3, runoff was not a predictor of decreased turnout. Age of democracy and percentage of completion of primary school were positively related at the .01 level, and the non-quadratic ENPP variable was negatively related and significant at the .10 level.

Thus, for any one year, presidential-election rule has an in impact on the level of democracy in a country. We are interested also in the effects of presidential-election rule over time. To explore this question, we operationalized plurality and runoff as a count of the number of years that the rule was in place.

Table 2.4 shows the relationship between years of plurality and the Freedom House and V-Dem indices between 1990 and 2016. Indeed, years of plurality was negative and statistically significant at the .01 level for the Freedom House index and almost at the .01 level for the V-Dem index. The Gini coefficient was also statistically significant at the .01 level. There was no statistically significant relationship between years of plurality and turnout.

These results forecast a key point in Chapters 3 and 4: in many elections, plurality does not have a negative impact; but, as time accumulates, in one election (usually an election with a larger number of parties and a president who is not perceived as legitimate or harbors authoritarian proclivities), plurality does have a negative impact, and in some countries this negative impact lasts for years. In other words, the longer that plurality is in effect, the greater the chance that a disadvantageous election will take place.

As Figures 2.1 and 2.2 suggest, years of runoff was not as significant a predictor of superior trends in levels of democracy; the longer runoff is in effect, the chance is not greater that a particularly advantageous election will take place. The trend was to better scores under runoff through about 2005 but level after 2005. Still, years

Table 2.2 **Presidential-Election Rule and Freedom House and V-Dem Indices: Random Effects Model Estimations**

	Freedom House Index (1990–2016)	V-Dem Liberal Democracy Index (1990–2016)
Presidential-Election Rule (Runoff rather than plurality)	1.800** (0.814)	0.006** (0.003)
Age of the Democratic Regime	−0.029 (0.025)	−0.000 (0.000)
GDP per Capita	0.000 (0.000)	−4.170 (4.660)
GDP Growth(%, annual)	0.179* (0.095)	0.000 (0.000)
Gini Coefficient	0.108 (0.084)	0.001*** (0.000)
% Completion of Primary School	0.029 (0.030)	0.000 (0.000)
ENPP	1.021 (1.217)	−0.003 (0.004)
ENPPq	−.1447 (0.137)	−0.000 (0.000)
Lag of Freedom House Index	0.951*** (0.018)	
Lag of Liberal Democracy Index		1.010*** (0.008)
Constant	−8.967 (5.585)	−0.077 (0.020)
Number of Observations	382	382

*$p < 0.1$, **$p < 0.05$, ***$p < 0.01$ (two-tailed tests).

Note: Entries are coefficients with standard errors in parentheses. The statistical significance of the effect of presidential-election rule was robust to both a cluster-corrected and robust standard error specification when using the Freedom House index but not the V-Dem index.

Table 2.3 **Presidential-Election Rule and Voter Turnout: Random Effects Model Estimations**

	Voter Turnout
Presidential-Election Rule (Runoff rather than plurality)	.334 (0.495)
Age of the Democratic Regime	−.035** (0.017)
GDP per Capita	.000 (0.000)
GDP Growth(%, annual)	.043 (0.058)
Gini Coefficient	−0.029 .053
% Completion of Primary School	.047*** (0.018)
ENPP	−1.445* (0.749)
ENPPq	.122 (0.084)
Lag of Turnout	.919*** (.019)
Constant	6.043 (5.674)
Number of Observations	382

*$p < 0.1$, **$p < 0.05$, ***$p < 0.01$ (two-tailed tests).
Note: Entries are coefficients with standard errors in parentheses.

of runoff was positive and statistically significant at the .10 level for the Freedom House index (but not the V-Dem index or turnout).

Various objections might be raised to our analysis. In particular, is there a problem of endogeneity? Is it, first, that Latin American nations are committed to democracy, and that they then adopt runoff? This point has considerable validity for some countries. For example, in Colombia in 1991, runoff was adopted as one among a package of reforms that were hoped to have a democratizing effect; and,

Table 2.4 **Years of the Plurality Rule and Freedom House and V-Dem Indices: Random Effects Model Estimations**

	Freedom House Index (1990–2016)	V-Dem Liberal Democracy Index (1990–2016)
Years of Plurality	−.131***	−0.000**
	(0.041)	(P = .012)
Age of the Democratic Regime	−.009	−0.000
	(0.024)	(0.000)
GDP per Capita	.000*	−1.700
	(0.000)	(5.280)
GDP Growth (%, annual)	.188***	0.000
	(0.094)	(0.000)
Gini Coefficient	.109	0.001***
	(0.083)	(0.000)
% Completion of Primary School	.023	0.000
	(0.030)	(0.000)
ENPP	.985	−.002
	(1.203)	(0.004)
ENPPq	−.149	−0.000
	(0.136)	(0.000)
Lag of Freedom House Index	0.930***	
	(0.020)	
Lag of Liberal Democracy Index		1.003***
		(0.009)
Constant	−6.331	−0.070
	(5.567)	(0.020)
Number of Observations	382	382

*$p < 0.1$, **$p < 0.05$, ***$p < 0.01$ (two-tailed tests).

Note: Entries are coefficients with standard errors in parentheses. The statistical significance of the effect of the for years of plurality was robust to both a cluster-corrected and robust standard error specification when using both the Freedom House index and the V-Dem index.

in Nicaragua in 2000, qualified plurality was adopted as one among a package of reforms that were hoped to have an anti-democratizing effect.

However, not every reform has the effect that its designers expect. Plurality advocates do not charge that runoff is adopted to hurt democracy; they charge only that it does and that its advocates are misguided. Further, in the most rigorous study to date of constitution-making in Latin America, Negretto (2013) argues that a key determinant of constitutional choice is the strategic interest of the relevant political actors.

Sources for Other Data and Information Frequently Cited in the Text

A variety of information mentioned in subsequent chapters is consistently drawn from the same sources; to avoid repetition, I indicate these sources here.

Parties' tallies in presidential and legislative elections are regularly provided. These tallies are from Nohlen (2005), www.pdba.georgetown.edu/Elecdata/elecdata.html, and, when necessary, the country's electoral commission.

The "number of political parties" is the "effective number of parties" variable calculated through the index developed by Murkku Laakso and Rein Taagepera (1979); the data are drawn from the sources cited previously in this chapter. The average "number of parties" for a country was calculated from its first democratic election through 2014.

I refer often to pre-election opinion polls. These figures are discussed in Chapter 3 and, unless otherwise indicated, are available in Appendix 4.

Economic variables are also mentioned frequently and, unless otherwise indicated, the data are from the same sources as cited earlier in this chapter. Additionally, crude oil prices between the 1970s and 2013 are cited in the text about Ecuador and Venezuela and are available at www.inflationdata.com/Inflation/Inflation_Rate/Historical_Oil_Prices_Table.asp.

A great deal of the information about the elections in subsequent chapters, including predictions about the likely results of runoffs, party alliances and endorsements, and candidates' biographies and possible outsider status, is drawn from the *Latin American Weekly Report* and *Latin American Regional Report*. These publications are cited as LAWR and LARR respectively. Throughout, LAWR was published weekly and the day as well as the month and the year were included in the publication date; however, after February 2005, LARR was published monthly for each region (i.e., the Andes, the Southern Cone, Brazil, Central America and the Caribbean, and Mexico) and only the month and year were included in the publication date. Prior to 1980, LAWR was entitled the *Latin American Political Report* and is cited as LAPR. Published by Latin American Newsletters, these reports provide consistent weekly and monthly information and are increasingly used by scholars (Mainwaring and Pérez-Liñán, 2013; Negretto, 2006; Pérez-Liñán, Lodola, Castagnola, Su, Polga-Hecimovich, Negri, and Quebral, 2011). The predictions about the likely results of runoffs are particularly valuable because such predictions are rare in scholarly work and, in contrast to newspaper articles and most journalistic sources, considerable consistency can be expected.

3

Why was Runoff Superior? Theory and Cross-National Evidence

This chapter first reviews plurality advocates' arguments and assesses the cross-national evidence for and against them and, next, discusses runoff advocates' arguments and the cross-national evidence. It probes conceptual and empirical questions about the number of parties and democracy, presidential legitimacy, and ideological moderation.

The third and fourth sections examine topics germane to both plurality and runoff advocates. In the third section, the question of authoritarian proclivities by Latin American political parties is assessed. Although this question is very relevant to the desirability of higher or lower barriers to entry into the political arena, to date it has not been addressed by plurality or runoff advocates. In the fourth section, the height of barriers to entry is further examined. The problems of strategic coordination by opposition parties, including inaccurate opinion polls, are emphasized.

The final section adds to the evidence in Chapter 1 that, indeed, entry into the top ranks of power was facilitated by runoff.

Plurality Advocates' Case: Arguments and Cross-National Evidence

As Chapter 1 noted, plurality is favored by the vast majority of scholars, including Juan J. Linz, Arturo Valenzuela, Mark Jones, and Aníbal Pérez-Liñán, and their primary argument is that runoff enables a larger number of parties, which endangers democracy. This section shows that, just as previously, in Latin America during the third wave the number of parties was indeed larger under runoff than plurality. However, it also cites the finding in the statistical analysis in Chapter 2 that a larger number of parties was not a statistically significant predictor of inferior levels of democracy.

Why was a larger number of parties not a significant predictor of inferior levels of democracy? This section next explores plurality advocates' expectations and the cross-national evidence. First, the number of parties under plurality was larger than plurality advocates expected, raising challenges. Second, several expected risks of runoff—a larger number of outsiders and voter fatigue—did not occur. However, plurality advocates' concern about legislative minorities was warranted.

The Number of Political Parties and Levels of Democracy

Originating in the 1954 work of Maurice Duverger, the argument that plurality favors a two-party system but runoff a multiparty system is long-standing (Clark and Golder, 2006: 681). Indeed, Colomer (2005) and Negretto (2013) show that, when political leaders revised electoral rules during the third wave, most assumed that plurality raises barriers of entry, benefiting extant larger parties, and that runoff lowers barriers of entry, benefiting nascent smaller parties.

The principle is endorsed by a multitude of scholars. Scott Mainwaring and Matthew Shugart (1997b: 467–468) state, "The run-off system ... encourages fragmentation of the field of competitors for both presidency and assembly.... The plurality rule, in contrast, encourages only two 'serious' contenders for the presidency in most cases." Martín Tanaka (2005: 127) argues that "runoffs ... stimulate fragmentation rather than combat it ...." As Shugart and Carey (1992: 212) point out, a salient example is the United States: "The United States has functioned effectively as plurality throughout nearly all of its history, encouraging broad coalitions that, on average, have garnered 51.6% for the front-runner and 43.3% for the runner-up."

Why are barriers to entry lower under runoff than plurality? As mentioned in Chapter 1, the first round and the runoff become two different stages of an electoral process; elections are not just one "single-payoff game" but a "two-level game." In a first round, citizens can vote sincerely for the candidate whom they like the most, whereas under plurality they must vote strategically for the candidate whom they think has a chance to win whom they prefer (Norris, 2004: 49; Riker, 1992: 214–215; Van de Walle, 2006: 88–89). Usually, a new party is not strong at its start, and must have sincere votes to win. A new party moving into contention is a party moving up in the polls; but voters will only know this if polls are accurate. However, in Latin America, polls are frequently inaccurate.

The two different "stages" of the election is itself an advantage for also-ran parties. Incumbents and frontrunners are exposed to the risks inherent in not one election, but two.[1] Even when a party does not reach the runoff, it gains power. In particular, a party can decide whether or not to make an endorsement (Jones, 1995: 92–93; Linz, 1994: 21–22; Negretto, 2007: 221).

Finally, most simply, there are greater chances of finishing either first or second than finishing first (Carey, 2003: 14; Jones 1995: 96–102; Linz, 1994: 21–22). As

Valenzuela (1993: 8) stated, "many parties can run candidates with reasonable hopes of making the second round."

Empirical evidence for the correlation between plurality and a smaller number of parties is ample. For an eclectic set of countries in Latin America and Western Europe from the 1930s until 1990, Shugart and Carey (1992: 220) found that the average number of parties was 3.4 under plurality but 5.15 under runoff. For Latin American nations from the 1930s to the mid-1990s where legislative and presidential elections were concurrent, Mainwaring and Shugart (1997a: 405–407) calculated that the average number was 2.53 under plurality versus 5.14 under runoff. For sixteen Latin American nations from the 1940s through the mid-1990s, Jones (1995: 90) found that plurality countries were likely to have fewer than 2.50 parties but runoff countries more than 2.50 parties.

I too found a positive relationship. Figure 3.1 shows the average number of parties in elections under plurality versus runoff for 1990–2016: about 2.90 under plurality versus approximately 4.50 under runoff. Under plurality, the average number was relatively steady between 1990 and 2016 but, under runoff, fluctuated between 1990 and 2004 and then steadied between 2004 and 2016.

However, Figure 3.1 shows too that the relationship between presidential-election rule and number of parties is complex. First, the number of parties is greater under runoff than under plurality at the start in 1990. As Michael Coppedge (2000) and Gabriel Negretto (2006 and 2013) point out, a larger number of parties may result from runoff, but it also causes runoff; countries adopt runoff because they already have a larger number and want to assure that the winner is the candidate

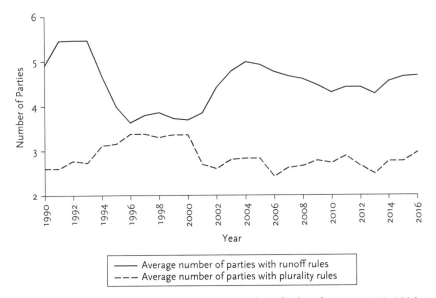

Figure 3.1 Presidential-Election Rules and the Number of Political Parties, 1990–2016

with the most popular support. I calculated that, whereas the number of parties in the five countries consistently using plurality averaged 2.81 from 1978 to 2006, the number in majority-runoff countries in the presidential, legislative, or constituent-assembly election just prior to the adoption of the runoff averaged 4.07; the number was at least 3.0 in every country (However, the number in the election just prior to the adoption of qualified runoff was 2.27.).[2]

Second, Figure 3.1 shows considerable oscillation in the number of parties under runoff. In particular, between 1994 and 2000, the number of parties declined under runoff. The primary reason was change in the countries in the dataset. In 1990, almost all the countries under runoff were countries that traditionally had a large number of parties: Brazil, Chile, Ecuador, Guatemala, and Peru. Then, between 1994 and 1999 several countries that traditionally had a small number of parties—Argentina, Colombia, the Dominican Republic, El Salvador, and Uruguay—implemented runoff. Although the number of parties increased after 2000, it was never as large as in the early 1990s.

The oscillation in the number of parties under runoff suggests that presidential-election rule is part of the story about the number of parties, but not the full story. As subsequent chapters show, variation among runoff countries was considerable. Despite runoff, the number decreased in the Dominican Republic, El Salvador, and Uruguay. The largest jump after the adoption of runoff was in Colombia; the number also rose considerably in Costa Rica. The number increased in Argentina, but was greater for midterm legislative elections than legislative elections concurrent with presidential races. Similarly, the number was exceptionally large in Brazil (more than 10 parties as of 2011) and in Chile (more than 5.5 parties as of 2002); but, for presidential elections, two broad coalitions emerged. This important change is not reflected in Figure 3.1. In Ecuador (until 2008), Guatemala, and Peru, the traditionally large number of parties merely continued.

Accordingly, the number of parties in a country reflects factors beyond presidential-election rule. When incumbent parties are unpopular, social demand for new parties increases. Another factor is domestic political cleavages. Traditionally, cleavages emerge on the issues of religion, political ideology, and regions within a country; cleavages around a polarizing party or leader, such as Argentina's Juan Perón, have also been common. The number of parties was considerable under both plurality and runoff due in part to other electoral rules. In particular, the vast majority of Latin American countries use proportional representation rather than first-past-the-post for the election of the legislature, and proportional representation is associated with a larger number of parties. Also, in some Latin American countries, presidential and legislative elections were sometimes non-concurrent, and non-concurrent presidential and legislative elections are also associated with a larger number of parties.

Plurality advocates argue not only that runoff increases the number of parties but also that a larger number is dangerous for democracy (Mainwaring and Scully, 1995: 33; Mainwaring and Shugart, 1997a: 435; Mainwaring and Shugart, 1997b: 465). Indeed, not only plurality advocates but many scholars argue that a larger number of parties is dangerous.[3] For many years, this argument was supported by the Latin American experience: traditionally, the number of parties was approximately 2.5 or fewer in Costa Rica, Colombia, and Venezuela, and these three countries were the region's longest-standing democracies.

However, in Latin America during the third wave, there was no statistically significant relationship between the number of parties and Freedom House or V-Dem scores (see Tables 2.2 and 2.4 in Chapter 2). Indeed, for 1990–2014, the correlation coefficient between the effective number-of-parties variable (ENPP) and the Freedom House index was .378 and between the number-of-parties variable and the V-Dem index .518; in other words, a larger number of parties was correlated not with inferior levels of democracy but with superior levels.

As Chapter 2 mentioned, when we looked closely at the relationship between ENPP and levels of democracy, we found that it is non-linear. Figure 3.2 shows the discontinuous relationship between ENPP (rounding the numbers to the nearest whole) and V-Dem Liberal Democracy scores. The graph for rounded ENPP and Freedom House scores was analogous.

Other scholars have found similar results. José Antonio Cheibub (2007: 97) found that, worldwide between 1946 and 2002, there was no relationship between the number of parties and the breakdown of presidential democracies. Cynthia McClintock and James Lebovic (2006: 51–53) found no relationship between the number of political parties and Freedom House scores in Latin America during the 1990s.

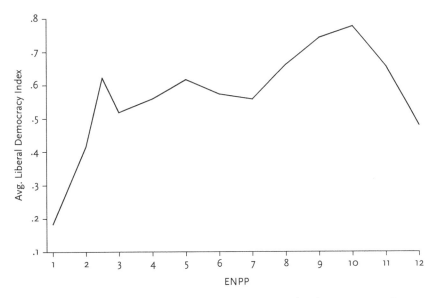

Figure 3.2 The Number of Political Parties and the V-Dem Liberal Democracy Index, 1990–2016

Plurality Advocates' Unrealized Expectations: The Number of Parties, Outsiders, and Voter Fatigue

Among plurality advocates' explanations for the superiority of plurality, most were not borne out. Under plurality, the number of parties was larger than expected and the incidence of outsiders was lower; under runoff, voter fatigue did not ensue.

Plurality advocates expected that, under plurality, the average number of parties would approximate 2.0. They acknowledge that, under plurality, three or more parties is dangerous, risking the election of presidents with less than 40%; they argue that this event is rare (Jones, 1995: 187–188; Mainwaring and Shugart, 1997b: 468); Shugart and Carey, 1992: 216; Shugart and Taagepera, 1994: 343).[4]

But Figure 3.1 showed that the number of parties under plurality neared 3.0. Indeed, between the first third-wave election and 2016 in all countries that either had or have plurality, the number of parties exceeded three in at least one election. Yet, with three parties, the election of the president with less than 40% is likely. During the third wave, elections were won with 41% or less in the Dominican Republic in 1990, Honduras in 2013, Mexico in 2006 and 2012, Nicaragua in 2006, Panama in 1994, Paraguay in 1993 and 2008, Uruguay in 1989 and 1994, and Venezuela in 1993—and were often deleterious to democracy for many years thereafter.

Plurality advocates also worry that runoff enables presidential victories by new parties and that some of the winners may be "outsiders" (Carey, 2003: 14–15; Hartlyn, 1994b: 47–48; Jones, 1995: 91–102; Pérez-Liñán, 2006: 132–140; Valenzuela, 2004: 7–8). I follow the definition of "outsider" used by Corrales (2008: 5): no prior electoral experience running for office and no major public administration experience. By definition, an outsider is risky for democracy (Carreras, 2014: 74–75).

Table 3.1 **The Incidence of Outsiders: Plurality versus Runoff Presidential Elections, 1978–2012**

Electoral Rule	Number of Presidential Elections	Number of Outsiders Who Tallied 10%–50%*	Percent of Elections in Which Outsiders Tallied 10%–50%*	Number of Outsiders Who Won	Percent of Elections Won by Outsiders
Plurality	45	5	11	3	6.66
Runoff	65	5	8	4	6.15

*I am again following Corrales (2008: 26) in the application of 10% as the threshold for candidate viability.

Note: For the definition of "outsider," see text.

Sources: See Appendix 2.

Plurality advocates fear that an outsider can attract media attention, slip into the runoff, and go on to win. An outsider can benefit from the tendency of the gamut of opposition candidates to "gang up" against a frontrunner.[5] An outsider wins because he or she is "anyone-but-X" [the first-round winner]; the victory is based primarily on "negative" votes against the first-round winner. These scholars again cite the cases of Fujimori in Peru, an outsider, and Serrano in Guatemala (who was not an outsider by my definition but was relatively unknown).

In fact, outsiders have been rare under both plurality and runoff. Table 3.1 shows that, in free and fair elections between 1978 and 2012, outsiders secured between 10% and 50% of the vote in approximately 10% of elections under both plurality and runoff and won approximately 6% of elections under both sets of rules. Three outsiders won plurality elections: Violeta Barrios de Chamorro in Nicaragua in 1990, Fernando Lugo in Paraguay in 2008, and Hugo Chávez in Venezuela in 1998. Four outsiders won runoff elections: Lucio Gutiérrez in Ecuador in 2002, Antonio Saca in El Salvador in 2004, Mauricio Funes in El Salvador in 2009, and Alberto Fujimori in Peru in 1990. Five outsiders tallied between 10% and 50% in plurality elections: in Colombia, Antonio Navarro Wolff in 1990; in Panama, Rubén Blades in 1994 and Alberto Vallarino in 1999; and, in Paraguay, Guillermo Caballero Vargas in 1993 and Pedro Fadul in 2003. Likewise, five outsiders tallied between 10% and 50% in runoff elections: in Chile, Francisco Javier Errázuriz in 1989; in Ecuador, Freddy Ehlers in 1996; in El Salvador, Facundo Guardado in 1999; in Peru, Mario Vargas Llosa in 1990 and Ollanta Humala in 2006.

I favor the definition of outsider by Corrales because no subjective judgment is necessary and information about candidates' backgrounds is readily available in such sources as LAWR and LARR. However, with other mainstream definitions of "outsider," the results would be similar. For example, Miguel Carreras (2012: 1456) adopts an additional criterion: "participation" as independents or in association with new parties. This criterion requires subjective judgments about independent and new parties. With such a criterion, Violeta Barrios de Chamorro (the widow of a prominent political leader) would not be classified as an outsider; but Ricardo Martinelli in Panama's 2009 election under plurality might be. In elections under runoff, Rafael Correa in Ecuador in 2006 might be classified as an outsider, but Antonio Saca and Mauricio Funes would not be. Subsequently, Carreras (2014: 72) revised his criteria, defining an outsider as a president with "less than two years of political experience." The results are again similar, with the omission of Saca and Funes but the inclusion of Correa and Alejandro Toledo.[6]

Another concern is that runoffs would be inefficient, wasting government resources and voters' energy (Norris, 2004: 49; Thompson, 2010). Scholars' concerns were shared by some political leaders; in my survey of Latin American legislators, 56% of the forty-five Latin American legislators who preferred plurality cited "excessive expenditure of time and money" as one of their reasons (see Appendix 1).

It was the most commonly cited reason. A considerable percentage cited "voter fatigue" as well.

The fear of "voter fatigue" reflects the fact that voters are likely to have to go to the polls twice in rapid succession. For a considerable number of voters, their preferred candidate might no longer be in the race. Indeed, in an analysis of turnout between 1974 and 2004 in a large set of presidential elections worldwide, turnout in plurality elections and the first round of runoff elections was similar, but, relative to the first rounds, turnout declined in runoffs (Dettrey and Schwindt-Bayer, 2009: 1329–1330).

By contrast, runoff advocates believe that the opportunity for a "vote with the heart" is likely to increase turnout in the first round. Further, runoff provides voters a second opportunity to assess candidates; voters may be more motivated in a runoff (Sartori, 2001: 98).

Chapter 2 showed that "voter fatigue" did not ensue under runoff in Latin America between 1978 and 2016. Voter turnout was steady under runoff but dipped slightly under plurality. Looking closely at the data for each country, I found that patterns of turnout for the first round versus the runoff were country-specific. Turnout between the first round and the runoff usually declined in some countries (Costa Rica, El Salvador, and Guatemala); was quite similar in most (Brazil, Chile, the Dominican Republic, Peru, and Uruguay); and usually increased in a couple (Colombia and Ecuador).

I was not able to secure data about expenditures for elections and cannot provide cross-national evidence about this concern.

A Warranted Concern: The Risk of Legislative Minorities

Plurality advocates believe that a smaller number of parties reduces the risk of minority government, which is in turn a prelude to executive-legislative gridlock and, ultimately, democratic breakdown (Chasquetti, 2001: 47; Diamond, 1996: 80–81; Huntington, 1968: 422; Linz, 1990a: 50–69; Linz, 1990b: 84–91; Weiner and La Palombara, 1966: 408; Mainwaring and Scully, 1995: 33; Mainwaring and Shugart, 1997a: 435). During the third wave, democratic breakdown has been rare in Latin America, but scholars have shown that legislative minorities "increase the likelihood of presidential failure [presidents' resignation, removal, or impeachment]" (Edwards, 2015: 111). Scholars' concerns were held by Latin American political leaders too; in my surveys with legislators (see Appendix 1), 53% of the legislators who favored plurality cited the greater likelihood of legislative majorities.

Plurality advocates' fear of legislative minorities is expressed within a context of concern about presidentialism.[7] Scholars worry that, since both the executive and the legislature are popularly elected, there is "dual legitimacy"; conflict between the two institutions is likely and, especially given that terms are fixed and inflexible, democracy may break down (Linz, 1990a, 1990b). By contrast, in parliamentary regimes, executive and legislative powers are combined; deadlock can be averted through the prime minister's dissolution of the parliament or the parliament's vote of no confidence in the prime minister. Scholars' concern about presidentialism is heightened by the use of proportional representation for the election of the legislature in most Latin American nations, which tends to increase the number of parties.

Plurality advocates acknowledge that the president's party may form alliances to achieve a majority, but they warn about the hazards of this process. Cautions Valenzuela (2004: 13), "The smaller the president's own party, the greater becomes the challenge of cobbling together a majority ruling coalition." Alliances established after the first round for the purpose of the runoff are feared to be "hastily manufactured" (Jones, 1995: 186) and "shaky and fleeting" (Valenzuela, 1993: 8). Such alliances are also feared to be based on payoffs, such as cabinet seats, rather than ideological principle, and to be haunted by animosities from the first-round campaign (Valenzuela, 1993: 8; Diamond, 1996: 80–81; and Pachano, 2006: 117).

Especially worrisome for plurality advocates is the president's victory through a "reversal" of the first-round result—when the runoff is won not by the first-round victor but by the first-round runner-up (Carey, 2003: 14–15; Jones, 1995: 96–102; Pérez-Liñán, 2006: 137; Valenzuela, 2004: 7–13). Given that legislators in all Latin American countries under runoff are elected on the basis of the first-round vote, the party of the first-round winner is likely to be the largest in the legislature; accordingly, in the case of a reversal, the president's party will probably have fewer legislative seats than the party of the first-round winner. A coalition established for the runoff is no match against the party that won the first round: "the main opposition party ... is likely to control the largest single bloc in congress and it may play legislative politics with a vengeance" (Pérez-Liñán, 2006: 137). In short, executive-legislative gridlock is very likely (Carey, 2003: 14–15; Hartlyn, 1994b: 46–49; Jones, 1995: 91–102; Pérez-Liñán, 2006: 137–140; Valenzuela, 2004: 7–13).

Table 3.2 shows that, indeed, the incidence of legislative majorities is lower in runoff countries than in plurality countries. A majority was achieved in 36%

Table 3.2 **Results of Legislative Elections Plurality versus Runoff Countries, 1978–2012**

Presidential-Election Rule	Elections in Which the President's Party Had Less than 40.0% (Percent)	Elections in Which the President's Party Had 40.0%–49.9% (Percent)	Percent of Elections in Which the President's Party Had at Least 50.0% (Percent)
Plurality (N = 44)	14	36	50
Runoff (N = 64)	44	20	36

Note: Percentage of the seats in the lower (or only) house of the legislature won by the president's party. Mid-term elections are excluded. For classification rules, sources, data by country, and also the data for upper houses (which are very similar), see Appendix 3.

of elections in runoff countries versus 50% of elections in plurality countries. Further, in runoff countries, the president's party held less than 40.0% of the seats in a worrisome 44% of elections. Not surprisingly, countries with larger numbers of parties were more likely to elect presidents without a legislative majority or without 40% of the seats (see Appendix 3).

Accordingly, plurality advocates' fears that legislative minorities are more common under runoff were borne out. Yet, evidently, the problem of legislative minorities was not as negative for democracy as plurality advocates anticipated. Why not?

First, legislative minorities usually do not result in executive-legislative gridlock or democratic breakdown. For democracies worldwide between 1946 and 2002, Cheibub (2007: 82) showed that, the larger the number of parties, the more likely were coalition governments. As Gabriel Negretto (2006) documents, minority presidents whose ideological or policy positions are similar to those of most legislators have an advantage in the formation of coalitions. Also, minority presidents do have "trade-worthy coalition goods," in particular cabinet appointments, and can form coalitions (Negretto, 2006; Pereira and Melo, 2012; Zucco and Power, 2013). A cabinet appointment can be a "payoff"—but also an opportunity for principled consensus policy-making.

Second, as the number of parties increases and new parties enter the political arena, parties are not the behemoths poised for conflict and gridlock posited by plurality advocates. Rather, party leaders may be "amateurs" (Levitsky, 2013: 300). Reversals are not especially dangerous because the party of the first-round winner is likely to be just as makeshift as the runoff winner's coalition (Clark and Golder 2006, 706).[8] For example, in Peru after the victory of Alan García through a reversal in 2006, executive-legislative relations were conflict-free:

> Politically, García and his APRA party face no organized, meaningful opposition. The one-time major opposition figures have all but self-destructed. Ollanta Humala's following has withered away. Lourdes Flores Nano is busy running the university where she is Rector. Alberto Fujimori has again decided that he is Japanese. And, Alejandro Toledo is trotting the globe.... With all four effectively out of the picture, no one has yet stepped forward to present a coherent national alterative to the current Administration.[9]

Third, the process of alliance formation may not be that different under plurality and runoff. An alliance forged between the first round and the runoff might be tenuous; but, after a first round, there are strong incentives for alliances for the runoff whereas, after a plurality election, there are not (Martínez, 2004: 548). Under both plurality and runoff, most Latin American presidents have considerable power over the legislature. For example, even minority presidents are often granted honeymoon periods with decree powers. Said former Brazilian president Fernando Henrique

Cardoso, "Everyone still looks to the president.... If you have the capacity to talk to the country and an agenda, Congress falls into line. When you have neither, it doesn't."[10]

None of this is to deny plurality advocates' concerns about legislative minorities. I would have liked to track the trajectory of alliances between the president's party and other parties, but the total number of parties was large and many of the parties small, often including yet smaller factions, and sufficient information was not available.

To make their case, plurality advocates cited the cases of Alberto Fujimori in Peru and Jorge Serrano in Guatemala, both of whom were runners-up in the first round, with their parties securing less than 20% of the seats, who nonetheless won the runoff and then executed *autogolpes* (self-coups, in other words by themselves, in which they suspended the constitution and closed their countries' legislatures). Chapter 6 explores these cases and shows that the problems were complex, going beyond the low percentages of legislative seats to the elections overall. Perhaps the best example of plurality advocates' concerns is the 2016 election of Pedro Pablo Kuczynski in Peru; with only 18 of 130 legislative seats, the president's inchoate party faced dangerous confrontation with an institutionalized party led by Keiko Fujimori, which held a legislative majority (see Chapter 6).

Runoff Advocates' Case: Arguments and Cross-National Evidence

To date, scholarship favoring runoff has been scant. There are two scholars who have advocated runoff with any detail: Rafael Martínez and Josep Colomer. I build on the argument by Rafael Martínez that runoff enhances the legitimacy of the elected president. And I also build on the argument by Josep Colomer that runoff leads to a president who is supported by a country's centrist voters. I elaborate the two concepts of legitimacy and ideological moderation and incorporate cross-national data bolstering the arguments.

The Legitimacy of the Elected President

Although the principle of majority consent is long-standing in democratic theory, its application to the elected president is minimal. To my knowledge, Martínez (2004: 541–561) is the only scholar who has elaborated the concept of the legitimacy of the elected president. Martínez points out that under majority runoff, a president wins the support of a majority of voters—but frequently under plurality he or she does not. For Martínez, a reversal is advantageous because it prevents the victory of a candidate who is not supported by a majority of voters. And in turn, the legitimacy of the president is a key bulwark against democratic breakdown. As the indicator of presidential legitimacy, Martínez (2004: 551–555) proposes the increase in the president's vote tally between the first round and the runoff and the size of his or her final tally. In this subsection, I specify a different indicator.

Usually, the concept of legitimacy is applied to the state. A standard definition is Bruce Gilley's "the degree to which citizens treat the state as rightfully holding and exercising political power" (Gilley, 2008: 260). Similarly, John A. Booth and Mitchell A. Seligson (2009: 6) consider legitimacy "citizen support for government."

Usually, the legitimacy of the state is measured through survey research about trust in government and support for democracy. Unfortunately, however, citizens' responses to these questions reflect in part their views about the incumbent government's performance and are affected by short-term events like corruption scandals, hurricanes, and earthquakes (Booth and Seligson, 2009: 10–11). Other common indicators are social protest and voter turnout (Booth and Seligson, 2009; Dettrey and Schwindt-Bayer, 2009).

A few scholars have applied the concept of legitimacy to elections in general. The most common indicator has been losers' acceptance of the results, usually in turn indicated by an absence of partisan disputes after the election (Anderson, Blais, Bowler, Donovan, and Listhaug, 2005). However, this indicator was not helpful in Latin America during the third wave. Defining "dispute" as (a) a losing party's charges of fraud sustained for more than two weeks, (b) a demand for a recount, and (c) some street mobilization, I found that, during the third wave through 2014, disputes were rare under both runoff and plurality.[11] There were five disputes; one was under runoff (Peru in 2000) and four under plurality (the Dominican Republic in 1986, 1990, and 1994 and Mexico in 2006). Two of these elections—Peru in 2000 and the Dominican Republic in 1994—did not meet the bar for freedom and fairness set by the Organization of American States (OAS) and, accordingly, opposition protests were appropriate. Charges of fraud that were sustained for more than two weeks but not accompanied by street mobilization were more common but some were rather pro forma, without major media coverage, and therefore difficult to research and code.

Although the concept of the elected president's legitimacy is not well developed, the perception that the president's legitimacy is based on winning a majority of the vote is widespread. In my surveys of Latin American legislators (see Appendix 1), of the 133 legislators who preferred runoff, 84% cited greater legitimacy for the president as a reason for their preference (from a list of at least three reasons); it was the most commonly cited reason for legislators in all countries. Statements to this effect are legion. Wrote former Peruvian president Alejandro Toledo (2015: 132), "[in Latin America during the third wave] the number of two-round runoff systems has risen ... [and] countries have moved in the direction of increasing the *legitimacy* [italics mine] of presidential elections." Said Peru's Ambassador to Honduras about the possible results of Honduras's 2013 election, "What kind of *legitimacy* [italics mine] would a president have with 30% of the vote? None."[12] Colombia's newsweekly *Semana* explained the origin of runoff in France to be "amid the proliferation of political parties, the authorities believed that greater *legitimacy* [italics mine] for the elected candidate was necessary."[13]

It could be rebutted that leaders' perceptions that majority support for a president enhances the president's legitimacy is merely a perception—not reality. But, in this case, is it not? In other words, if Latin American elites and citizens perceive the president's legitimacy to be derived from a majority of the vote, then, in fact it is (Pérez-Liñán, 2006: 145).

Latin American leaders' perceptions that a president's legitimacy is important and is derived from an electoral majority are based in part on their analyses of the causes of military coups in Chile in 1973, Brazil in 1955, Peru in 1962, Argentina in 1963, and Ecuador in 1968. Latin American analysts frequently invoked the concept of legitimacy to help explain both the military coups and subsequent adoptions of runoff.

First, in Chile, more than thirty years after the 1973 military coup, debate about whether or not Allende would have won a 1970 runoff remained intense.[14] Leticia Ruiz Rodríguez (2004: 153–159) commented:

> [Runoff was advocated] amid the recollection of the election . . . of Allende with support inferior to the weight of the electorate in opposition, which many Chileans put at the origin of a process that unraveled . . . . In the memory of many Chileans what happened with Allende remains the argument for the benefits of the runoff . . . especially the hypothetical greater *legitimacy* of the elected president [italics mine].

Chile's 1973 coup was traumatic for the entire hemisphere because Chile's democracy had been longer-standing and more robust than in most European countries. Citing the "Allende effect," Guido Canchari Obregón (2010: 31) reported concerns that "plurality opens the doors to the eventual election of minority presidents, lacking an origin of *legitimacy* [italics mine] that protects them . . . ."

In Brazil, three of the four elections between 1945 and 1964 were won with a minority of the vote. The implications were explained by Jairo Nicolau (2004: 129):

> In three of the four presidential elections . . . the President-elect received less than 50 percent of the votes: Getúlio Vargas . . . with 49% in 1950; Juscelino Kubitschek . . . only 36 percent in 1955 and Jânio Quadros . . . 48 percent . . . . These results never failed to produce criticism, as the defeated parties questioned the *legitimacy* [italics mine] of the results.

Added David Fleischer (2017: 2), "The seeds were there in the post-1946 democratic period regarding the necessity of an absolute majority in presidential elections to give the president *legitimacy* [italics mine]."

In Peru in 1962, Víctor Raúl Haya de la Torre was less than one point shy of a 33.33% threshold, and the runner-up was less than a point behind. After intense lobbying and strident charges, the candidate who had finished third with 28%—a former dictator—was poised to be selected as the next president by Peru's congress. This fiasco dismayed the military (Payne, 1968: 54). A prominent professor of constitutional law, Francisco Eguiguren (1990: 145), highlighted that a key argument for runoff was that "the president enjoys the support of a real majority of citizens' votes, which increases his political and moral *legitimacy* [italics mine]."

In Ecuador, the 1968 winner had only 33%, less than two points more than the runner-up and less than three points more than the third-place candidate. Although the winner served for four years and was ousted for many reasons, Andrés Mejía Acosta (1997: 1) stated that "the close outcome of the 1968 election … inspired reformers to adopt a majority runoff [to] help reduce the number of parties and endorse the presidential mandate with greater electoral *legitimacy* [italics mine]." Seconded Flavia Freidenberg (2004: 233), "[Runoff was introduced] to incentivize the construction of majority governments … that could count on enough *legitimacy* [italics mine] …."

After Argentina's 1963 election, scholars regularly noted that the elected president, Arturo Illia of the Radical Party, tallied "only" 25% (Snow and Manzetti, 1993: 22), "just" 25% (Wynia, 1986: 129), a "mere" 25% (Rock, 1985: 344), or a "scant" 25% (McGuire, 1995: 215). Stated Wynia (1986: 129–130), "[Illia's] small plurality invited complaints of *illegitimacy* [italics mine] throughout his tenure." Radical leaders in particular believed that Illia's low percentage of the vote and dubious legitimacy posed challenges for his presidency and factored into the 1966 military coup.[15]

The concept of the legitimacy of the elected president has been applied beyond Latin America. For example, with respect to several Asian elections, Francis Fukuyama, Björn Dressel, and Boo-Seung Chang (2005: 113) note that:

> Korea, Taiwan, and Indonesia all elected presidents who received a minority of the popular vote and whose *legitimacy* [italics mine] the opposition questioned. The alleged *legitimacy* [italics mine] deficit was the direct motivation for impeachment efforts.

As Chapter 1 mentioned, my indicator for the legitimacy of the elected president is majority support; the elected president suffers a legitimacy deficit if it is uncertain whether or not he or she would have won a majority.

Let me elaborate. Pérez-Liñán (2006: 130) states that it is important that "a threshold of legitimacy" be established for a president's election. Pérez-Liñán (2006: 134 and 144) finds that, in 67% of the runoffs in Latin America between 1979 and 2002, the first-round winner was "confirmed" as the victor, and so "in most cases, the president could have been elected by plurality rule without altering the final outcome and with minimal costs in terms of presidential legitimacy or credibility." Pérez-Liñán (2006: 129) continues: "The need for runoff elections is dubious when the most voted candidate in the first round has obtained enough votes to become a legitimate winner."

But how many votes are "enough" to be "a legitimate winner"? I infer that votes are "enough" when they indicate that the candidate is very likely to be the winner. But could it be that, even if most first-round winners ultimately prevail, their victories are uncertain? And, if an outcome is uncertain, it follows from my discussion here that the runoff enhances the elected president's legitimacy.

As Chapter 1 indicated, I identified sixty-six elections, including both first-round elections under runoff and plurality elections, in Latin America between 1978 (or the first free and fair election of the third wave) and 2012 that were won with less than 50% (see Appendix 6). Then, I assessed whether (a) the first-round winner's victory in a runoff was or (under plurality) would have been virtually certain or (b) the first-round winner's victory in a runoff was or would have been uncertain or (c) a reversal of the first-round result was likely or virtually certain. Table 3.3 provides further information about the high incidence of uncertainty and likely or virtually certain reversals mentioned in Chapter 1.

I acknowledge that my indicator for presidential legitimacy is imperfect. It is likely that there are degrees of deficits of presidential legitimacy that matter. By definition, a president who wins in a runoff was not the first choice of most voters. Plurality advocates' argument that, in a runoff, a runner-up may win merely because he or she is not the widely disliked first-round winner is correct. A legitimacy deficit is also likely if the elected president is widely believed not to have been the "Condorcet winner"—a candidate who was probably the second choice of a large number of voters but the first choice of very few.

Table 3.3 **Elections Won with Less than 50% of the Vote, 1978–2012: What Was the Likely Result of a Runoff?**

	Elections under Plurality (N = 24)	First-Round Elections under Runoff (N = 42)	All Elections (N = 66)
Victory by the First-Round Winner Was Virtually Certain	9 (37.5%)	9 (21%)	18 (27%)
Result Was Uncertain	8 (33%)	29 (69%)	37 (56%)
A Reversal of the First-Round Result Was Likely or Virtually Certain	7 (29%)	4 (9.5%)	11 (17%)

Sources: See Appendix 6.

Still, as indicated in Chapter 1, the concept of legitimacy is closely tied to the concept of majority consent. My indicator accounts for the most egregious violation of this principle: the election of a president who was virtually certain not to have enjoyed majority support or unlikely to have enjoyed majority support.

Ideological Moderation

Various analysts have posited that runoff is "a force for moderation" (Smith, 2005: 157–158). Said a Chilean legislator, "The runoff obliges candidates to adopt a discourse that is inclusive, appealing to a majority of voters rather than to only thirty percent."[16] José Antonio Cheibub (2007: 109) praised the runoff as "an incentive to [the candidates] to reach beyond their own constituencies in order to be ranked relatively high in other groups' preferences." However, only Colomer has developed the argument in detail, including empirical evidence.

These analysts and I assume that a president whose ideology is assessed as "extreme" will be problematic for the country's democracy in some respects. However, we recognize that exceptions for a particular "extreme" ideology in a particular time or place will occur. We also recognize that moderation may not be viable. Some parties and leaders are well known; they can try to change their brand and may succeed, but may not. An ideological shift can endanger a leader's credibility and be impeded by party activists (Sides, 2006: 408–409).

The validity of the concept of "moderation," and indeed left-right classifications in general, has been questioned. It is argued that political issues are varied and may not be captured by a single left-right dimension; indeed, left-right positions among Latin American citizens have been shown to be not particularly coherent (Zechmeister and Corral, 2013). In other words, citizens may have a "left" position on one issue, a "right" position on another, and a third position that cannot be classified within the left-right framework at all. Voters may not know their positions and may misclassify themselves (Sides, 2006: 408–409).

Still, the concepts of left and right are used very often by scholars. A recent definition of the left is offered by Murillo, Oliveros, and Vaishnav (2011: 53): "The Left refers to political actors who seek, as a central programmatic objective, to reduce social and economic inequalities . . . ." Similarly, Juan Pablo Luna and Cristóbal Rovira Kaltwasser (2014: 4) state that the difference between left and right is the belief that the "main inequalities between people" are "artificial and therefore should be counteracted by active state involvement" or are "natural and outside the purview of the state."

Colomer's approach to the concept is to gauge whether or not a president enjoys the support of the "median voter"—the voter at the center of the ideological spectrum. Argues Colomer (2004: 39), "If no candidate obtains an absolute majority of votes at the first round, majority runoff creates double the probability of plurality rule that the final winner will be the candidate with the median voter's support."

To identify the median voter, Colomer (2007: 16) uses Latinobarometer data for voters' placements of their own ideologies on a 1–10 left-right scale.

My approach is different. I measure not the ideologies of voters but, as Chapter 1 indicated, the ideological positions of leaders and parties. My most important source is the survey data in the Parliamentary Elites of Latin America (PELA) project at http://americo.usal.es.oir (*series temporales* and *eliteca*), directed by Manuel Alcántara at the Universidad de Salamanca. Beginning in 1993, but carried out consistently only by the late 1990s, legislators in eighteen Latin American nations were surveyed near the start of their terms on a wide array of issues. Unfortunately, the surveys did not invariably include all parties and leaders; also, surveys for some countries (in particular Brazil and Venezuela) are scanty and others are missing for some years (for example, Ecuador for 2006). Further, some samples are small and not representative of the shares of legislative seats held by the parties (Kitschelt et al., 2010: 348–351).

Still, the PELA surveys "represent a quantum leap in our knowledge" (Kitschelt et al., 2010: 341). They are exceptionally fine-grained. Also, in the PELA surveys the legislators of a country are classifying a party or leader as "extreme" or "moderate" within the ideological context of their country, and it is arguably these leaders' perceptions that matter most. The survey results have been used and reported by numerous scholars (Alemán and Saiegh, 2007; Carlin, Singer, and Zeicheister, 2015: 15–16; Kitschelt et al., 2010: 59, 65–67, 341–343; Luna, 2014: 122–139; Mainwaring, Torcal, and Somma, 2015: 95; Singer, 2016).

For data prior to PELA surveys and for purposes of comparison, I also use left-right placements by other experts. These include Murillo, Oliveros, and Vaishnav (2010: 108–109), Coppedge (1997), and the World Bank (2013). Unfortunately, the number of classifications in the three datasets is small: right, center-right, center, center-left, and left in the first two datasets and only left, right, center and "O" or "Otherwise" (usually, ambiguous or unascertainable) in the World Bank (2013). Somewhat similarly, Mainwaring and Pérez-Liñán (2013: 77–83) develop measures for "radical policy preferences" with three points on the scale and "normative preferences for democracy" with five points on the scale.

By comparison, the PELA classifications are nuanced. For example, with respect to the Liberal and National parties in Honduras (see Chapter 4), Murillo, Oliveros, and Vaishnav (2010: 108–109) classify all Liberal presidents at the center-left and all National presidents at the center-right, and the World Bank (2013) classifies both parties at the right. Coppedge (1997) omits Honduras (and most Central American countries). By comparison, PELA puts the Liberal Party at the center-left in 1994, the center-right in 1997 and 2002, and the center in 2006 and 2010; it puts the National Party at the right with the exception of 2006, when it was at the extreme right. As would be the case for any dataset, some of PELA's figures can be questioned (see, for example, those for Mauricio Funes and Rafael Correa in Table 3.4). However, the PELA dataset is by far the most nuanced and comprehensive available.

Table 3.4 **Leftist Presidents and Top Presidential Candidates in Latin America: Plurality versus Runoff Countries, 2000–2012***

		"Extreme Left" (1.0 through 3.20)**	*"Moderate Left"* (3.21–4.99)**
Plurality	Honduras	Zelaya 2010 2.48***	None
	Mexico	López Obrador 2006 2.21	None
	Nicaragua	Ortega 2007 1.96	None
	Panama	None	None
	Paraguay	None	Lugo 2008 3.35
	Venezuela*	Chávez 2000 3.18	None
Runoff	Argentina	None	Kirchner 2004 4.18
	Brazil*	None	Lula's PT 2005 4.44 Lula 2010 4.69 Rousseff 2010 3.97
	Chile	None	Lagos 2002 3.95 Bachelet 2006 3.28
	Colombia	None	None
	Costa Rica	None	Solís 2006 4.67
	Dominican Republic	None	None
	Ecuador****	None	PSP 5.42/MUPP–NP 3.70 2002**** Correa 2009 3.44****
	El Salvador	Funes 2009 3.11	None
	Guatemala	None	Colom 2008 4.57
	Peru	None*****	Humala 2011 4.14
	Uruguay	None	Vázquez 2005 3.46 Mujica 2010 3.26

*Prior to 2000, there were few leftist presidents and top candidates, and PELA surveys were less frequent. Unfortunately, PELA surveys are not comprehensive. The only surveys for Venezuela were for 2000 and 2005, and the only surveys for Brazil were for 2005 (which unfortunately did not include Lula, only his party) and 2010.

**I modified the original PELA classification in which 1.00–2.49 is "extreme left," 2.50–3.99 is "left," and 4.0–4.99 is "center-left."

***Between Zelaya's election and 2010, he moved sharply left.

****There was no survey for Ecuador for 2006 (when Correa first won), and the 2002 survey includes only the two parties that formed a coalition behind Gutiérrez, not Gutiérrez himself.

*****In 2006, Humala, at 2.70, finished slightly more than five points behind the winner.

Note: Either presidents or presidential candidates tallying within five points of the winner (in the election in plurality countries or in the decisive round in runoff countries) are included. The dates in the table are the years of the PELA survey. For the full names of the leaders, see the text in subsequent chapters.

Source: PELA at http://americo.usal.es.oir (*series temporales* and *eliteca*).

Table 3.4 reports the presidents and top presidential candidates classified by PELA at either the "extreme left" or the "moderate left" under plurality and runoff. I limit the table to the apex of leadership because my goal is to compare the ideological positions of those who won the presidency or those who were so close to it that they might have won if, say, the election had been one day earlier or later. As Chapter 1 mentioned, a president or top presidential candidate was at the extreme left in four of the six plurality countries but in only one of the eleven runoff countries. (And, the one under runoff was El Salvador's Mauricio Funes, who was arguably misclassified.) Further, a president or top presidential candidate was at the moderate left in only one plurality country (Paraguay) but in eight of the eleven runoff countries.

Runoff reduced the possibility that not only a candidate at the extreme left would be elected but also a candidate at the extreme right. (Of course, the moderate right had been incorporated into the electoral arena from the start.) For the period 2000–2012 under plurality and runoff, Table 3.5 identifies presidents and top presidential candidates classified at the "extreme right" by PELA. As mentioned in Chapter 1, presidents at the extreme right were elected in three of the six plurality countries but only three of the eleven runoff countries. Presidential candidates at the extreme right came close to election but were defeated in the runoff in two additional countries.

Latin American Political Parties: A Variety of Authoritarian Proclivities

Plurality advocates tend to assume that long-standing Latin American parties are not disadvantageous to democracy—that the stability offered by long-standing parties is superior to the uncertainties provoked by new parties. I indicate that, unfortunately, numerous long-standing parties harbored authoritarian proclivities and excluded newcomers and, accordingly, lower barriers to entry were an advantageous leveling of the electoral playing field. This section underscores three types of authoritarian proclivities of numerous long-standing parties: (a) authoritarian pasts; (b) the formation of "cartels"; and (c) the perpetuation of old-timers.

Authoritarian Legacies

Many Latin American parties were founded in earlier eras when authoritarianism was prevalent; these parties bear the weight of the authoritarian practices of the past (Hicken and Martínez Kuhonta 2011; Loxton, 2015). As in other parts of the world, amid low educational levels and limited suffrage, democratic norms were inchoate and political exclusion common. It is often hard for these parties to forsake their past habits and hard too for other parties to forgive the past habits. Further, a considerable number of parties were influenced by ideologies specific to the era, especially the Cold War era, which did not endorse democratic principles.

Table 3.5 **Extreme Rightist Presidents and Top Presidential Candidates in Latin America: Plurality versus Runoff Countries, 2000–2012**[*]

		"Extreme Right"[**] *(8.00–10.00)*
Plurality	Honduras	Maduro 2001 8.18
	Mexico	None
	Nicaragua	Bolaños 2001 8.35
	Panama	Martinelli 2009 8.64
	Paraguay	None
	Venezuela[*]	None
Runoff	Argentina	None
	Brazil[*]	None
	Chile	Lavín 2002 8.22 (defeated in the runoff)
	Colombia	Uribe 2003 8.17
	Costa Rica	None
	Dominican Republic	None
	Ecuador[*]	None
	El Salvador	Saca 2006 9.03 ARENA 2009 9.67 (defeated in the first round)
	Guatemala	Berger 2004 8.20 Pérez Molina 2012 8.47
	Peru	Fuerza 2011 2011 8.52 (defeated in the runoff)
	Uruguay	None

[*]Prior to 2000, PELA surveys were less frequent. Unfortunately, PELA surveys are not comprehensive. The only surveys for Venezuela were for 2000 and 2005, and the only surveys for Brazil were for 2005 and 2010; there was no survey for Ecuador for 2006.

[**]I modified the PELA classification slightly, extending "extreme right" from 8.50 to 8.00.

Source: PELA at http://americo.usal.es.oir (*series temporales* and *eliteca*), except the figure for Martinelli, which is from Alcántara (2012: 29).

Note: Either presidents or presidential candidates tallying within five points of the winner or, if this data is not available, winning parties or parties tallying within five points of the winning party (in the election in plurality countries or in the decisive round in runoff countries) are included. The dates in the table are the years of the PELA survey. For the full names of the leaders, see the text in subsequent chapters.

In six of the seventeen countries, either one or both of the parties that won the largest percentages of the legislative vote in the first election of the third wave were founded prior to 1920 (see Table 3.6). In Nicaragua, the Partido Liberal (Liberal Party), the party of the brutal Somoza-family dynasty, was founded in the 1830s. In Paraguay,

Table 3.6 The Two Leading Parties at the Start of the Third Wave and the Year of Their Founding

Country and Year of First Third-Wave Election	Party #1	Party #2
Argentina, 1983	Radical Party, 1889	Peronist Party, 1944
Brazil, 1989	PMDB, 1965	PFL, 1985
Chile, 1990	PDC, 1957	RN, 1987*
Colombia, 1978	Conservative Party, 1848–49	Liberal Party, 1848–49
Costa Rica, 1978	PUSC, 1983⁺	PLN, 1951
Dominican Republic, 1978	PRSC, 1963⁺	PRD, 1939
Ecuador, 1978–1979	CFP, 1949	ID, 1978
El Salvador, 1994	ARENA, 1981	FMLN, 1980
Guatemala, 1985	Christian Democratic Party, 1955	National Center Union (UCN), 1983
Honduras, 1982	Liberal Party, 1891	National Party, 1916–1919
Mexico, 2000	PAN, 1939	PRI, 1929§
Nicaragua, 1990	Liberal Party, 1830s#	FSLN, 1961
Panama, 1994	PRD, 1979⁺	Arnulfista Party, 1932⁺
Paraguay, 1993	Colorado Party, 1887	PLRA, descendant of the Liberal Party, 1887
Peru, 1980	Popular Action, 1956	APRA, 1924
Uruguay, 1985	Colorado Party, 1836	National Party, 1836
Venezuela, 1978	Democratic Action, 1942	COPEI, 1946

*This status did not reflect the RN's strength within the rightist coalition; Chile's electoral rules were anomalous. See Chapter 5.

⁺The PUSC brought together various parties were founded between 1953 and 1978 that were opposed to the PLN (Rivas, 2004: 210).

⁺The PR was founded in 1963 and became the PRSC in 1986. It was built on the political bases of the Dominican Party, the vehicle of the dictator Rafael Leonídas Trujillo, founded in 1931. Although as of 1986 the term "Social Christian" was in the party's name, Christian Democratic principles were not salient in the party (Mainwaring and Scully, 2003).

§The name PRI was given in 1938; the party had two previous names.

#At the start of the third wave in 1990, the Liberal Party was divided; various factions joined a coalition opposed to the FSLN. But the coalition broke down even before the next election and, for Nicaraguans, the salient party was the Liberal Party, despite its various iterations (Morris, 2010: 181).

⁺The Arnulfista Party had various names; for many years it was the personal vehicle of Arnulfo Arias. In 1994, both this party and the PRD were the major parties in coalitions but it was these parties that survived.

Note: The year of the founding of the two parties with the largest percentages of the vote in the legislature (or, if applicable, in the lower house of the legislature) during the first election of the third wave. The most common name in English or the common acronym for the party is used; for the formal name, see the first reference to the party in this book.

Sources: See text in subsequent chapters for scholarly work on each country's history.

both the Colorado Party (officially named the Asociación Nacional Republicana or National Republican Association, ANR) and the Partido Liberal (Liberal Party) were founded in 1887. In Argentina, the Unión Cívica Radical (Radical Civic Union, usually called the Radical Party) was founded in 1889. In Colombia, Honduras, and Uruguay, two parties were founded prior to 1920 and became "duopolies;" they tolerated competition with each other but sought to exclude other parties.

Prior to 1920, parties' programmatic differences were often about the role of the Catholic Church or the interests of rural versus urban sectors. Subsequently, in the 1920s, 1930s, and 1940s—after the Russian Revolution and amid the rise of Adolf Hitler and Benito Mussolini—parties emerged that were influenced by the debates about Marxism and fascism. The Dominican Republic's Partido Revolucionario Dominicano (Dominican Revolutionary Party, PRD), founded in 1939 by Juan Bosch, rejected Communism but endorsed Marxism; Peru's APRA advocated leftist social reforms but rejected Marxism. The leaders of the parties that were predecessors to Panama's Arnulfista Party, founded in 1932, and Argentina's Peronist Party were influenced by fascism. Indeed, as an Argentine military officer, Juan Perón was stationed in Italy in 1939–1941 and, like a considerable number of Argentine officers, he studied fascism.

Christian Democratic parties were also common. Christian Democratic parties founded in the 1930s and 1940s, such as Mexico's Partido Acción Nacional (National Action Party, PAN) and Venezuela's Comité de Organización Política Electoral Independiente (usually called the Christian Democrats or Social Christians, COPEI), as well as Ecuador's Partido Social Cristiano (Social Christian Party, PSC), founded in 1951, were in part reactions to successful secular, leftist or populist parties and were usually considered to be toward the center-right. Also, Costa Rica's Christian Democratic party, founded in the 1950s, joined more conservative parties and the coalition was defined in good part by its opposition to the dominant center-left party.

Subsequently, as the Cold War intensified in the 1950s, many Christian Democratic parties highlighted Catholic values and promised change—but legal and peaceful change—and presented themselves as a "third way" between capitalism and Communism (Mainwaring and Scully, 2003). These parties were successful in many European countries and Germany's party in particular promoted Christian Democracy in Latin America. Amid the Second Vatican Council (1962–1965), the Catholic Church was becoming more progressive, and most Christian Democratic parties founded around this time—including the parties in Chile, El Salvador, and Guatemala as well as Ecuador's Popular Democracy, founded in 1977—were considered to be to the center-left. However, in the twenty-first century, Latin America has become more secular and more Protestant, and the Catholic Church has become more guarded about participation in politics; Christian Democratic parties have receded.

By the 1960s, the Cold War was casting a large shadow on Latin America. Marxist parties emerged, and two of these parties were among the two largest parties in their country's legislature at the start of the third wave: the Frente Farabundo Martí de Liberación Nacional (Farabundo Martí National Liberation Front, FMLN) in El Salvador and the Frente Sandinista de Liberación Nacional (Sandinista National Liberation Front, FSLN) in Nicaragua. During the Cold War, political polarization was intense; supported by the United States, some rightist parties resorted to repression against Marxist sectors and, supported by the Soviet Union or Cuba, militants in some Marxist parties also resorted to violence. In El Salvador and Nicaragua, the intense polarization of the Cold-War period endured; not only was a Marxist party one of the two strongest in the first third-wave legislatures of the two countries, but the other strongest party was at the extreme right in PELA surveys—the Alianza Repúblicana Nacionalista (Nationalist Republican Alliance, ARENA) in El Salvador and the Liberal Party in Nicaragua.

Unfortunately, democratic principles were frequently abused. Table 3.7 provides a rough guide—the consensus scholarly view—to authoritarian actions by leading Latin American political parties prior to the third wave. (It is beyond the scope of this book to rigorously measure the extent of authoritarianism in Latin American political parties in the past.) Three types of authoritarian actions are considered: (a) complicity in a military coup or military government, (b) abuse of checks and balances (for parties in power), and (c) complicity in serious violations of human rights. As the notes at the bottom of the table indicate, I did not set bars too high.

The table reports that, of the two leading parties in each country at the start of the third wave, at least one of the two had committed at least one authoritarian action in thirteen of the seventeen countries. In five—Colombia, El Salvador, Nicaragua, Panama, and Paraguay—both parties had committed at least one authoritarian action. Only in Brazil, Chile, Costa Rica, and Guatemala had neither leading party committed at least one authoritarian action. There is a considerable correlation between older parties and more authoritarian pasts: as noted previously, both of the two parties in Colombia and Paraguay were founded in the nineteenth century, as was the Partido Nacional de Honduras (National Party) in Honduras, the Liberal Party in Nicaragua, and the Colorado Party in Uruguay. Other parties with authoritarian pasts that were founded prior to or during World War II include Argentina's Peronist Party, founded in 1944 as the Partido Laborista (Labor Party) and named the Partido Justicialista (Justicialist Party) in 1973; Mexico's PRI (Partido Revolucionario Institucional, Institutional Revolutionary Party); Panama's Arnulfista Party; and Peru's APRA (Alianza Popular Revolucionario Americana, American Popular Revolutionary Alliance, founded in 1924 by Víctor Raúl Haya de la Torre).

Cartel Parties

In the conceptualization developed by Richard Katz and Peter Mair (2009), numerous parties became "cartel parties." Cartel parties may be a single party or they may be two parties that "cooperate and collude" (Katz and Mair, 2009: 754).

Table 3.7 Did One or Both of the Leading Parties in the First Third-Wave Election Have an Authoritarian Past?

Country	Leading Parties with No Authoritarian Action	Authoritarian Action: Complicit in Military Coup or Military Government?	Authoritarian Action: Complicit in Abuse of Checks and Balances (if in Power)?	Authoritarian Action: Complicit in Serious Violations of Human Rights?
Argentina	Radical Party	Peronist Party	Peronist Party	Peronist Party
Brazil	PMDB and PFL	Neither[*]	Neither[*]	Neither[*]
Chile	PDC and Renovación Nacional	Neither[†]	Neither[†]	Neither[†]
Colombia	Neither	Conservative and Liberal Parties	Conservative and Liberal Parties	Conservative and Liberal Parties
Costa Rica	PLN and PUSC	Neither	Neither	Neither
Dominican Republic	PRD	PRSC	PRSC	PRSC's predecessor
Ecuador	ID	Neither	Neither	CFP[‡]
El Salvador[§]	Neither	Neither[§]	Neither	ARENA, FMLN
Guatemala[§]	DCG and UCN	Neither[§]	Neither	Neither
Honduras	Liberal Party	National Party	National Party	National Party
Mexico	PAN	Neither	PRI	PRI
Nicaragua	Neither	Liberal Party[#]	Liberal Party[#]	Liberal Party,[#] FSLN
Panama	Neither	PRD	PRD; Arnulfista Party[+]	PRD; to a lesser degree, the Arnulfista Party[+]

Paraguay	Neither	Colorado Party; to a lesser degree, the Liberal Party	Colorado Party; to a lesser degree, the Liberal Party	Colorado Party
Peru	Popular Action	Neither	Neither	APRA
Uruguay	National Party	Colorado Party	Colorado Party	Colorado Party
Venezuela	Democratic Action	COPEI**	Neither	Neither

*However, the PFL was a breakaway party from the PDS, which was complicit with Brazil's military government.

†However, Renovación Nacional joined a coalition with the UDI, which was close to the Pinochet dictatorship. Also, although the Christian Democratic Party did not cooperate with the 1973–1990 government, most party leaders foreswore dialogue with the Popular Unity government shortly before the coup; although the party did not anticipate the military's brutality, it was perceived in many quarters to have given a green light to the coup.

‡When CFP leader Assad Bucaram was mayor of Guayaquil, he was responsible for "brutal" suppression of students (Martz, 1987: 85).

§My bar for complicity in military governments or military coups is low for both El Salvador and Guatemala. Although neither ARENA nor the UCN was explicitly complicit in military governments or military coups, they were both considered the party of the mainstream military. Also, in Guatemala, the party of former General Efraín Ríos Montt was not first or second in the first third-wave election but it was nonetheless a key party; as the head of a military government, Ríos Montt was responsible for serious human-rights violations.

¶At the start of the third wave in 1990, the Liberal Party was divided; various factions united in an opposition coalition. But the 1990 coalition broke down even before the next election and, for Nicaraguans, the salient party was the Liberal Party, despite its various iterations (Morris, 2010: 181).

#The Arnulfista party has had various names. See Chapter 4.

**In contrast to, for example, the Christian Democratic Party in Chile, COPEI not only gave a green light to a military coup in 1948 but participated for a short period in the military government. See Chapter 4.

Note: For the two parties with the largest percentages of the vote in the legislature (if applicable, the lower house of the legislature) during the first election of the third wave. The most common name in English or the common acronym for the party is used; for the formal name, see the first reference to the party in this book.

Sources: See text in subsequent chapters for scholarly work on each country's political history.

Political parties "function like cartels, employing the resources of the state to limit political competition and ensure their own electoral success" (Katz and Mair, 2009: 753). Parties are "increasingly part of the state, and increasingly removed from society" (Katz and Mair, 2009: 756). In the traditional discourse about party organization, they are well institutionalized and "strong," but, closing alternative channels of political participation, they are also exclusive (Coppedge, 1994). As Chapter 1 mentioned, parties are not bridges between state and society but castles with vast moats.

Fused with the state, cartel parties frequently secure electoral laws and decisions to their advantage. Among the salient examples is the introduction of onerous requirements for the registration of coalitions by the PRI government after successful coalition-building by Mexico's opposition in the 1988 election (see Chapter 4). Another is the annulment of a conviction of a potential presidential candidate during the Colorado government shortly before Paraguay's 2008 election so that the candidate would take votes from the leftist priest, Fernando Lugo (see Chapter 4).

Further, cartel parties control the electoral machinery. They can tilt the playing field to their advantage in numerous ways, such as how easily citizens are registered to vote and how fairly voting places are distributed across the country. Often in Latin America, honest vote counts are expected to be assured through the presence of representatives of every party at the vote count in each voting place; but, small parties can rarely recruit enough representatives for all the voting places, and in various countries, in particular Honduras, the practice of the cartel parties was to divide between them the vote of the small parties (see Chapter 4). And, traditionally, cartel parties simply bought votes.

As Steven Levitsky (2001) emphasizes, cartel parties also enjoy vast patronage resources. For example, in Uruguay during "co-participation" between the Partido Colorado (Colorado Party) and the Partido Nacional (National Party, usually called the Blancos) from the 1920s through the 1950s, "the two traditional parties more and more saw the state and its apparatus as something to which they were entitled.... The growing state bureaucracy ... was both a source of votes and a payoff for the loyalty of party factions.... [There was a] total politicization of public employment and bureaucracy" (Weinstein, 1975: 65, 67, and 69). After 1952, of five positions on the boards of all state enterprises, three were given to the majority party and two to the minority party (McDonald, 1996: 276).

Further, for these parties, patronage rather than program was the key to the party's links to its supporters. Michelle Taylor-Robinson (2010: 116–117) describes the importance of patronage to the Liberal and National Parties in Honduras:

> Traditional parties still bind supporters to the party with clientele networks.... They are the way to gain access to the state's scarce resources, whether for elites who want government contracts or for poor people who

need a political patron to get them a job or welfare assistance.... The need for connections to gain access to even basic government services (e.g., schooling, health care, cash transfers) makes it very costly for poor people to leave a traditional party if they are frustrated by its platform.... Small parties ... are unlikely to give activists access to state resources.

In addition, as Kenneth Greene (2002 and 2007a) highlights, the control of resources by the cartel party pushes opposition parties to emphasize ideology and leads them to become "niche parties." Cartel parties attract and retain ambitious, pragmatic politicians; it is only ideological militants who risk activism in opposition parties. This emphasis on ideology impedes both subsequent ideological shifts and coordination among opposition parties.

Successful cartel parties include the Peronist Party in Argentina, the PRI in Mexico, the Colorado Party in Paraguay, and all the duopolies that endured at the start of the third wave: the Conservative and Liberal Parties in Colombia; the Liberal and National Parties in Honduras; the Colorado and Blanco Parties in Uruguay; and Acción Democrática (Democratic Action, AD) and COPEI in Venezuela.[17] After the 2006 election, the FSLN became a cartel party (see Chapter 4). Precise thresholds have not been established; for example, by the 2000s the Partido de la Liberación Dominicana (Party of Dominican Liberation, PLD) in the Dominican Republic was considered a cartel party by some analysts but not others.[18]

By some accounts (Lehoucq, 2005), the Partido Liberación Nacional (National Liberation Party, PLN) and the Partido Unidad Social Cristiana (Social Christian Unity Party, PUSC) in Costa Rica approximated a duopoly. As of the 1990s, programmatic differences between the two parties had eroded and both parties espoused "a centrism so bland that it has alienated large chunks of voters" (Lehoucq, 2005: 147). The parties were not perceived to be open to citizen input (Lehoucq, 2005: 146–147 and Seligson, 2002: 180). Costa Rica hosted a large number of "autonomous institutions" for the provision of medical care, electricity, telephone service, and the like; increasingly the two parties "began to collude at the task of colonizing the autonomous bodies with their respective loyalists" (Lehoucq, 2005: 148). Overall, however, I agree with Levitsky (2001: 99) that "cartel-like collusion between the parties ... [was] not as strongly present" in Costa Rica as in other countries. The two parties were relatively young and, into the 1980s, program was more important than patronage (see Chapter 7). Ultimately, the two parties were not able to exclude new parties from the political arena (see Chapter 7).

The Perpetuation of Old-Timers

Many Latin American parties have been dominated by caudillos. As Javier Corrales (2008) argued, while scholars are concerned about the emergence of "outsiders," a plethora of caudillos is worrisome also. Scholars have not established a precise definition of "caudillo" or "old-timer"; following the research by Corrales (2008), I consider "old-timers" to be ex-presidents who pursue presidential comebacks and, to a lesser degree, candidates with an ex-president's last name who compete.

The primary concern about old-timers is that they block the ascent of newcomers within the party and are likely to impede change in the party overall. They do not mentor younger politicians and do not yield to them. Said a Peruvian political analyst, "A caudillo freezes a party."[19] As a result, up-and-comers may bolt from their parties (Corrales, 2008: 18–19).

Yet, old-timers have large electoral advantages over newcomers. As Chapter 1 mentioned, they have loyal donors, loyal campaign teams, and loyal friends in high places. They are brand names; it is easy for them to get media attention and easy to fare well in opinion polls (which reflect, in part, name recognition). They draw all the political oxygen to themselves. At the same time, the obstacles facing newcomers are greater in Latin America than in the United States or Europe. Into the 1990s, many Latin American states were highly centralized; local and state political offices were not available. The range of political offices available remains small and the range of respected political offices smaller yet. In many countries legislatures are disdained and legislators are rarely able to achieve records that would be to their credit in a presidential race.

Corrales (2008) showed the prevalence of "neo-caudillismo" in Latin America for the period 1988–2006. Comparing old-timers in Latin America and in both presidential and parliamentary regimes in Europe, he found that ex-presidents or ex–prime ministers and candidates with an ex-president's or ex–prime minister's last name competed much more often in Latin America than in Europe (see Table 3.8).

I extended the years of Corrales' dataset for Latin America—beginning in 1978 rather than 1988 and ending in 2012 rather than 2006 (and with slight variations in the countries in the dataset). As Table 3.8 indicates, I too found a high incidence of neo-caudillismo in Latin America. Ex-presidents competed in 50% of the Latin American elections in which they were allowed to compete in Corrales' dataset and 44% in my dataset, versus only 17% of the European elections. Candidates with an ex-president's last name competed in 16% of the elections in Latin America in Corrales' dataset and 27% in my dataset, but were "virtually non-existent" in Europe.

As of 2006, the last year in Corrales' dataset, incumbent re-election was rarely allowed in Latin America and indefinite incumbent re-election was never allowed; accordingly, Corrales was not concerned about the impact of incumbents (Corrales, 2008: 6). However, during the course of the third wave, rules about incumbent re-election were dramatically relaxed.

As of 2015, any re-election of a president remained banned in Honduras, Guatemala, Mexico, and Paraguay and incumbent re-election remained banned in Chile, Costa Rica, El Salvador, Panama, Peru (except 1993–2000), and Uruguay. But, in the other seven countries, rules were relaxed. Since the mid-1990s, one

Table 3.8 **Old-Timer Candidates in Latin America versus Europe***

	Latin America, 1978–2012	Latin America, 1988–2006	Europe, 1988–2006*
Number of Elections Allowing Ex-Presidents to Compete	84	66	46
Number of Elections in Which Ex-Presidents Competed	34	33	8
Percent of Elections in Which Ex-Presidents Were Allowed to Compete & Won 10%	40%†	50%	17%
Percent of Elections in Which a Candidate with an Ex-president's Last Name Won 10%	27%‡	16%	"virtually non-existent"

*Most of the countries in Corrales' dataset for Europe were not presidential (Austria, Belgium, Germany, Italy, the Netherlands, Norway, Spain, Sweden, and the United Kingdom).

†This calculation under-estimates the number of ex-presidents who competed because in several elections more than one ex-president competed (Argentina in 2003 and the Dominican Republic in 1982 and 1986).

‡This calculation under-estimates the number of candidates with an ex-president's last name who competed because in several elections more than one candidate with an ex-president's last name competed (Argentina in 2011; Chile in 1993; Ecuador in 2002 and 2006; and Panama in 1994).

Note: Following Corrales (2008), I included only candidates winning more than 10.0% of the vote in at least one third-wave election in my dataset. (The reasons are candidate viability and information availability.) However, the sets of Latin American countries are slightly different; for reasons mentioned previously, I excluded countries that were not colonized by Spain or Portugal and I also exclude Bolivia. Classification as ex-president includes elections prior to third-wave elections.

Sources: For Latin America 1978–2012, see Appendix 5. For Latin America and Europe 1988–2006, see Corrales (2008: 6–7).

re-election of the incumbent was permitted in Argentina and Brazil and, since the 2000s, one re-election of the incumbent was permitted in Colombia, the Dominican Republic, and two in Ecuador. As of 2015, indefinite re-election of the incumbent was allowed in Nicaragua and Venezuela, and this possibility loomed in Ecuador (and Bolivia) as well.

Incumbents' overwhelming advantages are evident in electoral results. During the third wave through 2012 in Latin America, incumbents ran for immediate re-election twenty times and won seventeen times (albeit twice in fraudulent elections). In only three attempts (15%) did incumbents lose: Joaquín Balaguer in the Dominican Republic in 1978, Hipólito Mejía in the Dominican Republic in 2004, and Daniel Ortega in Nicaragua in 1990. By contrast, ex-presidents who ran for re-election after one or two intervening terms usually failed. Of thirty-seven attempts at re-election after one or two intervening terms (in which the ex-president tallied at least 10%), twenty-nine (78%) failed and eight (22%) succeeded. The immense advantages wielded by incumbents suggest that permission of the indefinite re-election of incumbents poses serious risks to democracy. In European countries with presidential regimes (Finland, France, Lithuania, Portugal, and Romania), presidents are limited to two terms, with the exception of Portugal, where additional terms are allowed after an intervening term.[20]

When ex-presidents were allowed to compete after an intervening term, some did not yield to newcomers for more than two decades. Peru's Alan García was first elected in 1985; he lost in 2001, won in 2006, discouraged his party's nomination of another presidential candidate in 2011, and planned to be the party's standard-bearer in 2016. By 2011, APRA was García's "fiefdom.... No one in the APRA challenges him."[21] Venezuela's Rafael Caldera competed in 1947, 1958, and 1963 before winning in 1968, competed again but lost in 1983; when he did not win his party's nomination in 1993, he formed a new coalition and won.

Indeed, even losing presidential candidates often dominated their parties and blocked the emergence of new leaders. A large number of Latin American presidential candidates competed even though they had lost at least three consecutive times (see Appendix 5). The Dominican Republic's Juan Bosch competed five times and lost five times; Ecuador's Álvaro Noboa competed four times and lost four times. Uruguay's Jorge Batlle lost four times before winning on his fifth try, and Brazil's Lula lost three times before winning on his fourth try. After Daniel Ortega's 1984–1990 presidency in Nicaragua, he lost three times before winning again on his fourth try. Candidates running three times and losing three times were Colombia's Álvaro Gómez Hurtado, Costa Rica's Otto Guevara and Ottón Solís, Mexico's Cuauthémoc Cárdenas (albeit losing in 1988 probably due to fraud), Paraguay's Domingo Laíno, Uruguay's Líber Seregni, and Venezuela's Andrés Velásquez. In total, among 221 unique presidential candidates winning 10.0% of the vote at least once during the third wave in Latin America, 37 (17%) ran three times or more (see Appendix 5). In European countries with presidential regimes (Finland, France, Lithuania, Portugal, and Romania), the percentage was similar.[22] It is the United States, with its tradition that losers in presidential races step aside, that is the exception.

Old-timers were common in most Latin American countries (see Appendix 5). Correlations between caudillismo and levels of democracy were not evident. The region's democratic stars were vulnerable: in Chile, the 2009 re-election bid of ex-president Eduardo Frei divided his coalition and was a factor in its first loss of the presidency in almost twenty years; as just indicated, in both Costa Rica and Uruguay, the incidence of multiple attempts at the presidency and of candidates with an ex-president's last name was high. Caudillismo was least evident in El Salvador and Honduras, where, overall, scores only approximated Latin American averages.

Barriers to Entry: Focus on Pre-Election Opinion Polls

Given that many long-standing Latin American parties are not very democratic, lower barriers to entry would be positive for democracy. We have noted various higher barriers under plurality. But we have not described an additional barrier in plurality countries with more than 2.0 parties (in other words, almost all Latin American plurality countries): the defeat of entrenched, exclusive parties usually requires the unity of the opposition. As Larry Diamond (2011: B5) stated: "Even extremely corrupt rulers may generate significant electoral support—not the thumping majorities they claim, but enough to steal an election—when the opposition is splintered."

The formation of alliances among opposition parties can be very difficult. Well-known obstacles include disparate ideologies, leaders' ambitions and rivalry, and serious political cleavages within the country. Also, presidential and legislative races usually coincide; if a party does not field a presidential candidate in the first round, it is likely to hurt its legislative list. These obstacles are very evident in my analysis of the problems of plurality in Chapter 4.

Additional obstacles are much less well-known but are also evident in Chapter 4. Entrenched incumbent parties may engage in outright sabotage to divide and conquer the opposition. They may pass laws that impede alliances. They may introduce new candidates or "fake" candidates (such as sports stars) into the campaign.

Indeed, in some contexts, alliances are likely to be counter-productive. When ideologies are very disparate—as was the case with the two major opposition parties against Mexico's PRI—an alliance can provoke cynicism. And, when long-standing parties are alive but not well—as was the case in Venezuela after 1993—an alliance can burden the new party with the older party's baggage.

An important, less well-known barrier is inaccurate opinion polls. Noted one political analyst, "You can't make good alliances when things are not stable or clear."[23] When opposition parties do not ally, opposition voters may not know for which opposition party they should cast their ballot. Stated Kenneth F. Greene (2007a: 7) for a Mexican election, "anti-PRI voters who prioritized democracy were left to gamble on which challenger party had the better chance of defeating the incumbent in a given election."

I assessed the accuracy of pre-election opinion polls about voters' preferences for presidential candidates in Latin America between 1988 and 2012 as well as in Europe between 2000 and 2012 (see Appendix 4). My assessment began in 1988 because, prior to the late 1980s, reports of polls were sparse, especially for Central American countries. Some data remained missing for a few countries.

Table 3.9 shows that, in Latin America between 1988 and 2012, at approximately one month prior to the election, only 35% of the pre-election polls were correct

Table 3.9 **Pre-Election Opinion Polls about Voters' Preferences for Presidential Candidates in Latin America, 1988–2012 and 2000–2012, versus Polls about Presidential or Prime Ministerial Candidates in Europe and the United States, 2000–2012**

Region of the World	Correct within 5.0 Points at Approximately 1 Month before the Election	Correct within 10.0 Points at Approximately 3 Months before the Election	Correct within 10.0 Points at Approximately 6 Months before the Election
Latin America, 1988–2012	35% (N = 91)	39% (N = 89)*	27% (N = 66)*
Latin America, 2000–2012	34% (N = 47)	48% (N = 46)*	26% (N = 35)*
Europe and the United States, 2000–2012	71% (N = 17)	88% (N = 17)	82% (N = 17)

*For the period 1988–2012, data for 6 months were not available for two elections in Costa Rica, one in Ecuador, two in Honduras, and one in Uruguay. Data for 3 months were are not available for one election in Honduras. In addition, in several countries at 6 months and in one election in Guatemala at 3 months, the candidates were not clear and these elections were not included. Most of these elections were between 1988 and 1999, but a few were between 2000 and 2012.

Note: For the candidates who won at least 10.0% of the vote in the election (or the first round of the election).

Sources and discussion: For See Appendix 4.

within five points of the actual result; at approximately three months prior, only 39% were correct within ten points; and, at approximately six months prior, only 27% were correct within ten points. The very low percentage of correct polls at about six months is especially significant because usually alliance decisions would have to be made be at this time. The only countries in which the polls were accurate for a majority of the elections were Chile and Uruguay (see Appendix 4). For the period 2000–2012, only polls at roughly three months were somewhat more accurate.

By contrast, Table 3.9 shows that most pre-election opinion polls in Europe and the United States were accurate. For elections in France, Spain, Portugal, and the United Kingdom as well as the United States between 2000 and 2012, 71% of the polls were correct within five points at approximately one month, 88% correct within ten points at approximately three months, and 82% correct within ten points at approximately three months. Remarkably, in the United States, 100% of the polls were correct—correct for all three time periods for four elections. Joseph Katz and Kevin Quealy (2016: A3) indicated that polls have been correct within these thresholds in the United States since 1980.

Entrenched parties are likely to be advantaged in the polls. Not only do they enjoy name recognition, but the party's leaders usually have links to media companies that in turn are linked to polling agencies.[24] Said Mexican presidential candidate Andrés Manuel López Obrador, "The polls are like propaganda."[25] Added former Peruvian president Alan García, "The pollsters lie and they know that they lie."[26] Lamented a 2016 Peruvian presidential candidate, "The survey companies always err in favor of those with the money. It is necessary to audit the survey companies because there is corruption."[27]

Of course, there are additional reasons for the inaccuracies of the polls. Campaigns are volatile and many voters are undecided until very late in the campaign (LAWR February 28 2006, p. 4). Large percentages of citizens—approximately 40% in Mexico and 60% in Peru—refuse to open their doors to pollsters.[28] Pollsters' resources are short and rural areas are usually under-sampled, as in Chile (LAWR, January 14, 2010, p. 9), Colombia (LARR, June 2006, p. 5), Ecuador (LAWR, April 30, 2009, p. 1), and Paraguay (LAWR, February 21, 2008, p. 11). Citizens often register and turn out disproportionately by candidate (LAWR, January 14, 2010, p. 9). There are fewer previous elections than in the United States or Europe on which pollsters can develop their statistical models.[29]

The Rise of New Parties

The principle that barriers to entry are lower under runoff was confirmed by trends in Latin America during the third wave. To date, precise definitions and thresholds for the emergence of a "new" party have not been established (see Appendix 7). I report, first, a measure for new parties in presidential elections and, second, in legislative elections.

Table 3.10 shows that new parties become "significant contenders" in a considerably larger percentage of presidential elections under runoff than under plurality.

Table 3.10 **New Parties as Significant Contenders in Presidential Elections under Plurality versus Runoff, 1978–2012**

Electoral Rule	Presidential Elections in Which a New Party Achieved 15%
Plurality (N = 45)	14 (31%)
Runoff (N = 65)	31 (48%)

Sources: Appendix 7, which includes definitions and the parties in each country.

A new party became a "significant contender," achieving 15% of the vote, in 48% of the presidential elections under runoff but 32.5% of the elections under plurality.

Tables 3.11 and 3.12 compare the rise of new parties in legislatures under plurality and runoff. The two tables identify the two parties with the largest percentages of the vote in the legislature (or, if applicable, the lower house of the legislature) for the most recent election through 2012 and, comparing these two parties with the two leading parties in the country at the start of the third wave in Table 3.6, asks whether or not there was a change in the identity of the two leading parties.

Table 3.11 shows that, among the six plurality countries, the two leading parties in the most recent election were the same as at the start of the third wave in all except Venezuela.

By contrast, Table 3.12 reports that, among the eleven runoff countries, the two leading parties were the same only in Argentina and El Salvador. With the exception of the Unión Demócrata Independiente (Democratic Independent Union, UDI) in Chile and the PLD in the Dominican Republic, all these parties either emerged during the third wave or were founded explicitly as alternatives to the governing parties. A good number of these parties had been at one time quite far to the left but had moderated: Brazil's Workers' Party (Partido dos Trabalhadores, Workers' Party,

Table 3.11 **The Two Leading Parties in the Most Recent Legislative Election through 2012: Plurality Countries**

Country	Party #1	Party #2	Was There a Change from the First Election to the Most Recent?
Honduras	National Party, 1916–19	Liberal Party, 1891	No
Mexico	PRI, 1929*	PAN, 1939	No
Nicaragua	FSLN, 1961	Liberal Party, 1830s*	No
Panama	PRD, 1932†	Arnulfista Party, 1979†	No
Paraguay	Colorado Party, 1887	PLRA, descendant from the Liberal Party, 1887	No
Venezuela	PSUV, successor to the MVR, founded in 1997	Democratic Unity Roundtable, 2008‡	Yes, two parties

*See notes about these parties in Table 3.6.

†Competed within coalitions; these parties won the first and second largest percentages of seats. A new party that won the presidency was in third place in the legislative vote.

‡Includes Democratic Action and COPEI but also numerous other parties, including Radical Cause, a "new" party with 22% of the vote in 1993. See Chapter 4.

Note: The identity and founding year of the two parties with the largest percentages of the vote in the legislature (or, if applicable, in the lower house of the legislature) during the most recent election of the third wave through 2012. The most common name in English or the common acronym for the party is used; for the formal name, see the first reference to the party in this book.

Table 3.12 **The Two Leading Parties in the Most Recent Legislative Election through 2012: Runoff Countries**

Country	Party #1	Party #2	Was There a Change from the First Election to the Most Recent?
Argentina	Peronist Party (Victory Front faction), 1944	Radical Party, 1889	No
Brazil	Workers' Party, 1980	PMDB, 1965	Yes, one party
Chile	UDI, 1983	RN, 1987	Yes, two parties*
Colombia	Partido de la U, 2002†	Green Party, 2005	Yes, two parties
Costa Rica	PLN, 1951	PAC, 2000	Yes, one party
Dominican Republic	PLD, 1973	PRD, 1939	Yes, one party
Ecuador	Alianza PAIS, 2006	PSP, 2000	Yes, two parties
El Salvador	ARENA, 1981	FMLN, 1980	No
Guatemala	Patriotic Party, 2001	LIDER, 20110	Yes, two parties
Peru	Gana Perú, 2010	Fuerza 2011, 1990‡	Yes, two parties
Uruguay	Frente Amplio, 1971	Blanco Party, 1836	Yes, one party

*The largest-percentage of the vote indicator is a flawed indicator of the trajectory of Chile's parties. The percentages depend on the dynamics of the two coalitions; also, the 2009–2010 election was anomalous because it was the first in which the rightist coalition won and the leftist coalition was divided. The most important change in Chile's party system was the return of the Socialist Party (see Chapter 5).

†The Partido de la U was a successor to Primero Colombia, founded by Álvaro Uribe for the 2002 election.

‡Fuerza 2011 was one of many successors to Cambio 1990, the party founded by Alberto Fujimori for the 1990 elections.

Note: The identity and founding year of the two parties with the largest percentages of the vote in the legislature (or, if applicable, in the lower house of the legislature) during the most recent election of the third wave. The most common name in English or the common acronym for the party is used; for the formal name, see the first reference to the party in this book.

PT), the Dominican Republic's PLD, Peru's Gana Perú (Win Peru), and Uruguay's Frente Amplio (Broad Front, FA) (see Chapters 5 and 6). Anti-corruption themes were emphasized by Colombia's Green Party and Costa Rica's PAC (Partido Acción Ciudadana, Citizen Action Party) (see Chapters 6 and 7).

Were these new parties what their supporters were likely hoping— programmatic, democratic, building grassroots networks, and on the path to institutionalization? To date, although none of the new parties is unflawed, the record is varied. In some countries, the problem was not that new parties were inchoate, but that they became too dominant; in other countries, personalism and amorphousness were indeed problematic (see Chapters 5 and 6).

Conclusion

Plurality advocates' expectations were not borne out for various reasons. Although plurality inhibited the emergence of five, six, seven, or even more parties, the number of parties often neared three; as Chapter 4 shows in greater detail, the results were often presidents' legitimacy deficits and victories by presidents at ideological extremes. Also, under plurality, the advantages of entrenched parties with authoritarian proclivities were greater and usually new parties, responding to concerns about inequality or corruption, were not able to become competitive. Among the important barriers to entry were inaccurate opinion polls.

By contrast, runoff advocates' expectations were borne out. For more than half the elections won with less than 50%, the result of a runoff either was or (under plurality) would have been uncertain, and, in almost 20% of these elections, a reversal of the first-round result was likely or virtually certain; accordingly, the risk of presidential legitimacy deficits was considerable. Presidents and top presidential candidates at ideological extremes were more common under plurality than under runoff. Amid Latin America's numerous entrenched parties with authoritarian proclivities, the lower barriers to entry under runoff were an important advantage.

Still, under runoff, the presence of five, six, seven, or even more parties is far from ideal. In such contexts, as plurality advocates fear, some parties were inchoate and most presidents lacked legislative majorities.

4

Plurality

Problems in Honduras, Mexico, Nicaragua, Paraguay, and Venezuela (and the Panama Exception)

Overall, the trend in the level of democracy during the third wave among the six countries that retained plurality was subpar. In Venezuela, the democratic star of South America in the 1970s and 1980s, Freedom House and V-Dem scores plummeted to the regional nadir. Nicaragua's scores also fell precipitously and by 2011 were the second-worst in the region in both datasets. Mexico's scores fell too, although less precipitously. Honduras's Freedom House score deteriorated markedly. Although Paraguay's scores did not decline, they remained below regional averages. As of 2014, Panama was the only plurality country with scores above the regional average.

The trend for voter turnout was more mixed, but also inferior to the trend under runoff. In none of the six countries was average voter turnout considerably above the regional mean, and in none did turnout increase considerably. Most seriously, turnout plummeted in Honduras to the lowest rate in Latin America save Colombia (where the vote is not compulsory).

The six plurality countries are diverse. Both Venezuela and Honduras enjoyed superior historical records of democracy; Panama's was roughly average; Nicaragua's was at a nadir and Mexico's and Paraguay's were inferior also. Mexico and Venezuela were among the region's wealthiest countries, whereas Honduras and Nicaragua were among the poorest.

Plurality was complicit in the inferior levels of democracy. In all six countries, at least one election was won with 41% or less and, in four of the six countries, these elections were very problematic. In Venezuela, the 1993 election was won with only 30.5%, the second-lowest of any third-wave election; in many analysts' views the limited legitimacy and weak mandate of the president were the most important catalysts for the subsequent democratic plunge. In Nicaragua, the 2006 election was won with only 38% by Daniel Ortega, who was at an ideological extreme and led a party with an authoritarian past. In Mexico, the 2006 election gave the rightist candidate

35.89% and the leftist candidate 35.31%; the legitimacy deficit was severe. Paraguay's 1993 election was won with about 40% and was followed by an attempted military coup; its 2008 election was won with 41% and was followed by the impeachment of the president. In Honduras and Panama, the 2013 and 1994 elections, respectively, were won with less than 40% but were not particularly problematic.

Plurality was also complicit in problems of political exclusion. In five of the six countries (all but Panama), longer-standing parties were challenged by new, leftist parties. But traditional elites knew that these leftist parties did not need 50% to win and feared that they would play to bases at extremes. Concomitantly, the elites were more likely to resort to authoritarian tactics to maintain power. At the same time, various elections were perceived by leftist leaders to have been won by a long-standing party despite a lack of majority support. These elections—the 1993 election in Venezuela, the 2006 election in Mexico, the 1993 and 2003 elections in Paraguay, and possibly the 1996 election in Nicaragua (under qualified runoff)—provoked dismay among many leftists and may have shifted them further left. Ultimately, when leftist presidents were elected or almost elected in Venezuela, Nicaragua, and Mexico, they were at the extreme left (see Chapter 3).

In general, with higher barriers to entry, plurality facilitated the continuation in power of cartel parties. At the start of the third wave, cartel parties were dominant in most plurality countries. The duopolies in Honduras and Venezuela were cartel parties, as was the PRI in Mexico and the Colorado Party in Paraguay. Subsequently, in Nicaragua after 2006 and Venezuela after about 2000, incumbent parties at the extreme left became cartel parties. In Mexico, Nicaragua, Paraguay, and Venezuela, these cartel parties won elections in part because plurality posed serious challenges of strategic coordination for the opposition parties.

Given that it is the plummet in Venezuela's level of democracy and the deep decline in Nicaragua's that are most important to the negative trends under plurality, I analyze trajectories first in Venezuela and second in Nicaragua. Then I turn to Mexico, where the decline was also serious, and next to Honduras, where Freedom House scores plunged and voter turnout was low but V-Dem scores were relatively steady. Fifth is Paraguay; although overall Paraguay's level of democracy was steady, it was below the regional average; a toll was taken by the almost-uninterrupted dominance of the Colorado Party and concomitant difficulties in the incorporation of the left. Finally, I analyze the only country where plurality did not take a toll: Panama. Not coincidentally, Panama's electoral arena was open to new parties and a major challenge was not posed by a leftist party.

Venezuela

Venezuela's descent from democratic star to authoritarianism was one of the most precipitous in Latin American history. In 1978, Venezuela's Freedom House score was 3, the best in Latin America save Costa Rica; in 1989 it fell to 4; in 1992 to 6; in 1999 to 8; in 2009 to 9; in 2010 to 10; and in 2016 to 11. Similarly, Venezuela's V-Dem score fell from .664 in 1990 to .149 in 2016. Whereas voter turnout averaged above 85% between 1978 and 1988, it plummeted to 60% in 1993, 64% in 1998, and only 57% in 2000.[1] (After 1994, the vote was not obligatory.) Turnout recovered only as of the 2006 election.

The descent was surprising because, although Venezuela's history of democracy prior to 1958 was meager, its relative success after 1958 enabled its 1900–1977 Polity score to approximate the regional average. Venezuela's record was also surprising because its 2009 per capita income was well above the Latin American average (World Bank, 2011: 10–12), and indeed in earlier decades had been among the highest in Latin America.

The descent was attributed in part to plurality by many Venezuelan political leaders and analysts. Runoff was advocated by numerous presidential candidates, including Hugo Chávez in his 1998 campaign and Eduardo Fernández, Manuel Rosales, and Teodoro Petkoff.[2] In my interviews with scholars, runoff was advocated by the vast majority.[3] I planned interviews with Venezuelan legislators, but unfortunately the response rate was minimal (see Appendix 1).

Plurality was criticized due to its implications for Venezuela's calamitous 1993 election. Gradually, Venezuela's two dominant parties, AD and COPEI, became a duopoly; but, in 1993, the duopoly broke down and the election result was almost a four-way tie that yielded a president, Rafael Caldera, with a legitimacy deficit and a limited political base. Many political analysts and political leaders, including Michael Coppedge, Steve Ellner, Eduardo Fernández, José Antonio Gil Yepes, Teodoro Petkoff, Carlos Romero, and Luis Salamanca, believe that runoff would have helped.[4]

In 1998, after the unpopular Caldera government, a fiery outsider and extreme leftist, Hugo Chávez, was elected. Although Chávez achieved majorities, runoff might yet have helped. Plurality posed severe challenges of strategic coordination to Venezuela's opposition. Especially in 1998, the opposition candidate with the broadest appeal was more likely to have emerged from a first round than from the unity candidate anointed by the disparate opposition parties. Plurality imposed a catch-22 for Venezuela's opposition: if new parties did not ally with the traditional parties, they could not defeat Chávez; but this alliance was "the kiss of death" (LAWR, December 8, 1998, p. 565).

Prior to Chávez's election, political exclusion was facilitated not only by plurality but also by other rules. Presidential re-election was permitted after two intervening terms, and the role of two old-timer ex-presidents—Carlos Andrés Pérez in 1988 and Caldera in 1993—was pernicious. Legislative lists were closed and nominations tightly controlled by party elites. Primaries for the selection of the presidential candidate were held only as of 1993. There were no elections for mayors or governors until 1989. Executive and legislative elections were concurrent, further limiting the opportunities for new parties.

Of course, there were other reasons for Venezuela's descent. Between the 1980s and 1998, the fall in the price of oil, Venezuela's key export, was steep and Venezuela's economic crisis prolonged. Average real wages in 1998 were only one-third of average real wages in 1982; between the mid-1980s and the end of the 1990s, the percentage of the population in poverty more than doubled, from 25% to more than 60% (Morgan, 2011: 92). Poverty worsened more in Venezuela than in any other country in the region (Buxton, 2003: 123). Then, in the mid-2000s, the price of oil not only recovered but hit record highs, making possible the prodigious social programs of the Chávez government that facilitated re-elections.

Punto Fijo Democracy and the Three 1978–1988 Elections

In 1958, after a history of authoritarian rule, Venezuela's three major non-Marxist political parties signed a power-sharing agreement known as the Pact of Punto Fijo, which gave Venezuela's 1958–1998 regime its name, "Punto Fijo democracy." Although Venezuela's Communist Party also worked against authoritarian rule, it was excluded from the Pact of Punto Fijo; in the early 1960s, it took up arms against the new government and lost most of its previous support.

The three parties signing the Pact of Punto Fijo were AD, COPEI, and the Unión Republicana Democrática (Democratic Republican Union, URD). Founded in 1942 by Rómulo Betancourt, AD won Venezuela's first democratic election in 1947. But its government was considered aggressively leftist by Venezuela's traditional elites and its secularization initiatives angered the Catholic Church; it was overthrown in 1948. COPEI, founded in 1946 by Rafael Caldera on the base of a conservative Catholic student movement, was complicit in the coup; COPEI supported the new military junta and sought positions in the new regime (Ellner, 1988: 41). The URD revolved around its founder, Jóvito Villalba, but it included significant left factions and had a considerable base among the urban poor (Myers, 2004:14–16, 21–22, 28).

In Venezuela's first three Punto Fijo elections, AD and COPEI were not a duopoly; the URD was a major competitor. But AD and COPEI became a duopoly between 1978 and 1988. Barriers to entry were high. Due in good part to state ownership of Venezuela's vast oil resources, the duopoly dispensed immense patronage. It also controlled the electoral machinery; and, as the only parties that could staff all of Venezuela's voting tables, stole votes (Buxton, 2000: 8; LAWR, November 18, 1993, p. 538).

In this context, leftist parties "held a permanent minority status" (Corrales, 2002: 299). Gradually, AD lost its image as a center-left party, but the percentage of Venezuelans self-identifying as leftists increased from 20% in 1973 to 35% in 1984 (Haluani, 1987: 12–13). Yet, the leftist voter preferred "not to waste his precious vote on a lost cause and would rather 'negotiate' his vote in return for some concrete benefit (a new attractive post, promotion in his work) from one of the two parties who are certain to win the election: AD or COPEI" (Haluani, 1987: 13). In addition, without local or regional elections, leftist leaders had scant opportunities to demonstrate competence and build a political base. Facing these barriers, most leftist parties became resigned to accommodation with the cartel parties (Haluani, 1987).

In the 1978 election, COPEI's Luis Herrera Campíns won with 47% to 43% for AD's Luis Piñerúa Ordaz. The result of a runoff would have been uncertain. In a context of high oil prices, the incumbent AD government of Carlos Andrés Pérez was popular, and an AD victory was expected; but, AD divided between two factions, one loyal to Pérez and the second to Betancourt. The leftist party Movimiento al Socialismo (Movement toward Socialism, MAS), which in 1971 had broken from Venezuela's Communist Party to participate in electoral politics, tallied 5% and other small leftist parties almost 3%, and most of these votes were likely to have gone to AD. A runoff would have given MAS a stronger political voice.

The 1983 election was won by the AD's Jaime Lusinchi in a landslide with 58%. The debt crisis was beginning and the incumbent COPEI government's achievements were scant. MAS and other leftist parties again tallied about 8%. It had been predicted that they would tally as much as 15% (LAWR, October 28, 1983, p. 10), but probably some leftists decided not to "waste" their votes and other left votes were stolen at the voting tables.

In 1988, the Lusinchi government was not unpopular (despite the debt crisis). Former AD president Carlos Andrés Pérez promised a return to the prosperity of his 1973–1978 government and was re-elected with 53% of the vote. Immediately, however, Pérez faced financial crisis; reversing campaign promises, he advanced market reforms. Within weeks, increases in the prices of public transportation and gasoline ignited two days of rioting and looting in Venezuela's ten largest cities. When Pérez sent troops into the areas, at least 200 and possibly more than 1,000 people were killed. Yet, Pérez forged ahead with market reforms. Living conditions deteriorated sharply. Further protests erupted and they too were violently repressed.

Amid the broad and deep opposition, in February 1992 junior military officers led by Lieutenant Colonel Hugo Chávez attempted a coup, but it was blocked. Asked by the government to request that his supporters lay down their arms, Chávez went on television and electrified Venezuelans. Chávez proclaimed that his goals were to end corruption and achieve social justice. Hoping for these changes, as many as 59% of Venezuelans supported the coup (Myers and O'Connor, 1998: 198, 206). Said one young Venezuelan:

> My hope was that they [the coup-plotters] would kill [Pérez].... It would have meant one less corrupt thief here. Every day I earn more but can buy less. People know who the corrupt are, and we no longer believe in the politicians, and we no longer have any options.[5]

In November 1992, another coup attempt was led by air force and navy officers. Pérez's demise was imminent. In May 1993, his suspension and trial on charges of misuse of public funds were mandated by Venezuela's senate. A political independent, Ramón J. Velásquez, was designated interim president. In September 1993, Pérez was impeached. The legitimacy not only of the Pérez government but Punto Fijo democracy in general was damaged.

As the 1993 election loomed, AD and COPEI were ossified, insulated, and bereft of moral authority (Coppedge, 1994a; Crisp and Levine, 1998: 40; Bejarano, 2011: 207, 241). Representation was "bankrupt" (Morgan, 2011).

The Calamitous 1993 Election

In the 1993 election, Caldera prevailed in a tight four-way race; the president suffered a legitimacy deficit and was bereft of the alliances that might have enabled effective governance. The final official tally put Caldera at 30.5%, AD at 24%, COPEI at 23%, and the leftist La Causa Radical (or, La Causa R, The Radical Cause) at 22%. In 1994, Michael Coppedge (1994b: 39) opened an article with the sentence: "Venezuela, once the most governable democracy in Latin America, is now a very fragile democracy." Daniel Levine (1994: 148) cited a "long-term growth in public skepticism and disaffection." Jennifer McCoy and William Smith (1995: 114) wrote: "The challenges confronting Venezuela are the decomposition—or deconsolidation—of an established democratic regime."

At seventy-seven, Caldera was making his sixth presidential bid; he had competed in 1947, 1958, 1963, 1968, and 1983 but had won only in 1968. Still, when COPEI had nominated a younger presidential candidate, Caldera bolted and formed Convergencia, a last-minute, ad hoc coalition including MAS plus sixteen tiny parties, mostly to the left. Despite decades as a pillar of the political establishment, Caldera ran as an outsider, lambasting the traditional parties. He was keenly aware of the frustrations that had led to Venezuelans' support for Chávez's coup attempt; he "stopped just short of proclaiming that ... [Chávez's] cause was just" (Myers, 2008: 283). Caldera promised to pardon Chávez. He assailed the AD government's market policies and the IMF; but his platform was not detailed. Some of his top advisers were pro-market and there was "a lot of double talk."[6]

The vote count was suspect; possibly, Venezuela's elites vetoed a leftist victory. A few weeks before the election, Andrés Velásquez, the candidate of La Causa R, was moving up in the polls. La Causa R was based in Venezuela's trade union movement; its stronghold was in the industrial state of Bolívar, where Velásquez was a popular governor. He was placed at the moderate left (3.61) in the 1995 PELA survey. The possibility of a military coup against Velásquez was rumored (LAWR, November 18, 1993, p. 538; Philip, 2000: 16).

In the first official tally, Velásquez was the runner-up; but in the final tally, he was demoted to fourth. Velásquez protested that he had won; his charges resounded with a considerable sector of Venezuelans (Coppedge, 1994b: 57; Dietz and Myers, 2007: 71). Citing manipulation of the tally and vote-stealing, some political analysts also believed that Velásquez had won, although most did not.[7]

How might runoff have helped? Despite Caldera's low tally, he was almost certain to have won a runoff. If Caldera had opposed AD, he is likely to have solidified his position as an outsider at the center-left and achieved the support of La Causa R voters. Alternatively, if Caldera had opposed La Causa R, Caldera was likely to have advanced a center-right position and gained the support of AD and COPEI voters. Under either scenario, Caldera would have clarified his positions and built political bridges. Then, if Caldera's position were center-left, perhaps allying with La Causa R, his government would probably still have failed, but leftist positions were likely to have been discredited and AD or COPEI would have had a better chance in 1998. Alternatively, if Caldera's position were center-right, openly working with AD and/or COPEI factions, the government's market policies might have succeeded; many other Latin American governments were succeeding in the mid-1990s. Like other analysts, former COPEI presidential candidate Eduardo Fernández believed that "a runoff would have allowed Caldera to enhance his base of support and gain moral authority."[8]

In the event, however, Caldera was torn between left and right; the first eighteen months of his government were "marked by ambiguity and contradictions" (McCoy and Smith, 1995: 140). Trying to keep his campaign promise to reverse market reforms, Caldera introduced "a series of draconian yet confused measures that sharply diverged from neoliberal precepts" (Weyland, 2002: 215). Caldera's Convergencia had only 25% of the seats in the Chamber of Deputies and less than 20% in the Senate; Caldera was immersed in legislative intrigues (Corrales, 2002: 223; Weyland, 2002: 237).

By 1996, Venezuela was virtually bankrupt. In April, the Caldera government reversed course and, in return for a large IMF loan, adopted market policies. But only about two years remained until the 1998 presidential campaign; both the economic crisis and corruption scandals continued. Popular alienation was intense.

When Caldera shifted the government's economic policies, he also shifted its political alliances. Previously, Caldera had looked to La Causa R and MAS for support; he also had covert support from AD. But in 1996, Caldera lost the support of most La Causa R and MAS legislators and gained overt support from AD. At the same time, however, MAS leader Teodoro Petkoff became the head of Caldera's economic team, two other MAS leaders joined Caldera's cabinet, and La Causa R leaders continued their support (Ellner, 2008: 106). Accordingly, virtually no party emerged untarnished by the Caldera government (Buxton, 2003: 122; Morgan, 2011: 188; Seawright, 2012).

The 1998 Election of Hugo Chávez

Hugo Chávez won the 1998 election with 56% versus 40% for the runner-up, Henrique Salas Römer, a former COPEI leader. Yet, a Chávez victory was not inevitable. In 1998, less than 25% of Venezuelans placed themselves at any point to the left of center (Seawright, 2012: 115). In the month or two before the election, Chávez led opinion polls with about 42%; but together, opposition candidates had at least five points more. In regional elections about a month before, Chávez's party had tallied only roughly 33% (LAWR, November 24, 1998, p. 543). However, plurality required that a new party have the support of the traditional parties, which still had at least 15% between them; but when a new party allied with AD or COPEI, it was tainted.

During most of 1997, the opinion polls were led by Irene Sáez, a former Miss Universe who had been an effective mayor of a wealthy Caracas municipality. Leading her own party, Sáez positioned herself as an independent. Then, in May 1998, she accepted the nomination of COPEI. Her popularity plummeted (Ellner, 2008: 104).

By mid-1998, the leading opposition candidate was Salas Römer, a governor who had defected from COPEI and established his own party in 1995. In the opinion polls, he was closing the gap on Chávez. But about two weeks before the election, AD dropped its candidate and endorsed Salas Römer; withdrawing its support from Sáez, COPEI also endorsed Salas Römer. Just as support for Sáez had fallen, so it did for Salas Römer (LARR, December 15, 1998, p. 1). Salas Römer was cast by Chávez as "a phony independent who, in the end, was joining forces with the discredited, traditional organizations" (LAWR, December 1, 1998, p. 554).

If there had been a runoff, the traditional parties would not have withdrawn their candidates in favor of a unity candidate. Prior to AD's endorsement of Salas Römer, its nominee had been seventy-seven-year-old Luis Alfaro Ucero, "the quintessential machine politician" (LARR, July 28, 1998, p. 6); a more appealing AD candidate is likely to have won at least 15%, probably denying Chávez a majority in a first round (Philip, 2000: 35–37). If Salas Römer had finished second in a first round and gone on to a runoff, he would have had a chance to build momentum and gain the support of traditional voters without alliances that appeared unprincipled.

Still, Chávez was a strong candidate. Despite plurality, he was moderating since his 1992 coup attempt (LARR, April 7, 1998, p. 7). He promised not socialism but "a third way" (LARR, May 19, 1998, p. 2) and a "different democracy" (Myers, 2008: 298). He emphasized that he would design a new constitution and build social and political participation. His appeal was heightened by his ethnicity; Chávez was of mixed race and looked like most Venezuelans. His party, the Movimiento Quinta República (Fifth Republic Movement, MVR), was supported by MAS, La Causa R defectors in the new party Patria Para Todos (Homeland for All, PPT), and other leftist parties.

Chávez's 2000 and 2006 Landslides

The 2000 election was won by Chávez with 60% of the vote and the 2006 election with 63%. Chávez was popular and would have been hard to defeat under any electoral rule. Even though in 2000 Venezuela's economy was still sputtering and Chávez was placed at the extreme left (3.18) in the PELA survey, he was perceived as concerned about Venezuela's poor and committed to building a more inclusive democracy (Molina and Pérez, 2004). Then, after 2000, oil prices rebounded, and Venezuela's economy grew robustly. Social spending skyrocketed. Further, although Chávez's authoritarian proclivities became more evident, the rightist opposition was discredited by its support for a failed coup attempt in April 2002 and for a prolonged national strike in late 2003 (Corrales and Penfold, 2007: 102). Subsequently, its protests against Chávez's victory in a recall referendum in 2004 and its boycott of congressional elections in 2005 proved counter-productive.

In the 2000 election, the runner-up with 38% was Francisco Arias Cárdenas, a former lieutenant colonel who had been one of the four leaders of Chávez's 1992 coup attempt. In 1995, Arias had been elected to a governorship for La Causa R and, in 1998, had supported Chávez. But, in 2000, Arias criticized Chávez as authoritarian and unable to control corruption. Yet, with his leftist, military background, Arias could not entice a sufficient number of traditional AD and COPEI voters to his side; many stayed home (Molina and Pérez, 2004: 113–114). Turnout was only 57%, the lowest in Venezuela's history.

In the 2006 election, the runner-up with 37% was Manuel Rosales. Rosales was a former AD mayor who had left AD in 2000 to found his own party; he had been elected to a governorship in 2000 and again in 2004. As of 2006, the number of political independents or "ni-nis" (literally, "neither-nors," critical of both Chávez and the confrontational rightist opposition) was growing and composed almost 40% of the electorate (López-Maya and Lander, 2008: 339–340). In the campaign, Rosales tried hard to strike moderate tones and attract "ni-ni" votes, but he had been an AD leader and in 2002 had signed the "Carmona Decree," supporting the failed 2002 coup attempt against Chávez.

Although there was one additional candidate in 2000 and many in 2006, it was obvious that they had no chance, and both Arias and Rosales were perceived to be the unity candidates of the opposition. In both elections, runoff might have helped by not putting a premium on a unity opposition candidate and facilitating voters' consideration of alternatives.

The 2012 Election and the Possibility of an Opposition Victory

Once again, Chávez won, but with only 55%. Chávez was vulnerable. He was running for a fourth consecutive term; the end of term limits had been approved in a 2009 referendum—only after having been rejected in a 2007 referendum. The

Chávez government was increasingly authoritarian; some opposition leaders were arrested and major media were imperiled. Also, crime had skyrocketed and inflation was high. Stricken with cancer, Chávez could not campaign as vigorously as he had in the past. Although unfortunately no PELA surveys were carried out, Chávez was running for the Partido Socialista Unido de Venezuela (United Socialist Party of Venezuela, PSUV) and was widely perceived to be at the extreme left.

The runner-up with 44% was Henrique Capriles Radonski. Capriles was the candidate of the opposition coalition Mesa de la Unidad Democrática (Democratic Unity Roundtable, MUD). Only forty years old, he was energetic and optimistic. In 2000, Capriles had co-founded the party Primero Justicia (Justice First); he had been elected mayor of a municipality in Caracas and then governor of an important state. Capriles had not signed the Carmona Decree. Promising not only to maintain but to expand Chávez's social programs and to increase the minimum wage, Capriles sought to woo independent voters (LAWR, August 9, 2012, p. 1; LAWR, September 27, 2012, p. 3).

However, Capriles was imperfect. In 1998, he had been elected to the Chamber of Deputies for COPEI and had been a leader of COPEI until 2000; this prior affiliation irked AD voters and did not help him with "ni-nis."[9] Also, Capriles' father was a wealthy businessman and Chávez credibly charged that he was "a right-wing oligarch in disguise" who was lying about his commitment to social programs (Neuman, 2012: A9). Further, although Capriles consistently struck a moderate tone, the MUD was a disparate coalition that included many leaders to the right of Capriles. Ultimately, Capriles attracted more voters beyond the right than Rosales had (and turnout reached 81%)—but not enough.

The challenge for Venezuela's opposition was to find a candidate who could bridge its deep divides. Somehow, a winning candidate had to bridge Venezuela's confrontational, staunchly pro-market right, in which former traditional party leaders were active, and the new sector of "ni-nis" (Cannon, 2014). Such a candidate would have been more likely to emerge under runoff, in which various candidates would have competed in a first round and one might have gained momentum from a strong first-round finish. Although this candidate would have had to gain the support of other opposition parties for the runoff, the form of the support would have been an endorsement—much less exacting than an alliance.

Nicaragua

Although at the start of the third wave the level of democracy in Nicaragua was below the regional average, deterioration was yet considerable. The country's Freedom House and V-Dem scores were the second-worst in the region between 2011 and 2016. At the time of Nicaragua's transition in 1990, its Freedom House score was 6 and, through 2006, its score was also usually 6. But, soon after the election of Ortega, Nicaragua's score fell, hovering at 8 between 2008 and 2015 and falling to 9 in 2016. The trajectory for Nicaragua's V-Dem scores was similar but not identical. At the time of Nicaragua's transition, its V-Dem score was also slightly below the regional average but then rose and reached it, only to fall below it again as of 1997. Then, after the 2006 election of Ortega, Nicaragua's V-Dem scores plunged. However, Nicaragua's voter turnout averaged about 77%—above the regional average, despite a voluntary vote.

With the fall in Nicaragua's scores after the 2006 election, the negative impact of the election is evident, and plurality was in large part to blame. Experts agreed that, if Ortega, with a mere 38%, had faced a runoff, he would have lost (Close and Martí i Puig, 2012: 12; DeShazo, 2006; Lacey, 2006: A5; McConnell, 2012: 147; Morris, 2010: 201–202; Pérez Baltodano, 2012: 84).[10]

Not only did plurality give Ortega the presidency without majority support, but, raising barriers to entry, it did not help overcome the polarization between the Liberal Party and the FSLN, Nicaragua's two dominant parties (see Chapter 3). Averaging the 1990, 2001, and 2011 elections, Nicaragua's number of parties was below 2.0; only in the 2006 election did the number exceed 3.0. Between 1990 and 2012, no new party achieved 15%.

The Liberal Party and the FSLN had been key actors during the war that wracked Nicaragua during the 1970s and 1980s. The Liberal Party was the party of the Somoza dictatorship that ruled with an iron fist from 1936 until 1979. (Despite a variety of names and iterations between its founding in the 1830s and the twenty-first century, the party continued to be identified by most Nicaraguans as the Liberal Party [Morris, 2010: 181]). In 1979, the Liberals' Anastasio Somoza Debayle was overthrown by the FSLN; the FSLN governed until the first free and fair election in 1990. In the 1996 and 2002 PELA surveys, the Liberal Party was placed at the extreme right (9.16 and 9.01 respectively) and in the 2007 survey at the right (7.27); in all three surveys, the FSLN was placed at the extreme left (2.39, 1.86, and 2.34 respectively).

Nicaragua's inferior third-wave record is also in part attributable to its history and economy. The country's historical experience with democracy was negligible; its 1900–1977 Polity score was the worst in the region. Also, for much of this period Nicaragua was the poorest country in the hemisphere, with only 25% of the average per capita income in 2009 (World Bank, 2011: 10–12). Between 1990 and 2009, Nicaragua's average annual per capita GDP growth was the lowest in Latin America.

The 1990 Election: A Relatively Positive Start

To virtually everyone's surprise, the 1990 election was won with 55% for the Unión Nacional Opositora (National Opposition Union, UNO) to 41% for the FSLN. Of Nicaragua's four third-wave governments, it was only during the 1990–1996 UNO government that Nicaragua's V-Dem scores did not decline.

UNO's victory is generally attributed to Nicaraguans' desire to end the war of counter-revolutionaries supported by the United States against the FSLN government. In addition, the UNO's candidate, Violeta Barrios de Chamorro, symbolized the possibility of reconciliation. She was the popular widow of an opposition political leader assassinated by Somoza; she had children on both sides of the conflict. She hailed from a family of four former presidents but was a political newcomer—technically, an outsider. Under plurality, it was important that the UNO was a coalition of the entire Nicaraguan opposition; it included fourteen parties, from the Partido Liberal Constitucionalista (Liberal Constitutionalist Party, PLC) at the extreme right to the Communist Party at the extreme left. Placed at the right (7.32) in the 1997 PELA survey, Chamorro was between these extremes. Confident of victory, the FSLN did not make significant efforts to divide the UNO.

In office, the UNO faced major challenges. Nicaragua was wracked by the debt crisis; the Chamorro government adopted market reforms but austerity was painful and the reforms were challenged by the FSLN. The government sought to reduce opposition through allowing the FSLN to continue to lead Nicaragua's security forces and through bribes—with unfavorable results (Morris, 2010: 174–181).

Amid these challenges, both the UNO and the FSLN divided and new parties pursued a more open political arena. In 1995 disparate legislative groups allied to pass electoral reforms that reduced the power of the dominant parties. A runoff with a 45% threshold was introduced; re-election of the president was prohibited; and the presidential term was reduced from six years to five.

The 1996 Election under Qualified Runoff: Amid Political Opening, a Victory for the Extreme Right

In 1996, Arnoldo Alemán of the Alianza Liberal (Liberal Alliance) tallied 51% to 38% for the FSLN's Ortega. Alemán partnered his PLC, which he had been reviving, with several small Liberal factions (but not the faction headed by Chamorro's allies) to establish the Liberal Alliance. Qualified runoff is a likely factor in the roughly 10% that was won by new parties.

Elected to the mayoralty of Managua in 1990, Alemán was classified at the extreme right (8.72) in the 1997 PELA survey. Alemán's father had been an official in one of the Somoza governments; in Alemán's youth, he had supported Somoza (Colburn and Cruz S., 2012: 110). In the 1980s, Alemán was a leader of farmers and ranchers opposed to the FSLN government; he was imprisoned. As mayor, Alemán built high-profile public works and was popular. Also, he enjoyed resources for the PLC among wealthy Cuban-American friends in Miami.

Running for the third time for the FSLN, Ortega tried to establish a more moderate image (Serrill, 1996: 27). Ortega replaced the Sandinista anthem, which included the lines "We fight the Yankee, enemy of humanity," with Beethoven's "Ode to Joy." He chose a rancher whose lands had been confiscated by the FSLN as his running mate. He pursued a rapprochement with the Catholic Church. Yet, Ortega continued to be placed at the extreme left.

Alemán's margin of victory was due to significant electoral irregularities. In particular, in Managua and another city led by Liberals, large numbers of ballots were lost—or hidden—and vote counts were erroneous—or falsified (The Carter Center, 1997: 31–33; Morris, 2010: 184). The electoral result was disputed by Ortega; privately, however, Ortega apparently did believe that Alemán won (Morris, 2010: 184–185). Yet, the irregularities were likely to have increased Ortega's cynicism about the Nicaraguan right's claim to democratic principles.

Probably in part due to qualified runoff, new parties emerged. Almost all were positioned closer to the center; but the number of candidates competing was so large—twenty-three—that it was difficult if not impossible for one or two candidates to stand out (Butler, Dye, and Spence with Vickers, 1996: 14).

However, one new party in particular, the Movimiento Renovador Sandinista (Sandinista Renovation Movement, MRS), was perceived to be poised for a bright future (Morris, 2010: 181–183; Butler, Dye, and Spence with Vickers, 1996: 32). Increasingly frustrated by the FSLN's authoritarian tactics and by Ortega's caudillismo, Ortega's former vice-president broke with the FSLN and formed the MRS in 1995. The new party's ideology was social-democratic and emphasized internal democracy. But it was relentlessly disparaged by the FSLN (Butler, Dye, and Spence with Vickers, 1996: 33). In the event, the MRS won less than 1%.

The Alemán government was beleaguered. In 1998, Nicaragua was hit by Hurricane Mitch. The Alemán government was perceived to have mismanaged emergency-relief funds and Alemán was suspected of corruption. Alemán feared for his future.

Ortega also feared for his future. He had been charged with sexual abuse by his stepdaughter. Also, in the wake of the adoption of qualified runoff and the 1996 election results, he worried that the FSLN would be eclipsed by new parties.

In this context of these mutual fears, in December 1999 Alemán and Ortega forged "el pacto"—"the pact." Both leaders wanted and achieved the right of former presidents to a legislative seat, which would provide immunity from prosecution. Both leaders wanted and achieved the reversal of the 1995 reforms. Electoral rules became "the most exclusionary in Latin America" (McConnell, 2012: 147). The obstacles to legal recognition of a party, to the maintenance of recognition, and to party alliances became very high (McConnell, 2012: 147–149; Dye with Spence and Vickers, 2000: 8-9). The FSLN and the PLC gained control over Nicaragua's Supreme Court and over its national electoral commission.

In addition, qualified runoff was replaced by qualified plurality—thresholds of 35% with a 5% lead or 40%. Plurality was a key goal for Ortega (see Chapter 2).

The 2001 Election and the Subsequent Division of Nicaragua's Right

Supported by all Liberal Party groups, in 2001 the PLC's Enrique Bolaños, Alemán's vice-president, defeated the FSLN's Ortega easily, 56% to 42%. Nicaragua's economy was recovering somewhat and many Nicaraguans were concerned about the implications of an Ortega victory for democracy (Anderson and Dodd, 2002).

The exclusionary effect of "the pact" was very evident in the reduction of the number of parties. The onerous requirements for the registration of parties, the politicization of national and sub-national electoral commissions, and qualified plurality discouraged competition (Dye with McConnell, 2002). Only one party in addition to the PLC and the FSLN competed and it tallied less than 2%. For its part, demoralized by its meager tally in the 1996 election, the MRS returned to the FSLN fold.

Bolaños was placed at the extreme right in PELA surveys (see Chapter 3). He had been a successful businessman and had led Nicaragua's most important business association, and was criticized in some quarters as the favorite of the United States. However, he was considered honest.

To Alemán's dismay, Bolaños immediately called for an investigation of the allegations of corruption against Alemán. Evidence emerged; ultimately it was estimated that Alemán had embezzled $100 million (LAWR, July 21, 2011, p. 14). Breaking with Alemán's PLC, Bolaños's allies partnered in the legislature with the FSLN and Alemán was stripped of his legislative immunity, prosecuted, and sentenced to twenty years in prison for embezzlement. PLC leaders were angry.

The 2006 Election: A Disastrous Plurality Victory

Placed at the extreme left (1.96) in the 2007 PELA survey, Ortega tallied only 38% in the 2006 election but won because of the division of the Liberal vote. The division had been sparked by the conflict between Alemán and Bolaños and was exacerbated by the entry of a fake candidate and uncertainties about candidates' strength due to inaccurate polls.

Ortega continued to try to moderate his image. He took additional steps to gain the support of the Catholic Church. His vice-presidential candidate, Jaime Morales, had been not only a key advisor to Alemán but also a leader of the violent anti-FSLN counter-revolutionaries (LARR, May 2006, p. 14). Yet, his placement in PELA surveys did not budge.

The runner-up was Eduardo Montealegre of the Alianza Liberal Nicaragüense (Nicaraguan Liberal Alliance, ALN) with 29%. A critic of "the pact" and Alemán's corruption, Montealegre was a former minister in the Alemán and Bolaños governments. A successful businessman with a MBA from Harvard University, he was deemed a "modern" candidate whereas his rival among the Liberal groups, the PLC's José Rizo, was deemed a "traditional" candidate (Colburn and Cruz S., 2012: 112).

As indicated previously, if there had been a runoff, Ortega was virtually certain to have lost. Although "traditional" PLC voters were no fans of Montealegre, the vast majority would have preferred him to Ortega. Indeed, it was believed that Ortega would have lost in a runoff to any of his three rivals (LAWR, September 19, 2006, p. 13; LAWR, October 3, 2006, p. 13).

The PLC's Rizo finished third with 27%. Rizo was what has been dubbed a fake candidate. Throughout the campaign, Montealegre was leading Rizo in the opinion polls and it was clear that the division of the Liberals would throw the election to Ortega. But, although Rizo was the 2001–2006 vice-president for Bolaños, he was running to further the interests of Alemán. Apparently, Alemán believed that, if Ortega won, he would facilitate the vacating of Alemán's sentence (as indeed he did), whereas Montealegre would not, and accordingly Alemán preferred Ortega (Noriega, 2006: 3).

In fourth place with 6% was the MRS's Edmundo Jarquín. About five months before the election, the MRS had had bright prospects; its candidate, Herty Lewites, was a charismatic, popular former Managua mayor and led Ortega in the opinion polls (McConnell, 2012: 147; Morris, 2010: 202). But, four months before the election, Lewites died of a heart attack. His successor, Jarquín, was the vice-presidential candidate; formerly an economist at the Inter-American Development Bank, Jarquín was not well known in Nicaragua.

The MRS indicated its preference for Montealegre (or even Rizo) over Ortega (LARR, June 2006, p. 9). Possibly, if Jarquín had known that he would tally only 6%, he would have withdrawn and endorsed Montealegre. But opinion polls about three months before the election gave Jarquín about 20%, putting him in striking distance of Montealegre.

In office, the FSLN did not have a legislative majority but did gain a monopoly over state resources and control over the electoral authorities and was becoming a cartel party (Colburn and Cruz S., 2012: 114–116). Opposition parties were harassed and, in the 2008 municipal elections, fraud was charged (McConnell, 2012: 149). The judiciary was politicized. In 2009, the Constitutional Chamber of Nicaragua's Supreme Court suspended the constitutional provisions limiting a president to two terms and prohibiting immediate presidential re-election.

The 2011 Election and the Continuing Democratic Deficit

Running for the fifth time and a second consecutive term in 2011, Ortega won in a landslide. His tally—62%—was so large that, despite a paucity of freedom and fairness, the election was not repudiated by the OAS (LAWR, November 17, 2011, pp. 14–15).

Ortega was popular. Between 2006 and 2011, Nicaragua's GDP growth averaged about 4% annually, much better than in recent decades and better than its neighbors. Despite Ortega's leftist rhetoric, his government's policies were pro-market, and exports and foreign direct investment surged. Also, economic aid from Hugo Chávez was generous and the FSLN government implemented an unprecedented array of social programs. Further, crime rates were relatively low.

Ortega also benefited from weak competition. The runner-up with 31% was Fabio Gadea, a radio journalist who was almost eighty years old but without political-campaign experience. He was the candidate of a Liberal faction that led a coalition of opposition parties including the MRS and Montealegre's group. In third place with 6% was the PLC's Alemán, who had been absolved of his conviction for corruption but remained disgraced.

Subsequently, infringements against democratic principles increased. Ortega continued to control the judiciary and the electoral authorities and gained control over the legislature and the security forces (LARR, March 2014, p. 9; LARR, July 2014, p. 6). Ortega achieved legislative approval for electoral reforms allowing indefinite presidential re-election and eliminating the thresholds for a runoff, shifting Nicaragua from qualified plurality to plurality. The playing field for the 2016 election was so tilted that the major opposition parties called for abstention. After the 2016 election, the fall in Nicaragua's Freedom House and V-Dem scores continued.

Mexico

Mexico's level of democracy declined during the third wave. In 2000, the country's Freedom House score was very good at 4, but it fell to 5 in 2006 and to 6 in 2010, where it remained through 2016. Similarly but not identically, its 2000–2005 V-Dem scores approximated regional averages but fell gradually after 2006 and, by 2016, had fallen about 15%. At roughly 65%, voter turnout was below the regional average. Mexico's record was disappointing given that its 2009 per capita income was among the highest in Latin America (World Bank, 2011: 10–12). However, Mexico's historical democratic record was poor. Mexico did not enjoy a period of competitive presidential elections during the twentieth century; its 1900–1977 Polity score was among the lowest in Latin America.

Debate about plurality versus runoff has been intense in Mexico. As mentioned in Chapter 1, runoff is preferred by most Mexican political leaders. It is also preferred by most Mexican citizens; in a nationwide public-opinion survey in 2009, 63% of Mexican citizens favored runoff and, in 2017, the figure rose to 77%.[11] Most scholars whom I interviewed, as well as Jorge Castañeda and Marco Morales (2007:108–111), Denise Dresser,[12] George W. Grayson (2009), Jerry F. Hough (2006: A16), and Gabriel Negretto (2007), endorsed runoff.[13] But several scholars opposed it.[14] In any case, the PRI resisted runoff; although by 2013 the PAN and the Partido de la Revolución Democrática (Party of the Democratic Revolution, PRD) were united in favor and debate about runoff was heated, the PRI remained adamant and prevailed.[15]

Plurality was deleterious. Between 2000 and 2012, two of Mexico's three presidents were elected with less than 40%, none enjoyed a legislative majority, and executive-legislative gridlock was virtually constant. The 2006 election was traumatic; doubts about both the fairness of the election and the result if there had been a runoff were widespread. The leftist runner-up, Andrés Manuel López Obrador (AMLO), led street protests that disrupted Mexico City for months. In contrast to many of his successful counterparts in runoff countries at this time, AMLO built a reputation for obstructionism and remained at the extreme left in PELA surveys.

The PRI was an exceptionally strong cartel party. It not only endured but won the 2012 election—primarily due to the division of its opposition between the PAN and the PRD. Strategic coordination between the PAN and the PRD failed due to ideological differences, leadership rivalries, and inaccurate opinion polls. The number of political parties averaged above 3.0.

Mexico's Three Major Political Parties

As of 2000, Mexico's PRI had been in power for seventy-one years and was the longest governing political party in the world. Founded under a different name in 1929, the PRI claimed to represent the goals of the various groups that had fought in Mexico's 1910–1917 revolution—land reform, social justice, democracy, and sovereignty. Incorporating three major organizational sectors, the PRI was one of the most strongly institutionalized parties in Latin America. For decades, PRI governments achieved considerable peace and robust economic growth.

Founded in 1939, the PAN was the only significant opposition party until 1988. The PAN was rightist—close to the Catholic Church and business groups; prior to 1994, it was unable to muster as much as 20% in any presidential election.

After the onset of the debt crisis in the early 1980s, the PRI advanced market reforms; as a result, the party split. Led by Cuauhtémoc Cárdenas, critics of the reforms left the PRI and competed in the 1988 election. "Massive" fraud was committed against Cárdenas in this election (Magaloni, 2006: 53–54). In 1989, the PRD was founded. During the 1990s, the PRD suffered severely from repression by the PRI. At least five hundred PRD activists were assassinated (Mossige, 2013: 7). Many PRD candidates were robbed of victories in sub-national elections; AMLO was the victim of fraud in his race for governor.

The obstacles to the unity of the opposition parties were high (Magaloni, 2006). Although both the PAN and the PRD were considered pro-democratic relative to the PRI, their positions on economic issues were far apart. Throughout the 1990s and through 2010 (the last year for which PELA surveys were available), both the PRD and the PAN were placed at ideological extremes. Between 1997 and 2010, the PRD's average placement in the PELA survey was 2.62 and the PAN's average placement was 9.27. By contrast, the PRI was consistently at the center-right.

The problem of strategic coordination by the PAN and the PRD was exacerbated by the PRI. In 1988, the PRI promoted provisions that impeded party coalitions in presidential elections. Prior to 1988, parties were allowed to endorse another party's presidential candidate but run its own legislative candidates. Then, in 1988, after successful coalition-building by the PRD, the PRI added onerous new requirements for the registration of coalitions (Bruhn, 2004: 136). To compete as a coalition, political parties were required to present a common slate of legislative candidates in a total of 628 races. In 1999, the PAN and the PRD tried to modify these new rules, but change was blocked by the PRI (Magaloni and Poiré, 2004: 270). In both the 2000 and 2012 elections, the PRI was credibly accused of manipulating opinion polls.

The 2000 Election: An Opportunity Lost

Mexico's first free and fair election, in 2000, was won by the PAN's Vicente Fox with 43%. Fox defeated the PRI's Francisco Labastida by seven points. In third place was the PRD with 17%. It was virtually certain that Fox would have won most of the PRD vote in a runoff (Magaloni and Poiré, 2004: 279). For plurality advocates, the election was promising: Fox was trying to position the PAN closer to the center and the PAN and the PRD came near to an agreement. But the promise was not realized. A runoff might have facilitated bridges between the PAN and the PRD.

Fox was a formidable candidate (Grayson, 2000). A successful Coca-Cola executive, Fox had joined the PAN only in 1987 and remained on the fringes of the party. But he had been a legislator and a governor, and, at six-feet-five with trademark cowboy boots and earthy language, he was an effective campaigner. He considered the PAN "much too far to the right to win" and wanted to be at "the center-left" (Greene, 2002: 779–780). To this end, Fox took various positions traditionally opposed by the PAN, such as advocacy of a tax increase. He attracted prominent leftist intellectuals like Jorge Castañeda to his campaign and formed a broad coalition, called Alianza por el Cambio (Alliance for Change). The Alliance for Change included a splinter of the PRD led by Porfirio Muñoz Ledo. To gain its support, Fox promised not to privatize the state oil company PEMEX and not to allow greater sway for the Catholic Church in education or politics (Berman, 2000: 38). In both 1998 and 2001, whereas the PAN was at the extreme right in PELA surveys, Fox was only at the right.

The PRI was divided between "dinosaurs" (the old guard given to authoritarian practices and a large state) and "technocrats" (who had led the party since 1988 and promoted market reforms). The PRI's Labastida was closer to the technocrats than the dinosaurs.

The PRD's candidate was Cuauhtémoc Cárdenas, who had been the standard-bearer for the left not only in 1988 but also 1994. In his third try for the presidency at sixty-six, Cárdenas was dour. Cárdenas is likely to have continued to resent the fraud in the 1988 election; he remained committed to "an old-fashioned leftism."[16]

Despite Fox's strengths, his victory was a surprise. Labastida consistently led the opinion polls. Why, when it appeared that only through an alliance between the PAN and the PRD could the PRI behemoth be defeated, was an alliance not achieved?

Indeed, in September 1999, the two parties came close. They agreed on a joint platform and manifesto (LARR, October 26, 1999, p. 2). But the partnership foundered over presidential ambitions; the two candidates could not agree on the method for the selection of the presidential candidate (LAWR, May 23, 2000, p. 231). Campaign-finance rules were another factor (Bruhn, 2004: 136). These rules stipulated that state funds for a party were distributed according to its vote shares; if Cárdenas had withdrawn, it would have hurt the PRD's electoral tally and reduced state funds for the PRD in the future.

An alliance also failed due to inaccurate opinion polls. Based on the polls, most Mexicans—and in particular most PRD voters—believed that the PRI would win the election, and, if the PRI were going to win anyway, why should PRD voters sacrifice their principles and ally with the PAN?[17] Why should Cárdenas step aside for Fox? To foster PRD voters' misperception, the PRI quashed polls that forecast the PRI's defeat. Pollsters who predicted a Fox victory were harassed or worse and editors and publishers were pressured as well.[18] In addition, it was widely believed that the PRI would do better than the polls predicted due to election-day chicanery.

Over the course of the campaign, animosities intensified and personal insults were hurled (LARR, July 11, 2000, p. 5). Still, if there had been a runoff, the pressure upon Cárdenas to endorse Fox would have been great, and the endorsement likely to have facilitated rapprochement between the PAN and the PRD.

The Traumatic 2006 Election

The 2006 election was very damaging. In the official results, the PAN's Felipe Calderón tallied below 40% and defeated AMLO by less than a percentage point. The PRI, running an uninspiring candidate from its old guard, finished third with 22%. The election was perceived as illegitimate not only by the great bulk of the PRD but also, many surveys suggested, by a majority of Mexicans (Flores-Macías, 2013: 135; Bruhn, 2012: 105–107). The reasons for the perceptions of illegitimacy were doubts about the fairness of the election, the validity of the count, and the identity of the candidate who would have won a majority in a runoff. AMLO's resentment and mistrust intensified.

Elected mayor of Mexico City in 2000, AMLO was popular and was the long-standing frontrunner. Indeed, in 2005 AMLO was the target of a dubious legal accusation that would have disqualified his presidential candidacy; it was widely believed that the PAN government was making the accusation for this reason. Although AMLO's official positions were not particularly leftist (his key slogan was "For the good of all, the poor first"), at campaign rallies AMLO was given to populist discourse—references to a corrupt ruling elite and a morally superior "people" (Bruhn, 2012: 90–106; Mossige, 2013: 31–32).

Calderón was a mainstream PAN leader; his father had been a founder of the PAN. Three months before the election, Calderón trailed badly in the polls and decided to "go negative." In attack ads, Calderón charged that AMLO was "a danger to Mexico"; in one ad, AMLO's face morphed into Hugo Chávez's (Mossige, 2013: 30). These ads were illegal under Mexican law but the PRD's complaints to the electoral commission were addressed very slowly. AMLO's fiery discourse at campaign rallies enabled Calderón's negative campaign to succeed (Bruhn, 2012: 90–106).

The PRD's dismay at the electoral result was intensified by uncertainty about whether Calderón or AMLO would have had majority support in a runoff.[19] As Craig Arceneaux (2013: 248) put it, "Calderón's supporters dismissed López Obrador's claims of electoral fraud, but they found it much more difficult to reject the allegation that Calderón did not represent the popular will of the people, since he failed to collect votes from over 60% of the electorate."

The PRI vote was likely to have divided closely between the PAN and the PRD. In a runoff, some experts gave the edge to the PRD.[20] Others cited the PAN.[21]

The result was also uncertain in part due to the impact of minor parties in the election. Calderón had struck an alliance with the Partido Nueva Alianza (New Alliance Party, PANAL), founded by Elba Esther Gordillo, a former PRI leader and the head of the teachers' union. As legally required, PANAL had its own presidential candidate, Roberto Campa; however, Gordillo urged votes for Calderón. Calderón gained about 3% of the vote through Gordillo's endorsement.

By contrast, AMLO had not struck an alliance with another minor party, the Partido Alternativa Socialdemócrata y Campesina (Social Democratic and Peasant Alternative Party, PASC), which tallied 2.8%. The PASC was to the left not only on economic issues but also on social issues such as women's rights and gay marriage. Apparently, given AMLO's strong lead in the polls at the time that any discussion would have had to occur, he was confident of victory and felt no need to reach out to the PASC (Grayson, 2007: 259).

The official result was immediately rejected by AMLO. He charged, correctly, that the PAN had violated numerous election laws (not only provisions against negative ads but also against the incumbent president's intervention in the campaign). He also charged that many PRD ballots had not been counted. He demanded a "ballot by ballot" recount. Mexico's Federal Electoral Institute (IFE) agreed to only a partial recount; in this recount, no evidence of vote fraud emerged. AMLO continued to demand a full recount. It was not an outrageous demand under the circumstances, but the IFE was adamantly opposed (Mossige, 2013: 43).

While PRD militants occupied the main boulevard in Mexico City, notoriously AMLO proclaimed, "To hell with your institutions!" Virtually throughout Calderón's six-year term, AMLO claimed to be the "legitimate president." AMLO was prioritizing his ties to his political base; his intransigence resonated among staunchly leftist voters but not at the center of the political spectrum (Bruhn, 2012: 103–112; Flores-Macías, 2013: 137–138; Mossige, 2013: 47, 56).

Immediately after his inauguration, Calderón made the fateful decision to launch a military offensive against Mexico's drug lords. In many analysts' views, Calderón was concerned about his government's legitimacy and hoped that, with this decision, he would assert his authority (González, 2009: 74–75; Starr, 2012: 47).[22] During Calderón's six-year term, more than 50,000 people died in the ensuing violence. The increase in violence was a key factor in Mexico's declining level of democracy.

The 2012 Election: The Return of the PRI

The return to Mexico's presidency of its cartel party was worrisome. Gustavo Flores-Macías (2013: 138–141) showed that the PRI's claims of renewal were not supported by its sub-national leaders' records. In the event, amid continuing impunity, the presumed murder of forty-three trainee teachers in the town of Iguala in 2014 and subsequent cover-up became notorious worldwide.[23] Mexico's Freedom House scores were stable, but its V-Dem scores dipped slightly.

In the election, the PRI's Enrique Peña Nieto tallied only 38%, but was almost certain to have won a runoff. The runner-up was AMLO with 32%; in third place was the PAN's Josefina Vázquez Mota with 25%. By this time, the distance between AMLO and the PAN was vast; former PAN president Fox endorsed Peña Nieto and most PAN voters would likely have followed his lead. Still, the the PRI's low vote share was problematic. Jorge Castañeda lamented, "This guy [the PRI's Peña Nieto] was elected with 38% of the vote, and his party hasn't gotten anywhere beyond that during the past 20 years.... The country just doesn't like these guys."[24]

Peña Nieto was a popular governor. But, raised in a PRI family, he was close to the PRI's old guard. He was widely deemed an intellectual lightweight. In part because of his marriage to a star on the country's largest television network, media coverage was believed to be skewed in his favor. Biased media coverage was a key factor in the emergence of an anti–Peña Nieto movement called *Yo Soy 132* (I am number 132), in reference to solidarity with 131 university-student protesters who had shown their student IDs after Peña Nieto's campaign charged that they were working for a rival party.

Peña Nieto benefited from inaccurate polls. In the week or two before the election, most polls put the PRI ahead by about fifteen points, with the PRD and the PAN neck-and-neck for a distant second. The pollsters' exaggeration of Peña Nieto's lead was perceived in some sectors as an effort by elites to give the PRI an aura of inevitable victory, discouraging both the PRD and the PAN (Flores-Macías, 2013: 134, 136). Also, for Mexico's pro-democratic voters whose priority was the defeat of the PRI, it was not clear which opposition party to choose. It is unlikely—but not impossible—that correct polls would have changed the outcome.

AMLO moderated his discourse considerably; although unfortunately PELA surveys were not available, it appeared that his change was not credible. Said political scientist Denise Dresser, "A lot of people don't believe his transformation to a loving leftist."[25] Seconded scholar Sergio Aguayo, "The takeover of Reforma [the main boulevard in Mexico City] is part of his black legend. He has tried to exorcise it, but hasn't succeeded."[26]

Possibly, AMLO would have overcome his reputation for intransigence through a calm concession in 2012. But, citing vote-buying by the PRI, he charged fraud and asked that the IFE annul the election. AMLO's position was not supported by the PRD; AMLO left the PRD and formed his own movement.

Honduras

Until 2009, the level of democracy in Honduras was somewhat below regional averages; then, after a coup in June 2009, its level of democracy plunged. Amid a political crisis, President Manuel Zelaya was taken from his bed at gunpoint by 200-odd soldiers and exiled. The new de facto government was led by civilians, but it moved against leaders and groups allied with Zelaya. Although an election was held in November, restrictions on civil liberties continued. Between the start of the third wave in 1981 and 2008, Freedom House scores for Honduras had been slightly below regional averages, at either 5 or 6; its V-Dem scores had been considerably below regional averages. After the coup through 2016, Honduras's Freedom House scores dropped to 8 (tied in 2009 and 2010 with Guatemala and Nicaragua for second-worst in the region). Honduras's V-Dem scores also plunged but gradually recovered to pre-2009 levels.

Voter turnout plummeted. Although the vote was obligatory, turnout fell from 81% of the voting age population in 1985 to approximately 50% in 2005 and 2009.[27] The 31-percentage-point decline was the largest registered during the third wave for any country save Venezuela, and the 50% turnout in 2005 was the lowest save Colombia, where the vote is not obligatory. The low and declining turnout worried analysts (Taylor-Robinson, 2006: 120; Ruhl, 2007: 527; Booth, Wade, and Walker, 2010: 174). Turnout did finally improve in the 2014 election but remained considerably below the regional average.

The deterioration of democracy in Honduras was not consistent with the country's historical record. For the period 1900–1977, Honduras held the fourth-best Polity score in Latin America (Pérez-Liñán and Mainwaring, 2013: 381).

However, Honduras's 2009 per capita income was slightly less than 40% of the regional average (World Bank, 2011: 10–12).

Plurality was complicit in Honduras' low level of democracy. Plurality facilitated political exclusion by the two cartel parties. Even though citizens were deeply disaffected and new parties tried to emerge, they failed. Between 1990 and 2012, the number of parties averaged only 2.2; in no election did the number exceed 2.41. Stated Michelle Taylor-Robinson (2010: 113), "Plurality elections for president gave voters an incentive to vote for the traditional parties rather than waste their vote on a party with little chance of winning the presidency and the access to resources for clientelism it provides." With respect to a new party, the Partido Unificación Democrática de Honduras (Party of Democratic Unification, PUD), Michael Allison (2006: 154) commented, "This formula [plurality] has worked against the PUD. After the PUD's first presidential election, voters realized that they had cast 'wasted votes' for the party.... It seems likely that ... [a] higher proportion of voters would support the PUD in presidential elections if their vote would somehow influence a second round."

Amid the 2009 coup, however, Honduras's duopoly did break down. The coup catalyzed Honduras's left; when Zelaya returned to Honduras in 2011, he and his wife, Xiomara Castro de Zelaya, founded a leftist party that frightened many Honduran elites. As noted in Chapter 3, former president Zelaya was placed at the extreme left in the 2010 PELA survey. In this new political context, Honduran legislators debated the adoption of runoff and numerous respected scholars and officials called for the adoption of runoff.[28]

Political Parties in Honduras Until 2009: Decades of Duopoly

Traditionally, politics in Honduras was less violent than in most of Central America. Land was less scarce in Honduras and coffee became an important crop later, only in the middle of the twentieth century; conflict between peasants and large landowners was relatively limited. Honduras's military was not strongly institutionalized. Under various governments, some social and economic reforms were made.

In this context, two political parties with elaborate patronage networks were established. Founded in 1891, the Partido Liberal de Honduras (Liberal Party, PLH) was dominant until 1932; in 1916–1919, the Partido Nacional de Honduras (National Party, PNH) was founded (McDonald and Ruhl, 1989: 112; Taylor-Robinson, 2006: 112). At this time, the two parties were supported by rival U.S.-based companies (McDonald and Ruhl, 1989: 112). Between 1923 and 1932, several competitive elections were held. However, a National Party caudillo, elected in 1932, governed into the 1950s and repressed the Liberal Party. As the Cold War began and conflict over land increased, the military intervened. It governed from 1963 to 1971 with the participation of the National Party and governed outright from 1972 to 1981 (Booth, Wade, and Walker, 2010: 161–162).

In contrast to most political parties in Central America, the Liberals' and Nationals' clientelist ties incorporated peasants' and workers' unions and reached deeply into the countryside. Yet, they were not perceived to be governing in the interests of a majority of Hondurans. Commented Taylor-Robinson (2001: 594), "In general, neither party represented the interests of most of the population and they have tended to freeze out other parties that might have done so." Stated J. Mark Ruhl (2007: 532), "Most public officials have concentrated on capturing the legal and illegal spoils of office for themselves and their political networks rather than addressing the needs of one of the poorest populations in the Americas." After the 2009 coup, it was clear that Thomas P. Anderson (1998: 168), writing in the 1990s, had been prescient: "If one of the major parties had produced a dynamic candidate who captured the public imagination and the presidency, what would have been his fate? Had he tried any far-reaching changes, he most likely would have been forced to board a plane with a one-way ticket to Miami."

As Chapter 3 noted, the National Party was placed at points on the right by analysts, but classifications of the Liberal Party varied. Unlike the National Party, the Liberal Party included a social-democratic wing (Ruhl, 2010: 97-98; Taylor-Robinson, 2010: 88); in some Liberal governments, this wing was dominant, but in most it was not, leading to the fluctuation in the party's classification in the PELA surveys.

Although the National and Liberal parties were not dominated by one or two individuals or families (due in part to prohibition of presidential re-election and a four-year term), the parties' leaders enjoyed vast power. Frequently, the president of the congress went on to win the next election. The opportunities for citizen input were very limited. Until 1997, ballots for presidential and legislative candidates were not separate; voters cast only one ballot for both, simply choosing a party. Even after voters chose candidates for both the presidency and the legislature, only as of 2005 were the names of legislative candidates provided (Taylor-Robinson, 2006: 117). It was also only in 2005 that election to the legislature was no longer through closed lists and that primaries were introduced for the selection of the presidential candidate. Although the mayors of Honduras's 300-odd municipalities were elected, the governors of its eighteen departments (who held considerable authority over the mayors), were appointed by the president. There were no provisions for public finance for parties and, until 2005, no formal televised debates.[29]

Several new parties were established but none ever won as much as 3%. A vicious circle emerged: new parties were so far from power that many leaders were not seriously committed; given weak leadership, the new parties remained far from power.[30] Through the 1993 election, the small parties were the Partido de Innovación y Unidad (Innovation and Unity Party, PINU) and the Partido Demócrata Cristiano de Honduras (Christian Democratic Party of Honduras, PDC). In PELA surveys, PINU was usually placed at the center and the PDC at the center or center-left. As of the 1997 election, the PUD was established; it was placed at the left or extreme left in PELA surveys.

New parties were excluded by plurality and a host of other means. As Chapter 3 mentioned, an important means was fraud at the voting tables. The vote count was tallied at the tables by representatives of the parties. But small parties did not have sufficient numbers of representatives to staff all the tables; the representatives of the two large parties simply divided the smaller parties' votes up between them.[31] Also, although Honduras's electoral commission distributed voting-table credentials to all political parties, the two large parties bought the credentials of the smaller parties or acquired them through other means (National Democratic Institute [NDI], 2010: 11).

Also, as cartel parties, the Liberals and the Nationals dominated the conduct of elections. In principle the composition of Honduras's national electoral commission was not problematic: until 2004, its members were representatives of the Liberal and National Parties and the PINU and PDC plus a Supreme Court representative; after 2004, three members and one substitute were elected by two-thirds of the legislature. But, in practice, the commission was co-opted by the traditional parties (McDonald and Ruhl, 1989: 119; NDI, 2010: 17). The commission did not develop an accurate voter registry (NDI, 2010: 5–7). It included deceased voters, duplicate voters, and non-existent voters (LAWR, November 18, 1993, p. 533).

Further, concerns were widespread that the two parties were complicit with security forces in repression (LARR, October 28, 1997, p. 2). In the 1980s and 1990s, leftist candidates were harassed and sometimes killed (McDonald and Ruhl, 1989: 118). As drug-trafficking and violent crime exploded in the 2000s, the murder of political activists became more common. It was difficult to attribute precise responsibility, but suspicions of the complicity of the parties were widespread. In the 2013 election, more than twenty candidates, over half of whom were from the Zelayas' party, were killed.[32]

The 1981–2005 Elections

Amid Central America's violent conflicts, in the early 1980s the U.S. government was active in Honduras and was lobbying for elections. Honduras's first third-wave election was held in 1981; subsequently, regular elections were held every four years. As Table 4.1 shows, electoral tallies were remarkably consistent: in all seven elections, the winning party won between 49.9% and 55%; the second-place party, between 42% and 46%; and the small parties between 3% and 5%.

The Liberal Party was the more successful party, winning five of the seven elections. In the 1980s, the key campaign issues were the presence in Honduras of the U.S. military and anti-FSLN counter-revolutionaries, the debt crisis and market reform, and the subordination of the Honduran military to civilian authority. In the

Table 4.1 **Electoral Tallies in Honduran Elections, 1981–2005**

Election	Winning Party	Second-Place Party	Small Parties
1981	54%, Liberal Party	42%, National Party	4.5%, PINU & PDC
1985	51%, Liberal Party	46%, National Party	3.5%, PINU & PDC
1989	52%, National Party	44%, Liberal Party	4.4%, PINU & PDC
1993	53%, Liberal Party	43%, National Party	4.0%, PINU & PDC
1997	53%, Liberal Party	43%, National Party	4.6%, PINU, PDC, & PUD
2001	52%, National Party	44%, Liberal Party	3.5%, PINU, PDC, & PUD
2005	49.9%, Liberal Party	46%, National Party	3.6%, PINU, PDC, & PUD

1990s, the latter two issues remained salient. In the late 1990s and the 2000s, the problem of crime topped the agenda.

The 1981 election was won by the Liberals' Roberto Suazo. The region's civil wars were continuing and several small leftist guerrilla groups undertook armed opposition (Allison, 2006: 149–151). Human-rights violations increased and Suazo was unpopular. But he sought to stay in power; a constitutional crisis erupted.

Amid the constitutional crisis, the 1985 election was anomalous. It was agreed that all candidates' names would appear on the ballot and that the most-voted candidate of the most-voted party would win. In the event, although one of the National Party's candidates won the most personal votes, the Liberal Party won the most votes and its top candidate, José Azcona, became president.

The 1989 election was the first in the third wave won by the National Party. Its candidate, Rafael Callejas, was an appealing agricultural economist. But, during his presidency, U.S. aid to Honduras declined amid the democratic transition in Nicaragua; economic problems mounted.

The Liberal Party rebounded in the 1993 election. Its candidate, Carlos Roberto Reina, was a former president of the Inter-American Court of Human Rights who hailed from the party's social-democratic sector and was placed at the center-left in PELA surveys. The Reina government implemented various measures that subordinated the military and police to civilian authority. It also prosecuted former president Callejas and a variety of his colleagues for corruption.

The 1997 election was won by the Liberal Party's Carlos Flores Facussé, who hailed from its mainstream. The new leftist party, the PUD, participated; it included leaders of the country's most important former guerrilla groups (Allison, 2006: 150–151). One of its mayoral candidates was murdered and the party charged intimidation (LARR, October 28, 1997, p. 2).

In 1998, Honduras was devastated by Hurricane Mitch; amid the devastation, crime and corruption worsened. Pledging a crackdown, the National Party's Ricardo Maduro triumphed in the 2001 election. A Stanford-educated economist and former central bank chief, Maduro was at the extreme right in the PELA survey.

The 2005 election campaign was commonplace. It did not herald the polarization that was to come. The Liberals' candidate, Zelaya, was a rancher, a three-term legislator, and former minister of Honduras's social-investment fund. Zelaya was placed at the center in the 2006 PELA survey; for example, he endorsed the Central American Free Trade Agreement (CAFTA).

The 2005 election was the only third-wave election won with less than a majority: 49.9% for the Liberal Party versus 46% for the National Party. If the election had gone to a runoff, the Liberal Party would have been almost certain to win. To the National Party's left, the Liberal Party would have been likely to secure most of the votes of the PINU, PDC, and PUD.

Hondurans' Disaffection from the Regime

Despite the large percentages of the vote that went to the two dominant parties, Hondurans were unhappy with them. Stated Ruhl (1997: 86), "Unfortunately, ordinary Hondurans are beginning to lose faith in electoral democracy.... [They] have already concluded ... that democratic politics has little to do with them."

Hondurans' disaffection was indicated in various surveys. In a 2008 LAPOP survey, citizens' attitudes on a spectrum of items were more inimical to democracy in Honduras than in Costa Rica, El Salvador, Guatemala, or Nicaragua (Booth, Wade, and Walker, 2015: 248–249). In a 2004 LAPOP survey not only in these Central American countries but also in Panama, Mexico, and Colombia, the percentage of anti-system respondents for three survey items was the highest in Honduras; 24% of Hondurans approved participation in a group using arms to overthrow the government, 25% supported confrontational political tactics, and 56% said that a hypothetical coup could be justified (Booth and Seligson, 2009: 182, 187, 190). An index of "triple dissatisfaction" and "triple satisfaction" was developed; the ratio of "triply dissatisfied" to "triply satisfied" citizens was much larger in Honduras than in any other country (Booth and Seligson, 2009: 247).

Zelaya's Left Turn and the Breakdown of the Duopoly

In 2008, Zelaya shifted left. In March, Honduras entered PetroCaribe, a Venezuelan energy initiative that provided oil and derivatives under favorable conditions. In October, Honduras entered ALBA (Alianza Bolivariana para las Américas, Bolivarian Alliance for the Americas), a bloc of leftist countries led by Venezuela. Through support from the Liberal Party and the smaller parties, these entries were approved by the legislature. The entries were supported by the Liberal president of the congress, Roberto Micheletti, in part because ALBA was popular among the poor and in part because Zelaya agreed to support Micheletti's campaign for the

Liberals' presidential nomination (Ruhl, 2010: 99). In December, Zelaya increased the minimum wage by about 60%. This measure was not approved by the legislature and was vehemently opposed by companies (Ruhl, 2010: 99). Zelaya grew closer to workers' unions and criticized Honduran elites as "the oligarchy" (Ruhl, 2010: 98).

Why did Zelaya shift leftward? Clayton M. Cunha Filho, André Luiz Coelho, and Fidel I. Pérez Flores (2013: 523–536) provide four helpful explanations. First, fuel prices were skyrocketing in Honduras; while assistance from U.S.-led financial institutions was meager, the benefits from ALBA were huge. Amid the energy crisis, Zelaya may have been dismayed when his implementation of a competitive bidding process for the supply of oil and derivatives was criticized by the U.S. ambassador. (U.S.-based companies had enjoyed an oligopoly in Honduras and, as a result of the competitive bidding process, were replaced.) Second, the space on the political left was open in Honduras, and Zelaya decided—opportunistically—to occupy it. In addition, at the start Zelaya was sincerely more to the left than Hondurans realized; he had gradually shifted from rightist factions within the Liberal Party to the social-democratic faction and, as the head of Honduras's social-investment fund, had been critical of market policies.

Zelaya was forcibly deported on June 28, 2009. Zelaya had wanted to reform Honduras's constitution. Indeed, the constitution was unwieldy and reform was widely considered overdue. Zelaya planned a referendum about a constituent assembly, but it was blocked in the legislature. Instead of a referendum, Zelaya proposed "a non-binding consultation." The "non-binding consultation" was declared illegal by the Supreme Court, but Zelaya persisted, and it was to be held June 28. Although the hurdles between this "non-binding consultation" and the re-election of Zelaya were huge, Honduran political elites "had a deep-rooted fear of Zelaya's intentions" (LAWR, July 2, 2009, p. 1). Seconded Ruhl (2010:105), "Manuel Zelaya and Hugo Chávez sparked new fears of revolution among the nation's privileged political and economic elites."

Amid the elites' coup and subsequent repression, a leftist political movement emerged and the duopoly ended. The number of killings, beatings, and detentions by the security forces and the degree of media repression were debated, but were considerable (Ruhl, 2010: 102–103).

Still, the November 2009 election was held as scheduled. The election was boycotted by Zelaya's movement, led by Carlos Humberto Reyes. At first, Reyes planned to compete; but Zelaya remained in exile and repression continued and Reyes withdrew. Most pro-Zelaya Hondurans appeared to stay home; without the pro-Zelaya votes, the Liberal Party's Elvin Santos tallied a meager 38%. With 57%, the Nationals' Porfirio Lobo won a lopsided victory.

Amid the coup, Honduras was suspended from the OAS and, after the 2009 election, remained so. In 2011, to re-gain admission, the Lobo government reached an agreement with Zelaya; Zelaya returned to Honduras without fear of prosecution. Libertad y Refundación, Libre (Liberty and Refoundation, Free) was founded and, in the 2013 elections, its presidential candidate was Zelaya's wife, Xiomara Castro de Zelaya.

The breakdown of the duopoly was confirmed in the 2013 election. The election was won by the National Party's Juan Orlando Hernández with only 37%. Libre was second with 29%. The Liberal Party was third with 20% and the Partido AntiCorrupción (AntiCorruption Party, PAC), another new party led by television commentator Salvador Nasralla, was fourth with 14%. If there had been a runoff, the Nationals' Hernández would have been likely to capture most of the Liberal Party's vote and some of the PAC's vote and prevail.

The election catalyzed criticism of the plurality rule in part because, for some months, Libre's Castro de Zelaya led the opinion polls (LARR, September 2013, p. 2); a victory for the left without majority support appeared likely. Only in the final month was Castro overtaken in the polls by Hernández (LAWR, November 21, 2013, p. 15).

For most Honduran elites and some analysts, a Libre victory would have been a victory for the extreme left.[33] For these elites and analysts, Libre was "defiantly radical," praising "democratic socialism" (LARR, September 2013, p. 2). Calling for the "re-founding" of Honduras, Libre was adopting the favorite priority of ALBA presidents; Venezuelan flags flew at Libre events (LARR, November 2013, p. 6). Libre frequently criticized Honduras' electoral commission, provoking doubts that Libre would accept an electoral loss. Recall that Zelaya was placed at 2.48 in the 2010 PELA survey.

Was Libre in fact at the extreme left? For Libre leaders and most pro-Libre analysts, the answer was no.[34] They noted that, despite the coup against Zelaya and despite ongoing repression, the party was working within the electoral process and included business leaders among its vice-presidential and legislative candidates. In this view, if there was leftist extremism among some militants at some moments, it was only a response to the repression and smear campaign by the right.

Paraguay

Although Paraguay's level of democracy did not decline between 1994 and 2016, it was considerably below regional averages. The pattern for Freedom House and V-Dem scores was similar. Between 1994 and 2002, Paraguay's Freedom House score was 7; in 2003, it improved to 6, where it remained. Paraguay's first V-Dem score was .380; it gradually reached .492 in 2011 but subsequently receded, falling to .437 in 2016. Between 1993 and 2014, voter turnout averaged 69%, slightly below the regional average, without an upward trend. Relative to Paraguay's historical record, its poor third-wave performance was not surprising; its 1900–1977 Polity score was tied for third-worst in Latin America (Pérez-Liñán and Mainwaring, 2013: 381). Also, Paraguay's per capita income was less than half the Latin American average (World Bank, 2011: 10–12).

Plurality was a factor in Paraguay's low level of democracy. Both a former Paraguayan president and a head of its second leading party advocated runoff (see Chapter 1). Plurality facilitated political exclusion by the Colorado Party, a cartel party with an authoritarian past (see Chapter 3). The Colorado Party governed without interruption from 1947 to 2008; when its stranglehold on the presidency finally ended in 2008, it had been the longest-governing party in the world.

Although historically the Colorado Party and the Liberal Party were dominant, in the third wave the number of parties averaged 2.75 and increased steadily, reaching 3.42 for the 2008 election. In this context, the winning party tallied only about 40% in Paraguay's 1993, 2003, and 2008 elections, and presidents suffered legitimacy deficits. The president elected in 1993 barely survived a coup attempt. The president elected in 2008 was impeached.

Plurality posed serious problems of strategic coordination for the opposition to the Colorado Party. Although new parties entered the electoral arena, they were unlikely to win without an alliance with Paraguay's second largest party, the Partido Liberal Radical Auténtico (Authentic Radical Liberal Party, PLRA), which had broken from the Liberal Party in 1978. Alliance with the PLRA posed difficult strategic and ideological questions, further complicated by inaccurate opinion polls. They were yet further complicated by a charismatic, ambitious army commander, General Lino Oviedo, who at first a led a faction within the Colorado Party and subsequently his own populist party.

Especially prior to the end of the Colorado Party's stranglehold, Paraguayans were very dissatisfied with democracy. As a cartel party, the Colorado Party depended on pork and patronage; the government grew, but performed poorly (Abente Brun, 2007: 19–27). At a time of market reforms in most of Latin America, Paraguay was frequently in political turmoil; between 1993 and 2000 its annual GDP growth was the lowest in the region with the exception of the major oil-exporting countries, Ecuador and Venezuela. In 2003, Paraguay was ranked as the fourth-most corrupt country in the world by Transparency International (LARR, October 28, 2003, p. 13). In 2006, Paraguayans' preferences for democracy were tied for lowest in the region and their satisfaction with democracy was the lowest; between 1996 and 2006, preferences for democracy fell more in Paraguay than in any other Latin American country and satisfaction with democracy more than in any other except Ecuador.[35]

In part due to Paraguayans' deep dissatisfaction, in 2008 they elected Fernando Lugo, an outsider who led a new, leftist party. Although Lugo was the only leftist president elected under plurality during 2000–2012 classified at the "moderate left" rather than the "extreme left" in PELA surveys, Lugo was only barely within the "moderate left"—3.35 (see Chapter 3). As I indicate in the following subsections, in various respects Lugo's positions were quite far left and frightened Paraguay's elites.

Political Parties in Paraguay: The Historical Context

Founded in the nineteenth century, both the Colorado Party and the Liberal Party were complicit in a military coup or military government and both abused checks and balances. The Colorado Party's past was especially authoritarian; intertwined with Paraguay's armed forces, it was responsible for serious human-rights violations (Sanders, 1986: 2–3). For the most part, the Liberal Party's violations were only in the early decades of the twentieth century (Sanders, 1986: 2).

In 1947, the Colorado Party ascended when the military faction with which it was allied defeated rival factions. In 1954, General Alfredo Stroessner emerged as the leader of the Colorado regime; he ruled for almost thirty-five years. Unlike many dictators, Stroessner worked to institutionalize his party, and Colorado leaders' links to the grassroots were considerable.

During the Stroessner government, elections were held. However, blatant fraud provoked a split in the Liberal Party; the dissident PLRA) was formed. Its leader and 1993 and 1998 presidential candidate, Domingo Laíno, was arrested and tortured several times.

In the 1980s, Stroessner's regime weakened; the dictator was aging, pro-democratic middle classes were emerging, and the hemispheric context was pro-democratic. In February 1989, Stroessner was deposed by General Andrés Rodríguez. Three months later, snap elections were won by Rodríguez.

Ideologically, in PELA surveys in the 1990s, the Colorado Party was placed at the right and the Liberal Party at the center-right. The Colorado Party was considered more populist and nationalistic, favoring landowners' interests; the Liberal Party, more linked to classical liberalism, favoring urban commercial interests (Riquelme, 1994: 19). But, first and foremost, both parties were clientelistic. According to Diego Abente Brun (2007: 21), the two parties were "born clientelist, remain clientelist, and … are among the most clientelist in South America."

The 1993 Election: A Colorado Victory with Limited Legitimacy and Subsequent Coup Attempt

The 1993 election was won by the Colorados with approximately 40%.[36] The opposition vote divided between the PLRA with 32% and the new Encuentro Nacional (National Encounter) party with 23%. If there had been a runoff, the PLRA was almost certain to have won. The legitimacy of the Colorado president was scant.

In pre-election polls, National Encounter had led and it was not clear that the 1993 election was free and fair. The Colorados resorted to intimidation, manipulation of the registration rolls, selective distribution of polling places, and other tactics (Riquelme, 1994; Abente Brun, 2005: 575). At first, the irregularities were denounced by the opposition parties, but within a few weeks they decided to see the elections as a step forward in a democratization process and acquiesced (Riquelme, 1994: 50–61; Abente Brun, 2005: 575).

National Encounter and the PLRA failed to ally for various reasons (Riquelme, 1994: 28–29; LAWR, April 29, 1993, p. 185; LAWR, May 13, 1993, p. 213). First, as mentioned, National Encounter was ahead in the polls; party leaders thought they could win without an alliance. Second, National Encounter was presenting itself as a centrist alternative to both long-standing parties; its leader, Guillermo Caballero Vargas, was an outsider—a successful businessman. Third, the Paraguayan military was considered more likely to block a Liberal victory than a National Encounter victory, and so an alliance was not necessarily in the party's interest.

The lack of majority support for the Colorado president, Juan Carlos Wasmosy, was one among several reasons for Wasmosy's legitimacy deficit.[37] He was a political neophyte who had made fortunes questionably, through business contracts during the Stroessner regime. Wasmosy had served as minister of integration in the Rodríguez government and enjoyed Rodríguez's support; it was widely believed that Rodríguez manipulated the results of the Colorados' primary for Wasmosy against Luis María Argaña, who led the faction closer to Stroessner (Abente Brun, 2005: 575).

Not surprisingly in this context, Wasmosy's government was precarious. It was challenged in particular by General Lino Oviedo. From humble origins, fluent in the indigenous language of Paraguay, and a compelling speaker, Oviedo enjoyed strong support, especially among Paraguay's poor. Wasmosy's surge in the final weeks of the election was attributed in part to support from General Lino Oviedo. After Wasmosy's inauguration, Oviedo repeatedly sought to dictate policy to Wasmosy. In April 1996, a frustrated Wasmosy demanded Oviedo's resignation from his army command; Oviedo then attempted a coup. Wasmosy survived only because of immediate international action as well as the backing of the Paraguayan political opposition (Valenzuela, 1997: 49–52).

The 1998 Election: A Majority Victory but a Factionalized Colorado Party

The 1998 election was the only third-wave election won with a majority. The Colorados' Raúl Cubas tallied 55%. A businessman and political neophyte, Cubas was standing in for the popular Oviedo. Oviedo had won the Colorados' primary but was ruled ineligible by the Supreme Court and sentenced to prison.

The Colorado Party won despite an alliance between the PRLA and National Encounter; the PLRA's Domingo Laíno was the alliance's presidential candidate and National Encounter's Carlos Filizzola was its vice-presidential candidate. Having supported Wasmosy in his confrontation with Oviedo, the two opposition parties had lost popular support.

Despite Cubas's majority, the Colorado Party was divided. One faction was led by Cubas and Oviedo; the other—favoring Stroessner—was led by the Colorado Vice-President, Argaña. Delivering on a campaign promise, Cubas pardoned Oviedo. Argaña proclaimed that the pardon was illegal and sought the impeachment of Cubas. In March 1999, Argaña was murdered; his supporters blamed Cubas and Oviedo. The opposing Colorado factions took to the streets, killing at least six and wounding hundreds (Sondrol, 2007: 336). Amid intense negotiations led by Brazil, a national-unity government emerged and held on (barely) until the 2003 elections.

The 2003 Election: A Colorado Victory with Less than 40% but a Relatively Successful President

The Colorado Party was in dire straits; the factionalism and violence during its 1998–2003 government had taken a severe toll. The Colorado Party tallied a mere 37% but prevailed due to the division of the opposition among three parties: the PLRA, with 25%; a new anti-corruption party close to the Catholic Church, Movimiento Patria Querida (Beloved Fatherland Movement), with 22%; and a pro-Oviedo party, UNACE (Unión Nacional de Colorados Éticos, National Union of Ethical Colorados), with 14%. If there had been a runoff, the PLRA would have been the likely winner. Indeed, the Colorado Party might have lost to any of the three major opposition parties (LARR, April 15, 2003, p. 2; Hebblethwaite, 2003: 5).

Various alliances among the opposition candidates were possible but not realized. The reasons were various. First, in late 2002 and early 2003, the PLRA's candidate, Julio César Franco, led the opinion polls and thought he had a good chance to win on his own (LAWR, April 8, 2003, p. 162). The PLRA considered reaching out to UNACE, but UNACE was polling only about 5%; in the event, UNACE won 14%. The PLRA and Beloved Fatherland discussed an alliance, but neither party would accede to the other's preferred presidential candidate (LARR, April 15, 2003, p. 2).

The new president was Nicanor Duarte Frutos, a long-standing Colorado leader not closely associated with any faction. Especially in his first two years, Duarte was effective and popular. The economy was growing. Paraguay's Freedom House score improved to 6 and Paraguay's V-Dem scores were rising.

However, Duarte over-reached. He launched an aggressive bid for re-election, proposing constitutional changes (which included runoff). Duarte's proposed changes were blocked.

The 2008 Election: An Outsider Victory with Limited Legitimacy and Subsequent Impeachment

The leftist outsider and former bishop, Lugo, won the 2008 election with only 40.9% of the vote. Although Lugo was allied with the PLRA, the result of a runoff would have been uncertain. The Colorado Party's political machine endured and the party finished second with 31%. In third place with 22% was UNACE; if there had been a runoff, it was unclear to whom UNACE's votes would have gone. Lugo's position proved very tenuous and he was impeached in 2012.

In the mid-2000s, Lugo was a liberation-theology priest in Paraguay's poorest rural area. He championed agrarian reform and supported land invasions of large estates; his political movement was Tekojoja ("Justice and equality" in Paraguay's indigenous language). In early 2006, he led an opposition rally against the constitutional changes promoted by Duarte, and his charisma and moral authority were clear (Uharte Pozas, 2012: 26). In late 2006, he announced his presidential candidacy and quickly led the opinion polls.

In July 2007, Lugo came to an agreement with the PLRA; the new Alianza Patriótica para el Cambio (Patriotic Alliance for Change, APC) was forged. Lugo became the presidential candidate and Franco, the PLRA's 2003 standard-bearer, the vice-presidential candidate. Lugo and the PLRA ran their own candidates for the legislature. Ideologically, Lugo and the PLRA were distant; Lugo "held views far to the left" of the PLRA (Marsteintredet, Llanos, and Nolte, 2013: 112). In the 2008 PELA survey, Lugo was at 3.35 and Franco at 6.79 (center-right, but very close to the right). It appeared that both Lugo and the PLRA recognized that their alliance was opportunistic but yet had not thought through what would happen after they won (LARR, March 2007, p. 7; Lugo, 2009: 155).

For Paraguayan elites, Lugo's ideological priorities were frightening. Many Paraguayans worried that Lugo's model was Chávez (LARR, November 2007, p. 7). Indeed, Lugo said that his model was "between Chávez on the one side and Lula and Bachelet on the other" (LAWR, May 1, 2008, p. 2). Lugo did not shrink from classifying Paraguay's democracy as merely "formal" and from labeling the traditional parties as "mafias."[38] In a context of elites' anxiety, the attack ads against Lugo were vicious; for example, his complicity in the murder of a former president's daughter was alleged (LAWR, May 1, 2008, p. 2).

In Lugo's platform and in many speeches, his top priority was agrarian reform (Cerna Villagra and Solís Delgadillo, 2012: 4). Paraguay remained predominantly agricultural, but Brazilian soya farmers were acquiring Paraguayan holdings and land ownership was becoming more unequal. It was estimated that 1% of the landowners held 77% of the land.[39] In Lugo's proposals, he specified the number of beneficiaries and promised that "the Indians, the landless, the homeless, those deprived of educational and health services" would be "in the first place" in his government (Lugo, 2009: 156–157; Cerna Villagra and Solís Delgadillo, 2012: 4). By comparison, in Lula's 1990s campaigns, Lula made similar promises (Ondetti, 2008: 206); but, in Lula's winning 2002 campaign, he invariably qualified his land-reform proposal as "pacific" and "well-planned" with a "clear strategy to differentiate ... [the Workers' Party] from the controversial campaigns [of Brazil's landless movement]" (Gómez-Bruera, 2013: 50).

Lugo's hope that he would lead a united opposition was frustrated. As in the past, the Colorado Party worked to divide and conquer—in this election, through the inclusion of the controversial Oviedo in the race. Having returned to Paraguay in 2004, Oviedo was serving a ten-year sentence for his 1996 attempted coup. But, in late 2007, he was absolved by Paraguay's Supreme Court and free to stand. It was widely believed, although not proven, that the Duarte administration pressured the Colorado-dominated court to annul Oviedo's conviction (LARR, September 2007, p. 2). Of course, the advantage for the Colorado Party was that Oviedo would take votes away from Lugo among the rural poor (LARR, February 2008, p. 7).

Oviedo was cagey about his ideology. Among knowledgeable Paraguayans, it was evident that Oviedo stood to the right; UNACE was at 8.16 in the 2008 PELA survey. But, in his public statements, wanting to maintain support among the rural poor, Oviedo sent mixed messages. Accordingly, before Oviedo's release from prison, he said that, if he were not a candidate, he would support Lugo, and that, if he were a candidate, he would propose a joint ticket (LARR, July 2007, p. 13).

In office, Lugo's lot was difficult. Not only had Lugo's coalition tallied barely over 40%, but it was far from a congressional majority. The coalition had only twenty-nine of the eighty seats in the Chamber of Deputies and only seventeen of the forty-five seats in the Senate; of these seats, leftist parties had only two in the Chamber of Deputies and only three in the Senate (Nickson, 2009: 148). Often, Lugo was opposed not only by the Colorado Party and UNACE but also by the PLRA. Further, almost from the start, the PLRA's vice president, Franco, was angling for his ascendance to the presidency (Abente Brun, 2009: 152). In 2009, Lugo was weakened further by various paternity claims.

Not surprisingly, Lugo failed to achieve legislative approval for most of his campaign promises. Land-hungry peasants were increasingly frustrated; a guerrilla group, demanding land, emerged. In June 2012, seven police officers and nine peasants were killed during land invasions; Lugo was blamed for having failed to secure the countryside and was impeached. The impeachment was constitutional, but rushed. Franco achieved his goal: the presidency.

What would have happened if there had been a runoff rule? Probably, in the first round, Lugo and the PLRA would have competed separately. If so, the Colorado candidate was likely to have been the first-round winner and Lugo the runner-up; the result of the runoff would have been uncertain. Both the PLRA and UNACE would have faced difficult decisions. Although they could have stayed silent, they would have been pressured to take a stand. Probably, UNACE's true colors would have become more apparent. If Lugo had won the runoff, his legitimacy would have been greater and the pressures against him by the PRLA less intense; Lugo's vice president would not have been a PRLA leader. Alternatively, if Lugo had lost, he would have gained considerable experience and then perhaps have moderated somewhat and, possibly, won in 2013.

Lugo's impeachment did not decrease Paraguay's 2012 Freedom House score, but it did diminish its 2012 V-Dem score. V-Dem scores continued to drop with the return to power of the Colorado Party in the 2013 election. The Colorados' candidate, Horacio Cartes, won 48%; the PLRA was second; the left was divided and fared poorly. (A few months before the election, Oviedo died in a helicopter crash.) A businessman and outsider, Cartes had been briefly imprisoned for currency fraud and faced allegations of money laundering. In office, Cartes was unpopular. In October 2016, Cartes began to pursue a constitutional provision for presidential re-election that would allow him to run in 2018; for most Paraguayans, the effort showed Cartes' authoritarian proclivities, and it failed.

Panama

Among plurality countries, Panama is a star. At the start of its third-wave democracy, its ratings were a tad above the regional average and rose subsequently. Between 1994 and 1998, Panama's Freedom House score was 5; in 1999, it rose to 3; in 2013, however, it receded to 4. Panama's V-Dem scores also began a tad above the regional average and improved through 2012, but to a lesser degree, and then in 2013 returned to 1994–1998 levels. At about 75%, average voter turnout was above the regional average. Panama's third-wave record was superior to its historical record: its 1900–1977 Polity score was tied for ninth among eighteen countries (Pérez-Liñán and Mainwaring, 2013: 381). Also, Panama's 2009 per capita income was approximately the regional average (World Bank, 2011: 10–12).

Why was Panama's democracy not impaired by plurality? The reason was not that Panama had a small number of parties; to the contrary, between 1994 and 2014 the number of parties averaged 3.65. Rather, Panama's political arena was relatively open to newcomers. Although the two leading parties in its legislature were the same in its most recent election through 2012 as in its first, the two parties were not a duopoly. The winner of the 2009 presidential election did not hail from the one of the long-standing parties.

With no pattern of political exclusion, there was no vicious circle of exclusion and polarization. Neither of Panama's long-standing parties was classified at the extreme right; indeed, one of the two parties, the Partido Revolucionario Democrático (Democratic Revolutionary Party, PRD), was usually at the center-left in PELA surveys between 1994 and 2009. No new leftist party emerged. Panama's left was weak in part due to the country's stellar economic growth, the best in the hemisphere during the 2000s.

Not surprisingly, however, with a larger number of parties, three of Panama's four elections were won without 50% of the vote and, in two of the three elections, the result of a runoff would have been uncertain and presidential legitimacy was questionable. However, amid Panama's relatively low polarization and robust economic growth, Panama's democracy was not damaged.

Various electoral rules were relevant. As of 1994, past presidents were allowed to run for re-election after two intervening terms (previously, they were allowed to run after one intervening term). Presidential and legislative elections were concurrent. To retain legal registration, parties were required to reach 4% of the votes in the presidential election (Brown Araúz, 2013: 154).

Panama's Political Parties: The Historical Context

At the start of the third wave, two political parties—the PRD and the party founded by Arnulfo Arias—were dominant. But they were not a duopoly; they were rivals and quite distinct.

The stronger of the two parties, the PRD, was considered a cartel party by a few analysts (see Chapter 3). The PRD was founded in 1979 by General Omar Torrijos. From 1968 until his death in a plane crash in 1981, Torrijos led a populist, leftist military government. In its first decade, the Torrijos government achieved social reforms and a treaty with the United States for the recuperation of the Panama Canal and was popular. Subsequently, however, under General Manuel Antonio Noriega (1983–1989), the PRD government was blatantly authoritarian; Noriega was ousted in 1989 through a U.S. invasion.

The second party, which had different names, was founded by Arnulfo Arias in 1932. Between 1969 and 2005, it was the Partido Arnulfista (Arnulfista Party, PA); in 2005, it resumed its original name, the Partido Panameñista (Panameñista Party, PP). I use the name Arnulfista Party. Of lower-middle class, mestizo origins, Arias at first proclaimed an ultra-nationalist, racist ideology that had fascist overtones. Elected in 1940 and 1948, Arias was deposed by the military due to discriminatory policies and abuse of power (Ropp, 2007: 552–556). Arias was elected again in 1968 but was again quickly ousted, primarily on the grounds of what the military considered his intervention into its institution.

The two parties remained at disparate ideological places. Throughout, the PRD was based first and foremost on Panama's security forces; the Arnulfista Party was based on civilians. While the PRD was usually at the center-left in PELA surveys, the Arnulfista Party was at the right. However, both parties established clientelist networks on the basis of the appeal of their founding leaders (McDonald and Ruhl, 1989: 239–252). Steve C. Ropp (2007: 552) compared them to "two extinct populist volcanoes ... [that] "rest upon rigid underlying social and economic 'tectonic plates' that have historically kept Panama's rich very rich and poor very poor."

Indeed, while Panama's political arena was not highly exclusive, it was not entirely open, either (Leis, 2009: 19). Political insiders enjoyed huge clout; for example, in the 2004 election, the incumbent president was the widow of a former president; the winner was the son of a former president; and the runner-up was a former president. In this election, several small leftist parties denounced the lack of voter choice and appealed for blank votes (LARR, April 27, 2004, p. 1).

The 1994 Election: A Victory with Less than 40% but a Successful President

The election of 1994 was won with only 33% by the PRD's Ernesto Pérez Balladares. Arias's widow, Mireyra Moscoso, was the runner-up with 29%. Two other candidates tallied more than 15%: Rubén Blades of the new party Movimiento Papa Egoró (Papa Egoró Movement) and Rubén Carles of the Movimiento Liberal Republicano Nacionalista (Nationalist Republican Liberal Movement, MOLIRENA). If there had been a runoff, the result would have been uncertain. The legitimacy deficit of President Pérez Balladares was a factor in the subsequent proposal for runoff (see Chapter 1).

Pérez Balladares was a long-standing PRD leader. In his campaign, he positioned himself as the successor to Torrijos, who remained popular. Yet, Moscoso might have been the favorite in a runoff. She was burdened by her lack of political experience and the unpopularity of the incumbent Arnulfista government of Guillermo Endara (the opposition coalition's presidential candidate in the 1989 election, aborted by the Noriega government, but then installed as president after the U.S. invasion). But Moscoso was likely to have captured almost all of the votes of the party in fourth place, MOLIRENA. Founded in the early 1980s, MOLIRENA had often allied with the Partido Arnulfista and had done so with the Endara government. In 1994, however, the alliance had ruptured over the issue of its potential candidate (LAWR, January 20, 1994, p. 18). MOLIRENA was placed to the Partido Arnulfista's right in the 1999 PELA survey, and its voters were very unlikely to have cast their ballots for the PRD.

The beneficiary of the votes of the third-place finisher, Blades, would not have been clear. An outsider, Blades was an Emmy award-winning musician with a master's degree in international law from Harvard University. Six months before the election, he led the polls. However, he was perceived as quixotic. His leanings were somewhat to the left (LAWR, May 19, 1994, p. 205). Probably, he would not have endorsed either candidate (LARR, June 23, 1994, p. 3); in the 1999 election, the party split over its endorsement (LAWR, February 16, 1999, p. 81).

Despite Pérez Balladares's low tally and narrow margin, his government did not fare badly. Confronting the debt crisis, it implemented market policies; these were unpopular, but growth resumed and became robust. Pérez Balladares hoped for immediate re-election, and to this end introduced a constitutional-reform package (including runoff). The re-election bid provoked the opposition's anger and was easily defeated in a referendum in 1998.

The 1999 and 2004 Elections and Panama's Improved Levels of Democracy

Both the 1999 and 2004 elections were won by opposition candidates hailing from one of the two dominant parties with at least 45%. As noted, it was during this period that Freedom House and V-Dem scores improved.

In the 1999 election, Moscoso won with 45%. The PRD's Martín Torrijos, son of the former president, finished second with 38%. The outcome of a runoff would have been virtually certain. Moscoso was likely to have gained most of the votes of the candidate in third place, Alberto Vallarino, who tallied 17%. Originally, both Moscoso and Vallarino were Arnulfistas; but, a commercial banker and outsider, Vallarino lost to Moscoso in the Arnulfista Party's primary. Vallarino became the standard-bearer for an alliance led by Partido Democracia Cristiana (Christian Democratic Party, PDC).

The Moscoso government was unpopular. In the campaign, Moscoso had criticized market policies and promised new social and anti-corruption programs, but she did not deliver. For most of her term, she faced an opposition majority in the legislature.

The 2004 election was won by the PRD's Torrijos, the 1999 runner-up, with 47%. Although Torrijos was close to 50% and defeated the runner-up, Endara (the 1989–1994 Arnulfista president), by more than fifteen points, the outcome of a runoff would have been uncertain. On the one hand, Torrijos was a dynamic candidate who had strengthened the PRD's organization. On the other hand, just a few weeks before the election, political analysts were considering the possibility that a "tactical vote" by anti-PRD voters in favor of whichever of the three non-PRD candidates was the strongest would yield a victory for that candidate (LARR, April 27, 2004, p. 1). The three non-PRD candidates were not divided by ideology; they were all at the right (PELA). Rather, they were divided by ambition (LAWR, September 23, 2003, p. 13). One of the three candidates was Ricardo Martinelli, a supermarket tycoon running for a new party, Cambio Democrático (Democratic Change, CD), who finished fourth.

Although the result of a 2004 runoff would have been uncertain, the legitimacy deficit did not plague the Torrijos government. Averaging about 9% annually, Panama's economic growth was the strongest in the hemisphere. However, Torrijos failed to secure U.S. approval for a U.S.-Panama free trade agreement and crime increased.

The 2009 Election: A Landslide Victory for a New Party

The 2009 election was the first third-wave election won with more than 50% and also the first won by a candidate, Martinelli, who did not hail from one of the two long-standing parties. Martinelli tallied 60% to 38% for the PRD's Balbina Herrera.

Placed at the extreme right in the 2009 PELA survey, Martinelli campaigned as an outsider, taking advantage of Panamanians' fatigue with the two traditional parties (Shifter, 2011c: 116). In reality, Martinelli was far from an outsider; he was a former Director of Social Security and former Minister of Panama Canal Affairs. With a party built in part through his chain of supermarket stores, Martinelli lavished funds on his campaign. Moreover, he partnered with both MOLIRENA and the Arnulfista Party; the coalition was called the Alianza por el Cambio (Alliance for Change). The Arnulfista Party's Juan Carlos Varela became the vice-presidential candidate.

The PRD's Herrera provoked many Panamanians' fears about PRD militarism and corruption. She was perceived as having been close to Noriega and was also charged with having received campaign funds from a Colombian drug trafficker (LAWR, May 7, 2009, p. 2).

The Martinelli government scored important achievements. Economic growth remained the best in Latin America—about 8% annually. The U.S.-Panama free-trade agreement was finally approved by the U.S. legislature.

But many Panamanians worried that Martinelli was abusing power and, as noted, Freedom House and V-Dem did too. Corruption charges against Martinelli were growing, but the president was repressing his critics. Martinelli's interest in continuing in power became apparent. The partnership between Martinelli and his Arnulfista vice-president, Varela, ruptured; Democratic Change and the Arnulfista party went their separate ways.

In 2014, Varela was the surprise winner of a close three-way race. Once again, Panamanians elected an opposition leader—but not a leftist leader. However, Varela won only 39%; Democratic Change tallied 31% and the PRD 28%. In 2015, Martinelli moved to Florida; in 2017, he was arrested on corruption charges and Panama sought his extradition.

Conclusion

Plurality was disadvantageous in Honduras, Mexico, Nicaragua, Paraguay, and Venezuela. The rule was complicit in vicious circles of deleterious elections won with less than 41%, political exclusion, and ideological polarization. Only in Panama, where a new, leftist party did not emerge, was plurality not fraught.

In both Venezuela and Nicaragua, long-standing parties were governing amid the severe challenges of structural adjustment and their economic records were among the worst in the hemisphere. Charges of corruption resonated loudly. In Venezuela, the long-standing duopoly broke down, resulting in a problematic election in 1993, and, in Nicaragua, the long-standing Liberal Party divided, resulting in a calamitous election in 2006. In Venezuela, after decades of exclusion of leftist parties, it was Hugo Chávez at the extreme left who emerged; in Nicaragua, after what in Daniel Ortega's mind was probably a decade of exclusion, it was Ortega at the extreme left.

Subsequently, amid economic recoveries, Chávez and Ortega became popular and, exploiting state resources and politicizing institutions, continued in power for more than a decade. In this effort, Chávez in particular was helped by the difficulties of strategic coordination for Venezuela's opposition parties.

In Mexico and Paraguay, a cartel party—the PRI in Mexico and the Colorado Party in Paraguay—was very strong at the time of the third-wave transition. The PRI lost Mexico's first two third-wave elections but returned in 2012; the Colorado Party did not lose until the fourth, in 2008, and then returned in 2013. Both cartel parties exploited the difficulties of strategic coordination posed by plurality for opposition parties. In both countries, the major opposition parties included both a traditional, pro-market, pro-democratic party and a new, leftist party. And, in both, the new, leftist party was either at an ideological extreme or very close to it. In Mexico, the uncertain commitment of AMLO to the rules of the democratic game was weakened by what he perceived as the PAN's uncertain commitment to the rules of the democratic game—in particular in the 2006 election. In Paraguay, the Colorado Party's virtually constant machinations appeared to disillusion most everyone.

In Honduras, the duopoly of the Liberal and National parties survived structural adjustment but remained intensely exclusive and disaffection mounted. The duopoly broke down because a Liberal president himself, Zelaya, shifted left, alienating traditional political elites; in turn, these elites' repressive response galvanized the country's left. In Honduras's 2013 election, elites worried intensely about what they feared would be a plurality victory for an extreme left led by Zelaya's wife.

5

Runoff

Success in Brazil, Chile, the Dominican Republic, EL Salvador, and Uruguay

Overall, levels of democracy improved in Brazil, Chile, the Dominican Republic, El Salvador, and Uruguay. Between 1994 and 2016, Brazil's Freedom House score rose three points, Chile's two points, the Dominican Republic's one point, Uruguay's two points, and El Salvador's one point. All five countries' 2014 Freedom House scores were superior to the regional average. The trends for V-Dem scores were similar. In the Dominican Republic and Uruguay, runoff was adopted in the mid-1990s after more than a decade of plurality and the impact was positive. Voter turnout was steadily above the regional average in Brazil, stood at the regional apex in Chile and Uruguay, and increased in the Dominican Republic and El Salvador.

Several caveats are necessary, in particular for the Dominican Republic. The Dominican Republic's scores were consistently lower for V-Dem than for Freedom House and the country's V-Dem scores did not attain Latin American averages. Also, after 2014, the Dominican Republic's scores fell for both Freedom House and V-Dem. Further, V-Dem scores for Chile and Uruguay eroded slightly for 2015 and 2016 and scores for Brazil decreased for 2016.

The five countries are diverse. Although both Chile and Uruguay enjoyed superior historical records of democracy, the other countries did not. Also, although both Chile and Uruguay enjoyed per capita incomes above the Latin American average, the other countries did not.

Runoff was advantageous to the improvements in levels of democracy in all five countries. First, of course, no election was won with only about 40% and no presidents suffered legitimacy deficits. Between 1978 and 2012, the result of at least one runoff was uncertain and runoff provided a legitimacy advantage in every country except El Salvador; and, in El Salvador in 2014, the result of the runoff was uncertain and it was helpful. Several elections—in particular the 1996 election in the Dominican Republic and the 1999 election in Uruguay—were won in reversals that were arguably particularly favorable.

Second, runoff opened the electoral arena to new parties at the left but incentivized their moderation. As Chapter 3 indicated, this effect was evident in four of the five countries—all except El Salvador. Between 2000 and 2012, Brazil, Chile, the Dominican Republic, and Uruguay elected a president placed at the moderate left who hailed from a party that had not been one of the two leading parties in the first third-wave election and had initially been classified at the extreme left in PELA surveys. At the same time, moderation was not without costs; in Brazil and the Dominican Republic in particular, the leftist parties' shifts were in part principled, but in part opportunistic.

Plurality advocates' arguments about an excessive number of parties were not borne out in these five countries. First, in the Dominican Republic and Uruguay, the number of parties decreased through 2014—to a mere 2.01 in the Dominican Republic and 2.65 in Uruguay. In El Salvador, although the number of parties usually exceeded 3.0, legislative and presidential elections were not concurrent and presidential elections were invariably between two parties. In Brazil and Chile, the number of parties was large (indeed, in Brazil, very large) but two coalitions emerged for presidential elections. Indeed, in the Dominican Republic in particular and more recently in Brazil, the level of democracy was impaired due to a dominant party's continuation in power for more than a decade and the concomitant failures of new parties emphasizing ethical governance.

This chapter first contrasts the negative effects of plurality and the positive effects of runoff in the country that is a model for runoff advocates: Uruguay. Next, it shows the negative effects of plurality in another country that adopted runoff during the third wave: the Dominican Republic. Then, the chapter turns to Brazil and Chile, where the advantages of runoff for both legitimacy and the incorporation of the left were very evident. Finally, I turn to El Salvador, where until 2014 the advantages of runoff were least apparent.

Uruguay

After the adoption of runoff in Uruguay in 1996, its advantages for legitimacy and the incorporation of the left were exceptionally evident. Further, the number of parties decreased rather than increased. Scholars (Buquet and Piñeiro, 2013: 230–231; Cason, 2000; Mieres, 2004: 477–479) have been very enthusiastic.

Although the level of democracy was very good under plurality, it improved further under runoff. In the mid- and late 1980s, Uruguay's Freedom House score was 4; in the 1990s, 4 or 3; and, as of 2000 (after the first election under runoff), 2. Similarly, Uruguay's V-Dem scores were very good and improved, but by a much smaller percentage, through 2012. Averaging about 90%, voter turnout was also arguably the highest in Latin America.[1]

Uruguay's third-wave record was commensurate with its excellent historical record; its average 1990–1977 Polity score was the second-best in Latin America (Pérez-Liñán and Mainwaring, 2013: 381). Its record was also commensurate with its status as a wealthier Latin American country with high levels of education. Its 2009 per capita income was about 20% greater than the regional average (World Bank, 2011: 12).

Still, under plurality during 1984–1994, concerns mounted about the future of Uruguay's democracy, in particular about the risk of "an Allende-like situation" (González, 1995: 163). Support for Uruguay's two long-standing parties endured, but the left was gaining, and the number of parties averaged more than 3.0. In two of the three elections, the president was elected with less than 40% of the vote and, in the third, with 42%. A reversal would have been likely in 1984 and the result would have been uncertain in 1994. As Jeffrey Cason (2000: 88–90) commented, "relatively thin mandates called into question the legitimacy of the eventual presidential winner."

Runoff was one electoral reform in a package approved in 1996 first in the legislature and then in a plebiscite. A second particularly important measure was the replacement of Uruguay's anomalous "double simultaneous vote" rule, discussed further in the following subsection, by compulsory party primaries. Other important rules did not change. Legislative and presidential elections remained concurrent; there were no midterm elections. Immediate re-election of the president remained prohibited. In part because parties did not proliferate, rules about party registration were not salient.

Uruguay's Political Parties and the Three Elections under Plurality, 1984–1994

From 1836 to the 1990s, the Partido Colorado and the Partido Nacional (National Party or the Blancos) were dominant; they became a duopoly (see Chapter 3). Between 1950 and 1966, the share of the presidential vote won by these two parties did not fall below 89%. Historically, there were programmatic distinctions between the two parties. Based in Montevideo, the Colorados had favored the growth of the state and had ruled uninterruptedly for the first half of the twentieth century, whereas the Blancos were based in the countryside and were pro-Church. But these programmatic distinctions gradually faded. As certain political families remained at the helm, both parties were perceived to suffer "progressive oligarchization" (Luna, 2007: 17).

Uruguay's parties were unusually factionalized due to its "double simultaneous vote", a rule in place since the early twentieth century. Each faction within a party could field its own presidential candidate and voters cast two votes, one for the candidate and one for the candidate's party. The winner of the presidential election was the candidate of the faction that received the most votes within the party that received the most votes. In effect, Uruguay was holding primaries at the same time as the election.

Uruguay's 1971 election was exceptionally fraught; fraud was protested (González, 1995: 152). A violent leftist movement (the Tupamaros) had emerged. Also, the leftist Frente Amplio (Broad Front, FA), a coalition of Communists, Socialists, and Christian Democrats, was founded by retired General Líber Seregni; it competed and tallied 18%. The Colorado Party's candidate, Juan María Bordaberry, proposed a hard line. By contrast, the Blancos' candidate, Wilson Ferreira, promised a measured response. Despite major irregularities that favored Bordaberry, Ferreira tallied more votes than Bordaberry, winning 26% to 24%; but, due to Uruguay's "double simultaneous vote," Bordaberry was declared president. Bordaberry resorted to the military for support and, in 1973, it took over outright. A majority of the Colorado Party supported the military government (González, 1995: 152–154). The Blancos' Ferreira was exiled.

The 1984 election was marred by conditions demanded by the military government. The top leaders of the Blancos and the Broad Front, Ferreira and Seregni respectively, were prohibited from candidacy. The only top leader allowed to compete was the Colorados' Julio María Sanguinetti, who had taken the lead in the negotiations with the military for the democratic transition; he won with 42%. Without their top leaders, the Blancos tallied 34% and the Broad Front 21%. If there had been a runoff, in the context of the joint opposition against the military regime by Ferreira's Blancos and the Broad Front, a reversal would have been likely.

Amid the debt crisis, the Sanguinetti government was unpopular and the 1989 election was won by the Blancos' Luis Alberto Lacalle with 39%. The Colorados tallied 30% and the Broad Front 21%. If there had been a runoff, Lacalle's victory would have been almost certain. Lacalle would have benefited from the Broad Front's continuing opposition to the Colorados, from his party's not having been in office since 1962, and from his name; Lacalle was the grandson of a legendary president.

Uruguay remained mired in the debt crisis and support for the left grew. The 1994 electoral result was almost a three-way tie. Although the Colorados and the Blancos were placed at very similar points on the right in PELA surveys in 1995, their historical rivalry endured and—despite plurality—they did not ally. Led by former president Sanguinetti, the Colorados won 32%; led by Alberto Volonté, the Blancos polled 31.2%; led by Tabaré Vázquez, a leftist coalition led by the Broad Front polled 30.6%.

The result of a runoff would have been uncertain. At this time, the Broad Front was at the extreme left (placed at 2.67 in 1995 PELA surveys) and was likely to have repudiated both the Colorados and the Blancos; the beneficiary of any votes cast by its supporters would have been unclear (LARR, November 24,

1994, p. 6). The Colorado Party was more united, and it was not burdened by incumbency, but the Blancos' Volonté enjoyed momentum (LAWR, December 1, 1994, p. 542).

If Uruguay's left had not been divided, it would have won. In 1989, dismayed by the Broad Front's decision to approve the entry of former *Tupamaro* guerrillas, center-leftists withdrew and formed the Partido por el Gobierno del Pueblo (Party for the Government of the People, PGP). In 1994, some PGP leaders joined with dissidents from the long-standing parties to form the center-left Encuentro Progresista (Progressive Encounter, EP) (Luna, 2007: 5); Progressive Encounter and the Broad Front allied. But, other PGP leaders joined a second center-left group, Nuevo Espacio (New Space), which ran its own candidate. New Space tallied 5%.

Given the steady rise of the left, it appeared likely that, under plurality, it would win the 1999 election. The traditional parties were galvanized and sought the adoption of runoff. For its part, the Broad Front was divided about the rule (LARR, March 14, 1996, pp. 2–3; LARR, November 21, 1996, p. 7).

The Advantageous 1999 Reversal

Expectations for a Broad Front plurality were borne out in 1999. Progressive Encounter/Broad Front tallied 40% in the first round; the Colorados' candidate, Jorge Batlle, 33%; and the Blancos' candidate, 22%. But Battle gained the Blanco vote in the runoff and won by more than eight points. The reversal was virtually certain (Cason, 2000: 93–96; LARR, November 16, 1999, p. 6; LAWR, November 2, 1999, p. 505). Batlle was an old-timer, winning the presidency on his fifth try. (Previously, three Uruguayan presidents had been named Batlle.)

Aware of the implications of runoff, Progressive Encounter/Broad Front was moderating (Cason, 2000: 92–96). Its candidate, Vázquez, was a former oncologist and successful mayor of Montevideo. In the first round, he promised to service the foreign debt and to govern with other parties. For the runoff, he moderated further. Rejecting a leftist tax proposal, he emphasized that changes would be "gradualist" (LAWR, November 2, 1999, p. 505) and "cautious" (LARR, November 16, 1999, p. 6). He sent representatives to speak to diplomatic and financial authorities in Washington. He raised Uruguay's flag much more frequently (Espíndola, 2001: 654). The shift was registered in PELA surveys; whereas Vázquez had been placed at 2.68 in the 1995 PELA surveys, in 2000 he was placed at 3.20.

But 3.20 was still far to the left. Vázquez's moderation was questioned by the long-standing parties. They pointed to leaders of the Broad Front coalition who were to Vázquez's left and highlighted previous statements contradicting their current positions (Cason, 2000: 93). Also, although the leaders of the center-left New Space, which had been in fourth place with 5%, said they would vote for Vázquez, they did not formally endorse him (Cason, 2000: 93; Espíndola, 2001: 650).

Victory for a Moderate Left in 2004

Finally, running for the third time in 2004, Vázquez prevailed. It was the first time in more than 150 years that neither of the two traditional parties won the presidency. Vázquez won 52% in the first round.

It was clear that, to gain a majority, Vázquez would have to continue to moderate (Luna, 2007; Lanzaro, 2011: 352–356; Altman and Castiglioni, 2006: 150–153). He did. He emphasized that his models were the center-left presidents Ricardo Lagos of Chile and Lula of Brazil. Months prior to the election, Vázquez announced that his economy minister would be Danilo Astori, a long-standing Broad Front leader but much friendlier to the market than Vázquez. Further, Progressive Encounter/Broad Front allied with the center-left Nueva Mayoría (New Majority, NM), which included New Space and splinters from the long-standing parties. The new coalition was usually called the EP-FA-NM. In PELA surveys, Vázquez moved from 3.20 in 2000 to 3.46 in 2005.

Vázquez's candidacy gained from the discredit of the traditional parties. Under the Colorados' Batlle, the Uruguayan economy had been devastated first by the devaluation of Brazil's currency and then by Argentina's financial collapse, and it had declined about 3% annually.

A Legitimacy Advantage with Runoff in 2009

In the first round of the 2009 election, the EP-FA-NM's candidate, José Mujica, tallied 49%; his victory in the runoff was likely, but not certain (LAWR, October 29, 2009, p. 5; LARR, November 2009, p. 6). Although the runner-up, former Blanco president Lacalle, tallied only 30%, he was immediately endorsed by the third-place Colorados, with 18%. In the event, the EP-FA-NM candidate won the runoff by ten points.

In a context of market-friendly policies and robust economic growth with social inclusion, the Vázquez government had been popular. However, Mujica was a more controversial candidate than Vázquez; Mujica was a former leader of Uruguay's guerrilla movement, the *Tupamaros*. Mujica had been jailed for more than ten years during the military dictatorship. Mujica, an agriculture minister in the Vázquez government, was the leader of the largest faction within the EP-FA-NM, but this faction was to the left within the coalition. Mujica was not Vázquez's choice; Vázquez preferred his economy minister, Astori, and in the first round provided only halfhearted support to Mujica (LAWR, October 29, 2009, p. 6).

However, Mujica sought to moderate and to unify his coalition (LARR, August 2009, p. 14). He chose Astori as his running mate. Like Vázquez, Mujica emphasized that his role model was Lula, not Chávez. For the runoff, Mujica gave Astori a more prominent role in the campaign and tried hard to appease Vázquez (LAWR, October 29, 2009, p. 6). He emphasized his promise to work with the traditional parties on key policies such as crime, education, the environment, and energy (LAWR, November 19, 2009, p. 3). He was even more adamant that his role model would be Lula, not Chávez (Benjamin, 2009: 3). Mujica was placed at 3.26 in 2010 PELA surveys.

Although the traditional parties lambasted what they termed Mujica's dangerous radicalism, the hyperbole backfired (Buquet and Piñeiro 2013: 216–223). Neither Lacalle nor the Colorados' candidate, Pedro Bordaberry, was able to build broad appeal. At the extreme right in PELA surveys, Lacalle was "neoliberalism's booster-in-chief"; Bordaberry, the son of the president who had presided over the breakdown of democracy, failed to distance himself effectively from the 1973–1985 military government.[2]

The 2014 Election

After 2012, Uruguay's Freedom House scores were steadily stellar, but its V-Dem scores dipped. Concerns were mounting that, if Vázquez were re-elected, the Broad Front would be in power continuously for fifteen years. New parties were not emerging. Indeed, in the 2014 election, Vázquez easily won a second term, securing 49% in the first round and 57% in the runoff. The runner-up was the Blancos' Luis Alberto Lacalle, the former president's son; the Colorados' candidate was in third. Between 2000 and 2014, the number of political parties declined in Uruguay, averaging 2.7, and arguably the political arena was insufficiently open.

The Dominican Republic

Under plurality, levels of democracy plummeted in the Dominican Republic; but, under runoff, they recovered. The country's Freedom House score plunged from 4 at its first election in 1978 to 7 in 1994; but, between the adoption of runoff in 1995 and 2012, its Freedom House score re-gained the three points that it had lost, returning to 4. The trends in the country's V-Dem scores were similar, although the improvement was less dramatic and, even at their apex, scores did not reach the regional average. Similarly, under plurality voter turnout declined but, between 1996 and 2012, it averaged 74%, slightly above the regional average.

The primary reason for the plummet under plurality was the advantage that it provided a rightist caudillo, Joaquín Balaguer. In the 1986 and 1990 elections, Balaguer won with less than 50%; if there had been runoffs, he would have been very likely to lose (Hartlyn, 1990: 93–94 and 1998: 185). Balaguer went on to rig the 1994 election.

By contrast, runoff was advantageous. Of course, no president was able to win through dividing the opposition. Although only one election—the 1996 election—went to a runoff, it provided a legitimacy advantage. Stated Francisco

Cueto (2004: 449), "With runoff, we see reinforced the legitimacy of the elected president relative to that of a president emerging in a plurality system." Also, runoff helped open the political arena to the Partido de la Liberación Dominicana (Party of Dominican Liberation, PLD); founded as a quasi-Marxist party in 1973, under runoff the party moderated and won the presidency in a reversal in 1996.

Ultimately, however, the PLD's dominance was a critical factor in the country's declining Freedom House and V-Dem scores. As of 2016, the PLD had won four consecutive presidential elections and five of the last six. For most analysts, democracy would have been enhanced by the emergence of a new programmatic party.

Even at the Dominican Republic's relatively lower level of democracy in the 2010s, its level is a dramatic improvement over the country's historical record. The Dominican Republic's average 1990–1977 Polity score was seventeenth out of eighteen countries (Pérez-Liñán and Mainwaring, 2013: 381). Its level of democracy was also superior to what might be expected given the Dominican Republic's 2009 per capita income slightly below the Latin American average (World Bank, 2011: 10–12).

Runoff was one of several electoral reforms enacted after the fraudulent 1994 election. Immediate re-election of the president was banned (a ban that ended subsequently). Due to an agreement that new elections would be held within two years, presidential and legislative elections became non-concurrent. Probably because the number of parties has been small, rules about thresholds for a party's entry into the legislature were not salient.

The Historical Context and the 1978–1994 Elections under Plurality

Prior to 1978, the Dominican Republic's political regime was among the most authoritarian in Latin America. From 1930 until 1961, the notorious dictator Rafael Leónidas Trujillo ruled the country, either as its official president or as the strongman who directed puppet presidents. In 1961, Trujillo was assassinated, and his puppet president, Balaguer, took over. Building on Trujillo's political networks, Balaguer founded the Partido Reformista in 1963 (Hartlyn, 1998: 90); this party subsequently united with the Social Christian Party to become the Partido Reformista Social Cristiano (Reformist Christian Social Party, PRSC).

In the 1960s, there were two key parties: the PRSC and the Partido Revolucionario Dominicano (Dominican Revolutionary Party, PRD). The PRD was founded in 1939 by Juan Bosch in opposition to the Trujillo regime. After Trujillo's assassination, elections were held in 1962 and won by Bosch, a leftist. Like other Latin American leftists of his era, Bosch favored land reform and workers' rights; he said that he was a Marxist but not a Communist (LARR, May 9, 1986, p. 7; LAWR, April 28, 1994, p. 176). He was labeled "soft on Communism" by Dominican elites and many U.S. officials. After only seven months in the presidency, Bosch was overthrown by a military coup; in 1965, after an uprising against the military regime by officers loyal to Bosch, the United States invaded. In 1966, amid severe political repression, new elections were won by Balaguer.

Subsequently, Bosch argued that, in the context of repression, the principled position for the PRD was abstention. Bosch's view came to be opposed by other PRD leaders; Bosch broke with the PRD in 1973 and founded a new party, the PLD.

Amid intense international pressure for democracy, free and fair elections were held in 1978 and 1982 and won by the PRD. In both elections, Balaguer was the runner-up. In 1978, Bosch's PLD was tiny, tallying only 1%, and in 1982 was still minor, tallying only 10%. Although the PRD was slightly short of a majority in 1982, in a runoff the PRD would have secured most of the PLD's votes and its victory would have been virtually certain.

Neither PRD government was considered successful. Both presidents were accused of corruption. As Latin America's debt crisis began, economic problems mounted. Facing the 1986 election, the PRD was also hurt by a violent dispute for its presidential nomination between a long-standing leader, José Francisco Peña Gómez, and the eventual nominee, Jacobo Majluta.

Amid dissatisfaction with the PRD, Bosch's PLD grew. At the same time, Bosch's inclination toward Marxism slackened; in 1990, he said that Marxism was not "an organizational road map for Dominican society" but "a useful analytical tool" (French, 1990; Morgan, Hartlyn, and Espinal, 2008: 4–6).

As the ideological positions of the PRD and the PLD became more similar, it would be expected that, under plurality, the two parties would ally. But, historical tensions lingered. Also, Bosch and Peña Gómez were personal rivals. Further, in all three elections between 1986 and 1994, opinion polls gave the eventual runners-up comfortable leads and they probably doubted that they needed an alliance.

In the 1986 election, Balaguer defeated the PRD candidate, Majluta, by less than three points: 42% to 39%. The PLD won 18%. In a runoff, Majluta was virtually certain to have gained most of the PLD vote and prevailed.[3] The electoral tally was challenged by the PRD. Although agreements were reached between Balaguer and key PRD leaders in about ten days, protests by other PRD leaders continued for more than a month (María-Bidó, 2007: 91–94).

In 1990, in the official tally, Balaguer won with only 35.5%. The runner-up, the PLD's Bosch, was behind by less than two points. The PRD's Peña Gómez was third and Majluta, leading a new party, fourth. At the start of the campaign and as late as a month before the election, Bosch enjoyed more than a ten-point lead in the polls. Bosch was continuing to moderate; he even advocated market reforms (Hartlyn, 1994a: 24). But, in the final weeks, the PRSC intensified its charge that "he [Bosch] would install a Communist regime" (Hartlyn, 1994a: 25).

The PRSC exploited divisions not only between the PLD and the PRD but also within the PRD. When Majluta broke with the PRD, he and Peña Gómez agreed that they both would run as candidates for new parties; but, the Balaguer government appeared to facilitate a successful reclaiming of the PRD name by Peña Gómez (Hartlyn, 1994a: 24). This PRSC maneuver was a likely factor in an increase in support for Peña Gómez in the final weeks of the campaign; Peña Gómez's rise probably cost Bosch the election (Hartlyn, 1994a: 25).

Irregularities, in particular duplicate identity cards for likely Balaguer voters and the purchasing of identity cards from likely Bosch voters, were "multiple" (Hartlyn, 1994a: 34). Bosch immediately charged fraud. However, international election monitors were constrained by conditions that had been placed upon their work.[4] For months, Bosch encouraged civil disobedience; fourteen people died and hundreds were arrested in a strike in August and coup rumors abounded in November.[5]

The 1994 election was blatantly fraudulent. In the official result, Balaguer won 42%, less than one point more than Peña Gómez, with Bosch in third. The PRD immediately charged the omission of thousands of names of opposition supporters from voter lists. Agreeing, the OAS and other international election monitors repudiated Balaguer's victory claim.

Negotiations ensued among Balaguer, the Dominican opposition, and the international community. The upshot was the reduction of Balaguer's term to two years and the adoption of new electoral rules, including runoff.

The Pivotal 1996 Reversal

The impact of runoff in the 1996 election was major. First, it provided a legitimacy advantage for the PLD's Leonel Fernández, who won in a reversal (Sagás, 1997: 105–106; Cueto, 2004: 449; María-Bidó, 2007:137). Second, runoff increased the incentive for the PLD's moderation. But, while runoff was positive overall, there were disturbing dimensions. In particular, to win, Fernández secured the support of the caudillo, Balaguer. This unseemly ideological mismatch was a prelude to intensifying opportunism and clientelism.

The first-round winner with 46% was the PRD's Peña Gómez, running for the third time. For some analysts, Peña Gómez deserved the presidency because, with runoff, he would have won in 1994. However, to other analysts, Peña Gómez was "temperamental and sometimes unstable" (Hartlyn, 1994a: 27). Unbeknown to Dominicans at this time, Peña Gómez was stricken with cancer; he died in 1998.

The PLD's Fernández tallied 39% in the first round and won the runoff by two-and-a-half points. Although he had been the PLD's 1994 vice-presidential candidate, he was a relative newcomer. Raised for several years in New York City, he had joined the PRD in his late teens and then followed Bosch into the PLD; Fernández was perceived as a protégé of Bosch (French, 1990).

In the runoff, Balaguer was a kingmaker. The PRSC's candidate, Jacinto Peynado, had finished third with 15%. Balaguer had been barred from candidacy but did not want to yield control of the PRSC; he provided scant support for Peynado. Balaguer preferred Fernández to Peña Gómez because of the long-standing rivalry between the two older leaders and because of racism and anti-Haitian nationalism; the dark-skinned Peña Gómez was of Haitian descent.

For Fernández's part, beginning a dizzying ideological shift, he courted Balaguer. As mentioned, at its inception the PLD had been quasi-Marxist; but, in a 1995 PELA survey a few months before the 1996 election, the PLD was placed at the center-left (4.10). By contrast, the PRSC was at the extreme right (8.50). But, now, Fernández praised Balaguer: "The thought and work of Balaguer would be essential reference points for his presidency" (Cassa, 1997: 22, 26).

Resentment about the unseemly alliance between the PLD and the PRSC simmered (Morgan, Hartlyn, and Espinal, 2008: 6). Still, Fernández's government was considered relatively successful.

The Five Elections between 2000 and 2016 and the Emergence of the PLD as a Likely Cartel Party

The impact of runoff during the five elections from 2000 to2016 was minor. Amid the death of Balaguer, the PRSC withered. The five elections were won with a majority in the first round; the first in 2000 was won by the PRD and the next four by the PLD. The PLD appeared to become a cartel party and runoff was insufficient to enable a newcomer to become a significant contender. In this context, the Dominican Republic's Freedom House score reached 4 for 2000 and retained that score through 2012 (with one exception for 2003) but worsened to 5 as of 2012 and 6 as of 2016. Similarly, the country's V-Dem scores were at their peak in the early 2000s and declined after 2012.

The rules for re-election of the president changed several times. In 2003, a president was allowed to seek one additional term, consecutive or not. During the 2008–2012 government, an indefinite number of alternate terms was allowed. Finally, during the 2012–2016 government, one consecutive re-election was again permitted.

In the 2000 election, the first-round winner, the PRD's Hipólito Mejía, a former agriculture minister, was only a few thousand votes short of the 50% threshold. The runner-up with 25% was the PLD's Danilo Medina; although Balaguer was 93 and blind, he finished third. Aware that the result of a runoff was virtually certain to be a landslide for Mejía, Medina withdrew (Sagás, 2001: 495–496). However, amid low economic growth and considerable corruption, the Mejía government was unpopular.

In both the 2004 and 2008 elections, former president Fernández won in the first round with about 55% and the PRD candidate was the runner-up. In 2004, after the death of Balaguer, the PRSC divided; increasing numbers of PRSC leaders supported Fernández (LAWR, May 18, 2004, p. 10). In 2008, the PRSC candidate tallied only 5% and, in subsequent elections, it did not present a candidate.

The 2012 election was closer than the 2004 or 2008 elections, but the PLD again won in the first round. Its candidate, Medina (the 2000 runner-up), secured 51%, four points more than the PRD's Mejía. During his 2012–2016 election government, Medina co-opted many long-standing PRD leaders and the party split. In the 2016 election, without competition from the PRSC or the PRD, Medina won easily, with 62%; the breakaway faction of the PRD finished second with 35%.

Unfortunately, programmatic debate was scant. For example, presidential debates were rare (Sagás, 2005: 159; Hartlyn and Espinal, 2009: 335). The PLD and the PRD were placed at very similar points on the center-right in PELA surveys. Both parties were increasingly "clientelistic and patrimonial" (Morgan, Hartlyn, and Espinal, 2008: 7). In 2010, 22% of Dominicans said that they had been "offered a material benefit in exchange for their vote sometimes or often"—the highest in Latin America and almost twice the regional average (Muñoz, 2014: 80).

Indeed, the PLD appeared to be a cartel party, returning to the tactics of the PRSC in the early 1990s. The PLD exploited state resources; with public funds, the PLD bought voter cards from members of small parties so that they would not be able to vote (Meilán, 2014: 348). Public funding for political parties was very generous—but only for parties that reached a 5% vote threshold and only in proportion to votes won in previous elections (Payne, Zovatto G., and Mateo Díaz, 2007: 195–204; Hartlyn and Espinal, 2009: 336). Increasingly, potential new parties gave up. In 2012, some nineteen new or tiny parties decided to ally with the PLD or the PRD rather than run on their own (Hernández, 2012: 65). Four small parties did compete, but none won as much as 1.5%.

The dearth of programmatic debate was unfortunate because the PLD's dominance was not warranted by its record. Although economic growth was robust, social spending was low and the decline in poverty small (LARR, June 2012, p. 2).[6] In 2009, only 2.3% of GDP was spent on education—the lowest percentage among the Latin American countries reporting a figure (World Bank, 2011: 76–78). The Switzerland-based World Economic Forum ranked the Dominican Republic last among 142 countries for the wastefulness of government spending (LAWR, February 16, 2012, p. 15).

Brazil

Brazil's third-wave democracy was widely considered one of Latin America's brightest success stories.[7] At only 7 during much of the 1990s, Brazil's Freedom House score rose to 4 in 2006 and maintained this rating through 2016. Brazil's V-Dem scores also improved, but less dramatically; in 1990, they were already above the regional average (and the 2016 score fell). At about 80%, voter turnout was steadily above the Latin American average. By contrast, prior to the third wave, Brazil's experience with democracy was limited; its average 1900–1977 Polity score was twelfth of eighteen Latin American countries (Pérez-Liñán and Mainwaring, 2013: 381). Brazil's 2009 per capita income was similar to the Latin American average (World Bank, 2011: 10–12).

Runoff was advantageous both for presidents' legitimacy and for the emergence and moderation of a new left. Of Brazil's seven third-wave elections, five (1989, 2002, 2006, and 2010, and 2014) went to a runoff, and the results of four of the five were uncertain. Further, runoff both facilitated the ascent of the new Partido dos Trabalhadores (Workers' Party, PT) and incentivized the moderation of its leader, Luis Inácio "Lula" da Silva. In contrast to the Dominican Republic and Uruguay, the number of parties in Brazil, traditionally considerable, increased further. Between 1954 and 1962 (the last legislative election prior to a military coup), the number of political parties averaged 4.55 (Mainwaring and Shugart, 1997a: 407); between 1990 and 2010 it averaged 8.70, one of the largest in the world. Of course, the electoral arena was open to newcomers. In 1989, the electoral arena opened to Lula; in 2006 and 2010, it opened to former PT leaders demanding integrity, Heloísa Helena de Moraes and Marina Silva respectively.

However, among the plethora of parties, two coalitions emerged for presidential elections. One coalition was the Workers' Party and its allies; the second was the Partido da Social Democracia Brasileira (Party of Brazilian Social Democracy, PSDB) and its allies. Runoff did not obscure "the majoritarian requirements of winning presidential office" (Hunter, 2010: 126). Also, pragmatic alliances—for example, two parties on a ticket, with one candidate for president and another as vice-president—were traditional in Brazil.

During most of the third wave, various rules were complicit in the large number of parties in Brazil's lower house: open-list proportional representation, a large district magnitude (a large number of seats from one electoral district), and the absence of a specific threshold for representation (Fleischer, 2011; Mainwaring, 1995: 375). After the 1989 presidential election, the non-concurrence with the legislative election was problematic. In 1994, the two sets of elections became concurrent and presidential terms were shortened from five to four years.

Brazil's Political Parties and the Problematic First Third-Wave Election in 1989

In the late 1970s and early 1980s, Brazil was hard hit by the debt crisis. The 1964–1985 military government confronted massive protests. In 1985, the military government allowed an indirect presidential election; the election was won by an opposition leader, Tancredo Neves. However, Neves died unexpectedly before his inauguration. To widespread consternation, the vice-presidential candidate, José Sarney, who hailed from the military's party, the Partido Democrático Social (Social Democratic Party, PDS), assumed the presidency. The Sarney government was perceived as corrupt and incompetent.

During the Sarney government, the dominant parties were the PDS; the Partido da Frente Liberal (Liberal Front, PFL), a right-wing machine party that had split from the PDS in the mid-1980s and was particularly strong in Brazil's impoverished

Northeast; and the Partido do Movimiento Democrático Brasileiro (Party of the Brazilian Democratic Movement, PMDB), a former opposition party that had become heterogeneous. When the PDS was increasingly maligned, many of its members shifted to the PMDB for opportunistic reasons (Hagopian, 1990: 159–161).

As a direct election approached in 1989, Brazil's traditional parties were discredited. Both the 1989 winner and runner-up led new parties; both were far from a legislative majority. Although the 1989 winner was impeached, a victory for the runner-up is unlikely to have been fruitful, either. The most positive outcome might have been a victory for the candidate who finished fourth, the possible Condorcet winner.

The first-round winner was Fernando Collor de Mello with 31%. Collor's party was his personal vehicle: the Partido de Renovação Nacional (Party of National Reconstruction, PRN). Collor was a former PDS legislator and former PMDB governor. As a governor, he had slashed bureaucrats' salaries, catapulting his popularity. From a prominent political family, he owned a television network and was greatly helped by the Globo network, Brazil's telecommunications giant. But Collor did not have the confidence of organized political groups. He campaigned as an outsider and "ostentatiously asserted his distance from 'the elite,' whom he attacked in true populist fashion" (Weyland, 1993: 9). Collor was widely considered "rash and unpredictable" (Kingstone, 1999: 153).

The first-round runner-up with 17% was the PT's Lula. From a humble Northeastern background, with only a primary education, Lula had become president of a metalworkers' union in São Paulo and had organized major strikes against the military government. In 1980, he was one of the founders of the Workers' Party, which was quite different from Brazil's traditional leftist parties; it emphasized trade unionism and the power of the grassroots and long held a reputation for integrity. Since 1982, the PT had competed in congressional and municipal elections, but as of 1986 it held only 3.3% of the seats in the Chamber of Deputies. In 1986, Lula was one of the party's elected legislators.

Lula's second-place finish was a surprise; he benefited from sincere votes to overtake a leftist old-timer, Leonel Brizola. Claiming the mantle of the leading party of Brazil's left, the PT was "ecstatic" (Hunter, 2010: 112). But Lula was "a scruffy bearded figure calling for radical change under the symbol of his party's red star" (Hunter, 2010: 1). He called for a moratorium on Brazil's payment of its debt, the nationalization of Brazil's banks, and land reform. Said Lula at a conference in 1985:

> I will tell you that the Third World War has already started . . . . This war is tearing down Brazil, Latin America, and practically all the third world. Instead of soldiers dying, there are children; instead of millions of wounded, there are millions of unemployed . . . . It is a war by the United States against the Latin American continent and the third world. It is a war over the foreign debt, one which has as its main weapon interest, a weapon more deadly than the atom bomb, more shattering than a laser beam . . . .[8]

Old-timer leftist Brizola was third with 16.5%. A former mayor, governor, and legislator, Brizola had been the early frontrunner. But Brizola was perceived as fiery and uncompromising; he was criticized for poor judgment during the government of his brother-in-law, João Goulart (1961–1964, the last before the military coup).

The Condorcet winner might have been the fourth-place candidate, Mário Covas of the PSDB (which, as mentioned earlier, became the core party in the coalition opposed to the PT's coalition), with 12%. The PSDB had been formed by dissident PMDB leaders, led by Covas, who charged that the PMDB had become complicit with the Sarney government. A widely respected former mayor and senator for São Paulo, Covas sought to present himself as the leader of Brazil's "modern Left" (LAWR, July 13, 1989, p. 2). Yet he also enjoyed considerable support from business groups (Kingstone, 1999: 152–153). An indicator of the possibility that Covas was the Condorcet winner was Brizola's suggestion that Lula withdraw from the runoff in favor of Covas (LAWR, December 7, 1989, p. 4).

The result of the runoff was uncertain (LAWR, November 30, 1989, p. 4; LAWR, December 7, 1989, p. 4). In the first round, the combined tally for the two leftists, Lula and Brizola, surpassed the tally for Collor, and it was not clear to whom Covas' votes would go; for much of the period, Collor and Lula were close in the opinion polls. Lula quickly gained the support of Brizola's party and, more slowly and equivocally, the support of the PSDB (Keck, 1992: 159). However, Brazil's business and military elites "closed ranks under the specter of a Lula victory" and generously funded Collor (Hunter, 2010: 113). Collor won by six points.

In office, Collor confronted Brazil's continuing economic crisis but had minimal legislative support. Legislative elections were not held until October 1990; Collor's party won only 8% of the seats in the lower house and 6.5% in the upper house. Using decree powers and also dividing and co-opting opposition groups, Collor imposed painful austerity measures. Yet inflation was in quadruple digits.

In mid-1992, Collor and his entourage were charged with graft reaching a billion dollars. Collor's brother exposed a scheme of kickbacks that had enabled lavish expenditures, most notoriously including $2.5 million for the landscaping of Collor's mansion. Collor was impeached in late 1992. He was succeeded by his vice-president, Itamar Franco.

The 1994 and 1998 Elections: Two First-Round Victories for Cardoso

In the 1994 and 1998 elections, runoff had minimal impact. Fernando Henrique Cardoso won 54% in the first round in 1994 and 53% in 1998. In both elections, he defeated the runner-up, Lula, by more than twenty points. The two coalitions for presidential elections were emerging; no other candidate tallied as much as 15%.

Cardoso was a founder of the PSDB, a senator, and a world-class sociologist. In 1993, as Franco's fourth finance minister, Cardoso became Brazil's knight, slaying the dragon of hyperinflation. In what was called the *Plano Real* (Real Plan), a new currency, the *real*, was introduced; it was not tied legally to the dollar but was valued on par with the dollar. Cardoso's success was attributed to his effective work with Brazil's legislature as well as to Collor's previous market initiatives (Kingstone 1999: 196). Also, stabilization programs were beginning to bear fruit in many Latin American nations at this time.

For the 1994 election, Cardoso allied with the PFL. Given that in the past Cardoso had been critical of the PFL's clientelism, the alliance surprised many Brazilians. But Cardoso was aware that support for his PSDB was largely restricted to the urban middle class in the south and wanted to extend its appeal in the northeast (Power, 2010: 196–198). For the 1998 election, Cardoso doubled down on this strategy, achieving the support of the heterogeneous PMDB (LARR, March 17, 1998, p. 1).

After the 1994 election, the Cardoso government was riding high, benefiting from renewed growth and low inflation. Cardoso achieved a constitutional amendment so that he could run for immediate re-election. Then, in October 1997, Brazil was hit hard by financial crisis in Asia. Per capita GDP growth turned negative. Still, most Brazilians considered Cardoso "serious, honest, and competent" (Hunter, 2010: 130) and Lula was not able to capitalize on the economic downturn.

In both 1994 and 1998, Lula remained quite far to the left (Hunter 2010: 118–120; Baiocchi and Checa, 2008: 115). Timothy Power asked Brazilian legislators to place parties a ten-point scale identical to PELA's; in both 1997 and 2001 the PT was placed at the extreme left, 1.89 and 2.27 respectively (Machado, 2009: 99). Although many of Lula's positions—for example, on Brazil's debt and land reform— were not as far to the left, his discourse remained rather angry (Goertzel, 1999: 173; Hunter, 2010: 118).

The 2002 Election: Victory for Lula, Now a Moderate Leftist, in a Runoff

Lula tallied 46% in the first round of the 2002 election and was almost immediately endorsed by the third-place and fourth-place candidates; he was almost certain to win the runoff (LAWR, October 8, 2002, p. 471; LAWR, October 15, 2002, p. 483). Yet, given Lula's history, the runoff was important for presidential legitimacy. In the event, Lula secured a whopping 61%.

Between the 1989 and 2002 elections, Lula metamorphosed from radical upstart to moderate old-timer: the "old persona of gruff, incendiary leftist gave way to that of Lulinha paz e amor [little Lula, peace and love]" (de Souza, 2011: 78). In its platform, the Workers' Party promised to abide by Brazil's bailout agreement with the IMF and to respect agribusiness; the word "socialism" disappeared (Hunter, 2010: 138–139; Sola, 2008: 34–35). For the first time, an alliance was forged with a party that was right of center: the Liberal Party, which included large numbers of

Protestant evangelicals. The Liberal Party's José Alencar, a wealthy businessman, became the vice-presidential candidate. Whereas in previous years the PT was placed at about 2.0 in Power's surveys, in 2005 it was placed at 3.83 (Machado, 2009: 99); in the first PELA survey in 2005, the PT was placed at 4.44.

To a degree, Lula's shift was a response to a more positive perception of market policies among Brazil's voters. But scholars agree that Lula's shift also reflected his recognition that moderation was necessary to win a majority (Hunter, 2010: 137; Samuels and Shugart, 2010: 194–204; Sola, 2008: 34–35).[9] Stated Michael Reid (2007: 194), "... successive electoral defeats persuaded Lula ... to move to the centre and seek alliances." Echoed Peter Smith (2008: 349), "In order to win the presidency, he would have to trim his sails and move toward the center of the political spectrum. That he did." A similar assessment was made by other scholars.

The runner-up with 23% was the PSDB's José Serra. Close to Cardoso, Serra was an economist and former senator who had served as planning minister and health minister in Cardoso's government. He was considered a good manager, but lacking in charisma.

The 2006, 2010, and 2014 Elections: PT Victories Amid Runoffs

The 2002 result became a pattern in 2006, 2010, and 2014: the PT finished first and the PSDB second. However, in the three later elections, the candidates in third place were former PT leaders and religious women demanding ethical governance. It was not clear to which finalist their votes would go and the results of the runoffs were uncertain (LAWR, October 3, 2006, p. 1; LAWR, October 14, 2010, p. 3; LAWR, October 16, 2014, p. 6). Although in 2006 and 2010 the PT candidates won decisively, the runoffs enhanced presidential legitimacy. Indeed, in a statement by the president of Brazil's electoral court about the 2006 runoff, the concept of legitimacy was invoked (LAWR, October 31, 2006, p. 1).

In the 2006 and 2010 elections, amid robust growth and a successful anti-poverty program, the PT candidates were the frontrunners. Although Lula's economic orthodoxy disappointed many leftists, his giant conditional cash transfer program, Bolsa Família, was very popular among Brazil's poor. Yet, in the last few weeks of the campaigns, there were setbacks.

In the 2006 election, the key problem was that the PT, which had long been considered honest, had been tarnished amid what was called the *mensalão* scandal. The PT's coalition had been far from a majority in Brazil's 2002–2006 legislature; to gain support, PT leaders paid opposition legislators to switch parties— as much as $400,000 each plus a monthly stipend of $12,500 (Rohter, 2005: A3). Then, just before the first round, a new scandal erupted: the PT had tried (but failed) to buy documents intended to implicate Serra (running in a different election) in corruption.

In the first round, Lula won 47% to 42% for the PSDB's Geraldo Alckmin, a former mayor, legislator, and governor of São Paulo. The third-place candidate with 7% was Heloísa Helena de Moraes, running for the Partido Socialismo e Liberdade (Party of Socialism and Liberty, PSOL). A fervent Catholic and socialist, she said that her "creed is based less on Marx and Lenin than on the Bible"; she scorned both Lula and Alckmin as "two sides of the same filthy coin" (Rohter, 2006: A3).

Despite the uncertainty of the runoff result amid the new scandal, Lula came back to win an impressive 61%. Lula effectively claimed innocence in the new scandal and charged that Alckmin was a free-market extremist (LAWR, October 17, 2006, p. 8; Baiocchi and Checa, 2008: 121). Further, Lula assiduously sought support from PMDB and even PFL leaders (LAWR, October 17, 2006, pp. 8–9).

In the 2010 election, the PT's candidate was Dilma Rousseff—Lula's protégé, chief of staff, and handpicked successor, who had been imprisoned by Brazil's military government. Amid the continuing economic boom and additional redistributive measures, Lula's approval ratings were approximately 80%—among the highest in the world. But Rousseff had never previously run for office and was not charismatic (LAWR, July 8, 2010, p. 8). In the last few weeks of the campaign, she was hurt by controversy about previous statements favoring abortion rights, allegations of influence-peddling in her office, and charges of PT plans for regulation of the media (LAWR, September 30, 2010, pp. 8–9).

In the 2010 first round, the PT again tallied 47%; the PSDB's Serra, its 2002 candidate, had 33%. The third-place candidate was Marina Silva, running for the Partido Verde (Green Party) and winning 19%. Silva was a former environmental minister in the Lula government and an evangelical Protestant. Her life story was inspiring: she was one of eleven children of Amazonian rubber-tappers and had worked as a maid to finance her education. Although Green Party leaders favored Serra and Serra made strong overtures to Silva, ultimately Silva remained neutral (LAWR, October 21, 2010, p. 5). Aggressively criticizing Serra as a free-market militant, Rousseff won the runoff with 56%.

By 2014, Brazil's economic growth had slowed and Rousseff's charisma deficit was more apparent. Still, the PT was very popular among Brazil's poor; Rousseff tallied 42% in the first round and eked out a victory in the runoff with 51.6%. For months, it was expected that her primary challenger would be Silva, the standard-bearer for the Partido Socialista Brasiliero (Socialist Party of Brazil, PSB), succeeding Eduardo Campos after his death in a plane crash. As in 2010, Silva promised "new politics" and "change"; but her message was inconsistent and she was hard hit by PT advertising (LAWR, October 9, 2014, p. 1). Silva finished third with 21%. In contrast to 2010, Silva did endorse the first-round runner-up, the PSDB's Aécio Neves, and in the weeks before the runoff Neves topped Rousseff in the opinion polls (LAWR, October 16, 2014, pp. 6–7).

Amid the concerns about the integrity of previous PT governments, the prospect of a fourth consecutive PT government was a likely factor in dips in Brazil's

V-Dem scores in 2013 and 2014. By 2015, the corruption scandal at Brazil's state oil company, Petrobras, was taking a tremendous toll. In 2016, the toll was even greater and Rousseff was impeached, with a concomitant fall in Brazil's V-Dem score.

Chile

Since 1990, democracy in Chile has fared very well. The country's Freedom House scores were good during the 1990s, usually at 4, and in 2003 rose to the best possible, 2. The pattern for Chile's V-Dem scores was very similar. Also, averaging almost 90%, voter turnout was among the highest in Latin America. To a certain extent, Chile's excellent third-wave record was not surprising. Prior to Augusto Pinochet's savage military coup in 1973, democracy was also robust; its 1900–1977 Polity score was the third-best in Latin America (Pérez-Liñán and Mainwaring, 2013: 381). Chile's 2009 per capita income was about 30% greater than the regional average (World Bank, 2011: 10–12).

Runoff was adopted in Chile's 1980 constitution and political analysts and leaders, including former president Ricardo Lagos, were enthusiastic.[10] In my surveys, 92% of Chile's legislators favored runoff, the largest percentage among the various countries (see Appendix 1). One Chilean political scientist said, "Nobody in Chile thinks that a runoff is a waste of time and money, even though it's during our summer."[11] Not surprisingly, amid the "Allende effect" described in Chapter 3, the predominant reason for the enthusiasm was the president's legitimacy advantage (Ruiz Rodríguez, 2004: 160).[12] Indeed, the results of all three of Chile's runoffs between 1989 and 2012 were uncertain.

The effects of runoff on ideological moderation and political parties were more complex than in other countries. Between 1990 and 2012, the number of parties remained large—averaging about 5.0—and the ideological positions of the five major parties were constant in PELA surveys. But two coalitions emerged for presidential elections and, within both coalitions, the leading party was displaced and the ideological position of the coalition shifted. As runoff advocates would expect, in the rightist coalition, a party at the extreme right was displaced by a party at the moderate right. But, contrary to runoff advocates' expectations, in the leftist coalition, a moderate-left party was displaced by a party classified at the "extreme left" in PELA surveys.

The shift in a leftist direction in both coalitions reflected Chileans' increasing frustration with what was called an "unfinished transition" from the Pinochet regime (Siavelis, 2008: 178). The perception that a defiant, impetuous left during the Allende government had led to a brutal dictatorship, as well as the exclusive provisions of the 1980 constitution elaborated under the Pinochet regime, weighed heavily on Chile's transition. Gradually, however, in part as a result of close runoffs in 2000 and 2006, Chile's "extreme-left" and what I call the "further-left" were included on the main stage of the political arena.

The exclusive provisions of Chile's 1980 constitution were called "authoritarian enclaves." In particular, the constitution mandated that nine senators be designated (including four representing the four branches of the armed forces, three chosen by the Supreme Court, and two by the executive); these nine senators constituted roughly one-fifth of the Senate. For many years, this bloc of designated senators impeded initiatives by elected legislative majorities. Also, the approval of constitutional reforms required supermajorities, again impeding initiatives by elected legislative majorities. These provisions were terminated in 2005.

Another "authoritarian enclave"—the rule for the election of the legislature called the binomial rule—continued until 2014. Unique worldwide, this rule contradicted democratic principles in various respects and its termination was demanded by most of Chile's left. The binomial rule provided that, in each district, two candidates were elected to both the Chamber of Deputies and the Senate. A list with two candidates was presented by each party or coalition. If the winning list of candidates had more than double the number of votes of the second-place list (usually, approximately two-thirds of the vote), both candidates were elected. But usually the winning list did not double the number of votes of the second-place list; in this case, only one of its candidates was elected and the top candidate from the second-place list was elected. One effect of the binomial rule was to considerably increase the number of seats of the second-most powerful political force—in Chile's case, the right. A second effect was to exclude small parties—which in Chile's case was the Communist Party in particular—and accordingly to promote coalitions.

An additional effect of the binomial rule was that many electoral outcomes at the district level were predictable. Most legislators were, in effect, selected not by voters but by the coalition leaders who named their candidates for each district. Gradually, the parties' leaders and grassroots were estranged (Luna and Altman 2011; Valenzuela and Dammert, 2006: 77). Although voter turnout as a percentage of registered voters was high, registration was not mandatory and more and more Chileans did not register.

Other rules were important as well. Most of Chile's legislative elections were concurrent with presidential elections. Whether or not the legislative elections were concurrent reflected the length of the presidential term, which changed several times. [13] In the 1980 constitution, the presidential term was eight years (except for the first term, which was four); but in 1994 the term was shortened to six years and in 2005 to four years. The binomial rule voided any need for a threshold for representation in the legislature.

The Formation and Trajectory of Chile's Two Political Coalitions

The emergence of two coalitions was a major change for Chile. As noted previously, during the 1960s and 1970s there were three major political blocs in Chile—one at the left, a second at the center, and a third at the right. The bloc at the left included the Partido Socialista (Socialist Party, PS) and the Partido Comunista de Chile (Communist Party of Chile, PC); Allende was a leader of the Socialist Party, elected to the presidency as the candidate of the leftist bloc. At the center during the 1960s and 1970s was the relatively new Partido Demócrata Cristiano (Christian Democratic Party, PDC). At the right was the Partido Nacional (National Party).

The rightist coalition, which had different names, was composed of two parties: the Unión Demócrata Independiente (Democratic Independent Union, UDI) and Renovación Nacional (National Renovation, RN). In PELA surveys, the UDI was at the extreme right (roughly 9.5) and Renovación Nacional at the right (roughly 7.75). The two parties were often at odds. The UDI was much closer to the Pinochet government and, in Chile's first three elections, it was the stronger party. The UDI was more ideological, with strong conservative Catholic principles, but it also built robust clientelist networks at Chile's grassroots. By contrast, the RN was founded on the base of Chile's historical right—the Partido Nacional (National Party), from which RN took part of its name. The rightist coalition's only victory during this period came in 2010 with a candidate from RN.

Until 2013, the leftist coalition was the Concertación de Partidos por la Democracia (Coalition of Parties for Democracy, called the Concertación). It was founded on the basis of cooperation among the parties for the plebiscite on Pinochet's continuation in power in 1988. It was composed primarily by three parties. From left to right, these parties were the Socialist Party; the Partido por la Democracia (Party for Democracy, PPD, formed to overcome registration problems for Marxist parties in the 1988 plebiscite); and the Christian Democratic Party. Consistently in PELA surveys between 1993 and 2010, the Socialist Party was placed at the extreme left (about 2.5), the PPD at the left (about 4.0), and the Christian Democratic Party at the center-left (about 4.75).

At first, the Concertación was careful to nominate candidates from the Christian Democratic Party. But, acknowledging the role of the left in the coalition, in 1999–2000 it nominated a candidate from the PPD and in 2005–2006, from the Socialist Party.

Also, for many years the Concertación did not include the Communist Party (which was not classified in PELA surveys and which I call the "further left"). In the 1980s, the Communist Party rejected the 1980 constitution as the framework for the democratic transition and had been slow to renounce violence (Scully, 1995: 132). But, in the first rounds of most elections as of 1999–2000, the Communist Party (usually allied with other further-left parties) averaged roughly 5%. The elections were close and, to win runoffs, the Concertación needed further-left votes. The Concertación candidates did delicate dances to maintain Christian Democratic support but attract the further-left (LAWR, November 30, 1999, p. 557; LARR, December 2005, p. 2). Ultimately, in the 2013 election, Chile's leftist coalition, renamed Nueva Mayoría (New Majority), included the Communist Party.

The 1989 and 1993 Elections: First-Round Victories for the Concertación

In the 1989 and 1993 elections, the impact of runoff was limited. Both elections were won in the first round by a Christian Democratic candidate within the Concertación: in 1989, Patricio Aylwin with 55% and, in 1993, Eduardo Frei Ruiz-Tagle with 58%.

In 1989, Aylwin was the long-standing frontrunner; he had been at the helm of the opposition's plebiscite campaign. Aylwin had opposed Pinochet but also, to the disgruntlement of some Socialist leaders, Allende. The rightist coalition tallied only 29%. Its candidate, the UDI's Hernán Büchi, had been the Pinochet government's 1985–1989 finance minister and failed to distance himself effectively from the Pinochet government. Amid Büchi's scant prospects, the outsider and supermarket tycoon, Francisco Javier Errázuriz, entered the race. Calling his party the Unión de Centro-Centro (Union of the Center-Center), Errázuriz was in the mold of rightist populists; he finished third with 15%.

The 1993 election was won in a landslide by Frei, a successful businessman and 1990–1994 senator. Frei benefited from the popularity of the Aylwin government and from the prestige of his name; he was the son of Chile's 1964–1970 president. Frei's landslide was remarkable because the rightist coalition's candidate, Arturo Alessandri Besa, had appeared stronger than Büchi. Although Alessandri Besa was also from the UDI, he had not served in the Pinochet government and, like Frei, he enjoyed a prestigious name; he was the nephew of Chile's 1958–1964 president and grandson of another president.

The 1999–2000 Election: A Runoff Victory for the Concertación

The result of Chile's first runoff in the 1999–2000 race was uncertain (Drake and Winn, 2000; LAWR, December 14, 1999, p. 578). The first-round result was a photo-finish: Ricardo Lagos, a Socialist within the Concertación, had 47.96% and Joaquín Lavín, an UDI leader within the rightist coalition, 47.52%. Combined, further-left parties—the Communist Party, the Humanist Party, and a "green" candidate—tallied 4%. In the event, Lagos won with 51.3%. The Concertación's delicate dance to maintain the support of Christian Democrats but attract the further-left had begun.

The election was close in part because the rightist coalition was shifting away from its association with Pinochet and toward personalism and populism (Fontaine, 2000). Its candidate, Lavín, was the popular mayor of an upscale district of Santiago; although from the UDI and at the extreme right in PELA surveys, he was affable. He highlighted priorities such as job creation, day care subsidies, and student loans.

The election was close also because the Concertación's candidate was a Socialist. Lagos had been nominated as Chile's ambassador to the Soviet Union by Allende and he alienated some Christian Democrats. However, Lagos had also been a founder of the Party for Democracy and had impressive credentials. Further, more voters were chafing at Chile's authoritarian enclaves and, after two successive Christian Democratic candidates, it was the Socialist Party's turn.

Facing the challenge to attract the further-left vote but maintain Christian Democratic support, Lagos feared that reaching out to the further-left would reignite the traumas of Chile's past, so he prioritized the latter (Ruiz Rodríguez, 2004: 162).[14] He moved toward the center (Drake and Winn, 2000; Fontaine, 2000). He emphasized the positive achievements of the Christian Democratic governments and appointed a popular Christian Democrat as his new campaign manager. He did not pursue an endorsement from further-left parties and did not receive any. Still, he was not oblivious to the need to capture further-left voters, and the further-left parties were not oblivious to their clout.[15] Lagos wooed the further-left through house-to-house visits (Drake and Winn, 2000; Fontaine, 2000).

Lagos governed during the period after Pinochet's arrest in London, return to Chile, and subsequent criminal investigations and house arrest. It was revealed that Pinochet was guilty not only of the murder and torture of thousands of people but also of embezzlement, money laundering, and tax fraud. As Pinochet was increasingly repudiated, the Concertación was able to secure support for constitutional reforms, and most of Chile's "authoritarian enclaves" ended.

The 2005–2006 Election: A Concertación Victory amid Division on the Right

As in 1999–2000, the runoff in 2005–2006 helped to enhance the legitimacy of a president further to the left than previous Concertación presidents. Michelle Bachelet, a Socialist within the Concertación, won 46% in the first round; for the runoff, she was favored, but the result was yet uncertain (Siavelis, 2008: 190–191; Morales Quiroga, 2008; LAWR, January 3, 2006, p. 9). For the first time, one of the two coalitions divided; the UDI and the RN ran their own candidates. Whereas the UDI had been the dominant party in the coalition, the RN's Sebastián Piñera was the first-round runner-up. In the event, Bachelet won the runoff by seven points.

Bachelet had various advantages. The Lagos government had been successful; economic growth had been robust. Although the Concertación had been in power for more than fifteen years and Bachelet had been a minister in the Lagos government, she was a relative newcomer. For Chileans seeking reconciliation, her personal background was appealing: on the one hand, her father had been a military officer; on the other hand, he had died at the hands of the dictatorship and both she and her mother had been arrested and tortured. She was a pediatrician—a healer.

However, as a Socialist, Bachelet struggled to retain the Christian Democratic vote. The Christian Democrats' potential nominee, Soledad Alvear, had withdrawn from a primary upon opinion polls favoring Bachelet. A distance between the two leaders lingered. Also, Bachelet was an unwed mother and an agnostic.

On the right, the RN had been chafing at what it considered the UDI's presumptiveness that it was the senior partner in the coalition, and Piñera was ambitious. Lavín proposed a primary to decide the coalition's nomination, but Piñera declined. Originally a member of the Christian Democratic Party, a "no" voter in the 1988 plebiscite, and a relative moderate at 7.29 in PELA surveys in 2010, Piñera effectively pursued the Christian Democratic vote. A billionaire businessman with a Ph.D. in economics from Harvard University, he emphasized his personal competence. The UDI's nominee was Lavín, but he was not the fresh face that he had been in 1999–2000.

With 25% in the first round, Piñera had to gain not only the 23% that Lavín had tallied but also a few more Christian Democrat votes if he were to win the runoff. He did not. His criticisms of Pinochet attracted Christian Democrats but alienated the approximately 20% of Chilean voters who continued to support the former dictator (Reel, 2006: A20). The wealthy Piñera did not have the appeal among Chile's poor that Lavín did (Morales Quiroga, 2008; Siavelis, 2008).

By contrast, Bachelet retained her Christian Democratic vote and attracted most of the 5% tallied by the further-left coalition Juntos Podemos Más (Together We Can Do More). To retain the Christian Democrats, she emphasized the importance of democracy and featured PDC leaders much more prominently in her campaign (Gamboa and Segovia, 2006: 105–109; Boas, 2007: 44).

And, like Lagos, Bachelet did a delicate dance with the further-left. Bachelet did not negotiate with the further-left—an undertaking still widely considered the kiss of death—but she pointed out that she shared many of its key priorities. For example, she highlighted that she shared the Communist Party's goal of the end of the binomial rule (Paz, 2005). For its part, Juntos Podemos Más debated whether or not to endorse Bachelet. Its leaders perceived this decision as leverage (Paz, 2005). The Communist Party decided in favor of endorsement while another faction, the Humanist Party, decided against it.

The 2009–2010 Election—A Rightist Victory amid Division in the Concertación—and the 2013 Election

Once again, in 2009–2010, the election went to a runoff with an uncertain result (LAWR, December 17, 2009, pp. 1–3). Piñera won the first round with 44% and the runoff by three points.

This time, it was the Concertación that divided. After two consecutive Socialist Party nominees, it was arguably the turn of the Christian Democratic Party. The former Christian Democratic president, Frei, was eager to run. However, Frei was stolid and to the right within the Concertación; and, the PDC was losing support. In the first two elections, it had won more than 30% of lower-house seats; but in 2005, only 17%. Frei won two primaries by large margins, but with low turnouts (LAWR, April 8, 2009, p. 7). More primaries were planned for different regions of the country, but these were aborted and Frei was declared the Concertación nominee. To many Chileans, the Socialist Party was complicit in an insiders' political game that led to an old-timer candidate.

Several Socialist Party leaders bolted. Marco Enríquez-Ominami, a youthful, flamboyant Socialist member of the Chamber of Deputies and member of a well-known political family, entered the presidential race. Forming a coalition called La Nueva Mayoría para Chile (A New Majority for Chile), Enríquez-Ominami challenged the two-coalition system and called for political openness and participation. He adopted positions on various sides of the ideological spectrum; he favored gay marriage, legalized abortion, and environmental protection, but also the privatization of some state businesses. His appeal was strong among urban young people.

In the first round, Frei tallied 30% to Enríquez-Ominami's 20%. Together, these two candidates had more votes than Piñera; but, although Frei adopted a variety of Enríquez-Ominami's positions, Frei did not win Enríquez-Ominami's endorsement (LAWR, January 7, 2010, p. 10). For Piñera's part, he struggled to maintain the support of UDI voters, but ultimately he did (LAWR, January 14, 2010, p. 9).

It is possible that Enríquez-Ominami was the Condorcet winner of the election (LAWR October 22, 2009, p. 12; LARR, December 2009, p. 11). In some polls, he bested Piñera in a runoff (Ipsos, 2009). However, Enríquez-Ominami was inexperienced.

In the 2013 election, Bachelet gained a second term. She tallied 47% in the first round and won the runoff easily, with 62%. In the new coalition New Majority, the Communist Party was included. The rightist coalition's candidate was the runner-up.

Chile's two coalitions tried to respond to the increased demands for openness and participation. After the 2009–2010 election, party primaries became more effectively institutionalized. The vote was made voluntary rather than compulsory. Yet, the demands continued. In the 2013 election, not only the third-place candidate, Enríquez-Ominami, but also the fourth-place candidate, an independent, criticized the "duopoly" of the two coalitions and called for greater openness (LARR, December 2013, p. 2). Once again, after the election, the two coalitions sought to respond; in particular, the binomial rule was replaced by proportional representation. Still, the demands continued.

El Salvador

Since 1997, Freedom House has rated democracy in El Salvador at 5— approximately the regional average; El Salvador's score improved to 5 from a score of 6 during 1994–1996. El Salvador's V-Dem scores improved by about 20%—even more than its Freedom House scores—but its scores were lower at the start and its 2014–2016 V-Dem scores remained slightly below the regional average. Voter turnout improved most dramatically—from an average of 43% in 1994 and 1999 to an average of 66% in 2004 and 2009—but also remained slightly below the regional average.

El Salvador's historically low voter turnout is usually attributed to exclusive registration and balloting procedures (Spence, Lanchin, and Thale, 2001: 6–7). During the 1990s, registration required several trips. At the time of the first election after the civil war, roughly a third of the population was not registered, and this percentage was even higher among the country's poor (LAWR, November 18, 1993, p. 533). Voter rolls were egregiously inaccurate; "the dead were able to vote while many of the living could not."[16] Voters were assigned to balloting centers not by proximity to their residence but by their last name; they often had to travel long distances to cast their ballots. Gradually, the Salvadoran electoral commission became more professional and procedures more inclusive, but until the 2014 elections many voters were still assigned distant balloting centers.[17]

Overall, relative to El Salvador's historical experience, the country "has fared well in building a robust democracy" (Colburn, 2009: 152). The country's average Polity score for 1900–1977 was tied for the third-worst in the region (Pérez-Liñán and Mainwaring, 2013: 381). Although elections occurred, the left was repressed and outcomes were manipulated by military and civilian elites. The repression catalyzed a twelve-year civil war that took as many as 75,000 lives between 1980 and 1992. Although leftist militants have been murdered even in the 2000s, the number is a tiny fraction of the figure during the civil war (Meyer, 2009: 4). In addition, El Salvador's 2009 per capita income was only about 60% of the regional average (World Bank, 2011: 10–12).

Through the 2012 end year for the cross-national comparisons in this book, the impact of runoff in El Salvador was not as major as in most other countries. Of El Salvador's four elections through 2012, only one went to a runoff and its result was virtually certain. Also, as Chapter 3 indicated, polarization endured; two political parties were dominant and both were at extremes in PELA surveys. El Salvador's electoral arena did not open to new parties. El Salvador was one of only two runoff countries that did not experience a change in the two leading parties between the first third-wave election and 2012.

Yet runoff mattered. Said one Salvadoran analyst, "The 50% plus one vote [rule] was key to the evolution of the parties."[18] Although the parties themselves were not perceived to have moderated, to a considerable degree they recruited presidential candidates who hailed not from their original militaristic inner circles and could appeal to centrists. The extreme-right party won the 1999 and 2004 elections in part for this reason; when in 2009 the FMLN nominated a presidential candidate who had not participated in the civil war, it won.

Further, runoff was very important in the 2014 election. This election went to a runoff with an uncertain result and it was vital for the legitimacy of the elected FMLN president, Salvador Sánchez Cerén, a former guerrilla commander. And, there were indications of ideological moderation.

El Salvador's Political Parties: Continuity and Change

El Salvador's two major parties emerged as armed opponents in the civil war. During the war, both parties were complicit in numerous, serious violations of human rights. The two parties were the Alianza Repúblicana Nacionalista (Nationalist Republican Alliance, ARENA), founded in 1981 by death-squad leaders, in particular Major Roberto D'Aubuisson, and the Frente Farabundo Martí de Liberación Nacional (Farabundo Martí National Liberation Front, FMLN), founded in 1980 by socialist revolutionaries. D'Aubuisson is widely believed to have masterminded the assassination of Archbishop Oscar Romero, the most notorious assassination of the war. ARENA's anthem promised that "El Salvador will be the tomb where the Reds meet their end." The FMLN also endorsed violence.

Despite runoff, between 1994 and 2009 the two parties remained at opposite ends of the ideological spectrum in PELA surveys. ARENA remained at the extreme right, with scores averaging about 9.5, and the FMLN at the extreme left, with scores averaging about 1.5.

In other words, despite vast ideological space for a more centrist party, the battle lines drawn during the civil war endured. Perhaps most surprisingly, the country's centrist party, the Partido Demócrata Cristiano (Christian Democratic Party, PDC), which had governed between 1984 and 1989, withered amid intra-party disputes that were adeptly exploited by ARENA. ARENA also sidelined a more ideologically similar party, the Partido de Conciliación Nacional (Party of National Conciliation, PCN); close to the military and strong in the countryside, the PCN had governed during the 1960s and 1970s.

It is also surprising that a new centrist party did not emerge because presidential and legislative elections were non-concurrent. The presidential term was five years but the National Assembly term three years; when both elections were due in the same year, they were held in different months. Although the two major parties dominated presidential elections, other parties, including the PDC and the PCN, won a considerable percentage of National Assembly seats, and the number of parties averaged about 3.25. But ARENA usually negotiated alliances with the PDC and the PCN and neither these parties nor a new party achieved significant clout (Spence, Lanchin, and Thale, 2001:10).

ARENA was quick to realize the strategic implications of runoff. In elections held amid the civil war in 1984, ARENA's idol, D'Aubuisson, lost in the runoff to the Christian Democrats' Napoleon Duarte. D'Aubuisson realized that, if ARENA were to win a majority and achieve international acceptance, the party's image would have to change.[19] D'Aubuisson groomed Alfredo Cristiani, a civilian and successful businessman with a degree from Georgetown University, as ARENA's 1989 presidential candidate. Cristiani won the 1989 election and, as the president who signed the 1992 peace accord with the FMLN, gained prestige. ARENA came to be led not by D'Aubuisson (who died of cancer in 1992) but by a fifteen-member executive committee. Overall, the party bridged the differences among its various sectors—an anti-Communist-at-any-cost "old guard," the landowners complicit in violence, and a "country club elite" partial to commercial interests (Spence, Dye, and Vickers, 1994: 22).

By contrast, the FMLN was slow to adapt. For many years, a considerable number of FMLN leaders believed that the party's presidential candidates should be former guerrilla commanders. Unlike ARENA, at its founding the FMLN was a coalition of small parties; each party had its own leaders, practices, and perspectives and these differences continued. Many FMLN leaders were overly optimistic that a socialist-left project could achieve majority support; they attributed rightist victories to El Salvador's low turnout.[20] Some FMLN fighters remained loyal to their commanders.

In part for these reasons, ARENA was the more successful party in El Salvador's first three elections. Further, ARENA embraced tough-on-crime positions that appealed both to rural elites as well as to the urban poor (Holland, 2013). With close ties to business sectors, ARENA enjoyed financial resources vastly superior to other parties (Wood, 2000: 249). Favored by most Salvadoran media, ARENA consistently launched effective negative campaigns against the FMLN. ARENA regularly charged that the FMLN was unqualified to govern and that it was the party of Communism or, in later elections, Venezuela's Hugo Chávez.

The Path-Setting 1994 Election

The first election after the civil war set the pattern for the next two elections. Although ARENA's candidate tallied 49% in 1994's first round and the election went to a runoff, its result was virtually certain (LARR, May 19, 1994, p. 1); ARENA triumphed by more than a two-to-one margin. A coalition led by the FMLN was in second place; the PDC was in third.

ARENA's candidate, Armando Calderón Sol, benefited from Cristiani's prestige. Calderón Sol had been a legislator and mayor of San Salvador—but he had also served as D'Aubuisson's personal secretary.

Rubén Zamora was the candidate for a coalition of leftist parties led by the FMLN; Zamora tallied 26%. In the context of the FMLN's electoral inexperience as well as sporadic death-squad attacks and exclusive registration and balloting procedures, FMLN leaders were pleased that the party emerged as El Salvador's second-largest political force (Vickers and Spence, 1994: 10). In many respects, Zamora was an excellent candidate. He had been a leader of a group of civilians who had provided diplomatic support for the FMLN during the war; subsequently, he helped found the moderate-left Convergencia Democrática (Democratic Convergence, CD) and had been its 1989 presidential candidate. At that time, Zamora was bravely testing the openness of El Salvador's electoral arena.

However, Zamora's selection was contentious. One of the largest of the five FMLN parties, known during the war as the Ejército Revolucionario del Pueblo (Revolutionary Army of the People, ERP), argued that the FMLN should ally with the Christian Democrats and select a Christian Democratic candidate (Vickers and Spence, 1994: 10). Almost immediately after the election, the legislative leaders of the ERP and a second party, the Resistencia Nacional (National Resistance, RN), decided to vote for ARENA's candidate for the presidency of the Assembly and were rewarded with prime positions. Dismayed, the FMLN suspended these ERP and RN leaders; one was Joaquín Villalobos, the FMLN's best-known and probably most charismatic leader, albeit controversial. These leaders never returned to the FMLN; rather, they formed the Partido Democrático (Democratic Party, PD).

It was in part because both ARENA and the FMLN were vying for support from the PDC that it was divided and finished third with only 16%. A Christian Democrat in his youth, Calderón Sol worked to attract Christian Democratic leaders to ARENA (LARR, April 7, 1994, p. 1). In a bitter PDC primary, Fidel Chávez Mena, who was close to ARENA, narrowly defeated Abraham Rodríguez, who was close to the left (Spence, Dye, and Vickers, 1994: 22–23). Although the PDC did not endorse ARENA in the runoff, the PDC was moving toward ARENA.[21]

The Calderón Sol government did not fare well. Economic growth was paltry. In 1997, legislative and municipal elections were held and the FMLN made major gains, winning more than 35% of the municipalities. The new mayor of San Salvador was Héctor Silva, a former Christian Democrat who ran for a leftist coalition led by the FMLN.

The 1999 and 2004 Elections: First-Round Victories for ARENA

ARENA won the 1999 election with 52% in the first round and the 2004 election with 58% in the first round. The FMLN was second in 1999 with 29% and in 2004 with 36%. The PDC and the PCN were disappearing.

After its 1997 losses, ARENA was intent on the nomination of a presidential candidate who could attract centrist voters (Holland, 2013). The party's 1999 candidate was Francisco Flores, whose entry into politics was triggered only by the assassination of his father-in-law, the chief-of-staff for Cristiani. Flores served in the Cristiani government and was then elected to the National Assembly. With degrees from U.S. universities in political science and philosophy, Flores was considered intellectual; and, he was darker-skinned—not a traditional member of El Salvador's elite (LARR, February 24, 1998, p. 3).

ARENA's 2004 candidate was Elías Antonio ("Tony") Saca. Like Flores, Saca had played no role in the war. Saca was an outsider: a radio broadcasting entrepreneur who had headed El Salvador's business association. From a Palestinian immigrant family, he had gone to work at a radio station at age fourteen.

By contrast, both FMLN candidates were former guerrilla commanders. For the 1999 nomination, Silva was in a strong position, but was blocked by hardliners led by Schafik Handal, a former guerrilla commander leading El Salvador's Communist Party. Ultimately, after three raucous conventions, a compromise candidate was chosen: Facundo Guardado. A former guerrilla commander of peasant origin and a party insider, Guardado had little appeal beyond El Salvador's left (Holland, 2013: 58). Many FMLN leaders who had supported Silva were bitter and withdrew (Spence, 2004: 73).

The FMLN's 2004 nominee was Handal, who defeated a young, moderate FMLN mayor at an FMLN convention. Openly admiring Castro and Chávez, Handal was placed at 1.35 in a 2003 PELA survey—an extreme point in the extreme left classification; and, he was aging and gruff (Colburn, 2009: 147).

In both elections, the moderate left tried to gain a foothold but failed. In 1999, the Democratic Convergence partnered with the Democratic Party (established by FMLN dissidents after the 1994 election) to form the Centro Democrático Unido (United Democratic Center, CDU), with Zamora as its candidate. It finished third but with only 8%. In 2004, Silva was the candidate for a coalition of the CDU and the Christian Democrats but tallied less than 4%.

The 2009 Election: A First-Round Victory for the FMLN

After two successive losses, the FMLN in 2009 acknowledged that it could not win its first victory if its candidate were a hardliner.[22] As LAWR (March 19, 2009, p. 1) noted, "The FMLN finally accepted that guerrillas irrevocably linked to the past ... would never bring the party the victory it craved." The FMLN wanted "to rebrand itself" (Booth, Wade, and Walker, 2015: 157). It did so, and eked out a first-round win with 51% to 49% for ARENA.

The FMLN's nominee was Mauricio Funes, an outsider. He was a renowned television journalist who had investigated and denounced corruption in the ARENA governments; he became a member of the FMLN only a year before the election (Beeson, 2009). His views were social-democratic; he said he would respect private property, adhere to all free trade agreements, and seek a constructive relationship with the United States. He cited as his political models Barack Obama and Lula—not Chávez. He wore a white Guayabera shirt rather than the red shirts that the FMLN commanders had favored (LAWR, March 19, 2009, p. 1). Funes was placed at 3.11 in the 2009 PELA survey— the "extreme left," but much less so than the FMLN at 1.41. Funes was endorsed by both the PDC and the PCN, whose candidates withdrew (LAWR, February 12, 2009, p. 13). Funes gained the support of FMLN hardliners only through intense negotiations. Handal had died and the hardline faction was weakened, but it achieved the nomination of a vice-presidential candidate, Sánchez Cerén, from its ranks.

By contrast, ARENA's candidate, Rodrigo Ávila, was more of an ARENA insider than Flores or Saca. Although Ávila had not been active in the war, he had served as Director of National Civilian Police and his brother had helped found ARENA. ARENA's smear campaign against Funes was intense, featuring scenes of street chaos and charges that Funes would be a puppet of FMLN hardliners.

In 2009, the FMLN had advantages in addition to its candidate. The U.S. economic crisis had hit El Salvador hard. ARENA had governed for twenty years, and Salvadorans were eager for a change. More Salvadorans identified themselves as leftists (Azpuru, 2010:124).

The 2014 Election: A Runoff Victory for a Former FMLN Commander

In the 2014 election, the value of runoff was more evident. Even though the FMLN candidate, Sánchez Cerén, tallied 49% in the first round, his victory was uncertain; he won the runoff by a mere 6,364 votes with 50.1%. The runner-up with 39% was ARENA's Norman Quijano, a former San Salvador mayor. However, in third place with 11% was "Tony" Saca, ARENA's 2004–2009 president. Although Saca had been expelled from ARENA, it was expected that two-thirds of his vote would go to Quijano and that turnout would increase in the runoff (LARR, February 2014, p. 4). Given that ARENA refused to accept the FMLN's runoff victory for more than two weeks and called for the military to "make democracy," the legitimacy advantage of the runoff was vital (LARR, April 2014, p. 3).

In addition, moderation was evident. As of 2014, the two parties were no longer classified at the limits of the extreme right and the extreme left in PELA surveys; ARENA was at 8.14 and the FMLN at 1.96.[23] Commented Forrest Colburn and Arturo Cruz (2014: 151), "It was hard to find any traces of the FMLN's revolutionary ardor in the 2014 campaign." At 69, Sánchez Cerén resembled a grandfather, not a guerrilla commander. He even briefly considered an alliance with Saca (LARR, February 2014, p. 4).

Conclusion

In these five countries, runoff was advantageous for democracy. It provided major legitimacy advantages and helped to incorporate the left.

Uruguay was an exceptional model of success. In 1999, a reversal prevented a minority victory for the Broad Front when it was still classified at the extreme left and an "Allende-like scenario" was feared. For the next election, the Broad Front's candidate, Vázquez, moved to the moderate left and won in the first round. Overall, the Broad Front appeared to moderate ideologically without abandoning ethical principles.

In the Dominican Republic, plurality was extremely problematic, enabling victories in the 1986 and 1990 elections without majority support by the rightist caudillo Balaguer, who proceeded to blatantly rig the 1994 election. Between the adoption of runoff in 1995 and 2012, the Dominican Republic's level of democracy improved considerably. Runoff was particularly valuable in the 1996 election, incentivizing the moderation of the winning candidate, the PLD's Fernández, and, in the context of a reversal, providing legitimacy for the new president. However, Fernández's ideological shift was opportunistic. Despite runoff, the PLD became a cartel party and, after 2012, its level of democracy eroded.

The importance of runoff for the incorporation of the left was very evident in Brazil. Both Lula's ascent in the 1989 election and his trajectory from "gruff, incendiary leftist" to "little Lula, peace and love" were pivotal for the dramatic improvement in Brazil's level of democracy. However, as the Workers' Party moderated, it too relinquished ethical principles. In part as a result, two dissident Workers' Party leaders, Heloísa Helena de Moraes and Marina Silva, formed new parties emphasizing integrity and sent signals about the importance of ethical governance. Arguably, however, the signals should have been even louder.

In Chile, political leaders remained haunted by the traumas of the Allende government and Pinochet's coup and were emphatic about the legitimacy advantage of runoff. Indeed, the 1999–2000 and 2005–2006 runoffs provided important legitimacy advantages for the two Socialist presidents, Lagos and Bachelet. Further, runoff facilitated the decision of moderate-rightist Piñera to separate from the extreme right in 2005–2006—and ultimately win in 2009–2010. However, due to Chile's history, the challenge for its left was not moderation but the incorporation of parties to the Christian Democrats' left, and this gradually happened. Still, as Socialist Enríquez-Ominami's exit from the Concertación and independent runs in the 2009 and 2013 elections showed, demands for greater political participation continued.

Until 2014, the advantages of runoff were less evident in El Salvador. Between the first election after the civil war in 1994 and 2012, no election went to a runoff with an uncertain result. Also, as in Nicaragua, the polarizing effect of the civil war endured for decades; two parties at opposite ends of the ideological spectrum were dominant. Still, runoff was important to the recruitment by both parties of candidates who appealed to independent voters: ARENA's Flores in 1999, ARENA's Saca in 2004, and the FMLN's Funes in 2009. And, in the 2014 election, the advantages of runoff for legitimacy and the incorporation of the left were evident.

In these five countries, plurality advocates' concerns about a larger number of parties under runoff were not realized. Either the number of political parties did not increase, as in the Dominican Republic, El Salvador, and Uruguay, or two coalitions emerged for presidential elections, as in Brazil and Chile. Indeed, in the 2010s in the Dominican Republic, Brazil, and Chile in particular, the concerns were that the "new parties" of the late 1990s and early 2000s had become "old parties," impeding the rise of newcomers calling for transparency, integrity, and participation.

6

Runoff Amid a Plethora of Political Parties

Colombia, Ecuador, Guatemala, and Peru

In Colombia, Ecuador, Guatemala, and Peru, levels of democracy were rarely at regional nadirs but also rarely above regional averages. Levels fluctuated to a greater degree than in most plurality countries or the runoff countries in Chapter 5. Trends were most positive in Colombia and Guatemala, especially for V-Dem scores, although they did not reach regional averages. Levels were most uneven in Peru; scores surpassed regional averages in the 1980s, plummeted to regional nadirs in the late 1990s, and surpassed regional averages again after 2000. The trend was most negative in Ecuador; its scores were above regional averages in the 1980s but fell subsequently and, by the 2010s, were considerably below regional averages. Patterns for voter turnout were also mixed.

Why was the overall record of these four countries not more positive? Is it because the number of parties was large, averaging about 4.7 between 1990 (or the first third-wave election under runoff) and 2014? Were plurality advocates' concerns about runoff borne out in these four countries?

I argue that, for Colombia and Guatemala, the answer is no. The considerable number of parties in the two countries was not a major factor in inferior levels of democracy. In neither country was executive-legislative gridlock a severe problem. In neither country did an outsider secure as much as 10% in any election. In neither country was there a distinct possibility that an elected president was not the Condorcet winner. In Colombia, reversals in the 1998 and 2014 elections are likely to have been helpful for democracy. In Guatemala, the only reversal was in the 1990–1991 election won by Jorge Serrano; the negative effects were brief.

Rather, the major factor in the inferior levels of democracy in Colombia and Guatemala was political violence. During the Cold War, both countries were wracked by intense political violence, largely due to elites' political exclusion of leftist groups and the radicalization of these groups. I show that, in the 2000s in both countries, runoff facilitated the opening of the political arena to leftist groups and, in part as a result, political violence attenuated and, in Guatemala (although not Colombia), voter turnout improved.

For Peru, the answer is less clear. Parties were personalistic and volatile. Still, Peru's positive record since 2000 suggests that the large number per se has not been seriously problematic. The percentage of legislative seats held by the president's party in the 2001, 2006, and 2011 elections was low—between 30% and 40% in all three elections—but, as mentioned in Chapter 1, amid the overall weakness of political parties, executive-legislative conflict was not severe. (However, in the 2016 election, the percentage of seats was even lower, and executive-legislative conflict was severe.) Although in 1990 Alberto Fujimori won as an outsider, in 2006 Ollanta Humala, another outsider, won the first round but was defeated in the runoff. There was only a remote chance in one election that the elected president was not the Condorcet winner.

For Ecuador, the answer is yes. In six of nine elections, the president's party had less than 30% of the legislative seats; the average percentage of legislative seats held by the president's party was by far the lowest in Latin America (see Appendix 3). Three successive presidents, all of whose parties had less than 30% of the seats, were ousted. Two of three presidents who won in reversals proved deleterious to democracy. An outsider, Lucio Gutiérrez, won in 2002 and was removed by the legislature in 2005. There was a strong possibility in two elections that the president was not the Condorcet winner.

Although runoff is likely to have facilitated the continuation of a large number of parties in Peru and Ecuador, it also helped both countries cope with a problem that, as Chapter 3 noted, began before the adoption of runoff. Especially in the context of the low tallies of first-round winners, runoff provided major legitimacy advantages for presidents. Also, in Peru in particular, runoff attracted various presidential candidates to the political center (who subsequently stayed, more or less, at the center). Further, a smaller number of parties is not necessarily positive; as the number of parties declined in Ecuador after 2006 under Rafael Correa, levels of democracy fell.

This chapter analyzes the impact of runoff on the level of democracy first in the country in which it was most positive: Guatemala. It then turns to Colombia, in which the impact was also positive. Next, it analyzes the impact in Peru, in which the impact for the legitimacy and moderation of the president was very important, even as the weakness of parties was worrisome. Finally, it turns to Ecuador, where the large number of parties was problematic and runoff was not always sufficient for the country to cope.

Given the importance of the reversals and subsequent *autogolpes* by Serrano and Fujimori to plurality advocates' arguments, I analyze these two elections and their aftermaths in depth. Although these presidents' weak political bases were problematic, I argue that the primary reasons for executive-legislative conflict were the presidents' authoritarianism, corruption, and sharp deviation from their campaign positions, which led to the loss of their runoff allies.

Guatemala

The number of political parties was considerable in Guatemala, averaging 3.85 between 1990 and 2014, but its democratic trajectory was positive. At the time of the first third-wave election in 1985, Guatemala's Freedom House score was 8; in the aftermath of Serrano's *autogolpe* in 1993, it fell to 9; it recovered to 7 for 1996 and subsequently fluctuated between 7 and 8 (most often 7 but 8 in 2015 and 2016). However, Guatemala's V-Dem scores trended gradually but steadily up, rising from .218 in 1990–1992 to .481 in 2016. The trend for voter turnout was also very positive: whereas between 1990–1991 and 2003, turnout averaged only 48%, it reached 65% in 2011 and 64% in 2015. Raved Mitchell A. Seligson (2005: 205), "The transformation of Guatemala from an authoritarian, war-wracked society into an electoral democracy has been nothing short of miraculous." Seconded Edelberto Torres-Rivas (2012: 117), "Elections in Guatemala have become increasingly competitive, free, and inclusive."

Further, Guatemala's economic conditions and political history were not propitious. Guatemala's 2009 per capita income was less than half the Latin American average (World Bank, 2011: 10–12). Guatemala's average Polity score for 1900–1977 was thirteenth out of eighteen countries (Pèrez-Liñán and Mainwaring, 2013: 381).

Indeed, after a military coup in 1954, Guatemala's governments were exceptionally brutal. In the aftermath of the coup, Marxist guerrilla groups emerged; in 1982, they established the Unidad Revolucionaria Nacional Guatemalteca (Guatemalan National Revolutionary Union, URNG). Although the URNG was weakly organized and popular support was limited (Torres-Rivas, 2013: 462–469), a United Nations Truth Commission estimated that more than 200,000 people were killed and attributed 93% of the deaths to Guatemala's security forces (Booth, Wade, and Walker, 2015: 186). In particular, during the government of General Eraín Ríos Montt (1982–1983), entire Mayan villages were destroyed amid a scorched-earth campaign.

Severe political violence continued in Guatemala at the start of the third wave. Voter turnout was low in part because, after the 1985 election, the vote became voluntary, but also because fear persisted (Pallister, 2013: 130–131; Isaacs, 2010: 116). Turnout increased in the mid-2000s as the legacy of repression faded and also as the number of polling places in rural areas increased and procedures for registration in rural areas improved (Azpuru and Blanco, 2008: 223; Isaacs, 2010: 114).

Runoff was advantageous. It was favored by former president Vinicio Cerezo.[1] All of Guatemala's seven presidential elections through 2012 went to a runoff; in four of the seven, the result was uncertain and the runoff was likely to have enhanced the president's legitimacy. The one scholar assessing runoff in Guatemala, Álvaro Artiga-González (2004: 329), was favorable, emphasizing that it reinforced presidents' legitimacy. In two of the four elections going to a second round, runoff was especially helpful because the winners were candidates usually classified at the center-left in a country that had historically excluded the left. As Seligson (2005: 207) noted, it was very important that "the political arena has clearly been widened to include the left." In 1999, Álvaro Colom competed as the candidate of a coalition that included the URNG; then, forming a new center-left party and moderating, he was the runner-up in 2003 and, finally, the winner in 2007.

Although the considerable number of parties was a concern (Artiga-González, 2004: 329), to date most of the problems associated with a larger number of parties have not arisen. Sustained executive-legislative conflict was not evident; even Serrano maintained a governing coalition for most of the time that he was in office. As mentioned above, there is no indication that any president was not the Condorcet winner. No outsider tallied more than 10% of the vote in any election. Rather, voters got to know candidates. The 1990–1991 winner, Serrano, had finished third in 1985; the 1995 winner, Álvaro Arzú, had finished fourth in 1990–1991; and, remarkably, Alfonso Portillo in 1990, Oscar Berger in 2003, Colom in 2007, and Otto Pérez Molina in 2011 had all been runners-up in the previous election.

Several important rules were constant. Legal barriers to entry were low; parties were not required to win a certain percentage of the vote to be represented in the legislature. They were required to win 5%, up from 4% in 2004, to maintain their registration for the next election, but the signature requirement was modest (Pallister, 2013: 124). Any re-election of a president was prohibited. Throughout, legislative elections were concurrent, for a single chamber.

However, there were some modifications. In 1993, the length of the presidential term was cut from 5 years to 4 years. In 1999, the electoral calendar was shifted so that both the first round and the runoff would be held before the end of the year.

Ideological Cleavages and Guatemala's Political Parties

At first, the considerable number of parties in Guatemala reflected ideological cleavages that were hardened amid the decades of bloody internal war. In the twenty-first century, however, these cleavages gradually attenuated, and personalism became a key factor.

During the 1980s and 1990s, the right was divided by the former dictator, General Ríos Montt. In PELA surveys, Ríos Montt's party was consistently classified at the right or extreme right. However, Ríos Montt was often dubbed a populist; his party denounced the "oligarchy" and the "privileged elite" (LARR, November 1, 1990, p. 2). Despite his government's scorched-earth campaign, Ríos Montt was not without popular support; he was perceived to have provided roads, schools, cheap credit, low-cost fertilizer, land titles, and, in general, to stand with the poor (LAWR, August 19, 2003, p. 13).

At the same time, Ríos Montt's populism, as well as his Protestant evangelicalism and acrimonious relationship with the United States—not to mention his government's brutality—alienated other Guatemalans and large sectors of Guatemala's business and military elites (Trudeau, 1993: 63). His 1982 coup had ousted other military leaders and, after less than two years as president, he in turn was overthrown by the "military establishment" (Trudeau, 1993: 151). These sectors were represented first through the party Unión del Centro Nacional (National Union of the Center, UCN), then the Partido de Avanzada Nacional (Party of National Advancement, PAN), and next the Gran Alianza Nacional (Grand National Alliance, GANA).

Guatemala's left was also divided. The URNG had been brutally repressed and its anger, fear, and sectarianism endured for decades.[2] It was classified at the extreme left (2.87) in a 1998 PELA survey (the first for which data were available). It was not until 1999 that the URNG competed in the electoral arena; although it continued to compete, it never fared well. The leading party at the time of Guatemala's first third-wave election was the Democracia Cristiana Guatemalteca (Guatemalan Christian Democrats, DCG). The DCG was most frequently classified as "moderate left" (Trudeau, 1993: 67); influenced by liberation theology, the party had been active at Guatemala's grassroots in the 1960s and 1970s and had suffered repression by death squads (McDonald and Ruhl, 1989: 280–281).

The 1985 Election: Legitimacy for a Christian Democratic Government after a Runoff

In the four years prior to the 1985 election, there had been two military coups: the coup by Ríos Montt and then by "the military establishment." Violent conflict between the military and the URNG continued.

In this context, the legitimacy provided by the runoff for the Christian Democratic winner, Vinicio Cerezo, was very advantageous. Cerezo's lot was described by LAWR (November 8, 1985, p. 10): "An objective analysis would place Cerezo on the center-right. He has rejected the idea of agrarian reform and has pragmatically acknowledged the influence of the armed forces . . . . Nevertheless, the right have labeled him a 'communist.' . . ."

In the first round, Cerezo tallied 39%, almost double the share of the runner-up, the UCN's Jorge Carpio, a wealthy newspaper publisher. However, the other three candidates with more than 5% were to Cerezo's right and the result of the runoff was uncertain (LAWR, November 8, 1985, p. 10; LAWR, December 6, 1985, p. 2). The third-place candidate was Serrano, who led his own Movimiento de Acción Solidaria (Solidarity Action Movement, MAS) but was close to Ríos Montt. The fourth-place candidate was Mario Sandoval, who had supported the 1954 military coup and was also complicit in death squads (LAWR, December 6, 1985, p. 2). Still, hopes for peace and democracy were high and Cerezo won the runoff with 68%.

Despite the high hopes, neither Guatemala's military nor the URNG was responsive to the Cerezo government's calls for dialogue (Booth, Wade, and Walker, 2015: 182–183). The military was not subordinate to civilian authority. In addition, the Cerezo government was facing the Latin American debt crisis and significant corruption charges. Guatemalans were severely disappointed and the Christian Democratic Party did not ever recover.

A coup was attempted in 1988 and coup rumors swirled in 1989 (Ebel, 1990: 516, 1996: 446). Trudeau (2000: 501–502) concluded, "In the Guatemalan context ... it is of no small significance that Cerezo finished his term."

The 1990–1991 Reversal and 1993 *Autogolpe*

The problems in the 1990–1991 election were manifold and way beyond the reversal by Serrano and his legislative minority. Especially problematic were ambiguity about the candidacy of Ríos Montt and Serrano's corruption.

The prelude to the election was fraught. Both Guatemala's military and the URNG continued to commit human-rights violations; "over a dozen leading figures of various parties [were] murdered during the campaign" (Freedom House, 1992: 178–179). In part because of fear and in part because of the discrediting of the DCG amid the Cerezo government, there was no viable presidential candidate at the center, center-left, or left.

During the first round, the campaign was dominated by the question of the candidacy of Ríos Montt. Having formed a political party, the Frente Republicano Guatemalteco (Guatemalan Republican Front, FRG), Ríos Montt was the frontrunner. However, he had been ruled ineligible because he had previously become chief-of-state through a coup, which was prohibited under the constitution. Ríos Montt was appealing the ruling and it was only three weeks before the first round that it became clear that he would not be allowed to run. The beneficiary of this ruling was Serrano. Serrano had headed Ríos Montt's cabinet and, like Ríos Montt, was a Protestant evangelical and former Christian Democrat (LAWR, November 22, 1990, p. 2). Also like Ríos Montt, Serrano combined a law-and-order message with denunciation of corruption and the Guatemalan establishment (Cameron, 1998).

The first round was won by the UCN's Carpio with 26%; Serrano was the runner-up with 24%. If Carpio had won in the first round under plurality, he would have suffered a legitimacy deficit; a reversal appeared likely, although not certain, from the outset (Trudeau, 1993: 149; LARR, December 6, 1990, p. 2). In the first round, Serrano did not have the Ríos Montt vote; Ríos Montt had asked his supporters to spoil their ballots in the hope that the election would be annulled (LAWR, November 1, 1990, p. 3). But, after the first round, Ríos Montt supported Serrano

(LARR, December 6, 1990, p. 2). Carpio was not endorsed by either the third-place DCG or the fourth-place PAN (LARR, January 1991, p. 3).

Serrano went on to win the runoff in a landslide—68%. And, although Serrano's party had only 16% of the legislative seats, it maintained a coalition with the UCN and the Christian Democrats for more than two years (Cameron, 1998: 223–224). The Serrano government invited DCG, UCN, and even leftist leaders into its cabinets and provided immunity for DCG leaders from investigation into corruption (Barry, 1992: 7–8). Guatemalans' priority was the peace process, and all the major parties were working to this end (Cameron, 1998: 223–224). Also, amid the debt crisis, all the major parties favored market reforms and the Serrano government was adopting them (Barry, 1992: 8–9).

But, in February 1993, the Serrano government announced the third large jump in electricity rates in two years. The hike came amid other privatization initiatives; popular protests ensued. It was widely believed that Serrano was siphoning funds from the electricity agency and was deeply corrupt—more so than any of his predecessors (Villagrán de León, 1993: 118–119; Vargas Llosa and Aroca, 1995: 95–96). At the same time, peace negotiations were gridlocked and political violence was intensifying. The government's coalition with the DCG and the UCN broke down.

On May 25, 1993, Serrano announced the *autogolpe*. Scholars' primary explanations were Serrano's authoritarianism and corruption (Cameron, 1998; Villagrán de León, 1993). Stated LAWR (June 10, 1993, p. 253), "Serrano had acted to pre-empt the presentation in congress of a petition, bearing 5,000 signatures, for the president's impeachment on several charges of corruption."

The *autogolpe* was protested by the vast majority of Guatemalans as well as by the international community and, in June, Serrano fled. Ramiro de León Carpio, a former human rights ombudsman, was elected president by Guatemala's legislature.

The 1995–1996, 1999, and 2003 Elections: Governments at the Right but Political Inclusion

The three elections held between 1995 and 2003 were won in runoffs. All three presidents were the first-round winners; two of the three runoffs were inefficient. Although all three presidents were to the right, a peace agreement between the government and the URNG was signed in December 1996, and the left began to be incorporated into the political arena.

The 1995–1996 contest was won by the PAN's Álvaro Arzú, who tallied 37% in the first round to 22% for the FRG's Alfonso Portillo, a stand-in for Ríos Montt. Arzú was considered virtually certain to win the runoff, and he did (LARR, October 5, 1995, p. 1). A popular mayor of Guatemala City, Arzú was a former Christian Democrat and, in the runoff, he gained most of the votes of the DCG-backed coalition as well as of a new small leftist party (Ariga-González, 2004: 328).

The 1999 election was won by the FRG's Portillo. In the first round, Portillo tallied 48% and the PAN's Oscar Berger, a former businessman and former mayor of Guatemala City, 30%. As in 1995–1996, the first-round winner was deemed virtually certain to win the runoff and he did (Artiga-González, 2004: 328; LAWR, November 9, 1999, p. 518).

In third place with 12% was Colom, the candidate for the URNG—participating for the first time—and another small leftist party. Colom was an industrial engineer and textile businessman but also a leftist; his politically active uncle had been brutally killed by the military in 1979 and for most of the 1990s he had directed a government program for social development in poor Guatemalan communities. His vice-presidential candidate was Vitalino Similox, an evangelical pastor of indigenous descent and an advocate for peace and human rights.

As of 2000, Colom had withdrawn from the leftist coalition that included the URNG to form a new party, the Unidad Nacional de la Esperanza (National Unity for Hope, UNE), which did not include the URNG. Unfortunately, the UNE was not included in the 2002 PELA survey and the classification of Colom was flawed by an extremely large standard deviation that suggests a survey error.[3] However, Colom was shifting away from the Marxist left. "Softening his leftist rhetoric," Colom said that his model was Lula (Congressional Research Service, 2008: 4). His vice-presidential candidate was Fernando Andrade, the 1995 presidential candidate for the DCG-backed coalition, respected by Guatemala's business groups.[4]

The 2003 election was won by Berger, running for GANA rather than the PAN, with 34% of the vote. In second place with 26% was Colom. In third place with 19% was Ríos Montt, who had been declared eligible on the grounds that the law disqualifying candidates who had led coups could not be applied retroactively. Berger was considered the likely, but not certain, winner of the runoff (LAWR, November 11, 2003, p. 1; LARR, December 16, 2003, p. 7); he prevailed by eight points.

The 2007 Election: Victory for Colom after a Close Runoff

For the first time in Guatemala, a candidate who had worked with the Marxist left was elected president in 2007. The UNE's Colom won the first round with 28% to 24% for the runner-up, former General Otto Pérez Molina of the Partido Patriota (Patriotic Party, PP). The outcome of the runoff was uncertain; but Pérez Molina, at the extreme right in PELA surveys, was favored; the third-, fourth-, and fifth-place candidates were to the right (LARR, November 2007, pp. 1–2). Yet, ultimately, none of the three endorsed Pérez Molina.[5] Colom won by six points.

The number of parties was large: 4.88. At the right were the third-place GANA, the fourth-place party of a physicist, and the fifth-place FRG. Three parties to the left of Colom's UNE, including the URNG, competed but fared poorly. The biggest surprise was the mere 3% for Rigoberta Menchú, a Nobel Peace Prize winner and indigenous champion of human rights.

Colom's victory was attributed in part to the fact that he had "moderated his leftist platform over the last two elections and ran as a center-left candidate for the UNE" (Congressional Research Service, 2008: 4). Colom was placed at the center-left (4.57) in the 2008 PELA survey. Colom promised to build "a social-democratic country with a Mayan face" (Lacey, 2007b: A11) and "made fighting poverty his campaign's centerpiece" (Lacey, 2007a: A11). His vice-presidential candidate was a respected heart surgeon who had practiced among both the wealthy and the poor.

During the 1982–1983 Ríos Montt government, Pérez Molina was an army commander in an area of indigenous massacres and was seriously implicated in human-rights abuses. However, Pérez Molina was one of the military officers who had ousted Ríos Montt in the 1983 coup. He had also served in the 1993–1996 government of de León Carpio.

The most salient issue was crime. Pérez Molina's campaign symbol was a fist and he promised a hard line, including deployment of the military. By contrast, Colom promised to address the economic and social causes of crime. Between the first round and the runoff, Colom emphasized the importance of intelligence (Roig-Franzia, 2007: A11).

The legitimacy that Colom gained in the runoff was important. Coup threats against Colom's government were legion (Booth, Wade, and Walker, 2010: 154). In particular, a prominent lawyer was assassinated and, in a videotape prior to his death, blamed Colom if he were to be killed; only several years later did an investigation prove that the lawyer had in fact plotted his own assassination.

The problem of organized crime became more salient. In the view of most Guatemalans, Colom's policies failed. But, in key respects, the Colom government was trying. In 2010, Claudia Paz y Paz was appointed attorney general, and she became an acclaimed prosecutor against organized crime and the abuse of human rights.

The 2011 Election: The Return of the Right

Throughout, the Patriotic Party's Pérez Molina was the favorite. He tallied 36% in the first round and prevailed in the runoff by six points. Still, Pérez Molina was at the extreme right (8.47) and his victory in the runoff was uncertain (LAWR, September 15, 2011, p. 2; LAWR, November 3, 2011, pp. 14–15; González, 2013: 619). The third-place candidate with 16% was Eduardo Suger (the physicist who had competed in 2007); he made no endorsement for the runoff.

The first-round runner-up with 23% was Manuel Baldizón, running for his own party, Libertad Democrática Renovada (Democratic Liberty Renewed, Líder). Baldizón was a lawyer, hotel entrepreneur, and legislator—first for the PAN and then for the UNE. Placed a tad right of center in PELA surveys, Baldizón promised an extra month's bonus pay for workers and a reinstatement of the death penalty, with the televising of executions.

Possibly, the opposition to Pérez Molina would have fared better if it had been led by Sandra Torres, Colom's ex-wife. Close relatives of a president were banned from candidacy; to try to surmount the ban, Torres and Colom had divorced, but ultimately her candidacy was prohibited. Torres had overseen the Colom government's popular conditional cash transfer program and, as the candidate of an UNE-GANA alliance, had been in second place in the polls.

The candidates outbid each other to be tough on crime. Pérez Molina's experience as an army commander was an advantage. Still, concerns about human-rights violations were considerable. Pérez Molina emphasized that he had been the military's representative during the negotiation of the 1996 peace agreement and promised that he would continue the internationally supported efforts against impunity (LAWR, November 10, 2011, p. 3).

This promise proved important. A week before the first round of the 2015 election, Pérez Molina was arrested on corruption charges. Líder and UNE were implicated as well. An outsider, the actor and comic Jimmy Morales, was the surprise winner of the election, defeating Torres in the runoff by a huge margin.

Colombia

Civilian government in Colombia was among the longest-standing in the region; Colombia's average Polity score for 1900–1977 was fifth of eighteen countries (Pèrez-Liñán and Mainwaring, 2013: 381). Yet, periods of severe political violence were common. After 1978, violence worsened, and Colombia's level of democracy during the third wave was low.

The ratings by Freedom House and V-Dem varied. For Freedom House, Colombia's level of democracy between 2008 and 2015 was no better than it had been in the 1990s and was worse than in 1978–1988. In both 1994, the year of Colombia's first election under runoff, and 2015, Colombia's Freedom House score was only 7; in 2015, its score was among the five worst for the countries in this book. But, for V-Dem, Colombia's scores improved almost 10% between 2008 and 2015 and more than 15% between 1978 and 2015. Colombia's 2015 V-Dem score was similar or superior to that for the Dominican Republic, Paraguay, Mexico, and Ecuador—countries ranked above Colombia by Freedom House at that time. For 2016, however, Colombia's Freedom House score improved to 6.

Between 1990 and 2014, voter turnout averaged 46%—the regional nadir. In the 2010 and 2014 elections, turnout was not improving. Colombia's low turnout was in part a reflection of the fact that voting was not mandatory. Indeed, registration was not mandatory; during this period Colombia was the only Latin American country except Chile where registration was not mandatory (Payne, Zovatto G., and

Mateo Díaz, 2007: 247). But the low turnout was also a reflection of enduring fear and cynicism (García, 2010).⁶ Lamented John Dugas (2012: 532), "Colombian elections continue to be marred by outright vote-buying and by the armed intimidation of both voters and candidates in some areas, particularly by the guerrilla movements and paramilitary organizations."

Runoff was one among several reforms in a new constitution adopted by Colombia in 1991. At that time, Colombia's homicide rate was "staggering ... perhaps the highest ... in the world" (Posada-Carbó, 2013: 236). Scholars perceived a "crisis of political legitimacy" (Hartlyn and Dugas, 1999: 280; Bagley, 1990: 148). Popular demand for reform was significant and political leaders sought more inclusive rules (Negretto, 2013: 179–181; Posada-Carbó, 2006: 88). The new constitution "marked [Colombia's] formal transformation ... into a more democratic and fully competitive regime" (Hartlyn and Dugas, 1999: 281–282).

Runoff did indeed encourage political inclusion. One of Colombia's former guerrilla groups, the Movimiento 19 de Abril (Movement of April 19th, M-19), suffered severe repression when it tried to come in from the cold for the 1990 election but was ultimately incorporated into the electoral arena; in the 2006 election, the candidate of the Polo Democrático Alternativo (Democratic Alternative Pole, PDA), many of whose leaders hailed from the M-19, was the runner-up. Further, in 2010, the runner-up hailed from a new good-governance, pro-environment party, the Partido Verde (Green Party, PV). More controversially, in 2002 the political arena also opened to Álvaro Uribe, who became the first civilian president in roughly a century who did not hail from the Conservative or Liberal Party.

Runoff was also advantageous for the legitimacy of Colombia's elected presidents. In two of the four elections under plurality, the winner tallied less than 50% and his victory in a runoff would have been uncertain. By contrast, under runoff, two reversals were helpful. A reversal in the 1998 election prevented a result that was likely to have been disputed by the opposition and a reversal in the 2014 election prevented a result that would have derailed the ongoing peace process between the Colombian government and the remaining major guerrilla group, the FARC (Fuerzas Armadas Revolucionarias de Colombia, Revolutionary Armed Forces of Colombia).

At the same time, the number of parties increased; indeed, the increase under runoff was more dramatic in Colombia than in any other country. The number jumped from an average of 2.17 parties in the four elections between 1978 and 1990 to an average of 5.23 between 1994 and 2014; in 2014, the number was 6.19. The number was large in part because legislative elections were not concurrent with presidential elections but were two months earlier; whereas the Liberal and Conservative Parties were eclipsed in presidential elections, they endured in legislative elections.

To date, the large number of parties has not posed major problems. Although the presidents elected in 2002, 2006, and 2010 led new parties, they formed governing majorities. Commented Posada-Carbó (2013: 243), for example, "Any possible obstacle that the [new] emerging multiparty system might have posed to governance under a presidential regime was overcome by [Juan Manuel] Santos through the formation of the strong coalition that controls over 90% of the seats in congress."

Still, party fragmentation was a concern (Posada-Carbó, 2013: 242–243). Steps were taken. Traditionally, most Colombian political parties presented multiple lists of candidates for elected positions; as of 2003, only one list per party was allowed (Rodríguez Raga, 2006: 161). Also in 2003, a threshold for a party's registration and representation in both houses of the legislature was enacted (Posada-Carbó, 2006: 88). For the 2014 elections to the Senate, the threshold was raised to 3%. Although the number of parties has remained large, the threshold is considered positive (Albarracín and Milanese, 2012).

Colombia's 2009 per capita income was a tad below the Latin American average (World Bank, 2011: 10–12). However, in the mid-2000s its Gini coefficient for inequality was the worst in Latin America (World Bank, 2011: 68–70).

Colombia's Two Long-Standing Parties and the Emergence of the Duopoly

Colombia's two traditional parties, the Partido Conservador (Conservative Party, renamed the Social Conservative Party in 1987) and the Partido Liberal (Liberal Party), were exceptionally long-standing (see Chapter 3). Since 1849, the only military ruler in power for more than a year was General Gustavo Rojas Pinilla, who governed from 1953–1957.

Until the late 1950s, the Conservative Party and the Liberal Party were intense rivals and violence erupted frequently. As Reid (2007: 286) commented, "Party allegiance ran deep, being passed from generation to generation within families as a badge of identity, as if it were support for a football team." Although ideological differences were secondary to clientelism (Martz, 1991: 98), the Conservative Party was considered to be to the right of the Liberal Party (PELA).

In 1948, civil war erupted after a popular leftist Liberal leader, Jorge Gaitán, was assassinated. Approximately 200,000 lives were lost. The violence provoked the 1953 military coup by Rojas Pinilla, which was initially supported by both the Liberal Party and a faction of the Conservative Party (Hartlyn and Dugas, 1999: 264).

To end the Rojas Pinilla government, the Liberal and Conservative Parties formed the National Front (1958–1974). The National Front was a political pact that stipulated the alternation of the presidency between the two parties and parity between them in the division of all elected and appointed government positions. By definition, the National Front was a duopoly. The only competition was among the factions of each party. In the last election under the National Front in 1970, Rojas Pinilla competed as a candidate for the Conservative Party; in the official tally, he lost by less than two points. He charged fraud and sparked the formation of the leftist guerrilla group, the M-19 (for the date of the election).

The National Front coincided with the Cold War; leftist perspectives were gaining ground but were repressed. In 1964, after a military attack on a rural Communist enclave, the FARC was established. Stated Donald Herman (1985: 23), "Political forces felt excluded and turned to violence to express their differences."

The 1978–1990 Elections under Plurality and Increasing Political Violence

Between 1978 and 1990, the Liberal-Conservative duopoly was dominant. Political representation was deemed "bankrupt" (Morgan, 2011) and "oligarchical" (Martz, 1991: 99; Herman, 1985: 16). At the same time, the duopoly was threatened by the rise of the M-19, the FARC, and other leftist groups; political violence escalated. When the 1990 election showed that the duopoly was no longer hegemonic, the new constitution including runoff was adopted.

In the 1978 election, the Liberals' Julio César Turbay Ayala won with 49.5% to 46.6% for the Conservatives' Belisario Betancur. Turbay's victory was disputed for several days (LAPR, June 9, 1978, p. 174). The remaining percentage of the vote split among seven candidates at diverse ideological positions; it was likely, but not certain, that Turbay would have prevailed in a runoff (LAPR, May 26, 1978, p. 159). Turbay was the candidate of the Liberals' "party machine;" he had "no ideas of structural change" and was "a disastrously tedious public speaker and abysmal television performer," whereas Betancur was "attractive" (LAPR, May 26, 1978, p. 159; Kline, 1988: 31).

The 1982 election was won by Betancur with 47%. If there had been a runoff, the runner-up, the Liberals' Alfonso López Michelsen, would probably have won (Negretto, 2013: 181–182; LAWR, June 11, 1982, p. 10). In the first round, the Liberal Party was divided between López Michelsen, a former Liberal president, and Luis Carlos Galán, a dissident Liberal who tallied 11%. A leftist, Galán presented a detailed platform that included agrarian reform, sovereignty over natural resources, and human rights (Kline, 1988: 32–35). In a runoff, most of Galán's votes were likely to have gone to López Michelsen.

The 1986 election was the only one of the four won with a majority. The Liberals' Virgilio Barco defeated the Conservatives' Álvaro Gómez Hurtado by more than twenty points. Chastened by the result of the 1982 election and worried by Gómez Hurtado's hardline proposals, the Liberal Party was united. The election was the first in which a party with Marxist proclivities participated. Led by Jaime Pardo Leal, the Unión Patriótica (Patriotic Union, UP), a coalition of the Communist Party and the political wing of the FARC guerrillas, polled 4.6%.

Amid the UP's showing in the 1986 election, Colombia's rightist paramilitary was galvanized, and politically targeted assassinations exploded. From 1986 to 1989, approximately 3,000 UP members and roughly 300 UP leaders were murdered (Palacios, 2006: 211). The UP's Pardo Leal and then his successor as the UP's 1990 presidential candidate, Bernardo Jaramillo, were assassinated. The M-19 signed an agreement for demobilization with the Barco government; its leader in these negotiations and the AD/M-19's first presidential candidate, Carlos Pizarro León-Gómez, was assassinated in 1990. Galán, the leftist Liberal, was leading the polls for the election and was also murdered.

Amid this bloodshed, the 1990 election was held and won by the Liberals' César Gaviria with 48%. It was virtually certain that he would have won a runoff against the runner-up, hardliner Gómez Hurtado, with 24%. Gómez Hurtado had split from the Conservative Party to form his own Movimiento de Salvación Nacional (Movement of National Salvation). The eclipse of the duopoly was evident not only in the second-place position of a new party but also in the third place position of a leftist party, the Alianza Democrática/Movimiento 19 de Abril (Democratic Alliance/Movement of April 19th AD/M-19). Its candidate was the former M-19 leader Antonio Navarro Wolff; he tallied 13%. The official Conservative candidate finished fourth.

Within the political crisis and demands for change, Constituent Assembly elections were held in December 1990. The dominance of the Liberal and Conservative parties continued to erode; the AD/M-19 secured 27% of the seats.

In the new constitution, majority runoff was approved overwhelmingly, with 64 of 66 votes (Negretto, 2013: 181). Additional important reforms included: (a) the popular election of governors (added to the popular election of mayors, a 1988 reform); (b) a single national district for the election of senators (facilitating the election of movements without political bases in specific localities); (c) the official distribution of electoral ballots (previously distributed by the candidates themselves); and (d) numerous initiatives to reduce the power of the executive in favor of the legislature (Hartlyn and Dugas, 1999: 282–283).

The 1994 Election: An Illegitimate President (Despite Runoff)

The winner of the 1994 election, the Liberals' Ernesto Samper, did not enjoy a legitimacy advantage from his victory in a runoff; rather, he was immediately tarnished by charges of having financed his campaign with funds from drug traffickers.

Samper was a former legislator and cabinet minister; the runner-up, Andrés Pastrana, was a well-known former successful Conservative mayor of Bogotá and television journalist. Pastrana sought to distance himself from the duopoly by running as an independent under the label "Andrés Presidente" (Taylor, 2009: 97). In the first round, each won 45%, with Samper ahead by a mere three-tenths of a point. The runoff was forecast to be a dead heat (LAWR, June 23, 1994, p. 269). Samper prevailed by two points.

Within days, Samper was accused by Pastrana of having accepted millions of dollars from the Cali drug cartel for his campaign. Evidence against Samper accumulated and two impeachment attempts were launched. Samper had a congressional majority and survived, but his government was gravely undermined. Both left-wing guerrilla movements and right-wing paramilitary expanded.

The 1998 Election: An Advantageous Reversal

In the first round of the 1998 election, Pastrana was the runner-up by a paper-thin margin to the Liberals' Horacio Serpa, 34.0% to 34.4%. The result of the runoff was uncertain (LAWR, June 2, 1998, p. 241; LAWR, June 23, 1998, p. 277). In the event, Pastrana won by four points. The runoff was advantageous.

It is likely that, if Serpa had won the presidency under plurality, he would have suffered a legitimacy deficit.[7] Serpa's first-round victory was unexpected and it was attributed in part to the Liberal Party "machine"—which, in rural areas, meant vote-buying (LAWR, June 2, 1998, p. 241; Ulloa and Posada-Carbó, 1999: 448–449). It is very possible that a Serpa victory would have been challenged by Pastrana.[8] As noted previously, after the 1994 election, Pastrana had aggressively challenged Samper. In this challenge, Pastrana might have enjoyed considerable support; whereas Serpa had been Samper's friend and interior minister and was tainted by the association, Pastrana was viewed positively in the Colombian business community and in the United States.

As in 1994, Pastrana did not run for the Conservative Party but established a broader coalition, called the Gran Alianza para el Cambio (Great Alliance for Change). Whereas the Conservative Party was placed at 8.28 in PELA surveys, Pastrana's coalition was placed at 6.67. In the event, Pastrana won most of the votes of the third-place candidate, Noemí Sanín (Ulloa and Posada-Carbó, 1999: 449). Sanín formed her own movement for the election and campaigned as a critic of the two-party system, but previously she had been a leader in the Conservative Party.

The key issue during the runoff was peace negotiations. Pastrana and Serpa were competing about the generosity of the concessions to be made to the FARC. Both candidates endorsed a demilitarized zone for the guerrillas. Members of Pastrana's campaign team met in the jungle with the FARC and this gesture was widely believed to give Pastrana the victory.[9]

The Pastrana government's negotiations with the FARC failed. The FARC was perceived to exploit the peace process to increase its military strength. (Given that the blame is widely placed on the FARC, it is unlikely that the outcome would have been very different under a Serpa government.) The FARC began to pose a serious threat to the Colombian state. Whereas in 1998 Colombians had overwhelmingly favored negotiations, they came to favor a repressive strategy (Palacios, 2012: 193; Bejarano, 2012: 207–208).

The 2002 and 2006 Elections: The End of the Duopoly amid Landslides for Uribe

The 2002 victory of a president who was neither a Conservative nor a Liberal was a watershed in Colombia. Uribe built his own party and won both elections easily in the first round. The costs and benefits of Uribe's governments are vehemently debated. Uribe was placed close to the extreme right (approximately 8.0 in the 2003 and 2006 PELA surveys). In the view of most Colombian citizens and some political analysts, "Uribe proved to be an outstanding and committed leader" (Posada-Carbó, 2013: 238). However, for others, Uribe achieved security improvements at an excessive toll on civil liberties.

It is likely that Uribe's entry with his own party into the 2002 election was facilitated by runoff. Uribe broke with the Liberal Party and established his Primero Colombia (Colombia First) due to Serpa's stranglehold on the Liberals' nomination and the discredit of the duopoly (McLean, 2002: 1–2; Taylor, 2009: 170). In early 2001, Uribe was "an outsider in what was expected to be a two-horse race between Serpa [the Liberal candidate] and Sanín [the former Conservative leader]" (LARR, February 26, 2002, p. 8). Uribe may have strategized that, with sincere votes, he could reach the runoff. However, within about four months of the election, Uribe led the polls by almost thirty points. As Governor of Antioquia, Uribe was known for hardline policies; he had opposed peace negotiations from the start, and in most Colombians' views his position had turned out to be correct. Uribe was supported by most members of the Conservative Party, which did not run its own candidate.

Uribe won the 2002 election with 54% to 32% for the Liberals' Serpa. Serpa had hoped for an alliance with parties to his left, but this did not happen. Dismayed in particular by the market reforms under Samper's government, leftist groups chose to build their own party, the PDA.[10] Including former M-19 leaders Navarro Wolff and Gustavo Petro, it ran Luis Eduardo Garzón, a trade-union leader, and finished third with 6%.

Even though Uribe's party was inchoate and had no formal presence in Colombia's legislature, Uribe built support and at the time of his inauguration held a working majority in both houses. Strengthening the military and police and introducing civilian defense programs, Uribe achieved results: homicide and kidnapping rates declined dramatically.

Uribe was very popular and, in the 2006 election, he triumphed with 62%. For this election, the Partido Social de la Unidad Nacional (Social Party of National Unity), usually called the Partido de la U (Party of the U) with the play on Uribe's name, was formed.

The surprise of the 2006 election was the second-place victory of the leftist PDA, tallying 22%. The PDA's candidate was Carlos Gaviria, the 1996–2001 chief magistrate of Colombia's Constitutional Court and a 2002–2006 senator (for another small leftist party that subsequently joined the PDA). Gaviria was adamant that the

Uribe government was violating human rights and neglecting the social conditions that spawn insurgencies (Posada-Carbó, 2006: 86). He was classified at the extreme left (2.32) in PELA surveys.

Although in some respects security continued to improve during Uribe's second term, in other respects it did not. Serious government abuses were revealed and it became apparent that many of Uribe's close associates were tied to paramilitary networks.

The 2010 Election: A Popular Party of the U within a More Open Electoral Arena

Uribe's popularity transferred to his defense minister, Juan Manuel Santos (Party of the U). In 2010, Santos won 47% in the first round and 69% in the runoff. The runoff was inefficient; it was clear that Santos would gain the support of the parties that finished third and fifth in the first round (LAWR, June 3, 2010, p. 1).

Santos became the candidate for the Party of the U after a February 2010 ruling by Colombia's constitutional court against the legitimacy of a referendum on a second re-election for Uribe. Although Santos did not connect easily with everyday Colombians, he was respected. A one-time leader in the Liberal Party, he had been finance minister for Pastrana and defense minister for Uribe during a three-year period of major successes against the guerrillas. The grandson of a president and the cousin of Uribe's vice-president, Santos hailed from one of Colombia's most prominent families.

As in 2006, the surprise was the second-place finish of a new party, in this case the Green Party. Competing in a national election for the first time, it tallied 22% of the vote in the first round. Indeed, for a few weeks, it was tied with the Party of the U in the polls. The Green Party's candidate was a former popular mayor of Bogotá, Antanas Mockus. Like Marina Silva in Brazil and Marco Enríquez-Ominami in Chile, Mockus called for government accountability and transparency and respect for the rule of law (Shifter, 2011c: 119). His positions on socioeconomic issues were centrist rather than leftist; he did not pursue an alliance with the left.[11]

However, in the runoff, Mockus faded. The reasons were various.[12] Trying to establish the Green Party's brand, Mockus did not accept the support of the fourth-place party, the PDA. Mockus made errors—for example, statements of admiration for Hugo Chávez.

The 2014 Election: Another Advantageous Reversal

To Uribe's dismay, the Santos government vigorously pursued peace negotiations with the FARC. As the 2014 election approached, Uribe built a new party, and its candidate was Óscar Iván Zuluaga, a former minister in Uribe's government. Zuluaga won the first round, but with only 29%. Santos was the runner-up with

26%; for the runoff, he gained most of the votes of the fourth-place PDA and the fifth-place Green Party to prevail by six points. If Zuluaga had won in an election by plurality, he would have suffered a legitimacy deficit, and the peace process would have been derailed. The advances in the peace process under Santos were reflected in the improvements in Colombia's Freedom House and V-Dem scores during this period.

Peru

Overall, Peru's third-wave democratic record approximated the Latin American average. Peru's modal Freedom House score was 5 (a tad above the regional average); it was 5 upon the start of the third wave in 1980, upon its first election with runoff in 1985, and during 2002–2016. Peru's average voter turnout was an excellent 82%. But, Peru's Freedom House scores were at regional nadirs between 1992, when Fujimori executed his *autogolpe*, and 1999. In the V-Dem dataset, the scores and trends were very similar; the only slight variation was that, during 2002–2006, scores were as much as 10% above regional averages. In general, Peru's level of democracy was comparable its historical record and economic status; Peru's 1900–1977 Polity score was approximately the Latin American average (Pérez-Liñán and Mainwaring, 2013: 381) and Peru's 2009 per capita income was slightly below the Latin American average (World Bank, 2011: 10–12).

Runoff was adopted in Peru's 1979 constitution. As the party with the strongest political base, APRA favored plurality; but, especially after the 1962 election fiasco, the argument about the dangers of a minority president was compelling (García Belaúnde, 1986: 32–37; Handelman, 1980: 14–15). In a compromise, the threshold was put at 36% in the upcoming 1980 election but 50% subsequently.

The vast majority of citizens and analysts believed that runoff was favorable. In a 2005 survey of the Lima public, 75% preferred majority runoff.[13] At a conference, three of Peru's most noted social scientists—Henry Pease García, Martín Tanaka, and Fernando Tuesta—endorsed runoff (Acevedo, Ausejo, Rojas, and Sulmont, 2011: 89). Most of Peru's political leaders agreed. In 1994, all of the eight political leaders asked about runoff by Peru's newsweekly *Caretas* endorsed it.[14] President Alan García said, "The second round is vital."[15] In my surveys with legislators, 75% of the Peruvian legislators favored runoff, whereas only 15% endorsed plurality and 10% were not sure (see Appendix 1).

As elsewhere, the predominant reason for legislators' preference for runoff was legitimacy (McClintock, 2008). In Peru's 1990, 2001, 2006, 2011, and 2016 elections, the first-round winner tallied less than 40% and was unlikely to have enjoyed legitimacy without a runoff. This was especially the case in the three reversals; in 1990, it was quickly apparent that majority support for the first-round winner was very unlikely and, in 2006 and 2016, uncertain.

Runoff was also important to ideological moderation. In particular, the 2006 first-round winner, Ollanta Humala, was a fiery outsider who deeply polarized the country; he moderated dramatically to win in 2011. Also, in the 1985 election, Alan García subdued the sectarianism of APRA.

However, Peru's number of political parties was large: an average of 3.87 between 1985 and 2014 and 4.1 between 2001 and 2014. Peru's parties were among the most personalistic in the hemisphere (Cotler, 1995; Tanaka, 1998: 197). With the exception of APRA, parties were vehicles for their leaders, without a significant political base. The incidence of outsiders winning 10% or more was greater in Peru than in any other country (see Appendix 5).

The problem of a large number of parties did not begin with runoff. In Peru's qualified-plurality elections in 1962 and 1963, the number of parties was calculated at 3.39 and 2.98 respectively (Kenney, 2003: 1229). In Peru's 1978 Constituent Assembly election, the number of parties was 4.44. In 2002, regional elections were introduced under plurality, and the number of candidates was huge; in 2006, only twelve of twenty-five regional presidents tallied as much as 33% and one tallied a mere 19% (Tanaka and Vera, 2007: 242). As a result, a runoff is now required if no candidate wins 30%; the change enjoyed broad support.[16] Rather, the large number of parties reflected voters' dissatisfaction with incumbents and the variety of political cleavages, including cleavages about APRA, about ideology, and, most recently, ethnicity (Madrid, 2011).

Various rules in addition to runoff were relevant. Throughout, legislative and presidential elections were concurrent. Between 1980 and 1992, the legislature was bicameral, but became unicameral under the 1993 constitution. Immediate presidential re-election was prohibited under the 1979 constitution, allowed at first under the 1993 constitution, and prohibited again after the return to democracy in 2001.

Peru's Political Parties and the 1980 Election under Qualified Plurality

At the time of Peru's first third-wave election in 1980, its two leading parties were APRA and Acción Popular (Popular Action, AP). The longer-standing party, APRA, was polarizing. It was founded as a boldly reformist party by the charismatic Víctor Raúl Haya de la Torre, but, after a loss in an election in 1931, the party was intransigent (Cotler, 1978: 227–272). Rebelling in the city of Trujillo, party militants killed more than fifty soldiers; a party militant assassinated the elected president. These and other subsequent violent actions provoked repression of APRA by military and civilian elites and widespread perceptions that the party was not respectful of civil liberties. The party was sectarian; its slogan was: "Only the APRA will save Peru."

Popular Action was the second leading party. The party's founder was Fernando Belaúnde, an architect. Committed to democracy and promising social inclusion through the expansion of education and infrastructure, Belaúnde won Peru's 1963 election. However, he faced many challenges and was ousted by the military in 1968.

The 1980 election was won with 45% for Belaúnde to 27% for APRA's Armando Villanueva. The threshold was 33% and a runoff was not required; if it had been, Belaúnde's victory would have been virtually certain (LAWR, May 30, 1980, p. 4). Belaúnde continued to promise democracy and social reform; Villanueva was widely perceived as a machine boss who had worked with his party's goon squads (Sanders, 1984: 1–3). Together, six different leftist groups tallied 16%. In a runoff, most of these votes would have gone to Belaúnde, who was expected to respect civil liberties (LAWR, May 23, 1980, p. 1). Belaúnde was also virtually certain to get most of the votes of the third-place party, the center-right Partido Popular Cristiano (Popular Christian Party, PPC).

The 1985 Election: The Renovation of APRA

Amid the debt crisis and the emergence of the savage Sendero Luminoso (Shining Path) guerrillas, the Belaúnde government was unpopular; not only AP but the PPC, which had partnered with the government, was tarnished. In 1985, for the first time, APRA won a presidential election.

APRA's candidate, Alan García, tallied 53% of the valid vote in the first round. A runoff was required if the first-round winner did not have 50% of the valid vote plus the null vote and the blank vote; García did not reach this percentage. But the first-round runner-up with 25%, the leftist Alfonso Barrantes, knew there was no hope and withdrew. The mayor of Lima, Barrantes led Izquierda Unida (United Left, IU), a coalition of predominantly Marxist parties.

Only 35 years old but already a legislator, García renovated APRA. García decided that "he needed to 'open up' APRA in order to win the nation's vote" (Graham, 1993: 243). Cynthia Sanborn (1988: 26) noted that, in 1980, "APRA's appeal was too radical for moderates, too ambiguous for radicals, and too sectarian to appeal to independents;" but, by 1985, APRA was aware of "the need to build electoral majorities." García "moved the party to a clear center-left position" (Carrión, 1998: 59). APRA's slogan "Only the APRA will save Peru" was replaced with García's promise, "My commitment is to all Peruvians" and, to its traditional symbol of a star, a dove was added.

The 1990 Reversal and 1992 *Autogolpe*

Although the 1990 reversal leading to the presidency for outsider Fujimori is often cited as an example of the dangers of runoff, the election was problematic overall. A plurality victory for the first-round winner, Mario Vargas Llosa, would have been perilous as well.

The first problem was that Peru's traditional parties were deeply discredited. By 1990, Peru's economic crisis was worsening and the Shining Path was threatening the state. The percentage of Peruvians supporting the parties that had governed during the 1980s—APRA, AP, and PPC—had plummeted (Kenney, 2004: 47).

The second problem was that the left, which had appeared poised to win about eighteen months before the election (Kenney, 2004: 41), imploded. The 1985 IU candidate, Barrantes, was placed far to the left (Schmidt, 1996: 333); accordingly, he decided to moderate and run a personalistic campaign (LAWR, March 29, 1990, p. 11). However, Barrantes' shift alienated his colleagues, many of whom believed that Barrantes was disrespectful of IU principles and procedures. Ultimately Barrantes took his Izquierda Socialista (Socialist Left, IS) out of the IU; in the election, both fared badly.

The third problem was that Vargas Llosa, who replaced Barrantes as the frontrunner, was a "confrontational" and "uncompromising" outsider (Schmidt, 1996: 340; Cotler, 1995: 347–348). Although the novelist enjoyed great prestige, and in 1987 had led a successful movement in opposition to García's attempt to nationalize banks, he had no government experience. At "extreme right" (8.5) on a scale identical to PELA's (Schmidt, 1996: 333),[17] Vargas Llosa proposed an economic "shock," including immediate drastic reductions in public employment and government subsidies. Vargas Llosa's colleagues asked him to moderate, but he did not (Cameron, 1994: 123; Schmidt, 1996: 327).

In addition, enjoying personal ties with Belaúnde and expecting organizational support, Vargas Llosa decided to join his Movimiento Libertad (Liberty Movement) with AP and the PPC in the Frente Democrático (Democratic Front, FREDEMO); Vargas Llosa was tarnished by his association with discredited parties (Cameron, 1994: 116–123; Daeschner, 1993: 63, 270). FREDEMO legislative candidates spent lavishly on campaign advertising and the image of Vargas Llosa as a member of Lima's fair-skinned elite was reinforced.

In short, as Peruvians pondered their options before the first round, they were dissatisfied. Only a month before the election, Fujimori, the candidate of Cambio 90 (Change 90 [1990]), was a nonentity. He rose meteorically. Fujimori had 29% to Vargas Llosa's 33% in the first round and then won the runoff in a landslide with 62%. After the first round, it was so evident that Fujimori would win that, at first, Vargas Llosa wanted to withdraw (Daeschner, 1993: 215–222).

Fujimori was an appealing candidate. He had risen from modest circumstances to become an agronomist and university rector. Despite his Japanese descent, he appeared ethnically to be "a president like you," in the phrase of one of his campaign slogans. Another slogan, "honesty, technology, and work," resonated too. Fujimori described himself as a centrist and Peruvians perceived him as a centrist (Schmidt, 1996: 333); for the most part, his proposals were vague compromises between right and left (LAWR, March 29, 1990, p. 11). It was evident that, independent of both APRA and the left, Fujimori would be able to gain the votes from both of these parties in a runoff, and this was important to voters whose key goal was to defeat Vargas Llosa (Tanaka, 1998: 193; Sánchez, 2004: 415). In contrast to Fujimori's style after his inauguration, during the campaign he was "calm" and "low-key" (Constable, 1990a, 1990b).

If Vargas Llosa had won under plurality, the outcome was likely to have been deleterious. Commented Francisco Sánchez (1994: 410), "[In this case] the winner would have been a candidate who had only a third of the votes and who would have met resistance in large sectors of the population." Together, FREDEMO's parties had a plurality in both houses of the legislature—but only approximately 35%. All the other parties were to its left. Speculated one scholar about a Vargas Llosa presidency,

> things could have been worse [than with Fujimori] due to the confrontational style Vargas Llosa chose when he entered politics.... [He] would probably have continued to lash out at his political adversaries ... and would have thereby polarized the country.[18]

So, given the robust support for Fujimori in 1990, why did he execute the *autogolpe* only two years later? Why, in April 1992, did Fujimori, with the support of the armed forces, suspend the constitution, close the congress, dismantle the judiciary, and detain more than twenty journalists as well as numerous APRA leaders?

The blame was placed primarily on Fujimori's legislative minority by various scholars, including Kenney (2004: 246–260) and Tanaka (1998: 208–218). Fujimori's Change 90 had only 22% of the seats in the Senate and only 17% in the Chamber of Deputies. These scholars noted that the possibility of Fujimori's impeachment due to "moral incapacity" (which required only a majority vote) was floated in the legislature as early as February 1991. Also, amid the threat from the Shining Path, Fujimori advanced draconian security measures in November 1991 that met significant legislative opposition.

However, the blame was placed primarily on Fujimori's authoritarianism and corruption by most scholars (Cameron, 1994: 148–153; Conaghan, 2005: 29–32; Cotler, 1995: 350–351; Daeschner, 1993: 280–288; McClintock, 1993: 112–119; Stokes, 1996: 61–69). These scholars believe that Fujimori did not want to negotiate with opposition leaders or undergo congressional or judicial oversight. In the words of Julio Cotler (1995: 350), "Fujimori ceaselessly incited [friction] as he set a collision course, certain that he would ultimately win the confrontation between the already discredited parties." Said a former minister in Fujimori's cabinet, "It was clear that Fujimori hadn't the slightest interest in achieving a majority...."[19] In addition, as is known now but was not at the time, the Fujimori government was the most corrupt in Peru's history (Quiroz, 2008). In March 1992, Fujimori's wife accused members of the president's family of corruption; these charges were to be investigated by a congressional commission to be formed on April 7. This investigation ended with the *autogolpe* on April 5.

In these scholars' view, after Fujimori's election, the prospects of legislative majorities were good. During the campaign, Fujimori had support from García and, given Fujimori's ideological position, it seemed likely that he would secure votes from APRA and, to a lesser degree, the left. Together, Change 90 and APRA had roughly 45% of the congressional seats and Change 90, APRA, and the left about two-thirds. However, Fujimori quickly shifted his ideological position. Despite having campaigned against a drastic economic "shock," Fujimori executed one. Stated Susan Stokes (1997: 222), "Fujimori's switch was probably the sharpest divergence from mandate accountability on record."

Fujimori's shift doomed any alliance with Peru's left but opened the possibility of support from the parties that had composed FREDEMO (which dissolved soon after the election). Together, Change 90 and these parties had more than 50% of the seats in the Senate and 47% in the House of Representatives. Indeed, for the most part Fujimori did secure the support of these parties for his economic initiatives; Kenney (2004: 250) acknowledged that, until November 1991, Fujimori achieved most of his policy initiatives. In the view of most scholars, Fujimori's November 1991 security measures met legislative opposition because they galvanized widespread fear of abuses of civil liberties (Daeschner, 1993: 278–279).

Fujimori's 1995 Landslide and Its Aftermath

After the *autogolpe*, elections were held for a constituent assembly, and a new constitution allowed Fujimori to run for immediate re-election. The Fujimori government enjoyed important successes. In September 1992, the leader of the Shining Path, Abimael Guzmán, was captured; by 1995 the insurgency was decimated. Peru's economy was growing robustly for the first time in two decades. In this context, Fujimori—now the candidate for Cambio 90/Nueva Mayoría (Change 90/New Majority)—triumphed in the first round of the 1995 elections with a resounding 64%.

Opposition candidates faced an uphill battle. With 22%, the runner-up was Javier Pérez de Cuellar, who led his own new party, Unión por el Perú (Union for Peru, UPP). Although a distinguished former secretary general of the United Nations, Pérez de Cuellar was not well known in Peru. His primary emphasis was democracy (LAWR, October 6, 1994, p. 448). His policy positions and campaign team uncomfortably mixed left and right (Schmidt, 1999: 102–111).

A key question was the freedom and fairness of the election. Pérez de Cuellar and other opposition candidates charged that Fujimori's intelligence agency was sabotaging their campaigns (LAWR, November 24, 1994, p. 533, and LAWR, December 22, 1994, p. 586). Fraudulent vote counts and missing voting materials were reported; Change 90/New Majority's tally in the legislative contest—56% of the seats—was highly suspect (Conaghan, 2005: 100–104).

However, it was only in 1997 when Fujimori contorted Peru's re-election rule so that he could run for a third consecutive term that concerns about his authoritarian proclivities gained resonance (Conaghan, 2005: 117–130). Gradually, the government's misuse of public funds, violation of electoral laws, and manipulation of the media were dismaying broad swathes of Peruvians. Finally, just before the 2000 runoff between Fujimori and first-round runner-up Alejandro Toledo, the government introduced new computer software and declined to give the OAS election-monitoring team time to review it; as Chapter 2 noted, the OAS called the election "not free and fair" (McClintock, 2006: 262). Although Fujimori was inaugurated for a third time in July, scandals quickly erupted and he fled Peru in November.

The 2001, 2006, and 2011 Elections: Three Advantageous Runoffs

The results of the 2001, 2006, and 2011 runoffs were all uncertain and runoff added legitimacy and enticed candidates to the center. Also, the 2006 runoff led to a helpful reversal.

In 2001, Alejandro Toledo of Perú Posible (Peru Possible, PP) won the first round with 37% and the runoff with 53%. In 2000, Toledo had boycotted the runoff and organized large protests; he enjoyed respect as the democrat who had confronted a corrupt, authoritarian government. Toledo also had an impressive rags-to-riches story: dark-skinned and from humble origins, he had earned a PhD from Stanford University and had become a business-school professor. Toledo called for social inclusion but also respect for the market and was placed toward the center in PELA surveys.

Toledo's victory in the runoff was likely but far from certain (LAWR, May 29, 2001, p. 246); throughout, Toledo was dogged by personal scandals. The runner-up was García; despite García's failed 1985–1990 government, he appeared a statesman. Between the *autogolpe* and a few months before the election, García had been in exile; but, in the first round, he narrowly defeated Lourdes Flores, a former PPC legislator who led Unidad Nacional (National Unity, UN), an alliance between the PPC and various other groups. In PELA surveys, García was to the left and Flores to the right; they did not ally for the runoff.

The 2006 reversal was advantageous because the first-round winner with 31%, Humala, was an outsider placed at the extreme left in the 2006 PELA survey. Humala alarmed many Peruvians (Schmidt, 2007: 819; Tuesta, 2008: 136; LAWR, March 21, 2006, p. 4); indeed, in elite quarters, there was "hysteria" (ConsultAndes, 2011b: 10). If Humala had been elected under plurality, it is likely to have jeopardized Peru's democracy.

Although economic growth had been excellent, its benefits were not reaching most Peruvians. A retired army officer of mixed ethnicity (*mestizo*), Humala had come to Peruvians' attention through political rebellions. In 2000, as a lieutenant colonel, he had led an uprising against the Fujimori government; in 2005, he had appeared to support his brother's attack against a police station (an effort to provoke Toledo's resignation). Humala enjoyed the backing of Chávez. Humala advocated the nationalization of strategic industries and resources and repudiated a Peru-U.S. free-trade agreement. At the same time, Humala's family's ideology, called *ethnic cacerismo* after Andrés Cáceres, a mestizo hero in Peru's fight against Chile in 1879–1883, had fascist components. Humala had established his own party, but it did not achieve the number of signatures required for registration, and Humala became the standard bearer for the UPP (founded by Pérez de Cuellar).

As Humala's first-round victory loomed, many Peruvians asked: How could he be stopped from winning the runoff? The early frontrunner had been the UN's Flores. However, Flores was placed at the extreme right in the 2006 PELA survey. Meanwhile, García positioned himself at the center (PELA; Vergara, 2007); he introduced innovative, detailed proposals, such as *la sierra exportadora* ("the exporting highlands"), which integrated the left's concern for the poor and the right's respect for global markets. To many Peruvians, García had a better chance to defeat Humala than Flores, and in part for this reason García again edged out Flores to reach the runoff (Tuesta, 2008: 136).

Although García was favored in the runoff, his victory was uncertain (LAWR, April 4, 2006, p.1). His slogan was "responsible change," implying that Flores had stood for the status quo and Humala for reckless change. To attract the votes of Flores and the fourth-place finisher, a proxy for Fujimori, he became more business-friendly. García won by five points.

Plurality advocates might argue that, given elites' fears of Humala, under plurality Flores and García would have allied before the election. But this was unlikely. First, Humala surged in the polls only about three months before the first round. Second, due to personal ambition and the historical enmity between their parties, neither Flores nor García was likely to have ceded the nomination. In the polls, the relative strength of the two candidates was not clear.

In the 2011 election, the result of the runoff was again uncertain (Levitsky, 2011: 89). It was won by Humala—but, as of the 2011 PELA survey, he was at the center-left (4.14).

Although economic growth remained robust, Peruvians continued to doubt that they were receiving their fair share; also, they worried about crime and corruption (Meléndez, 2013: 526–532). Humala's party partnered with other leftist organizations to form Gana Perú (Win Peru). Humala's 2010 campaign platform, entitled "The Great Transformation," called for a new constitution and criticized the "neoliberal model" based on "cheap *cholo* labor."

Humala won the first round with 32%. Gradually before the first round, Humala moderated (Levitsky, 2011: 89; Shifter, 2011b). He recruited political advisers from Brazil's Workers' Party and emphasized that his political model was Lula, not Chávez. Humala no longer advocated the nationalization of strategic resources or the review of free-trade agreements but proposed social programs, in particular for pensions and daycare (ConsultAndes, 2011b: 8). Whereas in 2006 Humala was constantly grimacing in a red polo shirt, in 2011 he donned a suit and a smile.

The first-round runner-up was Keiko Fujimori, the former president's daughter. She was the candidate for Fuerza 2011 (Force 2011), built on her father's political base and placed at the extreme right in the 2011 PELA survey. She was supported by Peruvians who attributed the defeat of the Shining Path and Peru's economic recovery to her father and favorably remembered his government's social programs and public works.

For much of the period between the first round and the runoff, Fujimori led the polls. But her entourage included former advisers to her father, including a health minister considered responsible for the forced sterilization of more than 300,000 women, and reminders of abuses took a toll (LARR, June 2011, p. 1). Meanwhile, Humala continued to shift to the center (Tanaka, 2011:81; Levitsky, 2011: 89–90). Leftist leaders were "locked away for the runoff" (ConsultAndes, 2011b: 7). Humala announced that "The Great Transformation" was now "The road map." In mid-May, he was endorsed not only by Toledo but also by Vargas Llosa. Humala won by three points.

Both Humala and Fujimori were outside Peru's pro-market, pro-democratic mainstream and frightened considerable numbers of Peruvians (Basombrío, 2011: B1). They were the two finalists in part because Peru's right-of-center vote divided among three candidates. It is possible that one of these three candidates was the Condorcet winner (Shifter, 2011a). However, Schmidt (2012: 626–628) doubts this, and I agree. First, by 2011 Humala had "become a real politician, saying what people want to hear" and "honing his message to the issues that Peruvians care about—citizen security, corruption, and employment" (ConsultAndes, 2011c: 4). He had the entire center and left of the political spectrum to himself.

Second, the three right-of-center candidates were flawed. In third place was Pedro Pablo Kuczynski, the candidate for a four-party coalition that included the PPC. Rather surprisingly, given that Kuczynski was seventy-two and had served in important positions in numerous governments, he ran as a fun, hip outsider. However, Kuczynski was a U.S. citizen and his coalition was placed at the extreme right in the 2011 PELA survey. In fourth place was Toledo. Toledo was not as far from the center; most analysts believed that he would be the toughest rival against Humala in a runoff (Schmidt, 2012: 628). But, as in the past, Toledo faced charges of frivolous partying, heavy drinking, and the like. In fifth place was Luis Castañeda; although a successful two-term mayor of Lima, he was an ineffective campaigner and was not well known outside of the capital.

Under plurality, might these three right-of-center candidates have allied? Probably not. It was only two weeks before the first round that polls indicated the possibility that none of them would reach the runoff (Meléndez, 2013: 541). And it was unclear which of the three candidates was the strongest.

The Problematic 2016 Election

Kuczynski eked out a victory in the 2016 runoff versus Fujimori by less than a percentage point. It was a stunning reversal: in the first round, Fujimori had tallied 39.9% and Kuczynski only 21.1%. Although since 2011 Fujimori had been trying hard to dispel her father's ghosts and had led the polls for weeks, ultimately scandals erupted. For most analysts, the reversal was welcome; as Eduardo Dargent and Paula Muñoz stated, "[Kuczynski's] victory reduces the risk of a democratic reversal in the country, a risk that would have been high with [Fujimori's victory] (Dargent and Muñoz, 2016: 155).

At the same time, plurality advocates' concerns about reversals were evident. Fujimori's party gained a solid legislative majority—73 of 130 seats—and, in part because of anger at the runoff loss, proved obstructionist. Kuczynski won with the support of the left, which feared Fujimori's authoritarianism; but it was no surprise that the left did not support many initiatives by the center-right Kuczynski government.

The problems of the election went beyond the reversal. First, prior to the first round, many Peruvians were dissatisfied with the two frontrunners, Kuczynski and Fujimori, and wanted a center-left option (Dargent and Muñoz, 2016: 149). Into the arena jumped Julio Guzmán, who hailed from Peru's interior and had won scholarships for MA and PhD degrees at U.S. universities, leading to ten years at the Inter-American Development Bank; but, just as Guzmán surged past Kuczynski in the polls, he was disqualified by Peru's National Electoral Jury. Guzmán's disqualification was criticized on a host of grounds by Peruvian analysts and by Luis Almagro, the OAS Secretary General, but it stood. Second, Fujimori's party won 56% of the legislative seats despite having won only 36% of the legislative vote; the difference was due to the effects of Peru's proportional-representational formula and of the 5% threshold for legislative representation (Dargent and Muñoz, 2016: 151).

Ecuador

Ecuador was the only runoff country in which the level of democracy eroded. Ecuador's Freedom House score fell from 4 for 1979–1990, to 5 for 1991–1999, to 6 for 2000–2015, and finally to 7 for 2016. Similarly, Ecuador's V-Dem score fell from averages of .510 for 1991–1999 and .500 for 2000–2006 to .350 for 2007–2016. However, voter turnout was steady, slightly above the regional mean. Relative to Ecuador's historical experience, its third-wave record was similar; its average Polity score for 1900–1977 was roughly the Latin American average (Pérez-Liñán and Mainwaring, 2013: 381). Ecuador's 2009 per capita income was about 20% below the Latin American average (World Bank, 2011: 10–12).

Ecuador was the first Latin American country to adopt runoff during the third wave. The goal was to secure presidential legitimacy and reduce the country's traditionally large number of parties (Freidenberg, 2004: 268; Isaacs, 1991: 222; Martz, 1985: 2). In the 1968 election, the number of parties had been 5.66 (Maier, 1969: 82) and the president had won with only 33%. In the two previous presidential elections, in 1956 and 1960, no candidate had reached 50%; in the 1956 election, three candidates had tallied between 24% and 29%. A further measure for the reduction of the number of parties was a high threshold for party recognition—5% of the vote in congressional elections, including support in at least ten provinces; but it was not enforced (Gutiérrez Sanín, 2006; 270; Conaghan 1995: 447–448; Negretto, 2013:197, 215).

Runoff had important advantages. In Ecuador's 1998 constituent assembly, a proposal to eliminate runoff was rejected by all but one of fifty-one delegates (Negretto, 2013: 210). In Ecuador's first third-wave election in 1978–1979, its 1988 election, and its 2006 election, the results of runoffs were uncertain and legitimacy advantages were gained, and the runoffs encouraged various types of moderation.

However, in many respects plurality advocates' concerns were borne out in Ecuador. Among the countries where two broad coalitions did not form for presidential elections, the average number of parties between the first third-wave election and 2014 was the largest in Ecuador: 5.92. As mentioned previously, the immense number was complicit in very low percentages of legislative seats for the president's party, executive-legislative conflict, and elections in which the elected president was probably not the Condorcet winner—and, ultimately, complicit in the oustings of three consecutive presidents.

Further, the effects of runoff on ideological moderation were far from ideal. Ideological shifts by two presidents, Lucio Gutiérrez and Abdalá Bucaram, were so drastic that they were among the reasons for the presidents' oustings. Although the leftist president, Rafael Correa, moderated for the 2006 runoff, subsequently he was not perceived as moderate in many quarters. Further, several rightist leaders, including President León Febrés Cordero, did not moderate.

Scholars (Freidenberg, 2004: 268–269; Negretto, 2013: 202–208; Pachano, 2006: 106, 115–117) worried that runoff was a factor in the continuation of a plethora of parties. Political leaders worried too.[20] Accordingly, the 1998 constituent assembly adopted a reduced threshold: 40% with a 10 point lead, which was first applied in the 2002 election. Ecuador became the only country that started the third wave with majority runoff to reduce its threshold.

In the effort to increase incentives for party coalitions, Ecuador's 1998 constituent assembly adopted various other new rules: the elimination of midterm legislative elections, the end of term limits for legislators, and open lists for election to the legislature. Until the 2008 constitution, re-election of the president continued to be permitted only after one interim term; in the 2008 constitution, a second consecutive term was allowed.

Ironically, after Correa's 2006 election, the long-sought goal of a reduction in Ecuador's number of parties was achieved—and Freedom House and V-Dem scores fell.

Ecuador's Gigantic Number of Parties, 1978–2008

Why was the number of parties immense for decades? First, because of the number of political cleavages. One cleavage was geographic: the coast—in particular the country's largest city, Guayaquil—versus the highlands, in particular Ecuador's capital, Quito. To a degree, the geographic cleavage overlapped with an ideological cleavage: populism was stronger on Ecuador's coast and liberalism stronger in the highlands.

Between the 1930s and the early 1970s, Ecuador's political arena was dominated by José María Velasco Ibarra, a populist feared by civilian and military elites. Velasco Ibarra was elected five times and deposed four times. He did not build his own party but formed coalitions of diverse parties. Gradually, however, a populist party, the Concentración de Fuerzas Populares (Concentration of Popular Forces, CFP), was established under the leadership of Assad Bucaram.

As of the 1978 transition to democracy, there were four major parties in addition to the CFP. Of two liberal parties, the strongest was the Partido Social Cristiano (Social Christian Party, PSC), founded in 1951 and originally based in Quito. And there were two leftist parties, both based in the highlands: Izquierda Democrática (Democratic Left, ID) and Democracia Popular (Popular Democracy), linked to Christian Democracy.

In the mid-1980s, an additional cleavage emerged: indigenous versus non-indigenous. In 1986, indigenous groups established CONAIE (Confederación de Nacionalidades Indígenas del Ecuador, Confederation of Indigenous Nationalities of Ecuador). CONAIE demanded land reform, water rights, and cultural rights for indigenous peoples. CONAIE became the key political base for a new party, the Movimiento de Unidad Plurinacional Pachakutik/Nuevo País (Pachakutik Plurinational Unity Movement/New Country, MUPP-NP). The Quechua word *pachakutik* means "return in time" or "cultural rebirth."

Another reason for the large number of parties was social demand for new parties. Amid Ecuador's prolonged economic crisis, virtually all incumbent political parties became unpopular and, amid citizens' anger, new parties emerged. Although oil was not as large a percentage of exports in Ecuador as in Venezuela, it accounted for approximately half of Ecuador's export earnings in the 1970s (Martz, 1987: 157, 291). Amid the low prices for oil, the debt crisis was extremely challenging for Ecuador. GDP growth between 1985 and 2003 was among the lowest in the region.

The 1978–1979 Election: A Very Helpful Runoff

Ecuador's transition to democracy was precarious. The first round in July 1978 was won with 28% by the CFP's Jaime Roldós; the runner-up with 24% was the PSC's Sixto Durán, a former mayor of Quito. Roldós was the probable, but not certain, runoff winner (LAPR, August 11, 1978, p. 244). Without a runoff, elites were likely to have succeeded in exploiting Roldós's less-than-30% tally to cancel the election and interrupt the democratic transition.

In 1978, military and civilian elites had manipulated the electoral rules to exclude the CFP's Bucaram from candidacy. The CFP was advancing "the most explicit program of social and economic reform yet witnessed in Ecuadorian politics, along with a serious commitment to its implementation" (Schodt, 1987: 135). However, Roldós, a prestigious lawyer as well as a CFP veteran and Bucaram's nephew-in-law, stood in for Bucaram. In the first round, Roldós and Bucaram campaigned side by side and a key slogan was "Roldós to government, Bucaram to power" (Martz, 1983: 36–37).

The prospect of a Roldós victory panicked elites. Led by León Febrés Cordero, a multi-millionaire Guayaquil industrialist, rightist groups labeled the CFP Communist, charged fraud, and called for the cancellation of the election (Martz, 1983: 39–41; Schodt, 1987: 130–135; LAPR, August 11, 1978, p. 244). The result was a prolonged recount; nine months elapsed between the first round and the runoff in May 1979.

The runoff enabled a shift to the center by Roldós and bolstered his legitimacy (LAPR, May 4, 1979, p. 129). Roldós had already shown his ability to reach out to other parties by choosing as his running mate Osvaldo Hurtado of Popular Democracy, the center-left, highlands-based party. Now, he declared his independence from Bucaram on television (Martz, 1983: 39). Roldós won the runoff with a stunning 69%.

However, Latin America's debt crisis was beginning and the new government was challenged. In 1981, Roldós died in an air crash; he was succeeded by Hurtado. Coup threats lingered (Conaghan and Espinal, 1990: 165). Hurtado emphasized that "his main achievement" was the maintenance of "the new democracy" (Corkill, 1985: 73).

The 1984 Election: Victory for a Rightist in a Problematic Reversal

The 1984 election was held amid dire economic straits and an unpopular incumbent government. The presidency was won in a reversal that proved deleterious. In the first round, Rodrigo Borja, a former legislator from Quito and co-founder of the leftist ID, tallied 29%. The runner-up with 28% was the PSC's León Febrés Cordero, a businessman from Guayaquil. In the runoff, Borja was upset by Febrés Cordero, who eked out 51.5%.

Febrés Cordero was placed at the right by Murillo, Oliveros, and Vaishnav (2010: 108–109). A populist who arrived at rallies on horseback, he made extravagant promises. He was confrontational; after the first round, he charged fraud and intensified a smear campaign against Borja (Martz, 1985: 24).

Febrés Cordero's PSC held only 13% of the seats in the legislature and faced a concerted leftist opposition. Rather than negotiate, Febrés Cordero sought to bully it into submission (Conaghan, 1987: 1–4). Febrés Cordero was unpopular; coup threats continued (Isaacs, 1991: 230–231).

The 1988 Election: A Second Helpful Runoff

In 1988, the long-standing frontrunner, Borja, tallied 25% in the first round; the runner-up with 18% was Abdalá Bucaram of the Partido Roldosista Ecuatoriano (Roldosista Party of Ecuador, PRE). The result of the runoff was uncertain (LAWR, February 19, 1988, p. 10; LARR, April 7, 1988, p. 6). Borja won with 54%. The legitimacy advantage of the runoff was especially important because coup threats still continued (Isaccs, 1991: 230–233).

Borja's positions were more moderate than in the 1984 campaign. Classified at the center-left by Murillo, Oliveros, and Vaishnav (2010: 108–109), Borja proclaimed that he was the "candidate of peace and harmony." For the runoff, Borja pledged not to nationalize any companies and to include businessmen in his government (LAWR, February 18, 1988, p. 11).

Abdalá Bucaram was the nephew of the late Assad Bucaram and gained much of the CFP's political base; Abdalá's comportment worried Ecuador's military just as his uncle's had. As mayor of Guayaquil, Abdalá had insulted the armed forces and gone into exile in Panama; he identified himself with Jesus Christ, Simón Bolívar, and Adolf Hitler. However, especially among the poor on Ecuador's coast, his populist promises were appealing.

The 1992 Election: Ecuador's Only Inefficient Runoff

Once again in 1992, amid austerity policies, the incumbent administration was unpopular, and voters looked to an ideological alternative—in this case, the right. Sixto Durán, the 1978–1979 PSC runner-up, won the first round with 32% and triumphed in the runoff with 57%. Durán's runoff victory was virtually certain (LAWR, July 16, 1992, p. 1).

The key competition was within the right on issues of character. Fiery former president Febrés Cordero had achieved the nomination of his protégé, Jaime Nebot, as the PSC's candidate. As a governor, Nebot was widely perceived to have wielded an iron fist. He was the first-round runner-up.

After Nebot's nomination, Durán had broken with the PSC to found his own party. Durán considered himself the leader of the "rational and civilized right"— in contrast to Febrés Cordero's belligerent, Guayaquil-based clique (Conaghan, 1995: 443). Upon Durán's split from the PSC, he was widely perceived as a principled independent and became the immediate frontrunner. Staunchly pro-market, Durán was classified at the right by Murillo, Oliveros, and Vaishnav (2010: 108–109).

Durán barely finished his term. Durán's market reforms were painful, but GDP growth per capita was approximately zero. Corruption scandals erupted. Durán's party held only 16% of the legislative seats and executive-legislative conflict was intense.

The Problematic 1996 Reversal and Ousting of the President

Overall, the 1996 election, won by Bucaram in a reversal, was fraught. It is unlikely that Bucaram was the Condorcet winner.[21] Like Serrano and Fujimori, Bucaram was corrupt and shifted sharply rightward, alienating his runoff allies.

Voters were dismayed by the failures of the rightist Durán government, and candidates at the center, center-left, or left were expected to fare well. Borja would have been a strong candidate (LARR, March 7, 1996, p. 6). However, apparently, looking at polls, Borja believed—in the event incorrectly—that Nebot was the certain winner and did not compete (LARR, March 7, 1996, p. 6).

In the wake of Borja's decision, the left, center-left, and center divided between two candidates: Freddy Ehlers and Rodrigo Paz. Ehlers and Paz were intense personal rivals (LARR, May 23, 1996, p. 7). A businessman, Paz was the candidate for Popular Democracy; an investigative television journalist, Ehlers was the candidate for the new indigenous-based party, MUPP-NP. As of 1996, Popular Democracy was placed at the center (5.21) and the MUPP-NP at the left (3.63) in PELA surveys. Ehlers had been an ID adviser to Borja and was supported by Borja but was an outsider. Neither Ehlers, with 21% in the first round, nor Paz, with 14%, reached the runoff.

The first-round winner was the PSC's Nebot; he edged out the PRE's Bucaram, 27.2% to 26.3%. For the runoff, Bucaram was favored, but the result was uncertain (LAWR, May 30, 1996, p. 229). Bucaram won by nine points.

Bucaram, who was nicknamed "El Loco" ("the madman"), sought to moderate his image as an intemperate populist. He dismissed his most outrageous previous positions as "youthful excesses."[22] Bucaram worked to build alliances with local indigenous leaders and gained the support of Paz (LAWR, July 18, 1996, p. 313). Bucaram was classified at the center-right (6.25) in PELA surveys, the center-left by Murillo, Oliveros, and Vaishnav (2010: 108–109), and "otherwise" by the World Bank (2013).

After only six months, Bucaram was dismissed by a majority vote of the congress on the grounds of "mental incapacity." (Impeachment would have been the constitutionally correct process, but it required a two-thirds vote and would have taken time.) Although Bucaram's PRE held only 23% of the legislative seats, he had built considerable support for the runoff and it was possible that he could have fashioned a majority; but, almost immediately, Bucaram shifted sharply to the right.[23] He adopted austerity policies, which provoked nationwide strikes and alienated his former left and center-left allies. Moreover, he was widely considered to have led "the most corrupt government in [Ecuador's] history" (Escobar, 1997: A33).

Yet, a first-round victory for Nebot would also have been difficult. Nebot's tally was less than 30%; his PSC was placed at the extreme right in PELA surveys and all the candidates with more than 10% were to his left.

For Ecuador's political leaders, the problematic 1996 election and subsequent ousting of the president were traumatic. The events triggered the 1998 constituent assembly and electoral reforms.

Despite an Auspicious Election in 1998, a Second President Is Ousted

The 1998 election provided the winner, Popular Democracy's Jamil Mahuad, a good start. Mahuad won the first round with 35%. The result of the runoff was uncertain (LAWR, June 9. 1998, p. 256). Mahuad prevailed by slightly less than three points.

Mahuad was a Harvard-educated lawyer, a popular two-time mayor of Quito, and a long-time Popular Democracy leader. At the center in PELA surveys in 1996, Popular Democracy was shifting rightward. For the runoff, Mahuad secured all the major endorsements (LAWR, June 9, 1998, p. 256). By contrast, the first-round runner-up, the PRE's Álvaro Noboa with 27%, was a flashy banana tycoon; a populist, Noboa surged during the first round due to handouts of food, clothing, and the like.

As Mahuad took office, the price of oil hit rock bottom. Then, severe El Niño weather devastated crops, which in turn led to massive defaults on bank loans. In 1999, GDP fell by 7%; Ecuador's currency depreciated 200%; inflation reached 90%; and the fiscal deficit was 5% of GDP (Mejía Acosta, 2009: 129). Interest payments on Ecuador's debt consumed almost half the government budget.[24] However, the International Monetary Fund maintained stringent loan conditions (Hakim, 2000). Desperate, in early January 2000 the Mahuad government adopted the U.S. dollar as Ecuador's currency. But, at the rate of conversion of Ecuador's currency, the sucre, to the dollar, the value of savings and wages in sucres was devastated. Strikes were rampant.

On January 21, 2000, mobilized by Pachakutik and CONAIE, thousands of indigenous protestors stormed government buildings in Quito. They were joined by mid-level military officers led by Colonel Lucio Gutiérrez. These officers were angry at the Mahuad government's reduction of resources for the military and its 1998 border agreement with Peru, which they considered too generous to Peru. Indigenous and military leaders announced a new government; however, they were not supported by top officers. Pressured by the United States and other countries, within the day the armed-forces commander transferred power to the constitutional vice president, Gustavo Noboa.

Noboa achieved a degree of market reform and the IMF was somewhat forthcoming (Mejía Acosta, 2009: 131). However, many Ecuadorians, especially poor and indigenous Ecuadorians, remained angry.

The Fraught 2002 Election and the Ousting of a Third Consecutive President

The 2002 election was problematic overall. The winner was the 2000 coup leader, Gutiérrez. Gutiérrez was an outsider whose first-round victory with 21% was a major surprise (LAWR, October 15, 2002, p. 481). It is likely that Gutiérrez was not the Condorcet winner.

The Condorcet winner might have been one of the two mainstream center or center-left candidates (Quintero López, 2005: 75): León Roldós, the candidate for an eclectic coalition, finishing third with 15%, or the ID's Borja, finishing fourth with 14%. Roldós was the brother of the late former president Jaime Roldós and a former vice-president and university rector. Borja had been the frontrunner in the opinion polls and did not seriously consider an alliance with Roldós. (Also, Roldós was from Guayaquil and Borja from Quito.) Together, the two candidates' first-round tally was greater than the tally of the first-round winner.

Of mixed ethnicity, Gutiérrez appealed to those Ecuadorians who considered his 2000 coup attempt a heroic rebellion. Gutiérrez named his party after his coup attempt: Partido Sociedad Patriótica 21 de enero (Patriotic Society Party January 21, PSP). For the election, Gutiérrez's PSP allied with Pachakutik.

In the first round, Gutiérrez was four points ahead of the runner-up, Álvaro Noboa (the 1998 presidential candidate, not the 2000–2002 president). The outcome of the runoff was uncertain (LAWR, October 22, 2002, p. 493; Quintero López, 2005: 27). Noboa was running not for the controversial PRE but for a new vehicle of his own. Since 1998, he had undertaken popular initiatives such as low-cost health clinics. However, Noboa's business practices were unsavory; he was subject to numerous domestic and international suits and did not move easily among Ecuador's traditional elites. Noboa was placed at the extreme right in PELA surveys.

For the runoff, a vast ideological space opened for Gutiérrez; he began to shift to the center (Quintero López, 2005: 187–189). No longer did he praise Hugo Chávez or wear a green military-style uniform. He traveled to Washington and New York and struck a moderate tone. Although Gutiérrez was endorsed only by the sixth-place PRE, he worked with other parties and gained many of their votes (Quintero López, 2005: 189–191). Gutiérrez won the runoff by ten points.

In office, Gutiérrez faced the same pressures from the IMF that his predecessors had, and he too was perceived by his supporters to succumb to these pressures and shift sharply to the right. In late 2004, in pursuit of legislative allies, Gutiérrez dismissed the Supreme Court; but events spun out of his control and, as protests mounted in April 2005, his removal was called for by the legislature. He was succeeded by Vice President Alfredo Palacio.

The 2006 Election of Rafael Correa in a Reversal

Correa was the long-standing frontrunner for 2006, but Noboa, the 1998 and 2002 runner-up, was the surprise first-round winner (LAWR, October 3, 2006, p. 7). Correa won the runoff by almost fifteen points—a wide margin that points to the legitimacy deficit that Noboa was likely to have suffered had he won the presidency in the first round. But the less confrontational stance that Correa adopted for his runoff victory did not continue and, as a result, Ecuador's Freedom House and V-Dem scores declined.

Correa's first-round loss was widely attributed to fears about his leftist views, aggressive tone, and affinity with Chávez (Romero, 2006). A former professor who held a PhD in economics from the University of Illinois, Correa had served briefly as the economy minister in the Palacio government and was accordingly not an outsider by Corrales' definition. However, running for his own party, Alianza PAIS (Proud and Sovereign Fatherland Alliance), Correa campaigned like an outsider; he constantly berated Ecuador's traditional parties as a *partidocracia* ("dictatorship of the parties"). He promised the dissolution of Ecuador's legislature and a constituent assembly; to show he was serious, his party did not compete in the legislative election. Repudiating a free-trade agreement with the United States and threatening to default on Ecuador's debt, Correa promised a "citizens' revolution" that would end "the long neoliberal night."

At first, the outcome of the runoff was uncertain (LAWR, October 17, 2006, p. 102). Then, Correa moderated (Navia, 2006; LAWR, November 28, 2006, p. 1). He was less combative and more substantive. His previous slogan, *"Dale Correa"* ("Give them [the political establishment] the belt," in a play on *Correa*, which means "belt"), became *"Dale trabajo, desarrollo, y vivienda"* ("Give them work, development, and housing"). As mentioned previously, there was no PELA survey for Ecuador in 2006; but, in 2009, when Correa was maintaining his 2006 policy positions, he was placed at the "moderate left"—3.44.

Correa's 2009 and 2013 Landslides

For the first time during the third wave, runoffs were not necessary in 2009 or 2013. Correa's government was basking in high oil prices; it dramatically enhanced welfare programs and infrastructure. Correa won the 2009 election in the first round with 52% and the 2013 election in the first round with 57%. In the 2009 election, Gutiérrez was the runner-up with 28% and Noboa was in third place; in the 2013 election, the runner-up with 23% was a newcomer, Guillermo Lasso, a former banker.

Correa's landslides appeared to confirm the adage, "Be careful what you wish for." Ecuador's number of parties fell to 3.75 in the 2009 election; Correa's party enjoyed 48% of the seats. The number fell further to 1.83 in the 2013 election; Correa's party enjoyed a majority. However, whereas in the past democracy was hurt by the fragmentation of power, after 2006 it was hurt by the concentration of power. Correa was perceived to bully opposition leaders and harass opposition media in order to achieve his goals, such as a new constitution (approved in 2008).

Conclusion

Overall, in Guatemala, Colombia, Peru, and Ecuador, runoff provided important advantages. In the context of considerable numbers of parties, the first-round winners' tallies were usually low, and legitimacy advantages from runoff were significant. Several reversals, especially in the 2014 election in Colombia and the 2006 election in Peru, were very positive.

Also, runoff was helpful for the incorporation and moderation of the left. In particular, at the start of the third wave, political violence was severe in Guatemala and Colombia in part due to the historic exclusion of the political left. In Guatemala, runoff enhanced legitimacy for a Christian Democrat, Cerezo, in 1985 and facilitated the incorporation of the URNG and eventual triumph of Colom in 2007. In Colombia, this process remained incomplete, but an important advance was the incorporation of the M-19: in the 2006 election, Gaviria, the candidate for the leftist PDA, which included many former M-19 leaders, was the runner-up. Further, in Ecuador, runoff was helpful to the incorporation of the populist left during the country's democratic transition, and in Peru it was helpful to the moderation of Humala between his 2006 campaign and his 2011 victory.

However, in Peru and especially in Ecuador, plurality advocates' concerns were not unfounded. Runoff facilitated a plethora of parties and many parties were indeed "groups of friends"—and sometimes fair-weather friends. Presidents' first-round tallies were often very low and at times presidents might not have been the Condorcet winners. Especially when presidents were unpopular, executive-legislative conflict could be severe. Although I believe that the damages to democracy inflicted during the Serrano, Fujimori, and Bucaram governments were caused primarily by the presidents' own post-runoff ideological turnabouts and corruption, the stage was set by weaknesses in political parties that led in turn to fraught elections.

Yet, in Peru, political leaders continued to favor majority runoff and, in Ecuador, they continued to favor qualified runoff. These leaders knew that the problem of a large number of parties was complex. They knew both that plurality did not necessarily yield a small number of parties and that, as the case of Ecuador under Correa indicated, a small number was not necessarily positive. As I discuss in Chapter 8, there are alternative approaches to the problem of a plethora of parties that do not entail the risks of plurality.

7

Runoff

Is a Reduced Threshold Better? Argentina and Costa Rica

Might a reduced threshold open the electoral arena to newcomers—but not too much, containing party fragmentation? Might a reduced threshold prevent runoffs with virtually certain outcomes that waste resources but still also prevent presidents with small shares of the vote and legitimacy deficits? In short, might a reduced threshold—in particular, 40% with a ten-point lead—be a felicitous compromise between majority runoff and plurality? As Table 2.1 suggested, the trend in Latin America is toward the adoption of a reduced threshold. The two countries that most recently adopted or modified a runoff rule—Bolivia in 2009 and Ecuador in 1998—chose a 40% threshold with a ten-point lead.

Various scholars, including Tanaka (2005: 123), favor a reduced threshold. Also, in the author's surveys among Latin American legislators (see Appendix 1), a considerable number of legislators preferred a threshold of 40% or 45% with a five- or ten-point lead. The preference was more common in plurality than runoff countries. In Chile, 12.5% preferred such a threshold; in Peru, 26%; in Mexico, 39%; and in Paraguay, 56% (McClintock, 2008).

Unfortunately, the question cannot yet be definitively answered. To date, a reduced threshold has been used in only five Latin American countries—Bolivia, Nicaragua, Ecuador, Costa Rica, and Argentina. In Bolivia, Nicaragua, and Ecuador, the number of elections has been insufficient to provide a rigorous test. In Nicaragua, a 45% threshold was used in only its 1995 election. In Bolivia, it was initiated during the government of Evo Morales and, to date, his government endures.

In Ecuador, the reduced threshold has been applied only since 2002 and its impact was difficult to isolate from the impact of Rafael Correa, elected in 2006. In the 2002 and 2006 elections, Ecuador's large number of parties continued; further, the winning party was a new party in both elections. But, after 2006, Correa became very popular and was re-elected in 2009 and in 2013 by wide margins in the first round. The number of parties plummeted. But Correa was concentrating power in his own hands and Ecuador's Freedom House and V-Dem scores fell.

Correa's party is likely to retain a political base approximating 40% for some time, complicating the challenge for Ecuador's opposition parties. For example, in the 2017 election, Correa's party (under the leadership of Lenín Moreno) tallied 39.4% in the first round against a divided opposition and accordingly almost escaped a runoff, which Moreno won very narrowly (51% to 49%). In any case, the leadership of Correa was much more important to the political changes in Ecuador after 2002 than the reduced threshold.

The two countries that provide a rigorous test of the reduced threshold are Costa Rica and Argentina, but they are not ideal. Both Costa Rica and Argentina enjoyed at least average historical records of democracy; Costa Rica held Latin America's best record and it is difficult to distinguish the effects of its favorable heritage from the effects of its electoral rules. In Costa Rica, a moderate leftist party was already incorporated at the start of the third wave. Further, Costa Rica's reduced threshold is anomalous because it does not include a requirement for a lead.

Still, the two cases of Costa Rica and Argentina are suggestive. Barriers to entry were raised. The average number of parties in both Costa Rica and Argentina was below the average for the region. In Costa Rica, where the two long-standing parties were not widely deemed a duopoly, the barriers were not too high. But, in Argentina, where a cartel party with an authoritarian past was strong, the barriers did appear too high. As indicated in Chapter 3, Argentina was the only runoff country in which the dominant party prior to the third wave—the Peronist Party—was even more dominant in 2012. Also, Argentina was one of only two runoff countries in which the two leading parties were the same in the last third-wave election as in the first.

Further, in Costa Rica and Argentina, the reduced threshold voided runoffs that wasted resources but also runoffs that would have enhanced the president's legitimacy. In two of the four elections in which a reduced threshold voided a runoff—Costa Rica's 2010 election and Argentina's 2007 election—the result was virtually certain. In the other two elections—Argentina's 1995 and 1999 elections[1]—the result was uncertain and a runoff would have enhanced the president's legitimacy. In Argentina's 1999 election, the legitimacy deficit was serious.

The incentives for ideological moderation remained with a reduced threshold. In neither Costa Rica nor Argentina was a party winning more than 15% placed at an ideological extreme.

The 40% Threshold and Presidential Legitimacy

In the effort to assess whether or not a 40% threshold would void runoffs that waste resources but not runoffs that enhance presidential legitimacy, I examined elections in countries in addition to the country cases in this chapter. I re-visited the information in Appendix 6; previously, in Table 3.3, this information was the basis for determinations of the likely results of sixty-six elections, including both first-round elections under runoff and plurality elections, between 1978 (or the first free and fair election of the third wave) and 2012 that were won with less than 50%. For this chapter, I assessed whether or not a 40% threshold with a ten-point lead—the most common reduced threshold—came into play or would have come into play. In other words, I identified the elections in which the first-round winner tallied at least 40% with a ten-point lead but not 50% and, accordingly, a runoff either was not held or would not have been held if the threshold had been reduced. Then, I assessed whether or not the first-round winner's victory was virtually certain or whether the result was uncertain or a reversal was likely (see Appendix 6).

The number of elections in which a 40% threshold with a ten-point lead came into play or would have come into play was eighteen. I determined that, in nine of these elections, the first-round winner's victory was virtually certain. However, also in nine, the first-round winner's victory was not virtually certain. In eight the result was uncertain, and in one (Paraguay in 1993) a reversal was likely. In my view, a legitimacy deficit in half the elections is too many.

Since the 2012 end year for the elections I analyzed in depth, several elections have indicated the possibility of significant legitimacy deficits if thresholds are reduced. In El Salvador in 2014, the FMLN's candidate, former guerrilla commander Salvador Sánchez Cérén, tallied 48.93% in the first round to 38.96% for ARENA's candidate; El Salvador's electoral arena was polarized and a victory for a former guerrilla commander without 50% would have been questioned. Indeed, Sánchez Cérén won the runoff by less than one percentage point. In Peru in 2016, the first-round winner, Keiko Fujimori, the divisive daughter of the former authoritarian president, tallied 39.86%—only .14 from 40%, and almost twenty points more than the runner-up, Pedro Pablo Kuczynski. But, in a reversal, Kuczynski won the runoff by a razor-thin margin. Similarly, as just mentioned, in Ecuador in 2017, Moreno was less than 1 percentage point from 40% and, without a runoff, a legitimacy deficit.

Costa Rica

Costa Rica is Latin America's democratic star. It is one of three Latin American nations that did not suffer a military coup during the Cold War and, in comparison to the other two nations of this set (Colombia and Venezuela), its democracy fared much better during the third wave. For most of the third wave, Costa Rica enjoyed perfect Freedom House scores; its score was the second-best possible, 3, only during 1993–2003. Also, almost invariably, Costa Rica's V-Dem scores were at the regional apex; these scores were steady, without a 1999–2003 dip. On the other hand, although the vote is mandatory, turnout has been only about the Latin American average; between 1978 and 1994, it averaged roughly 80%, but between 1998 and 2010 fell below 70%, and the decline worried analysts.[2]

Costa Rica's excellent third-wave record is commensurate with its historical experience. Costa Rica's average Polity score for 1900–1977 was a perfect 10, by far the best in Latin America (Pèrez-Liñán and Mainwaring, 2013: 381). Costa Rica's 2009 per capita income was slightly above the Latin American average (World Bank, 2011: 10–12).

Costa Rica was the only Latin American country with runoff prior to the third wave. It adopted its 40% threshold, without a lead, in 1936. A 1926 rule for a runoff in the legislature if the first-round winner did not secure 50% was proving problematic. Accordingly, it was decided that a 40% threshold would increase the possibility that the election would be won in the first round but would prevent victory by a minority party; and, the runoff would be by direct popular vote (Lehoucq, 2004: 140–142).

Both scholars and political leaders have been enthusiastic about Costa Rica's rule. Lehoucq (2004: 133) stated, "Citizens and politicians alike agree that 40 per cent qualified-plurality with a second-round runoff is a great way to elect presidents." Both former President Miguel Angel Rodríguez Echeverría and Lehoucq believe that, in Costa Rica, qualified runoff encouraged a focus on "the median voter" (Rodríguez Echeverría, 2006: 163; Lehoucq, 2005: 144–145). Political leaders endorsing the runoff with a 40% threshold include former president Óscar Arias, former president Miguel Angel Rodríguez Echeverría, and former vice-president Kevin Casas-Zamora.[3] Although only one of Costa Rica's nine third-wave elections—the 2002 election—went to a runoff, it was very likely to have enhanced the president's legitimacy.

However, it is unfortunate that Costa Rica's 40% threshold is not accompanied by a lead. Both the winners and the runners-up in Costa Rica's 1998 and 2006 elections tallied between 40% and 49.9% in the first round and the results of runoffs would have been uncertain; but, without a lead, runoffs were not held. After the 2006 election, criticisms of the absence of a lead were common.

As noted already, Costa Rica's reduced threshold raised barriers to entry. Barriers to entry were raised too by closed legislative lists and seat-allocation rules (Wilson, 1999; 760; Lehoucq, 2005: 146–147). Indeed, they were raised further by campaign-finance rules; a party was required to win 4% of the national vote or a legislative seat in the previous election to qualify for public funds and these funds were allocated on the basis of the percentage of votes received in the previous election (Wilson, 2007: 713). Presidential and legislative elections were concurrent.

Some scholars (Lehoucq, 2005; Wilson, 1999: 759–760) worried that, from the mid-1990s through the early 2000s, Costa Rica's Partido Liberación Nacional (National Liberation Party, PLN) and Partido Unidad Social Cristiana (Social Christian Unity Party, PUSC) were a duopoly. The parties were not perceived to be open to citizen input (Lehoucq, 2005: 146–147; Seligson, 2002: 180). Costa Rica hosted a large number of "autonomous institutions" for the provision of medical care, electricity, telephone service, and the like; increasingly the two parties "began to collude at the task of colonizing the autonomous bodies with their respective loyalists" (Lehoucq, 2005: 148). Programmatic differences were eroding (Lehoucq, 2005: 147); amid the challenges of the debt crisis and structural adjustment, PLN leaders (although not the party itself) and the PUSC were placed at the center-right or right in PELA surveys.

However, other scholars (Levitsky, 2001: 99) argued that "cartel-like collusion between the parties ... [was] not as strongly present" in Costa Rica as in Latin American duopolies. The PLN, founded in 1951, and the PUSC (which had several precursors), founded in 1983, were relatively young. And between the two parties, if not among the leaders, there were programmatic differences. With its founder triumphant in a civil war in 1948, the PLN had implemented ambitious social reforms; traditionally, it was placed to the left of the PUSC. Through 1994, the PLN was at the center-left for Murillo, Oliveros, and Vaishnav (2010: 108) and Coppedge (1997: 20); for 1994–2002, it was at the center in PELA surveys.

In addition, party openness was encouraged by several rules. Between 1969 and 2003, re-election of the president was banned. In the 1980s, presidential primaries were not working well, but they were gradually conducted with greater transparency (Booth, Wade, and Walker, 2010: 73; Lehoucq, 2005: 146–147).

Ultimately, the PLN and the PUSC were not able to exclude new parties from the political arena. In the 2002 election, a new party, the Partido Acción Ciudadana (Citizen Action Party, PAC), which demanded ethical governance and criticized the market, finished third and, in 2014, it won. As of 2002, Costa Rica's two-party system ended; the number of parties across the 2002–2010 elections averaged 3.6 (versus the 1990–2014 regional average among runoff countries of 4.98).

There were reasons beyond electoral rules for Costa Rica's traditionally small number of parties. The only significant political cleavage was left-right ideology; there were no cleavages around a long-standing party with authoritarian proclivities or around geographic regions of the country. Also, between 1978 and 1994, Costa Rica's two major parties enjoyed overwhelming support because they were perceived to be governing effectively (Rivas, 2004: 209, 224–226; Seligson, 2002: 161). And, as mentioned, an opening to the center-left—the PLN—had already been made.

Presidential Elections 1978–1994: PLN and PUSC Dominance

Between 1978 and 1994, there were five elections; together, the PLN and the PUSC or its precursor won approximately 95% of the vote in all five. The winner secured at least 50% in all five. The PLN won three and the PUSC or its precursor, two. The number of parties did not exceed 2.50. Although some six to eight presidential candidates competed, most were irrelevant. As mentioned previously, both parties had clear ideological positions—roughly, the PLN at the center-left and the PUSC at the center-right.

A particularly successful president was Óscar Arias (1986–1990), who won the 1987 Nobel Peace Prize for his work for peace in Central America and also promoted the diversification of Costa Rica's economy. Pressure to allow the re-election of Arias was key to the 2003 change in Costa Rica's constitution.

But, the 1994–1998 PLN government of José María Figueres was unpopular. A toll was taken not only by the debt crisis and market reform, which dismantled welfare programs, but also by corruption scandals. Costa Ricans' support for the political system eroded (Seligson, 2002: 166–168).

The 1998 and 2002 Elections: The Erosion of PLN and PUSC Dominance

Both the 1998 and 2002 elections were won by the PUSC with the PLN in second place, but the two parties were not as dominant as previously. The economy was stagnant and Costa Ricans were dissatisfied: voter turnout dropped, the number of candidates from new parties jumped, and media criticism of the equivalence and corruption of the PLN and PUSC intensified (Corella, 1999).

The 1998 election was won by the PUSC's Miguel Angel Rodríguez with 47% to 45% for the PLN candidate, José Miguel Corrales. If a runoff had been required, its outcome would have been uncertain. Together, eleven candidates not from the PLN or the PUSC took 8%. Both the third-place candidate with 3%, Vladimir De La Cruz De Lemos, and a candidate tied for fourth with 1.4%, Sherman Thomas Jackson, were placed at the left (Corella, 1999: 304–309); most of their votes were likely to have gone to the PLN. However, the outcome was not disputed. Prior to the election, Rodríguez had been leading the opinion polls by more than ten points; his victory was expected.

After the 1998 election, Ottón Solís, a former PLN economics minister and legislator, broke from the party to form the PAC. Solís denounced the PLN as a "corrupt clique" (LARR, February 19, 2002, p. 1). Solís's PAC was classified at the center-left by PELA. Four months before the 2002 election, Solís had only 3% of voters' preferences in polls; but he performed well in a televised debate and, about three weeks before the election, had 20% (LARR, January 15, 2002, p. 3).

The 2002 election was the only election that went to a runoff. In the first round, Abel Pacheco of the PUSC tallied 39%; the runner-up, Rolando Araya of the PLN, 31%; and Solís, 26%. The outcome of the runoff was uncertain and it enhanced presidential legitimacy (Rivas, 2004: 224; LAWR, February 5, 2002, p. 67). Still, Solís might have been the election's Condorcet winner (Wilson, 2003: 513).

Given that there were only eight points between Pacheco and Araya, Solís's votes appeared likely to determine the outcome and, given that Solís was a former PLN leader, it would have been expected that most of his votes would go to Araya (LAWR, February 5, 2002, p. 67). However, Solís declined to endorse either candidate, proclaiming that "we can't continue voting for the lesser of two evils" (Wilson, 2003: 514). Apparently, Solís's message resonated. Many Solís voters stayed home (Wilson, 2003: 514).

Pacheco won the runoff handily, with 58%. Pacheco was not a traditional PUSC politician. Although Pacheco was a former legislator, he was best known as a psychiatrist and television personality. He campaigned with a folksy style on an anti-corruption platform.

However, during the Pacheco government, the PUSC was wracked by corruption charges. In 2004, its two most recent former presidents, Rafael Angel Calderón (1990–1994) and Miguel Angel Rodríguez (1998–2002), were arrested on corruption charges. The arrests provided further ammunition for the PAC.

The 2006 Election and 2010 Elections: The Eclipse of the PUSC by the PAC

The 2006 election was won by former PLN president Óscar Arias with 41%, but the PAC's Solís was in second place with 40%. The PUSC was a distant fourth. Arias ran on his first-term achievements but also advocated the Central American Free Trade Agreement (CAFTA-DR); by contrast, Solís opposed CAFTA-DR and market economics in general (Wilson, 2007: 714).

The victory with only 41% by less than one point led to a legitimacy deficit and criticism of the absence of a lead requirement (LAWR, February 14, 2006, p. 14). Most analysts believed that it was impossible to know the re-direction of the remaining 19% of the vote (LAWR, February 7, 2006, p. 13). In third place with 8% was Otto Guevara of the Movimiento Libertario (Libertarian Movement); although Guevara was placed at the extreme right by PELA, and accordingly closer to the PLN, the Libertarian Movement and the PAC had worked together in the legislature against PLN corruption. Similarly, despite ideological differences, the PUSC indicated its preference for the PAC (Wilson, 2007: 715).

Did the questions about Arias' legitimacy matter? On the one hand, the electoral result was by and large accepted by Costa Ricans (LAWR, February 21, 2006, p. 14; LARR, March 2006, p. 5). Despite vote counts that gave one candidate the victory one week and the other the next, both Arias and Solís were restrained (Vargas Cullell, 2007: 118–119). On the other hand, the view was widespread that a key issue of the election—Costa Rica's entry into CAFTA-DR—had not been decided. A legislative dispute ensued for months. Finally, it was agreed that Costa Rica's first referendum would be held; Costa Rica's entry into CAFTA-DR was narrowly approved in 2007.

Overall, Arias' second term was considered successful. He again won respect as a regional statesman, this time for his efforts to resolve the political crisis in Honduras after the 2009 coup. New conditional cash transfer, pension, and student and home loan programs were popular.

In the context of Arias' popularity, the 2010 election was won easily by his former justice minister and security minister and protégé, Laura Chinchilla, with 47%. With 25%, Solís was again the runner-up. The PUSC remained in disarray; the party tallied less than 4%.

A runoff would have been virtually certain to be won by Chinchilla (LAWR, February 11, 2010, p. 1). The Libertarian Movement's Guevara finished third with 21%. With Solís at the center-left, Chinchilla at the right, and Guevara at the extreme right in PELA surveys, it is extremely unlikely that Solís could have won most of Guevara's votes.

Solís fared less well in 2010 than in 2006 primarily because corruption was less salient and security more salient. Guevara focused on the problem of crime and advocated a hard line.

The 2014 Election: Victory for the PAC

Although the 2014 election is past the end date for my in-depth analysis, its result was important, confirming the openness of Costa Rica's political arena to a new party, the PAC. The election was the second in Costa Rica's third wave to go to a runoff.

Chinchilla's government was unpopular and the 2014 PLN candidate, Johnny Araya, faced a difficult race. For many months, it appeared that his major rival would be José María Villalta, an irreverent candidate with socialist roots leading a new leftist party, the Frente Amplio (Broad Front) (LAWR, January 23, 2014, p. 1). But Villalta was hit hard by the other candidates and the media, and nervous voters turned to the moderate left, represented by the PAC's Luis Guillermo Solís (no relation to the PAC's former standard bearer) (LAWR, February 6, 2014, p. 2). Defying the opinion polls, Solís won the first round with 31%. For the runoff, Solís was so far ahead of the PLN's Araya that Araya suspended his campaign. The runoff was held and gave Solís a whopping 78%.

Argentina

Argentina's level of democracy was considerably above the regional average. In the 1990s, Argentina's modal Freedom House score was 5; in the 2000s, 4. Argentina's V-Dem scores were steadily above .600 until dipping after 2007. Average voter turnout was 80%. This level of democracy was better than Argentina's historical record; Argentina's average Polity score for 1900–1977 was only middling for Latin American countries (Pérez-Liñán and Mainwaring, 2013: 381).

However, Argentina was wealthy, with its per capita income among the highest in Latin America (World Bank, 2011: 10–12). Arguably, Argentina's third-wave record was somewhat disappointing.

At the start of the third wave, plurality was in force, but was not problematic in either the 1983 or 1989 election. Runoff with a reduced threshold was adopted in 1994 within a package of electoral reforms negotiated by the incumbent president, the Peronist Carlos Saúl Menem, and the former president, Raúl Alfonsín of the Unión Cívica Radical (Radical Civic Union or Radical Party, UCR), and approved in a constituent assembly. As Table 2.1 indicated, there were two thresholds: either (a) 45% or (b) 40% with a ten-point lead.

The runoff with a reduced threshold was a compromise between the Peronist Party and the Radical Party. As the predominant party with the strongest political base, the Peronist Party preferred plurality; as the second leading party but prone to division, the Radical Party preferred majority runoff (Negretto, 2013: 158–161). Radical leaders also favored runoff because they continued to rue the debacle of the 1963 election, in which the Radical president, Illia, had been elected with only 32% (see Chapter 3). Further, the number of parties was increasing (2.23 in the 1983 election, 2.79 in the 1989 election, and 3.15 in the 1991 midterm election), galvanizing concerns in numerous quarters about presidential legitimacy (Cabrera, 1996; Negretto, 2004).

The advantages of runoff were particularly evident in the 2003 election. The first-round winner, Menem, had only 24.5% of the vote and so little support beyond his first-round electorate that he withdrew. It was very clear that Menem was not the choice of a majority and that a Menem presidency would have been devoid of legitimacy.

As mentioned above, Argentina's reduced threshold voided runoffs that would have been helpful in the 1995 and 1999 elections (Novaro, 2004). This was especially the case in the 1999 election; a legitimacy deficit was likely to have been one factor in the 2001 resignation of the president amid financial collapse and massive protests.

Further, Argentina's reduced threshold raised barriers to entry, favoring its predominant Peronist Party—an entrenched party with authoritarian proclivities—and its second leading party, the Radical Party (Novaro, 2004: 50–53; Mustapic, 2002: 169). In a context of two parties with political bases of about 40%, any new party that divided the opposition to the other party doomed the opposition to defeat. Yet, despite the reduced threshold and these implications, new parties emerged. Between 1995 and 2002, Argentina's number of parties averaged only about 2.75; but, between 2003 and 2014, it averaged approximately 4.30, only a tad below the regional average.

The reduced threshold was particularly advantageous to the Peronist Party. Said Sergio Berensztein in 2015, "The threshold was established to fit the requisites of Peronism."[4] In particular, for many years it appeared that a new opposition party could win only in alliance with the Radical Party. This belief impeded the rise of the new Frente para un País Solidario (Front for a Country in Solidarity, FREPASO), which had a promising start in the 1995 election but entered an alliance with the Radical Party for the 1999 election that proved fraught.

The predominance of the Peronist Party was facilitated by other rules also. In particular, the Peronist Party (and to a lesser extent the Radical Party) had robust clientelist networks in Argentina's provinces, and provincial party leaders were powerful (Jones and Hwang, 2005: 115–116). Until 2001, provincial legislators indirectly elected the country's senators for nine-year terms. Also, election to the lower house was through a proportional representation formula that was skewed in favor of small, remote provinces and the Peronist Party was strong in these provinces; in part as a result, between 1983 and 2012 the Peronists held a plurality of the seats in the Senate and, with the exception of the 1983–1989 Radical government, in the Chamber of Deputies also (Calvo and Murillo, 2005: 208–213). Argentina's two third-wave Radical presidents were weakened by limited support for their party in the legislature and by the Peronists' greater capacity to mobilize social protest (Calvo and Murillo, 2005: 208–210).

Amid the 1994 electoral-reform package, various new rules were adopted (Negretto, 2013: 155). Menem achieved his key goal: permission for one consecutive presidential re-election. In return, the Radical Party achieved direct election of the president (not through an electoral college) and the reduction of the president's term from six years to four. Also, as of 2001, senators were to be directly elected for six years (with one-third of the senators renewed every two years), rather than indirectly elected by provincial legislators for nine years. Other rules remained constant: legislative lists were closed and legal requirements for party formation were low (Levitsky, 2005: 84).

As a result of the reduction of the president's term from six to four years, the degree of concurrence between legislative and presidential elections was greater. Prior to 1994, legislative elections were held every two years and two of these elections were not concurrent with the presidential election; subsequently, legislative elections were still held every two years but only one was not concurrent with the presidential election.

Argentina's Two Leading Political Parties and the 1983 and 1989 Elections under Plurality

Both the Peronist Party and the Radical Party were flawed. As Chapter 3 indicated, the Peronist Party had an authoritarian past (Chen, 2014; Anderson, 2009). For most analysts, its authoritarian origins have not been overcome. Commented Michael Reid in 2015, "[Peronist] exercise of power is characterised by the strong leader and control of the Argentine street. Almost all Peronist presidents have concentrated power in their own hands."[5] Stated Leslie Anderson (2009: 769), "[The Peronist Party] began as an authoritarian, verticalist party tied to a single charismatic leader [Perón]" and "the authoritarian roots of the party still emerge periodically." Anderson (2009: 770, 773) also criticized the Radical Party as "elitist," with leaders who were "unable to compromise."

The Peronist Party was founded in 1944 by Colonel Juan Domingo Perón. In 1939–1941, Perón was assigned to Italy, and, like numerous Argentine officers, gave considerable thought to Benito Mussolini's ideology. Returning to Argentina, in 1943 Perón became the minister of labor in a military government; he prioritized the country's workers. He was elected president in 1946 and re-elected in 1952. However, in 1952 his popular wife, "Evita," died and Perón's support began to erode. The economy was troubled. Perón began to persecute opposition parties and censor independent media. A confrontation erupted between Perón and the Catholic Church, and Peronist militants set fire to several churches. Perón also sought to subordinate the military to his authority. Perón fell to a military coup in 1956; Perón was exiled and the Peronist Party prohibited from electoral competition. But the party retained considerable support, especially within Argentina's labor movement, and subsequent governments struggled to achieve legitimacy.

Finally, in 1973, a stand-in for Perón was allowed to run for president; he won, and soon Perón returned to the presidency. But he died in 1974 and was succeeded by his vice-president, his wife, Isabel Perón. Several revolutionary groups were active in Argentina and Isabel Perón became complicit with repressive forces. She fell to a coup in 1976.

The Radical Party, founded as the Unión Cívica in 1889, was one of the oldest leading parties in Latin America. In the late nineteenth century, Argentina's political regime was oligarchic. The Radical Party was the first to demand free and fair elections and universal male suffrage. The Radical Party was elected in 1916 but, amid the Great Depression, was ousted in a military coup in 1930. Emphasizing the values of honesty and democracy, the Radical Party returned to power in the 1958 election and, with Illia, won the 1963 election; but, in the context of the prohibition of the Peronist Party, effective democratic governance was difficult. Between 1995 and 2010, the Radical Party was consistently classified at the center-right in PELA surveys.

The 1983 election was won by the Radical Party with 52% to 40% for the Peronists.[6] The Radicals' candidate was Raúl Alfonsín, a human-rights lawyer and long-standing party leader; the Peronists' candidate was Italo Luder, a former senator and former acting president. More than ten other parties competed but fared poorly.

The result was a surprise. The Peronists had won every election in which they had been allowed to compete since 1946. But, after the military's massive human-rights abuses during what was called the "Dirty War" and its defeat in the Falklands-Malvinas war, the Radicals were helped by their democratic image. Also, the Peronists were bickering.

Amid the debt crisis, Argentina's economy was in dire straits. The Alfonsín government struggled. It introduced an austerity program, provoking massive protests led by the Peronist labor movement. It also initiated judicial processes against military officers for human-rights violations; these sparked military rebellions.

The Peronists' Menem won in 1989 with 49%; the Radicals' Eduardo Angeloz tallied 37%. In third place with 7% was the Alianza del Centro (Alliance of the Center), which included a new rightist party, the Unión del Centro Democrático (Union of the Democratic Center, UCeDé). In fourth and fifth places were two leftist parties. If the election had gone to a runoff, Menem's victory was likely but not certain (LARR, April 20, 1989, pp. 4–5).

Menem was a popular, flamboyant governor. He was a "populist" who represented 'old-style Peronism'" (LAWR, July 21, 1988, p. 8; LAWR, August 25, 1988, p. 2). He "built a coalition of 'the political cadavers of Peronism,' ... including old-guard unionists and rump cadre organizations of the left ... *and right* ... [italics in original] (Levitsky, 2003: 170). His platform was "vague and contradictory" (LAWR, May 11, 1989, p. 2). Menem was controversial even within the Peronist Party; in a 1988 primary, Menem only narrowly defeated another Peronist governor who represented the social-democratic sector of the party (Levitsky, 2003: 123).

The Radicals' Angeloz was also a popular governor. But, amid the severe economic crisis and the military rebellions that were wracking the Alfonsín government, the odds were against him. Still, Angeloz was gaining momentum and the number of undecided voters was large. In the month before the election, it appeared possible that Angeloz would win (LAWR, May 18, 1989, p. 2).

What would have happened in a runoff? If there were setbacks to Menem, a Radical victory was possible. The UCeDé fervently favored market reform; almost all of its votes would have gone to Angeloz (LARR, April 20, 1989, p. 5). Argentina's socialist left was no fan of Peronism.

Almost immediately after his election, Menem reversed his campaign promises and implemented market reform. Suddenly, the Peronist Party, with its political base in Argentina's labor movement, was shifting right—facilitated by the acquiescence of the labor movement (Levitsky, 2003: 150–157). To implement reform, Menem issued an unprecedented number of constitutionally dubious decrees and stacked the Supreme Court. Menem also pardoned top military officers convicted of human-rights violations.

By 1992, economic growth was strong and Menem was popular. It was in this context that Menem pursued the removal of the ban against immediate re-election of the president.

The 1995 Election: The Eclipse of the Radical Party by FREPASO

Menem won the 1995 election with 49.9% in the first round. The surprise of the election was the eclipse of the Radical Party by FREPASO. FREPASO Senator

José Octavio Bordón was the runner-up with 29%; the Radicals' Governor Horacio Massaccesi tallied 17%.

As the election approached, Menem was questioned. Economic growth was slowing, unemployment was at record levels, and the trade deficit was large. These problems as well as "excessive dependence on foreign capital inflows" were cited by the numerous Peronist leaders who, in general, were shocked by Menem's abrupt shift to the right (Levitsky, 2003: 173). Concern about corruption was widespread.

FREPASO was built by both dissident Peronists, dismayed by the Menem government, and dissident Radicals, dismayed by the concessions granted to Menem by Alfonsín in the electoral reform. FREPASO ran "a campaign with a strong moral and institutional slant" (Torre, 2005: 170). Placed at the center-left in the 1995 PELA survey, FREPASO was filling an ideological space that had been left empty by the Peronists and the Radicals. FREPASO's candidate, dissident Peronist Bordón, rose rapidly in the polls. Untainted by corruption, Bordón emphasized honesty, efficiency, and democracy—and also social sensitivity (LAWR, April 13, 1995, p. 158; LARR, June 1, 1995, p. 3).

The Radicals' Massaccesi faced an uphill battle. As governor, his handling of a budget crisis had been questioned. Also, the Radical Party was divided on the electoral reform; with Alfonsín, Massaccesi had favored it.

As in 1989, if the election had gone to a runoff, a Peronist victory was likely but not certain. There was "a potential majority against [Menem]" (LAWR, April 13, 1995, p. 158). Bordón would have secured most of the Radical vote. Indeed, Menem was "unsettled" about this possibility; as Bordón took the lead in the polls from the Radical candidate, Menem claimed that the polls were wrong (LAWR, April 20, 1995, p. 178).

The 1995 election showed that there was political space in Argentina for a social-democratic left (Torre, 2005: 170). It showed too that Bordón was an appealing candidate who had a good chance to win in 1999 (Mustapic, 2002: 169).[7] However, it also appeared to show that, if the Peronist Party were not to win 40% with a ten-point lead, an alliance between the Radical Party and FREPASO would be necessary (Novaro, 2004: 47–48). In the event, this was not the case, but it was the conventional wisdom at the time.

Bordón was not eager for an alliance with the Radical Party (Leiras, 2007: 140–142). It was very unlikely that the Radicals would cede the top spot on the 1999 ticket to FREPASO.[8]

A year or two after the 1995 election, Bordón left FREPASO to return to the Peronist fold. Not only was Bordón wary of an alliance with the Radical Party, but in 1996 he quarreled with FREPASO leader Graciela Fernández Meijide about the party's candidate for mayor of Buenos Aires. Also, with the imminent end to Menem's presidency, changes in the Peronist Party were again likely. Bordón's departure was "a hard blow" to FREPASO (Novaro, 2010: 264).

Menem's second term was problematic. Serious corruption scandals erupted and economic storm clouds gathered. These challenges were believed to have been complicated by concerns about Menem's possible lack of majority support (Novaro, 2004: 55).

The 1999 Election: A Problematic Victory with 48%

Amid division in the Peronist Party, the election of 1999 was won in the first round by the Radical Party's Fernando De la Rúa with 48%. De la Rúa was the candidate of a coalition between the Radical Party and FREPASO that was called the Alianza por el Trabajo, la Educación, y la Justicia (the Alliance for Jobs, Justice, and Education). Without 50%, De la Rúa suffered a legitimacy deficit (Novaro, 2004: 53).

De la Rúa was the mayor of Buenos Aires and an experienced Radical leader. However, De la Rúa was flawed. He was nominated as the Alliance's candidate through an open primary, which favored the Radical Party because its grassroots networks were much stronger than FREPASO's. De la Rúa was widely considered a "political lightweight."[9] Further, he was far to the right within the Radical Party and even further to the right within the Alliance as a whole (Novaro, 2004: 51).[10] He tended to be dismissive of FREPASO (Jones and Hwang, 2005: 132).

As in 1989 and 1995, in 1999 the first-round winner would have been likely but not certain to prevail in a runoff. The Peronist Party divided between a leftist critic of Menem, Governor Eduardo Duhalde, with 39%, and a rightist supporter of Menem, his former finance minister, Domingo Cavallo, with 10%. Probably, in a runoff Duhalde would have been endorsed by his fellow Peronist and would have won most of Cavallo's votes (LAWR, September 7, 1999, p. 409; Negretto, 2004: 118).

Within two years, Argentina was in turmoil. Argentina's economic storm clouds hit with devastating force. De la Rúa was poorly positioned to cope. He remained dismissive of FREPASO; for example, among his first ten key cabinet officials, there were only two FREPASO members (LARR, December 21, 1999, p. 2). Allegedly, in October 2000, the De la Rúa government bribed eleven senators for their votes for a labor reform bill; then, it resisted an investigation. The FREPASO vice-president, former legislator Carlos Álvarez, resigned; an ex-Peronist who was considered smart and dynamic (LARR, December 22, 1998, p. 2), Álvarez might have been an effective advocate for de la Rúa if the Alliance had held.

De la Rúa resigned in December 2001. His resignation is likely to have been "the final blow to Radicalism as a competitive electoral party"; it "made the party seem unable or unwilling to govern" (Anderson, 2009: 774). Still, despite the Radical Party's weakening, it remained the second largest party in Argentina's legislature (see Chapter 3). For its part, FREPASO "disintegrated" (Levitsky and Murillo, 2005: 40). After several interim presidents, the 1999 runner-up, Duhalde, was chosen president by Argentina's two legislative houses in January 2002. Argentina's 2001 Freedom House score plummeted three points.

The 2003 Election: An Invaluable Reversal

The Peronist Party was poised for victory in 2003 but was divided into four factions. The rightist faction was led by old-timer Menem; he won the first round, but with only 24.5%. The first-round runner-up, Néstor Kirchner, a Duhalde protégé and governor, led the second major faction, the Frente para la Victoria (Front for Victory), and was the runner-up with 22%. Fearing a defeat of humiliating proportions, Menem withdrew from the runoff and Kirchner prevailed.

By 2003, Menem was anathema to most Argentines (Jeter, 2003; Rohter, 2003). His economic policies were considered complicit in Argentina's 2001–2002 financial collapse. In 2001, he had been arrested on charges of arms trafficking. But Menem was bent on re-election.

Kirchner was forecast to win the runoff by forty points (Levitsky and Murillo, 2005: 41). Placed at the center-left in PELA surveys, Kirchner promised a renovation of Peronism and a tough line in negotiations with the International Monetary Fund. He was believed likely to win most of the votes of the Peronist candidate in fourth place and was endorsed by the candidate in fifth place, Elisa Carrió, a former beauty queen, multi-term Radical legislator, and anti-corruption and human-rights advocate (LAWR, May 6, 2003, p. 198).

Menem ceded victory to Kirchner less than a week before the runoff. Kirchner accused Menem of trying to weaken the incoming president's mandate. Kirchner's concern was shared by numerous analysts; even in a country where a runoff had never been held, it was widely perceived to be critical to a president's legitimacy after a close first round.[11]

The Kirchner government was popular. Kirchner's nationalistic defiance of the International Monetary Fund was widely credited with restoring economic growth. His government advanced human-rights initiatives.

The 2007 and 2011 Elections: Predominance for Cristina Fernández de Kirchner

Both the 2007 and 2011 elections were won in the first round by Cristina Fernández de Kirchner, Néstor's wife, running for the Front for Victory faction of the Peronist Party. In 2007, she tallied 45% with more than a twenty-point lead over the runner-up. In 2011, she tallied 54%.

In both elections, Fernández de Kirchner was the odds-on favorite. In 2007, she was not only the first lady but a former three-term senator. In 2011, she was a widow with a huge a sympathy vote. Despite setbacks (in particular a failed attempt to raise taxes on soybean exports), her government was popular. During 2003–2011, economic growth was stellar, averaging more than 7% annually, and the poor were helped by major redistributive policies. Her government continued human-rights advances.

However, there were concerns about Fernández de Kirchner's commitment to democratic principles. Although these concerns did not prompt a decline in Argentina's Freedom House score, they did prompt a gradual decline between 2002 and 2015 of about .100 in its V-Dem Liberal Democracy score. Fernández de Kirchner's abuses were described by Noam Lupu (2016: 47): "Over her two terms, she centralized ever more legislative and fiscal authority within the executive branch. She won emergency powers from Congress to make momentous fiscal decisions.... And her administration only selectively enforced the Supreme Court's rulings against it. Faced with heavy media criticism, ... she imposed new regulations on the country's media conglomerates. And when the independent INDEC [National Institute of Statistics and Censuses] published unfavorable economic figures and the Central Bank refused to provide the government with cash, she ousted their leaders."

Might majority runoff have made a difference? In the 2011 election, almost certainly not. The runner-up, Hermes Binner, a governor for the small Socialist Party, had only 17%. Possibly, however, it would have made a difference in the 2007 election. The 2007 runner-up with 23% was Carrió, the former Radical who had finished fifth in 2003, now running for the Coalición Cívica (Civic Coalition). It was virtually certain that Carrió would have lost a runoff. Her executive experience was limited. She was placed at the left in the 2004 and 2008 PELA surveys but would have had to court the third-place and fourth-place candidates, both Peronists to her right. Still, with a runoff, political space would have been opened. Opinion polls had underestimated the support for the opposition; with the presumption of victory, Fernández de Kirchner traveled outside the country and eschewed debates (LAWR, October 25, 2007, p. 6). After Carrió's first-round performance, she would have catalyzed discussion.

The 2015 Election

Although the 2015 election is past the end date for my in-depth analysis, its result is important for the implications of the reduced threshold. The reduced threshold did not impede a victory by the opposition to the Peronists' Front for Victory, but it was widely feared that it would.

By 2015, a Kirchner had governed Argentina for twelve years. During Fernández de Kirchner's second term, economic growth sputtered; inflation and crime rose. Also, as the continuing dip in V-Dem scores indicated, questions about political abuses intensified. In 2014, Fernández de Kirchner was suspected of complicity in the death of a prosecutor, Alberto Nisman.

Still, only a few weeks before the first round, it appeared very possible that the Front for Victory candidate, Daniel Scioli, would reach 40% with a ten-point lead (LAWR, September 10, 2015, p. 10; LAWR, October 15, 2015, p. 9).[12] The opposition was divided between the center-right mayor of Buenos Aires, Mauricio Macri, running for the coalition Cambiemos (Let's Change) including Macri's own party and the Radical Party, and a dissident Peronist on the right, Sergio Massa. Macri promised "change": market reforms and honest democratic governance.

In the event, however, Scioli tallied only 37% in the first round. Macri was the runner-up with 37% and Massi was third with 21%. For the runoff, Macri was favored but his victory was far from certain (LAWR, November 5, 2015, p. 9). In a reversal, Macri edged out Scioli by three points.

Conclusion

Although the evidence is not definitive, a reduced threshold appears risky. Although it voids runoffs that would have been unnecessary, it also voids runoffs that would have added presidential legitimacy. Raising barriers to entry, a reduced threshold is likely to be disadvantageous if a cartel party or a party with an authoritarian past is strong, as in Argentina between 1983 and the present. A reduced threshold might be advantageous if the number of parties in the country is very large, as in Ecuador between 1978 and 2006; yet, a large number of parties continued in Ecuador after the introduction of the reduced threshold and declined only amid the popularity of the Correa government. The case of Ecuador reminds us that the reasons for a larger or smaller number of parties are manifold.

Overall, the reduced threshold worked well in Costa Rica, although a lead requirement would have been helpful. The reduced threshold voided a runoff that was unnecessary in 2010 but did not void a runoff that was valuable in 2002. Between the mid-1990s and the early 2000s, some scholars worried that barriers to entry were too high; but, in the 2002 election, the center-left PAC emerged and it advanced and won in 2014.

By contrast, the reduced threshold was problematic in Argentina. Fortunately, the reduced threshold did not void a runoff in the 2003 election, when the re-election of Menem with a scant 24.5% in the first round would have been calamitous. But the reduced threshold did void a runoff in 1995, when it might have helped the emergence of a social-democratic left under Bordón. And it voided a runoff in 1999, when a reversal of De la Rúa's victory—with major political implications—was possible and a runoff would have added legitimacy. Especially during the 1995 and 1999 elections, barriers to entry were too high, posing serious challenges of strategic coordination for the opposition to the Peronist Party.

8

Conclusion and the Future of Presidential-Election Rules

Although stability is a goal esteemed by many scholars, change is constant and adaptation is necessary. In recent decades, educational levels and social media expanded in most countries; larger numbers of people understand politics and are interested in it. Pre-election opinion polls matter in multiple, often unexpected, ways. Power is more diffuse. Presidential elections dominated by one or two entrenched parties that are unresponsive to the concerns of popular majorities are seriously questioned. These questions reverberate and catalyze new movements and new parties. If old-timers try to exclude newcomers and prevail with low percentages of the vote, their legitimacy is questioned. Amid economic recessions, corruption scandals, or simply stressful times, these questions intensify.

As societies evolve and politics changes, democratic institutions should adapt. In particular, presidential-election rules should adapt. In the past, the frequent changes in constitutions in Latin America were at times ridiculed; but it is commendable that, in recent years, Latin American leaders examined democratic experiences in their countries and elsewhere and were able to adopt new rules that would enhance democracy. Runoff has been an effective innovation.

In this concluding chapter, I first review my argument in favor of runoff (and also point to conceptual issues that would gain from future research). Next, with the recognition that runoff is not a panacea and that it permits an excessive number of parties, I discuss a variety of innovations that could ameliorate this problem. Finally, with the recognition that the United States is an outlier, retaining many electoral rules that are widely considered anachronistic and sclerotic, I ask whether or not the advantages of runoff would travel to the United States. I also ask whether or not "ranked-choice voting" (also called an "instant runoff," the "alternative vote," and the "instantaneous vote"), which has been adopted for elections in several countries worldwide and for some local elections in the United States, might be a superior alternative.

The Superiority of Runoff in Latin America

No electoral rule is a magic bullet. No electoral rule is without its negative implications. No electoral rule operates independently of a country's entire set of electoral rules.

Still, runoff is superior to plurality. Although the number of parties was smaller under plurality than under runoff, these parties were often entrenched, with authoritarian proclivities; despite plurality, new parties tried to enter. Often, strategic coordination among older and newer opposition parties was difficult to impossible. In this context, it was not rare that an election under plurality yielded a president who was uncertain to have won a runoff, suffered a legitimacy deficit, and proved deleterious for democracy. Further, in Latin America during the third wave, the higher barriers to entry under plurality impeded the incorporation of new leftist parties and a vicious circle emerged: the leftist parties doubted the value of democracy and were more likely to remain at ideological extremes; concomitantly, they were more frightening to elites—who in turn were more likely to resort to ugly tactics against them, which further alienated the leftist parties.

By contrast, although the number of parties was larger under runoff, the president won a majority and did not suffer a legitimacy deficit. Further, lowering barriers to entry, runoff was helpful for the incorporation of new leftist parties into the political arena. A virtuous circle emerged: lower barriers to entry increased respect for the democratic process; with greater respect as well as awareness that a majority was necessary for victory, leftist parties moderated and were less frightening to rightist elites, who did not resort to ugly tactics.

Various caveats are necessary. First, presidential legitimacy is a new concept and should be elaborated in greater detail and measured more thoroughly. It is clear that a president who was unlikely to have won a majority suffered a legitimacy deficit. It is not clear whether or not there are gradations among legitimacy advantages. For example, does a president winning in a runoff through votes from other parties enjoy less of an advantage? This president was the voters' first choice in the runoff, but not in the first round. Further, does a president winning very narrowly enjoy less of an advantage?

Second, ideological moderation is a concept that should also be elaborated in greater detail and measured more thoroughly. When parties moderated, why did some but not others lose their ethical principles? And, when candidates presented centrist views during political campaigns, why did a few veer far to the right in office, provoking political crises? Further, while candidates at both leftist and rightist ideological extremes moderated their discourse during political campaigns, why were some shifts credible to voters, but not others?

Third, of course, new parties are not invariably positive. Of course, new parties usually add to the total number of parties, and a large number can be challenging.

And, new parties are virtually, by definition, inchoate. Accordingly, the ideal—a small number of parties that, with strong ties to voters, respond to their concerns and achieve their desired policies—remains elusive.

In quantitative analysis, between 1990 and 2016, levels of democracy improved for countries under runoff but plummeted in countries under plurality. In regression analysis, runoff was positively related and statistically significant at the .05 level to superior Freedom House and V-Dem scores (and of course plurality negatively related and significant at the .05 level). Further, the number of years of plurality was negatively related and statistically significant at the .01 level for the Freedom House index and almost at the .01 level for the V-Dem index; and, the number of years of runoff was positively related and statistically significant at the .10 level for the Freedom House index. Although rule was not statistically significant to voter turnout, turnout was steady under runoff but slightly down under plurality.

The Inferiority of Plurality

Six countries that began the third wave with plurality used it in 2016: Honduras, Mexico, Nicaragua, Panama, Paraguay, and Venezuela. Freedom House and V-Dem scores declined in Honduras, Mexico, Nicaragua, and Venezuela and remained inferior in Paraguay. Voter turnout did not increase considerably in any plurality country; it was below the regional average in Mexico and Paraguay and plunged in Honduras and, for a period, in Venezuela. The only favorable democratic trajectory was in Panama. What went wrong (but right in Panama)?

In many Latin American countries, parties with political bases of approximately 40% of the vote but authoritarian proclivities—or duopolies with roughly 90% of the vote—were entrenched. Yet, new leftist parties (and, later, new good-governance parties) wanted to compete and, despite high barriers to entry under plurality, the number of parties approached 3.0—a much larger number than plurality advocates anticipated.

The high barriers to entry facilitated the continuation in power or return to power of the entrenched parties. To defeat an entrenched party, it was necessary that opposition parties ally. But, amid ideological differences, leadership rivalries, and inaccurate polls, coordination among opposition parties was difficult. Argentina's Peronist Party, Mexico's PRI, Nicaragua's FSLN, Paraguay's Colorado Party, and Venezuela's PSUV all exploited the difficulties posed to the opposition by coalition formation. To defeat a duopoly was even more difficult; both the AD-COPEI duopoly in Venezuela and the Liberal-National duopoly in Honduras ended amid internal division.

In this context, presidents' victories without majority support were more frequent than plurality advocates anticipated. Often, these victories wreaked havoc on democracy. First, such victories discredited democratic principles and disillusioned opposition parties, which moved toward ideological extremes or did not shift away from them. Concomitantly, in a vicious circle, the extremism of the opposition parties frightened elites—exacerbating polarization. When leftist leaders did emerge—Zelaya in Honduras, AMLO in Mexico, Lugo in Paraguay, and Chávez in Venezuela—they were perceived to be far to the left.

Second, presidents' victories without majority support diminished their legitimacy. Some presidents overcame these legitimacy deficits but others did not. After Mexico's 2006 election, Calderón struggled; after Paraguay's 1993 election, Wasmosy was almost overthrown; after Paraguay's 2008 election, Lugo was impeached; after Venezuela's 1993 election, Caldera struggled.

The deepest plunge was in Venezuela. Although during the 1970s and into the 1980s Venezuela was a democratic star, its two dominant parties, AD and COPEI, became a duopoly, excluding leftist parties. When the duopoly broke down in 1993 and Caldera, an old-timer leading a motley coalition of small parties, won a narrow, suspect victory, Venezuela's left was deeply disillusioned. With only 30.5% of the vote, Caldera's presidency suffered a serious legitimacy deficit. The path was set for the 1998 victory of the fiery anti-system outsider, Chávez. Thereafter, plurality imposed difficult problems of strategic coordination for opposition parties: although AD and COPEI were widely discredited, they retained some support, and new parties had to ally with them if they were to defeat Chávez. An opposition candidate with broad appeal was more likely to have emerged from an open first round than from a unity candidate anointed by the disparate opposition parties.

The plunge was also deep in Nicaragua. Although Nicaragua's democratic history was negligible, the country appeared to be off to a good start in 1990. In part to achieve a more open political arena, runoff with a 45% threshold was introduced. But, the Liberal Party, a cartel party, and the FSLN, which had ousted the Liberal dictator Somoza in 1979 and governed at the extreme left until 1990, remained Nicaragua's leading parties. In 1996, the Liberal Party regained the presidency; in a 1999 pact between the Liberal Party and the FSLN, qualified plurality and exclusionary electoral rules were adopted. The unscrupulousness of the pact galvanized splits in both the Liberal Party and the FSLN. The beneficiary was FSLN old-timer Ortega; tallying only 38%, Ortega won even though he would have been virtually certain to have lost a runoff. Increasingly, the Ortega government repressed the opposition and compromised elections.

The level of democracy fell in Mexico. The PRI was a strong cartel party and, despite its defeat in 2000, worked to increase the distance between the two opposition parties, the PAN and the PRD; in 2012, the PRI returned to power amid a divided opposition. The distance between the PAN and the PRD increased markedly amid the 2006 election, when the PAN's Calderón won with 35.89% to the PRD's 35.31% and, for the PRD's AMLO in particular, the PAN president was bereft of legitimacy. After 2006, AMLO was intransigent.

In Honduras, the level of democracy was low before the 2009 coup against Zelaya, and, after the coup, fell considerably. For decades, the Liberal-National duopoly achieved the exclusion of new parties, in particular leftist new parties. Amid Hondurans' dissatisfaction, it was perhaps not surprising that the duopoly was betrayed from within. But, Zelaya's left turn panicked Honduran elites. In the 2013 election, a minority victory for Zelaya's new party was very possible—but would have been extremely polarizing.

In Paraguay, the level of democracy did not decline but remained low. Between its transition to democracy in 1993 and 2016, Paraguay was governed for all but four years by the Colorado Party, a cartel party. The Colorado Party was particularly adept at dividing and conquering its opposition. Paraguayans' disillusionment was intense, leading to the 2008 election of the leftist outsider, Lugo. However, despite an alliance with the PLRA, Lugo won only 40.9% of the vote and was impeached in 2012.

Among three of the four nations that shifted from plurality to runoff during the third wave—Argentina, Colombia, the Dominican Republic, and Uruguay—plurality was also problematic. In the Dominican Republic's 1986 and 1990 elections, a rightist caudillo, Balaguer, won with less than 50% and was unlikely to have won runoffs; he went on to rig the 1994 election. In Uruguay, a duopoly was increasingly challenged by leftist parties; between 1984 and 1994, one of the two traditional parties triumphed in two elections with less than 40% and in a third with less than 42%; concerns mounted about "an Allende-like situation." In Colombia, the Conservative and Liberal parties were an exceptionally long-standing duopoly perceived as "bankrupt," "oligarchical," and exclusive. Polarization was intense and the duopoly was challenged by leftist parties (and violent insurgencies).

Panama was an exception that to a certain extent proved the rule. The average number of parties in Panama was the largest among the six plurality countries; its political arena was relatively open to newcomers. Perhaps because of the relative openness of the political arena, the country's stellar economic growth, and the leftist historical credentials of the PRD, no leftist party emerged. Polarization was limited. Concomitantly, although the 1994 and 2004 elections were won without 50% and the results of runoffs would have been uncertain, questions about the presidents' legitimacy were not salient.

The Superiority of Runoff

As of 1999, runoff had been adopted in Argentina, Brazil, Chile, Colombia, Costa Rica, the Dominican Republic, Ecuador, El Salvador, Guatemala, Peru, and Uruguay. Between the adoption of runoff and 2016, Freedom House scores improved for Argentina, Brazil, Chile, Colombia, the Dominican Republic, El Salvador, and Uruguay. Scores for Costa Rica were quite steady, at regional apexes; scores for Guatemala were also quite steady, somewhat below regional averages. Scores for Peru decreased under Fujimori but were roughly similar at the start of the third wave and in 2016. Only in Ecuador did scores decline. For V-Dem, levels and trends were similar, with some exceptions: scores were lower, or trends less positive, for Argentina and the Dominican Republic; trends were more positive over a longer period for Colombia and Guatemala.

Without runoff, at least one president would have suffered a legitimacy deficit in every country. A considerable number of first-round winners who lost runoffs were likely to have provoked widespread dismay and possibly serious political crises. These presidents would have been Menem in 2003 and Scioli in 2015 in Argentina; Zuluaga in 2014 in Colombia; Noboa in 2006 in Ecuador; Carpio in 1991 in Guatemala; Vargas Llosa in 1990, Humala in 2006, and Fujimori in 2016 in Peru. Although several reversals—Bucaram's in Ecuador in 1996, Serrano's in Guatemala in 1991, and Fujimori's in 1990 in Peru—were problematic, the elections were fraught overall, and victory for the first-round winner would have been problematic too. Also, for most of the candidates who won runoffs but whose parties had been perceived to be significantly leftist or populist in their countries at the time—Lagos in 1999–2000 and Bachelet in 2005–2006 in Chile; Fernández in 1996 in the Dominican Republic; Roldós in 1978–1979 and Borja in 1998 in Ecuador; Sánchez Cerén in 2014 in El Salvador; Cerezo in 1985 and Colom in 2007 in Guatemala; Humala in 2011 in Peru; and Mujica in 2009 in Uruguay—the legitimacy advantage of the runoff was very important.

The lower barriers to entry under runoff facilitated the emergence of new significant contenders that were responding to social demand. In the first decades of the third wave, these contenders were usually parties at the left that were likely to have perceived political exclusion if the rule had been plurality. Such parties included the Workers' Party, which became a significant contender in Brazil in 1989; the Democratic Alternative Pole, a significant contender in Colombia in 2006; the FMLN in El Salvador in 1994; and Álvaro Colom's UNE in Guatemala in 2003. In the twenty-first century, the new significant contenders were usually focused on ethical governance: the Green Party in Brazil in 2010; Marco Enríquez-Ominami's New Majority for Chile in Chile in 2009–2010; the Green Party in Colombia in 2010; and Ottón Solís's PAC in Costa Rica in 2002.

Also, the requirement of 50%-plus-one vote for victory enticed candidates of parties at leftist extremes toward the center, and a good number went on to win. These candidates were Lula in Brazil; Fernández in the Dominican Republic; Roldós, Borja, Bucaram, Gutiérrez, and Correa in Ecuador; Sánchez Cerén in El Salvador; Colom in Guatemala; Humala (in 2011) in Peru; and Vázquez and Mujica in Uruguay. As presidents, most stayed at the center or center-left and governed without negative effects on the level of democracy. The exceptions were several presidents in Ecuador—Bucaram and Gutiérrez, who both veered sharply right, and Correa, who reverted to his pre-runoff confrontational stance. Also, under several presidents—Lula and Fernández in particular—the newly significant parties became entrenched parties that violated ethical principles.

In Chile and El Salvador, the trajectories of moderation were complex. In Chile in 1989, the democratic transition was "unfinished"; the end to "authoritarian enclaves" was gradual. As the traumas of the Allende government and the Pinochet regime receded, Chile's rightist coalition moderated but its leftist coalition brought the Socialist Party to center stage and, in 2013, incorporated the Communist Party.

In El Salvador, ARENA and the FMLN—both established during a civil war that had raged into the 1990s—remained dominant and remained at ideological extremes. Still, immediately or eventually, both ARENA and the FMLN nominated presidential candidates who were closer to the center (Flores and Saca by ARENA and Funes by the FMLN). And, although the 2014 FMLN president, Sánchez Cerén, was a former guerrilla commander, indicators of his moderation were numerous.

However, runoff is imperfect. Plurality advocates are correct that runoff enables a larger number of political parties. The average number of parties under runoff neared 5.0. Runoff was a factor in the increase in the number of parties in Brazil, Chile, Colombia, and Costa Rica, and in the continuation of a large number in Ecuador until 2008, Guatemala, and Peru. However, in other countries—the Dominican Republic, El Salvador, and Uruguay—the number of parties did not increase; and, in Brazil and Chile, broad coalitions formed for presidential elections. (Indeed, even under runoff, the dominant party after 2004 in the Dominican Republic appeared to become a cartel party.)

Plurality advocates are also correct that a large number of parties can be problematic. Although plurality advocates' concerns about the incidence of outsiders were not borne out, their concerns about the incidence of legislative minorities were borne out. Between 1978 and 2012, the president's party did not achieve a legislative majority in 64% of elections under runoff versus 50% under plurality; further, the president's party did not achieve 40% of the seats in 44% under runoff versus 14% under plurality. Usually, in a context of a considerable number of inchoate parties and the president's "trade-worthy coalition goods," a legislative minority was not as negative as plurality advocates feared. In Peru in 1992 and Guatemala in 1993, the presidents who executed *autogolpes* would not have confronted hostile legislatures if they had not veered to the ideological right and lost the alliances that they had built for the runoffs.

Still, inchoate parties and the distribution of "trade-worthy coalition goods" are far from democratic ideals. "New parties" are not necessarily superior to "old" parties. Runoff facilitated the emergence of many parties that were responding to social demands and were positive for democracy, but also parties such as Uribe's Colombia First and Fujimori's Change 90 that were responding to social demands but, in most scholars' views, were ultimately negative for democracy.

And a very large number of parties can provoke other problems. In particular, it increases the incidence of elections in which the Condorcet winner does not reach the runoff. There was a strong possibility that the Condorcet winner did not reach the runoff in Brazil's 1989 election and Ecuador's 1996 and 2002 elections; a possibility in Chile's 2009–2010 election and Costa Rica's 2002 election; and a remote possibility in Peru's 2011 election. It was not coincidental that the presidents elected in Brazil in 1989 and Ecuador in 1996 and 2002 were ousted.

Remedies for the Problem of A Proliferation of Parties

Various strategies for the amelioration of the problem of a proliferation of parties have been proposed. The goal is for the achievement of a "sweet spot" where the political arena is open to new parties—but not too open. More research is necessary for the determination of the advantages and disadvantages of these strategies.

A Strategy: Runoff with a Reduced Threshold

A common recent recommendation is a reduced threshold (usually, 40% with a ten-point lead). However, for most Latin American countries, I doubt that a reduced threshold would be advantageous.

First, a reduced threshold is a blunt instrument against a complex problem. A reduced threshold may raise barriers "too little." After the introduction of a reduced threshold in Ecuador for the 2002 election, the number of parties did not fall below 5.5 until 2009. In at least one election in Argentina and one in Costa Rica, the number was almost 5.0 or more. Yet, a reduced threshold may also raise barriers "too much." Even under majority runoff, barriers to entry appeared too high in the Dominican Republic and El Salvador. Further, cartel parties and parties with authoritarian proclivities—such as the Peronist Party in Argentina, PAIS, the PRI in Mexico, the FSLN in Nicaragua, the Colorado Party in Paraguay, the Fujimorista party in Peru, and the PSUV in Venezuela—endured in Latin America and often commanded approximately 40% of the vote and accordingly, a reduced threshold might enable these parties to win without a majority if the opposition divided.

Second, with a reduced threshold, the risk of legitimacy deficits is considerable. In Latin American elections between 1978 and 2012 for which a 40% threshold with a ten-point lead would have come into play, victory in the runoff for the first-round winner was virtually certain in only 50% of the elections. The risk of legitimacy deficits was evident in several recent elections. In El Salvador in 2014, a former FMLN commander tallied 49% in the first round, but, in the country's polarized context, would have lacked legitimacy without a runoff. In Argentina in 2015, Peru in 2016, and Ecuador in 2017, the first-round winners were very close to 40% but did not quite reach it; two of the three first-round winners lost.

Strategies Focusing on the Legislative Election

Strategies focusing on rules for the legislative election are more promising. The "number of parties" is, of course, a measure of the number of parties in the legislature. Recall for example that, in Brazil and Chile, two broad coalitions emerged for presidential elections but yet the number of parties in the legislature remained large. Accordingly, a focus on the legislative election is logical.

One common remedy is concurrent scheduling of presidential and legislative elections. The trend in both runoff and plurality countries has been toward concurrent scheduling, usually by the elimination of midterm elections.[1] In Costa Rica, Guatemala, Honduras, Nicaragua, Panama, Paraguay, Peru, and Uruguay, they were concurrent at the start of the third wave; in Brazil, Chile, and Ecuador, they became concurrent during the third wave. In Argentina, the frequency of midterm elections was reduced in 1994. However, they remained non-concurrent in Colombia and became non-concurrent in the Dominican Republic and El Salvador. Mexico retained midterm elections for its lower house.

This remedy could be taken a step further: scheduling the legislative election not at the time of the first round but subsequently or at the time of the runoff (Acevedo, Ausejo, Rojas, and Sulmont, 2011: 89).[2] To date in Latin America, all concurrent legislative elections are at the time of the first round; a change to after the first round was debated in Ecuador's 1998 constituent assembly but was rejected, primarily due to parties' short-term interests (Negretto, 2013: 212–215). The expectation is that citizens would vote more strategically in a legislative election after the first round, favoring parties that fared well in the first round. (Also, parties that did not reach a threshold in the first round could be eliminated in the legislative race.)

In France, as of 2002, the legislative election was scheduled after the presidential election, with the expected positive result: all four presidents since 2002 have enjoyed a legislative majority, even including the president elected in 2017, Emmanuel Macron. An outsider, Macron won the first round with only 24% in April, leading his own new centrist party; but he won the runoff with 66% in May and, in June, his party achieved a resounding legislative majority. The disadvantage appears to be that, given a first round plus a runoff for the presidential contest and then, in France, a first round plus a runoff for the legislative contest, voters could go to the polls four times within two months and voter fatigue could ensue.

Another promising recommendation is a threshold of the vote for the securing of a seat in the legislature.[3] In other words, if a certain percentage of the vote is not achieved, a party does not secure a seat. A party might also lose its registration and have to re-register to compete in the next election; in some countries, registration requirements are onerous, including not only signatures from a significant percentage of voters throughout the country but also evidence of local committees.

Thresholds for representation were established in numerous countries. As Chapter 6 noted, a threshold of the vote was established in Colombia in 2003, raised subsequently, and considered successful. Thresholds between 2% and 5% of the vote were established in Bolivia, Mexico, Peru, and Nicaragua (Payne, Zovatto G., and Mateo Díaz, 2007: 47). And, in Argentina, a threshold of 3% of the voter registry of the candidate's district was established (Calvo and Murillo, 2012: 149).

However, parties have found ways to circumvent these rules, usually by lobbying their allies in electoral commissions for exceptions or postponements, and threshold requirements have not been regularly enforced. In some countries, parties made shotgun alliances to reach the threshold.[4] In Brazil, a threshold provision was ruled unconstitutional.

Another recommendation is a shift away from proportional representation for election to the legislature, or a shift from larger districts (with more seats) to smaller districts (with fewer seats), or a shift from the Hare Quota to the D'Hondt formula for the calculation of seats. Such shifts have been debated and some adopted in several countries, in particular Brazil and Ecuador, where of course the number of parties was exceptionally large (Payne, Zovatto G., and Mateo Díaz, 2007: 40–55; Fleischer, 2011; Negretto, 2013: 209–215).

A Strategy: The Allocation of Public Goods

Increasingly, Latin American countries have established rules for public funding of campaigns, free media access, entry into presidential debates, and similar public goods, and these rules can be restrictive—or not. Usually, allocations are based on the percentage of the votes received in the previous election—disadvantaging new parties. It was previously noted that, in both Costa Rica and the Dominican Republic, the dominance of long-standing parties was facilitated by restrictive campaign-finance rules. Of course, the degree of impact varies with the amount of public funding and free time or space in the media and with the number of debates.

Runoff for The United States? or, Ranked-Choice Voting?

The United States is the only democracy in the world in which a candidate can win the popular vote but not be elected (Bormann and Golder, 2013: 360). U.S. states continue to use plurality for the selection of the Electoral College. Change in the United States is difficult. To most analysts and most U.S. voters, U.S. electoral rules are anachronistic, sclerotic relics. Yet, among others, the U.S. Constitution is revered as if it were a quasi-biblical revelation.

Demands for change have mounted. Among the proposals are runoff, which has been used for party primary elections in various states, and ranked-choice voting, which has been used for numerous mayoral elections.

The Need for Electoral-Rule Reform

For many years, plurality was more deleterious in Latin America than in the United States. The problem of political exclusion was particularly severe in Latin America, where many entrenched political parties were misshapen by authoritarian pasts and where old-timers were especially likely to continue to compete. Pre-election opinion polls were more frequently inaccurate in Latin America, further complicating voters' strategic choices and increasing surprise presidential victories with more serious legitimacy deficits. The problem of ideological extremes was also particularly important in Latin America; in many countries after the Cold War, a long-standing authoritarian right needed to accommodate a left with various degrees of Marxist pasts. Also, in the context of ideological extremes, it was more likely that a president elected without majority support would face widespread dismay and opposition.

In recent years, however, the problems of plurality have become more salient in the United States. U.S. citizens' dissatisfaction with U.S. government has mounted. In 2002, only 39% of respondents in a Gallup poll were "dissatisfied" with "the way the nation is being governed"; in 2016, the figure was 67% and, in 2017, 71%."[5] In the 2016 poll, 21% cited "dysfunctional government" as the most important problem facing the United States. Citizens whose respect for political institutions was "none" or "minimal" jumped from 16% in 2006 to 29% in 2016–2017, and citizens' whose respect for political parties was "none" or "minimal" jumped from 27% in 2006 to 50% in 2016–2017.[6]

Dissatisfaction was due in part to increasing polarization between the Republican and Democratic parties and concomitant executive-legislative gridlock. Whereas in 1947–1948 about 30% of salient legislative issues were mired in gridlock, in 2011–2012 roughly 70% were (Binder, 2014).

The increasing polarization resulted in part from gerrymandering. Due to gerrymandering by partisan electoral commissions, most U.S. congressional districts were dominated by one of the two parties and the electoral tally was lopsided. In the 2010 elections for the U.S. House of Representatives, only 19% of the races were deemed "competitive"—won by less than ten points; the average margin was thirty-three points.[7] (As of the 2010s, the beneficiary was the Republican Party; due to both gerrymandering and Democrats' concentration in cities, in the 2016 election for the U.S. House, Republicans tallied just under 50% of the votes but gained 55% of the seats.[8] The result had been yet more disproportional in the 2012 election.[9])

In the twenty-first century, the election that candidates feared was the party primary. But, in primaries, turnout was low; in contested primaries for U.S. House seats in 2006 and 2010, turnout averaged only about 20% of registered voters.[10] Party activists, pulling candidates to ideological extremes, were over-represented among primary voters.

The problems of plurality and old-timer advantage were especially evident in the 2016 U.S. presidential election. Only 27% of the eligible U.S. population voted in the primaries (Parlapiano and Pearce, 2016: A16). During the campaign, favorability ratings for both Donald Trump and Hillary Clinton were below 50% and they were deemed "the least popular candidates in the last thirty years."[11] The victory of Trump—an outsider—in the Republican Party's primaries was attributed in part to plurality rules in a multi-candidate field and in part to the party's swerve toward its rightist base amid low turnout. Clinton's victory in the Democratic Party's primaries was attributed in part to old-timer advantage. The nominations were "the largest failure of the two-party system since . . . 1968" (Gerson, 2016: A21).

Further, in both the 2000 and 2016 elections, the elected president lost the popular vote and won in the Electoral College in part due to the impact of third-party candidates; the legitimacy deficits were serious (Shugart, 2004: 652; McLean, 2006; Clement, 2016). In 2016, it was the fifth time in U.S. history that a president had lost the popular vote but won the Electoral College and the second time in sixteen years. In both elections, third-party candidates—in this context, called "spoilers"—were likely to have cost the popular-vote winner the election.

In 2000, George W. Bush prevailed in the Electoral College due in part to his very narrow plurality over the Democrats' Al Gore in the state of Florida. Bush's legitimacy was tarnished by doubts both about the vote count in Florida and about the likely presidential victory of Albert Gore if there had been a runoff in the state. The third-party "spoiler" on the left, Ralph Nader, won more votes in Florida than third-party "spoiler" Patrick Buchanan on the right; without these two candidates in the race, Gore was likely to have won Florida and the presidency. In several Gallup polls in 2001, roughly 30% of respondents did not consider Bush's election "legitimate" and less than 50% believed that Bush had won the election "fair and square."[12]

In 2016, Trump won without 50% in numerous states, including Florida, Michigan, Pennsylvania, and Wisconsin; most votes not cast for Trump or Clinton were for the Libertarian Party and some were for the Green Party. It was estimated that half of the votes for the Libertarian Party would have gone to Clinton and all the votes for the Green Party, and in this case Clinton would have won all four states cited above as well as the Electoral College.[13] (Also, almost certainly, if more voters had been willing to cast sincere votes, third parties would have fared much better; in mid-2016, the Libertarian Party topped 10% in pre-election polls but in the event tallied below 4%.)

U.S. citizens wanted change. A large majority favored abolishing the Electoral College.[14] In a 2008 Pew Research Center poll, almost 75% favored new rules for nominating presidential candidates (Tolbert and Squire, 2009: 28). In Gallup polls between 2013 and 2016, more than 55% of respondents consistently said that they "believe a new party is needed."[15]

Proposals for Electoral-Rule Reform

Interest in electoral reform is longstanding; elimination of the Electoral College has been debated more than once in the U.S. Congress. And various alternatives to plurality, including both runoff and ranked-choice voting, have been tried at subnational levels.

Proposals for Electoral-College reform were initiated as early as 1800 and, between 1800 and 1966, 513 amendments for presidential-election rules were introduced (Peirce and Longley, 1981: 131–132). Direct popular vote was first proposed in 1816.

Debate in the U.S. Congress about a direct popular vote was intense in both 1969 and 1977. In the 1968 election, George Wallace emerged as a formidable third-party candidate and the possibility that neither Richard Nixon nor Hubert Humphrey would gain a majority of Electoral-College votes loomed. In a November 1968 poll, 81% of respondents favored a direct popular vote (Peirce and Longley, 1981: 187).

One contentious issue in the Congress was states' rights, but a second was plurality versus runoff. The questions were similar to the questions addressed in this book (Peirce and Longley, 1981: 170–190 and 211–222). Under plurality, would a president be elected with only 30% or 35% and be at an extreme or suffer a legitimacy deficit? Under runoff, would a large number of parties enter the race and upend the two-party system? In 1969, a 40% threshold was proposed in the bills before both the U.S. Senate and the U.S. House of Representatives. The threshold had been recommended by the American Bar Association, which "suggested that the 40% figure ... would assure a reasonable mandate for any elected president and function to discourage splinter parties" (Peirce and Longley, 1981: 221).

Since the first decades of the twentieth century, runoff has been used in the party primaries of various U.S. states. As of 2016, it was used in these primaries in eight states (Alabama, Arkansas, Georgia, Mississippi, North Carolina, Oklahoma, South Carolina, and Texas). The threshold was 50% with the exception of North Carolina (40%). In most states, runoff was adopted because the Democratic Party was dominant and its nomination was tantamount to election. During the 1980s, it was argued that the rule was used to block the victory of African-American candidates who finished first but without a majority in a field of multiple Caucasian candidates.

Studies of these runoffs have been limited. Charles Bullock and Loch Johnson (1992) analyzed its effects in 1,900 Democratic and Republican primaries for governor, senator, and legislator between 1970 and 1986 in all the states with the rule during this period. Their assessment was favorable, emphasizing the positive effects for the legitimacy of the winners; however, African-American first-round winners were disadvantaged (Bullock and Johnson, 1992: 6, 118, 175). Relative to Latin America, the incidence of runoffs was lower (only about 25% of contested primaries) but the incidence of reversals of the first-round result similar (about 30% of runoffs) (Bullock and Johnson, 1992: 35, 59).

Richard L. Engstrom and Richard N. Engstrom (2008) are rather neutral. Analyzing Democratic and Republican primaries for governor and senator from 1980 and 2002 in most U.S. states with the rule, they focus on the incidence of majority-vote winners and reversals. Their findings are similar to Bullock and Johnson's. The incidence of runoffs was about 33% of the contested primaries and the incidence of reversals about 25%; most surprisingly, the number of candidates was only slightly greater under runoff than under plurality (Engstrom and Engstrom, 2008: 411–415).

More recently, what is most commonly called the "top-two primary" or the "jungle primary" has been adopted in several U.S. states. In a top-two primary, all voters, regardless of their party registration, vote in one primary, and the top two vote-getters, regardless of their party, compete in the general election. As of 2016, it has been used for many offices in California since 2012, Louisiana since 1975, and Washington since 2008.

The impact of the top-two primary has been unclear because it is recent and because additional rules, including non-partisan electoral commissions for the setting of district boundaries, were adopted at the same time in California, the state where it has been most salient. However, it appears that, as intended, the top-two primary is an incentive for ideological moderation.[16] The impact on political parties has not yet been analyzed.

Currently, the electoral rule that is most frequently recommended in the United States is ranked-choice voting.[17] With this rule, voters rank the candidates on their ballot in the order of their preference; usually, voters rank only their top three or four choices. If no candidate wins more than 50% of the first-choice votes, the candidate with the fewest first choices is eliminated. Voters who chose this candidate have their ballots added to the totals of their second-ranked candidate and the ballots are re-tabulated. If there is still no candidate with more than 50%, this process continues.

Ranked-choice voting has been adopted for presidential elections in Ireland; some legislative elections in Australia, India, Papua New Guinea; and many sub-national elections. In the United States, as of 2016 it had been adopted for local elections in cities in California (including Oakland and San Francisco), Colorado, Minnesota (including Minneapolis and St. Paul), Maine, Maryland, and Massachusetts. In 2016, Maine citizens approved ranked-choice voting for elections for state offices and the U.S. Congress, but the rule was deemed in violation of the state's constitution by Maine's Supreme Court. Ranked-choice voting is also used by various non-governmental organizations, including the U.S. Academy of Motion Picture Arts and Sciences for its Oscar awards.

Although research on ranked-choice voting is scant, it is evident that ranked-choice voting has advantages similar to runoff: it upholds the principle of majority support but accommodates voter choice. A new party is not a "spoiler"; citizens can vote sincerely. And ranked-choice voting has advantages over runoff. First, with ranked-choice voting, there is almost no chance that a Condorcet winner does not prevail; as we have seen, at times under runoff the two candidates who reach the runoff are not the strongest contenders. Second, with only one election rather than two, administrative costs are reduced. Third, although the effects on ideological moderation have not been assessed, candidates are pursuing second-preference and third-preference votes and, in U.S. cities under ranked-choice voting, negative campaigning declined (John and Douglas, 2017).

The primary concern about ranked-choice voting is complexity. Even among well-educated voters in the United States, ranked-choice voting can be daunting. Indeed, more than five years after the implementation of ranked-choice voting in San Francisco, the city's mayor said he was "confused by the system."[18] The complexity is the likely reason that ranked-choice voting has not been overwhelmingly popular in cities that have used it; in a 2014 survey in cities in California, 57% of respondents favored it (John and Douglas, 2017: 26).

There are several sources of complexity. First, rounds of ballot-counting and re-orderings of candidates can be numerous and confusing. Second, rather than simply identifying their preferred candidate, voters must rank multiple candidates. As a result, decision-making can be difficult; some voters may rank only one or two candidates (Burnett and Kogan, 2015). In Pierce County in Washington in 2008, almost 50% of voters failed to cast a complete ballot and more than 10% listed the same candidate in more than one rank (Burnett and Kogan, 2015: 46). Ballots with only one or two rankings can be "exhausted"—in other words, all of the voters' choices have been eliminated and their ballots are discarded—before a candidate receives a majority; accordingly, the victorious candidate may have won not a majority of the votes but a majority of the votes that were not discarded.

Accordingly, at this time, ranked-choice voting is not favored by most Latin American analysts. In the author's survey of Latin American legislators, most legislators feared that it would be rejected by voters (McClintock, 2008: 10). Said one expert in Mexico, "People don't know about it and don't understand it."[19] However, as education levels and public information continue to improve, ranked-choice voting could be welcomed.

Final Reflections

Runoff is an advantageous presidential-election rule. Plurality often facilitates political exclusion by long-standing dominant parties and, in turn, exacerbates polarization among political leaders and cynicism among both leaders and citizens. By contrast, in Latin America during the third wave, runoff established a virtuous circle: amid lower barriers to entry to the electoral arena, opposition parties and new parties held greater respect for the democratic process and this respect facilitated elites' toleration of their entry. Although the larger number of parties under runoff was at times problematic, the number of parties was often considerable under plurality. Runoff enabled democracies to cope with three or more parties; it enticed presidential candidates toward the political center and reduced the incidence of serious deficits in presidential legitimacy. Although the problem of party proliferation under runoff can be serious, it can be ameliorated through such measures as the scheduling the legislative election after the first round and thresholds for a party's entry to the legislature.

Appendix 1

AUTHOR'S SURVEY OF LATIN AMERICAN LEGISLATORS

To explore Latin American leaders' views about plurality and runoff, I distributed surveys in Chile, Mexico, Paraguay, Peru, and Venezuela. I planned to select two countries with runoff and two with plurality; however, when I achieved only four responses in Venezuela, I added Paraguay. Further explanation of the country cases is provided in McClintock (2008).

The survey was carried out in two different formats. First, between May 2006 and January 2007, through the good offices of Dr. Henry Pease in Peru, Dr. Rafael Fernández de Castro in Mexico, and Dr. Claudio Fuentes and Gonzalo Alvarez in Chile, hard-copy questionnaires were distributed to legislators through their professional networks. Then, between June and December 2007, an electronic questionnaire was forwarded to all legislators in Chile, Mexico, Paraguay, Peru, and Venezuela. In Paraguay, Dr. Diego Abente followed the electronic request with a personal appeal to former colleagues. For further information about the format of the questionnaire and about the partisan affiliations of the legislators, see McClintock (2008).

Overall, runoff was preferred. In Chile and Peru, where runoff was in place, the percentages favoring runoff were 75% or more (see table below there were no differences in rule preferences by partisan affiliation. In Paraguay, where plurality was in place, the percentage favoring runoff was 61% whereas in Mexico it was 44% (see table below). In Mexico and Paraguay, legislators who did not hail from the traditionally dominant parties were more likely to favor the runoff.

Why was the runoff preferred? From lists of possible reasons, an overwhelming majority of the legislators cited greater legitimacy (see table below); at least 80% of legislators in each country cited this reason. About half the legislators (with a particularly large percentage in Chile) cited a second reason, and several chose all the reasons.

Appendix 1

Electoral Rule Preferences: Nations with Runoff

	Chile (N = 48)	Peru (N = 61)
Runoff	92%	75%
Plurality	4%	15%
Not sure, or preference depends on the combination of rules	4%	10%

Electoral Rule Preferences: Nations with Plurality

	Mexico (N = 71)	Paraguay (N = 18)	Venezuela (N = 4)
Runoff	44%	61%	25%
Plurality	41%	17%	75%
Not sure, or preference depends on the combination of rules	15%	22%	0

Reasons for Preferences for the Runoff Rule

	Legislators (N = 133)*
Greater legitimacy for the president	84%
Given majority approval, the president is closer to the center of the political spectrum.	34%
For a win in a runoff, a president will make alliances and clarify his or her political agenda.*	34%
The political arena is opened to a candidate who is good but not well known.	19%
There is a second opportunity to evaluate the top two candidates.*	19%
The first round functions like a primary for parties with difficulties choosing their candidate.*	13%
Other	3%

*The asterisked reasons were available only on the electronic questionnaires and the N was 32. Otherwise, differences in responses for the hard-copy questionnaires and the electronic questionnaires were minor.

Note: Percentages based on the number of respondents; about half the legislators gave more than one reason and accordingly percentages do not add to 100.

Appendix 1

Similarly, why was plurality preferred? From lists of possible reasons, two were cited by more than half the legislators: excessive expenditure of time and money and a reduced likelihood that the president would have an absolute majority of legislative seats and that alliances made for the runoff are precarious.

Reasons for Preferences for Plurality

	Legislators ($N = 45$)
Excessive expenditure of time and money	56%
The president is less likely to have a majority in the legislature and alliances for the runoff are precarious.	53%
The runoff induces voter fatigue.*	32%
The runoff does not favor a "centrist" president; the "right"-"left" spectrum is too simple.*	21%
It's too easy for an outsider to win.	5%
The runoff takes the important function of candidate selection away from the political party.*	11%
Other	4%

*The asterisked reasons were available only on the electronic questionnaires and the N was 19.

Note: Percentages based on the number of respondents; most legislators gave more than one reason and accordingly percentages do not add to 100.

Appendix 2

OUTSIDERS IN LATIN AMERICAN ELECTIONS, 1978–2012

The following tables identify outsiders securing 10%–50% of the vote and winning in third-wave elections. As indicated in Chapter 3, my definition of "outsider" and my application of a 10% threshold follow Corrales (2008: 5). Unless otherwise indicated, my sources are LAWR, LARR, and, like Corrales (2008: 6), candidates' published biographies. The sources for vote tallies are indicated in Chapter 2.

Outsiders in Elections with Plurality

Country	An Outsider with 10%–50%?	An Outsider Winning?
Argentina, two elections	None	None
Colombia, four elections	Antonio Navarro, 1990	None
Dominican Republic, four elections	None	None
Honduras, eight elections	None	None
Mexico, three elections	None	None
Nicaragua, four elections	None	Violeta Barrios de Chamorro, 1990
Panama, four elections	Ruben Bladés, 1994; Alberto Vallarino, 1999	

(continued)

Appendix 2 213

Continued

Country	An Outsider with 10%–50%?	An Outsider Winning?
Paraguay, four elections*	Guilllermo Caballero Vargas, 1993; Pedro Fadul, 2003	Fernando Lugo, 2008
Peru, one election	None	None
Uruguay, three elections*	None**	None
Venezuela, eight elections	None	Hugo Chávez, 1998

*In Paraguay, candidates for the party of General Lino Oviedo are excluded given that they were stand-ins for Oviedo. In Uruguay, stand-in candidates for banned leftist leaders in the 1984 election are excluded.
**However, information for Alberto Volonté, with 14.9%, /in 1994, was scant.

Outsiders in Elections with Runoff

Country	An Outsider with 10%–50%?	An Outsider Winning?
Argentina, five elections	None	None
Brazil, six elections	None	None
Chile, five elections	Francisco Javier Errázuriz, 1989	
Colombia, five elections	None	None
Costa Rica, nine elections	None	None
Dominican Republic, five elections	None	None
Ecuador, nine elections*	Freddy Ehlers, 1996**	Lucio Gutiérrez, 2002
El Salvador, four elections	Facundo Guardado, 1999	"Tony" Saca, 2004; Mauricio Funes, 2009
Guatemala, seven elections	None	None

(continued)

Continued

Country	An Outsider with 10%–50%?	An Outsider Winning?
Nicaragua, one election	None	None
Peru, six elections	Mario Vargas Llosa, 1990; Ollanta Humala, 2006	Alberto Fujimori, 1990
Uruguay, three elections	None	None

*Rafael Correa was often called an outsider but he had served as economy minister.

**Source:* www.voltairenet.org.

Appendix 3

LEGISLATIVE MAJORITIES IN LATIN AMERICAN ELECTIONS, 1978–2012

This appendix indicates percentages of the vote (less than 40.0%, 40.0%–49.9%, or 50% or more) won in legislative elections by the president's party. Because the goal is to assess the effects of plurality versus runoff on legislative majorities, but not the effects of other rules, mid-term elections are excluded and seats or branches not elected through a popular vote (Argentina's Senate prior to 2001 and the "designated senators" stipulated in Chile's 1980 constitution) are excluded. If presidential and legislative elections are non-concurrent and/or there are mid-term elections, the legislative election closest in time to the presidential election is the cited election. The legislative election in Venezuela in 2005 is omitted because it was boycotted by the opposition.

In the case of party coalitions, the identification of the "winning party" is often difficult. In general, if two or more parties were allied in the presidential contest, I designate the seats of the "winning party" as only the seats of the president's party if the other party or parties in the alliance ran their own legislative candidates. (If parties ran their own candidates for the presidency, they are not considered to be in an alliance.) However, my goal is to identify legislative majorities, and in various countries the alliances for the presidential race did indeed function as alliances in the legislature and endured for more than one election; in these cases, it violates common understandings to assess that there was not an alliance in the legislature. For example, in Nohlen (2005: 280–284) the parties of Chile's Concertación, consistent through numerous elections, are included as an alliance. Similarly, in 2002, Colombia's Uribe formed a coalition that endured through 2006. By contrast, although various alliances for Brazil's presidential elections were not impromptu, they did not endure.

The column for "legislative branch" is included only if the country's legislature is bicameral. Although in Chapter 3 I define "legislative majority" as a majority in the lower house, data for both the upper and lower houses are provided here for comparative purposes.

Unless otherwise indicated, my sources are http://pdba.georgetown.edu/Elecdata/elecdata.html and Nohlen (2005), supplemented by LAWR, LARR, and country-specific sources (indicated in source notes beneath the tables).

Presidential Elections under Plurality

ARGENTINA

Election	Less than 40%	40%–49.9%	At least 50%
1983			51%
1989		47%	

COLOMBIA

Election	Legislative Branch	Less than 40%	40%–49.9%	At least 50%
1978	Lower House			56%
	Upper House			55%
1982	Lower House			58%
	Upper House			55%
1986	Lower House		49%	
	Upper House			51%
1990	Lower House			60%
	Upper House			58%

DOMINICAN REPUBLIC

Election	Legislative Branch	Less than 40%	40%–49.9%	At least 50%
1978	Lower House			53%
	Upper House		49%	
1982	Lower House			52%
	Upper House			63%
1986	Lower House		47%	
	Upper House			70%
1990	Lower House	34%		
	Upper House			53%

HONDURAS

ELECTION	Less than 40%	40%–49.9%	At least 50%
1981			52%
1985			50%
1989			55%
1993			55%
1997			52%
2001		48%	
2005		48%	
2009			55%

MEXICO

Election	Legislative Branch	Less than 40%	40%–49.9%	At least 50%
2000	Lower House		41%	
	Upper House	36%		
2006	Lower House		41%	
	Upper House		40%	
2012	Lower House		48%	
	Upper House		48%	

Sources: For 2006, Amparo Casar (2010: 119–120); for 2012, Flores-Macías (2013: 135).

NICARAGUA

Election	Less than 40%.	40%–49.9%	At least 50%
1990			56%
2001			51%
2006		42%	
2011			68%

PANAMA

Election	Less than 40%	40%–49.9%	At least 50%
1994		42%	
1999	25%		
2004			53%
2009			52%

PARAGUAY

Election	Legislative Branch	Less than 40%	40%–49.9%	At least 50%
1993	Lower House		47.5%	
	Upper House		44%	
1998	Lower House			56%
	Upper House			53%
2003	Lower House		46%	
	Upper House	36%		
2008	Lower House	39%		
	Upper House	38%		

Source: For 2008, LARR, May 2008, p. 2.

PERU

Election	Legislative Branch	Less than 40%	40%–49.9%	At least 50%
1980	Lower House			54%
	Upper House		43%	

URUGUAY

Election	Legislative Branch	Less than 40%	40%–49.9%	At least 50%
1984	Lower House		41%	
	Upper House		43%	
1989	Lower House	39%		
	Upper House		40%	
1994	Lower House	32%		
	Upper House	35%		

VENEZUELA

Election	Legislative Branch	Less than 40%	40%–49.9%	At least 50%
1978	Lower House		42%	
	Upper House		48%	
1983	Lower House			57%
	Upper House			64%
1988	Lower House		49%	
	Upper House		49%	
1993	Lower House	26%		
	Upper House	12%		
1998	Lower House	17% (35% including the parties supporting the MVR for the presidency)		
	Upper House	15% (33% including the parties supporting the MVR for the presidency)		
2000	N.A.			56%
2010	N.A.			58%

Presidential Elections under Runoff

ARGENTINA

Election	Legislative Branch	Less than 40%	40%–49.9%	At least 50%
1995	N.A.			51%
1999	N.A.		46%	
2003	Lower House			50.2%*
	Upper House			57%*
2007	Lower House			60%**
	Upper House			61%**
2011	Lower House			60%**
	Upper House			50%**

*Although the Peronist Party divided in the presidential election, it remained intact in most legislative elections. Legislative elections were held on various dates in different parts of Argentina.

**Of the seats contested.

Sources: For 2007, Singer and Fara (2008: 758–759); for 2011, Tagina (2013: 594).

BRAZIL

Election	Legislative Branch	Less than 40%	40%–49.9%	At least 50%
1990	Lower House	8%		
	Upper House	7%		
1994	Lower House	35%		
	Upper House	17%		
1998	Lower House	19%		
	Upper House	15%		
2002	Lower House	18%		
	Upper House	19%		
2006	Lower House	16%		
	Upper House	19%		
2010	Lower House	17%		
	Upper House	17%		

Note: The 1990 election was not concurrent. Terms in Brazil's Senate are eight-years long. In alternate elections, two-thirds and one-third of the Senate are contested. Percentage refers to percentage of seats contested.

Sources: For 2006, LAWR, October 3, 2006, p. 2; for 2010, LAWR, October, 14 2010, p. 4.

CHILE

Election	Legislative Branch	Less than 40%	40%–49.9%	At least 50%
1989	Lower House			58%
	Upper House			58%*
1993	Lower House			58%
	Upper House			55%*
2001	Lower House			52%
	Upper House			50%*
2005	Lower House			52%
	Upper House			55%*
2009	Lower House		48%	
	Upper House			50%*

*Percentages are for contested seats.

Note: Please see the introductory note for the guidelines for the identification of coalitions as "parties". Both the Concertación and the rightist alliance are counted as a "party."

Sources: For 2005 and 2009, LAWR, December 17, 2009, p. 2.

COLOMBIA

Election	Legislative Branch	Less than 40%	40%–49.9%	At least 50%
1994	Lower House			54%
	Upper House			55%
1998	Lower House	17%		
	Upper House	15%		
2002	Lower House			Uribe's Primero Colombia did not compete. But, as of Uribe's inauguration, he had the support of the Conservative Party and proliferating "Uribista factions" and had 97 of 166 seats (Ulloa and Posada-Carbó, 2003: 787).
2002	Upper House			Uribe's Primero Colombia did not compete. But, as of Uribe's inauguration, he had the support of the Conservative Party and proliferating "Uribista factions" and had 62 of 102 seats (Ulloa and Posada-Carbó, 2003: 787).
2006	Lower House			"Uribe's coalition of the PSUN, CR, the Conservatives, and three small parties obtained ... 90 of the 166 seats" (Posada-Carbó, 2006: 89).
	Upper House			"Uribe's coalition of the PSUN, CR, the Conservatives, and three small parties obtained ... 61 of the 122 Senate seats" (Posada-Carbó, 2006: 89).
2010	Lower House	29%*		
	Upper House	27%*		

*In 2010 (in contrast to 2002 and 2006), the Conservative Party and Radical Change ran their own presidential candidates.

Note: Legislative and presidential elections are non-concurrent.

Sources: For 2002, Ulloa and Posada-Carbó (2003: 787); for 2006, Posada-Carbó (2006: 89); for 2010, Posada-Carbó (2013: 243).

COSTA RICA

Election	Less than 40%	40%–49.9%	At least 50%
1978		47%	
1982			58%
1986			51%
1990			51%
1994		49%	
1998		47%	
2002	33%		
2006		44%	
2010		40%	

Sources: For 2006, Vargas Cullell (2007: 122); for 2010, LARR, February 2010, p. 2.

DOMINICAN REPUBLIC

Election	Legislative Branch	The winning party had less than 40% of the seats	The winning party had 40%–49.9%	The winning party had at least 50%
1998	Lower House	33%		
	Upper House	13%		
2002	Lower House		49%	
	Upper House			91%
2006	Lower House			54%
	Upper House			69%
2010	Lower House			57%
	Upper House			97%

Note: Legislative elections became non-concurrent in 1996; the "winning party" is the party that won the preceding presidential election.

Sources: For 2006, Sagás (2006: 155); for 2010, Meilán (2014: 347).

ECUADOR

Election	Less than 40%	40%–49.9%	At least 50%
1979		CFP 45%	
1984	13% (rightist parties as a whole 23%)		
1988		42%	
1992	16%		
1996	23%		
1998	27%		
2002	12% (Gutiérrez's party and coalition partners)		
2006	Zero (Correa's party did not run congressional candidates.)		
2009		48%	

Sources: For 2006, LAWR, November 7, 2006, p. 4; for 2009, LARR, July 2009, p. 1.

EL SALVADOR

Election	Less than 40%	40%–49.9%	At least 50%
1994		46%	
2000	35%		
2003	32%		
2009		42%	

Note: Legislative elections were held every three years and were non-concurrent. I include the four legislative elections closest in time to the four presidential elections. The "winning party" is the party that won the presidential election closest in time to the legislative election.

Source: For 2009, Córdova Macías and Ramos (2012: 94).

GUATEMALA

Election	Less than 40%	40%–49.9%	At least 50%
1985			51%
1990	15.5%		
1995			54%
1999			56%
2003	31%		
2007	32%		
2011	36%		

Sources: For 2007, Azpuru and Blanco (2008: 232); for 2011, González (2013: 618).

NICARAGUA

Election	Less than 40%	40%–49.9%	At least 50%
1996			57%

PERU

Election	Legislative Branch	Less than 40%	40%–49.9%	At least 50%
1985	Lower House			59%
	Upper House			50%
1990	Lower House	18%		
	Upper House	23%		
1995	N.A.			56%
2001	N.A.		38%	
2006	N.A.		30%	
2011	N.A.		36%	

Sources: For 2006, Tuesta (2008: 139); for 2011, Lupu (2012: 624).

URUGUAY

Election	Legislative Branch	Less than 40%	40%–49.9%	At least 50%
1999	Lower House	33%		
	Upper House	33%		
2004	Lower House			54%
	Upper House			57%
2009	Lower House			51%
	Upper House			53%

Source: For 2009, Altman (2010: 536).

Appendix 4

PRE-ELECTION OPINION POLLS ABOUT VOTERS' PREFERENCES FOR PRESIDENTIAL CANDIDATES IN LATIN AMERICA, 1988–2012, AND EUROPE, 2000–2012

This appendix reports the accuracy of the pre-election opinion polls for candidates who won at least 10.0% of the vote in the election (or the first round of the election). The spread must be accurate for all candidates (not only, for example, the winner). Candidates who ultimately won less than 10.0% but were predicted to win more than 10.0% are included if they affected the accuracy or inaccuracy of the polls. If it is clear that there was a percentage of undecided respondents, this percentage is allocated proportionally among the candidates. If more than one poll is available, an average is reported; precise dates or estimated dates of the polls are available from the author. The full names of most candidates are available in the text.

My goal was to report the pre-election polls at one month before the election, three months before the election, and six months before the election. Unfortunately, data were often not available for precisely these months. Accordingly, I extended the periods to zero to two months, two to four months, and five to nine months, respectively. For a few polls, to be as comprehensive as possible, I relaxed the date parameters slightly. For the Latin American countries, the date of the election and the top three candidates' tallies are reported in the first column of the election-by-election table.

Usually, for Latin American countries, the sources are LAWR and LARR. (Note that LARR was published with a precise date until February 2005 but subsequently only with the month; the year of the poll is provided only if it is different from the year of the election.) Most sources are cited directly in the box in the table, but at times the sources are provided at the end of the table and, in this case, sources: "see below" is in the box in the table. Also, some sources are cited directly in the table. These include sources from the Latin America Database at the University of New Mexico through notisur or noticen, cited with the document number

For the European countries, the sources are indicated at the end of the table.

Appendix 4

Pre-Election Opinion Polls about Voters' Preferences for Presidential Candidates in Latin America, 1988–2012: Summary by Country

Country	Total Number of Elections	Correct within 5.0 points at 0 to 2 months before the election	Correct within 10.0 points at 2 to 4 months	Correct within 10.0 points at 5 to 9 months
Argentina	6	4 of 6	2 of 6	2 of 3
Brazil	6	2 of 6	2 of 6	0 of 5
Chile	5	4 of 5	5 of 5	3 of 5
Colombia	6	0 of 6	3 of 6	1 of 5
Costa Rica	6	3 of 6	2 of 6	1 of 4*
Dominican Republic	7	3 of 7	4 of 7	2 of 6
Ecuador	7	1 of 7	0 of 7	0 of 2*
El Salvador	4	3 of 4	1 of 4	1 of 4
Guatemala	6	1 of 6	2 of 5	0 of 3
Honduras	6	1 of 5*	4 of 5*	1 of 3*
Mexico	3	1 of 3	1 of 3	0 of 3
Nicaragua	5	1 of 5	0 of 5	1 of 5
Panama	4	0 of 4	2 of 4	1 of 4
Paraguay	4	0 of 4	2 of 4	1 of 4
Peru	5	0 of 5	0 of 5	0 of 3
Uruguay	5	4 of 5	4 of 5	3 of 4*
Venezuela	6	4 of 6	3 of 6	1 of 5
TOTAL	91	32 of 91 (35%)	35 of 90 (39%)	18 of 66 (27%)

*Polls in which the candidates were not yet fully specified or for which data were not available are not included in the count of number of elections.

Pre-Election Opinion Polls about Voters' Preferences for Presidential Candidates in Latin America for Each Election, 1988–2012: Each Country

The column to the left reports the actual electoral result. I use the following words and abbreviations:

YES: Accurate within the indicated spread.
NO: Inaccurate within the indicated spread.

C.N. Candidates not yet fully identified. More detailed information is available in the text or from the author.

N.D.: No Data Available.

As mentioned above, when "source: see below" is in the box in the table, the source is at the end of this table.

ARGENTINA

May 14, 1989 **Menem 49.3%** **Angeloz 37.2%**	YES Menem 33% Angeloz 28% (LAWR, May 4, p. 4)	NO Menem 37% Angeloz 30% (LAWR, Jan. 26, p. 4)	YES Menem 30.5% Angeloz 16% (LAWR, Sept. 29 1988, p. 3)
May 14, 1995 **Menem 49.5%** **Bordón 28%** **Massaccesi 17%**	YES Menem 43% Bordón 25% Massaccesi 18% (LAWR, April 20, p. 178)	NO Menem 47% Massaccesi 21% Bordón in third (LAWR, Feb. 16, p. 63)	C.N.
October 24, 1999 **De la Rúa 48.4%** **Duhalde 38.7%** **Cavallo 10%**	NO (albeit barely) A margin of 15 points was predicted between De la Rúa and Duhalde (LAWR, Oct. 12, p. 470).	YES De la Rúa an 8-point lead over Duhalde (LAWR, Aug. 17, p. 379)	NO De la Rúa 33% Duhalde 32% (LAWR, Feb. 9, p. 67)
April 27, 2003 **Menem 24.5%** **Kirchner 22.2%** **López Murphy 16%** **Rodríguez Saá 14%** **Carrió 14%**	YES Kirchner 19% Menem 18% Rodríguez Saá 17% Carrió 12% López Murphy 10% (LAWR, April 8, p. 157)	YES Kirchner 16% Menem 14% Carrió 12% (LAWR, Feb. 4, p. 50).	C.N.
October 28, 2007 **Fernández de Kirchner 45%** **Carrió 23%** **Lavagna 17%**	NO Fernández de Kirchner 44% Carrió 15% Lavagna 11% (LAWR, Oct. 25, p. 6)	NO Fernández de Kirchner 46.5% Lavagna 10.5% Carrió was not yet declared. (LAWR, July 26, p. 12)	C.N.

(continued)

Appendix 4

Continued

October 23, 2011	YES	NO	YES
Fernández de Kirchner 54%	Fernández de Kirchner 49%	Fernández de Kirchner 39%	Fernández de Kirchner 41%
Binner 17%	Binner 15%	Alfonsín 23%	Alfonsín 12.6%
Alfonsín 11%	Alfonsín 11%	(LAWR, June 2, p. 11)	Binner 5.6%
	(LAWR, Oct. 13, p. 8)		(Source: See below)

BRAZIL

November 15, 1989	NO	NO	NO
Collor 28.5%	Collor 29%	Collor 40%	Collor 43%
Lula 16%	Brizola 13%	Brizola 12%	Brizola 11%
Brizola 15%	Lula 10%	Lula about 6.5%	Lula 8%
Covas 11%	(LAWR, Oct. 26, p. 8)	Covas about 6.5% (LARR, Aug. 3, p. 9)	(LARR, July 6, p. 2)
October 3, 1994	YES	NO	NO
Cardoso 54%	Cardoso 47%	Lula 34%	Lula 37%
Lula 27%	Lula 23%	Cardoso 25%.	Cardoso 21%
	Fleischer (1998: 35)	Fleischer (1998: 35)	Fleischer (1998: 35)
October 4, 1998	YES	YES	NO
Cardoso 53%	Cardoso 44%	Cardoso 42%	Cardoso 34%
Lula 32%	Lula 25%	Lula 25%	Lula 25%
Gomes 11%	(LAWR, Sept. 8, p. 412)	Gomes 3rd (LAWR, July 14, p. 320)	Gomes 9% (LAWR, May 26, p. 231)
October 6, 2002	NO	NO	NO
Lula 46%	Lula 35%	Lula 33%	Lula 31%
Serra 23%	Serra 17%	Gomes 22%	Garotinho 2nd
Garotinho 18%	Gomes 17%	Serra 15%	Serra 7%.
Gomes 12%	Garotinho 4th (LARR, Oct. 15, p. 1.)	No reference is made to Garotinho. (LAWR, July 23, p. 340)	(LARR, Jan. 2, p. 1.)
October 1, 2006	NO	YES	C.N.
Lula 49%	Lula 53%	Lula 45%	
Alckmin 42%	Alckmin 35%	Alckmin 32%	
	(LAWR, Oct. 3, p. 1)	LAWR, July 4, p. 12)	
October 3, 2010	NO	NO	NO
Rousseff 47%	Rousseff 50%	Rousseff 40%	Serra was ahead by about 10 points
Serra 33%	Serra 28%	Serra 35%	(LAWR, April 29, p. 4)
Silva 19%	Silva 8-10% (LAWR, Sept. 9, p. 1)	Silva at 8-9% (LAWR, July 1, p. 7)	

CHILE

December 14, 1989 **Aylwin 55%** **Buchi 29%** **Errázuriz 15%**	YES 56% to 28% (although no Errázuriz) (LAWR, December 14, p. 10)	YES Aylwin 54% Buchi 28% (although no Errázuriz) (LARR, Sept. 7, p. 6)	NO Aylwin 53% Buchi 40% (although no Errázuriz) (LAWR, July 20, p. 3)
December 11, 1993 **Frei 58%** **Alessandri 24%**	YES Frei 60% Alessandri 20% (LARR, Dec. 23, p. 2)	YES Frei 57.6% Alessandri 18.4% (Source: See below)	YES Frei was ahead 2:1. (LAWR, March 4, p. 100)
December 12, 1999 **Lagos 48%** **Lavín 48%**	YES "Dead heat" (LARR, Nov. 16, p. 3)	YES Lagos and Lavín even (LARR, Oct. 12, p. 2)	YES Lagos 40% Lavín 30% (LARR, Sept. 7, p. 6)
December 11, 2005 **Bachelet 46%** **Pinera 25%** **Lavín 23%**	YES Bachelet 39% Piñera 22% Lavín 21% (LARR, Nov., p. 14).	YES Bachelet at 38%, Piñera and Lavín both at 17% Morales Quiroga (2008: 12)	NO Bachelet 41% Lavín 18% Piñera 13.5% (LARR, May, p. 1).
December 13, 2009 **Piñera 44%** **Frei 30%** **Enríquez-** **Ominami 21%**	NO Piñera 38% Frei 23% Enríquez-Ominami 20% *El Mercurio-Opina*, December 9, 2009	YES Piñera 38% Frei 23% Enríquez-Ominami 22% *El Mercurio-Opina*, October 18, 2009	YES Piñera 38% Frei 25% Enríquez-Ominami 14% (LAWR, Oct. 22, p. 12)

COLOMBIA

May 27, 1990 **Gaviria 48%** **Gómez Hurtado 24%** **Navarro Wolff 13%**	NO Navarro Wolff 6% (LAWR, June 7, p. 1)	YES Gaviria 53% Gómez Hurtado 24% Navarro Wolff 13% (Latin America Database notisur/1990/03/15-072016)	YES Gaviria 40% Gómez Hurtado ~20% Navarro Wolff ~20% (Latin America Database; docview 1440997619).

(continued)

Continued

May 29, 1994 **Samper 45%** **Pastrana 45%** **Navarro Wolff 4%**	NO Samper 49% Pastrana 42% Navarro Wolff 3% (LARR, May 26, p. 3)	YES Samper 38% Pastrana 33% Navarro Wolff 11% (LAWR, March 3, p. 87)	NO "Pastrana has been far ahead in the opinion polls for months" (LAWR, Feb. 24, p. 74)
May 31, 1998 **Serpa 34%** **Pastrana 34%** **Sanín 26%**	NO Pastrana 40% Serpa 29% Sanín 14% (LAWR, May 26, p. 236)	NO Pastrana 24% Serpa 22% (LAWR, March 17, p. 125)	NO Serpa 26% Pastrana 23% Valdivieso in 3rd 12% (LAWR, Oct. 21, p. 496)
May 26, 2002 **Uribe 54%** **Serpa 32%** **Sanin 6%**	NO Uribe 53% Serpa 23% Sanin 4th (LARR, May, p. 4)	YES Uribe at 53% Serpa at 24% (LARR, Feb., p. 3)	NO Serpa 37% Sanín 25% Uribe 22% (LARR, Dec. 2001, p. 8)
May 28, 2006 **Uribe 62%** **Gaviria 22%** **Serpa 12%**	NO Uribe 57% Gaviria 13% Serpa 10% (*El Tiempo*, April 19)	NO Uribe at 54% Serpa 20% Gaviria not yet in the polls (LAWR, March 7, p. 6)	NO Uribe's big lead was indicated, but the runner-up was not (LAWR, Jan. 31, p. 4)
May 30, 2010 **Santos 47%** **Mockus 22%** **Vargas Lleras 10%**	NO Santos and Mockus essentially tied (LARR, May, p. 9)	NO Santos 34% Sanín 23% Mockus 10% (LAWR, Mar. 25, p. 3)	N.C.

COSTA RICA

February 4, 1990 **Calderón 46%** **Castillo 42%**	YES Calderón 51% Castillo 47% (Latin America Database; docview 10863340)	YES PUSC ahead by 4 points (LAWR, Feb. 8, p. 9)	N.D.

(continued)

Continued

February 6, 1994 **Figueres 50%** Rodríguez 48%	YES Figueres 48% Rodríguez 41% (Source: See below)	YES "Slight lead in polls for PUSC's Rodríguez" (Source: See below)	N.D.
February 1, 1998 **Rodríguez 47%** Corrales 45%	NO Rodríguez 35% Corrales 25% (LAWR, Jan. 20, p. 29)	NO Rodríguez 35% Corrales 25% (LARR, Sept. 23 1997, p. 3)	YES Rodríguez 42% Corrales 35% (LARR, July 15, 1997, p. 3)
February 3, 2002 **Pacheco 39%** Araya 31% Solís 26%	YES Pacheco 32% Araya 24% Solís 20% (LARR, Jan. 15, p. 2)	NO Pacheco 32% Araya 31% Solís 3% (LARR, Jan. 15, p. 2).	NO Pacheco 29.5% Araya 22% Solís not included (Latin America Database; noticen/2002/01/10-053228)
February 5, 2006 **Arias 41%** Solís 39.8% Guevara 8.48%	NO Arias more than 20-points ahead of Solís (LAWR, Jan. 10, p. 14)	NO Arias 45% Solís 16% Guevara 11% (LAWR, Oct. 25 2005, p. 15)	NO Arias 62% Solís 14% (LAWR, Aug. 23, 2005, p. 15)
February 7, 2010 **Chinchilla 47%** Solís 25% Guevara 21%	NO Chinchilla 41% Guevara 30% Solís 14% (LARR, Jan. 14, p. 3)	NO Chinchilla 43% Guevara 30% Solís 16% (LAWR, Dec. 3, 2009, p. 4)	NO Chinchilla 47% Solís 10% Guevara 9% (LARR, Aug. __ 2009, p. 15)

DOMINICAN REPUBLIC

May 16, 1990 **Balaguer 35.5%** Bosch 33.8% Peña-Gómez 23%	NO Balaguer was "consistently at least 10 points behind in polls in recent weeks" (*New York Times*, May 17, p. A6).	NO Bosch "seemed a certain winner" (*Washington Post*, May 17, p. A29)	C.N.

(continued)

Appendix 4

Continued

May 16, 1994 **Balaguer 42.3%** **Peña-Gómez 41.6%** **Bosch 13%**	NO Peña-Gómez 39% Balaguer 33% Bosch 16% (LARR, May 19, p. 3)	NO Peña-Gómez 42% Balaguer 30% Bosch 13% (Hartlyn, 1994b: Table 3)	NO Peña-Gómez 36% Balaguer 29% (LAWR, Sept. 9 1993, p. 411)
May 16, 1996 **Peña-Gómez 46%** **Fernández 39%** **Peynado 15%**	NO (albeit close) Peña-Gómez 39% Fernández 38% Peynado 15% (LAWR, March 28, p.144)	YES Peña-Gómez 43% Fernández 33% Peynado 18% (LARR, April 4, p. 8)	YES Peña-Gómez 36% Fernández 30% Peynado 15% (Latin America Database Article 0055941)
May 16, 2000 **Mejía 49%** **Medina 24.9%** **Balaguer 24.6%**	YES Mejía 43% Medina 28% Balaguer 23% (LAWR, May 9, p. 209)	YES Mejía 43% Medina 25% Balaguer 24% (LAWR, March 14, p. 122)	YES Mejía 44% Medina 26% Balaguer 19% (LAWR, March 14, p. 122)
May 16, 2004 **Fernández 57%** **Mejía 34%**	YES Fernández 55% Mejía 27% (LAWR, April 27, p. 13)	NO Fernández 58% Mejía 13% (LAWR, Feb. 17, p. 3)	NO Fernández 65% Mejía 20% (LAWR, Feb. 17, p. 3)
May 16, 2008 **Fernández 54%** **Vargas 40%** **Aristy Castro 5%**	NO Fernández 54% Vargas 31% Aristy Castro 9% (Angus Reid Global Monitor, May 14)	YES Fernández 55% Vargas 34% Aristy Castro 6% (LAWR, March 19, p. 15)	NO Fernández 40% Vargas 31% Aristy Castro 17% (Angus Reid Global Monitor, December 9, 2007)
May 20, 2012 **Medina 51%** **Mejía 47%**	YES Medina 49% Mejía 44% (Latin News Daily, May 1, 2012)	YES Medina 50% Mejía 42% (LAWR, Feb. 16, 2012, p. 14)	NO Mejía 48% Medina 33% (LARR, Sept. 2011, p. 5)

ECUADOR

January 31, 1988 Borja 25% Bucaram 18% Durán 15%	NO Borja 20% Durán 15% They are the "top two presidential candidates" (Bucaram is not mentioned) (LAWR, Jan. 28, pp. 10-11)	NO Borja 21% Durán 15% Duarte 13% Bucaram 12% (LAWR, Dec. 3, 1987, p. 9)	NO Borja 45% Duarte 13% Bucaram 12% (LARR, May 21, 1987, p. 8)
May 17, 1992 Durán 32% Nebot 25% Bucaram 22%	YES But precise figures not provided (LAWR, May 28, p. 1)	NO Durán 35% Nebot 31% Bucaram 10% (LARR, April 9, p. 7)	N.D.
May 19, 1996 Nebot 27.2% Bucaram 26.3% Ehlers 20.6% Paz 13.5%	NO Nebot 33% Ehler 18% Statistical tie between Paz and Bucaram: Paz 13% Bucaram 14% (LARR, May 23, p. 7)	NO Nebot "mid 30% range" Ehlers 16% No data for third place; very uncertain (LARR, March 7, p. 6)	NO "Paz had been in second place with around 20% support in all the polls since last November" (LARR, May 23, p. 7)
May 31, 1998 Mahuad 35% Noboa 27% Borja 16% Ehlers 15%	NO Mahuad 36% Noboa 21% Ehlers 13% (LAWR, May 19, p. 219)	NO Mahuad 22% Ehlers 20% (LAWR, March 3, p. 104)	C.N.
October 15, 2002 Gutiérrez 21% Noboa 17% Roldós 15% Borja 14% Neira 12% Bucaram 12%	NO Borja was first with 17% or 18%, Noboa 2nd and Gutiérrez #3 with a "five-point difference between Borja and Gutiérrez" (LAWR, Oct. 15, p. 481)	NO Noboa 29% Borja 16% Gutiérrez 7% (LAWR, August 13, p. 380)	C.N.

(continued)

Continued

October 15, 2006 **Noboa** 27% **Correa** 23% **Gutiérrez (Gilmar)** 17% **Roldós** 15%	NO Correa 26% Roldós 18% Noboa's percentage is not given; he was not even in 2nd place (LAWR, Sept. 26, p. 3) Gutiérrez's candidacy was still uncertain but one prediction was 5th (LAWR, Sep. 5, p. 6)	NO Roldós 23% to 25% Noboa 15% to 20% Correa 10% -15% (LAWR, July 4, p. 8)	C.N.
April 26, 2009 **Correa** 52% **Gutiérrez** 28% **Noboa** 11%	NO Correa 55% Gutiérrez 15% Noboa 13% (LAWR, April 8, p. 4)	NO Correa 47% Gutiérrez 6% Noboa 5% (LAWR, March 12, p. 5)	N.C.

EL SALVADOR

March 20, 1994 **Calderón Sol** 49% **Zamora** 26% **Chávez Mena** 16%	NO ARENA 35% Zamora 17% Chávez Mena 11% (Instituto Universitario de Opinión Pública, "La opinion de los salvadoreños sbore las elecciones. La última encuesta pre-electoral," Universidad Centroamericana, San Salvador, February 1994)	YES Calderón Sol 41% Zamora 27% Chávez Mena 7% (Latin America Database; notisur/1993/12/17–057113)	YES Calderón Sol 37% Zamora 16% Chávez Mena 12% (LAWR, Nov. 18 1993, p. 533)
March 7, 1999 **ARENA** 52% **Guardado** 29% **Zamora** 7%	YES Precise numbers not provided but overall prediction correct (LAWR, March 9, p. 109)	NO ARENA 41% Zamora 12 % Guardado 11% (LARR, Jan. 19, p. 2)	NO FMLN and ARENA were roughly tied. (LARR, May 12, 1998, p. 3)

(continued)

Continued

March 21, 2004 **Saca 58%** **Handal 36%** **Silva 4%**	YES Saca 54% Handal 34% (LAWR, March 9, p. 15)	NO Saca 43% Handal 29% Silva 4% (Source: Latin America Database; notisur/1993/12/17–057113)	NO Polls were correct that ARENA would trounce the FMLN. But Silva and Handal were tied with about 15% (LAWR, Nov. 4, 2003, p. 14)
March 15, 2009 **Funes 51.3%** **Avila 48.7%**	YES Funes a 6-point lead (LAWR, Feb. 5, p. 14)	NO Funes a 17-point lead (LAWR, Jan. 8, p. 3)	NO Funes a 21-point lead (LARR, June 2008, p. 5)

GUATEMALA

November 11, 1990 **Carpio 26%** **Serrano 24%** **Cabrera 18%** **Arzú 17%**	NO Carpio 26% Arzú 17% Serrano 9% Cabrera 8% (LAWR, Oct. 25, p. 2)	C.N.	C.N.
November 11, 1995 **Arzú 36.5%** **Portillo (for Ríos Montt) 22%** **Andrade Díaz-Durán 13%**	NO Arzú 43% Andrade Díaz-Durán 4% Portillo 1% (Source: Latin America Database; notisur/1995/09/29–055922))	YES Arzú leads Ríos Montt 2nd with 31% (LAWR, Aug 17, p. 368).	NO Ríos Montt (37%) Arzú 27% Andrade Díaz-Durán 2% (LARR, June 2, p. 2)
November 7, 1999 **Portillo 48%** **Berger 30%** **Colom 12%**	YES Portillo 48% Berger 36% Colom 8% (LARR, Nov. 2, p. 2)	NO Portillo 29% Berger 27% Colom 5% (LARR, Aug. 24, p. 3)	NO Berger and Portillo tied with 25% Colom 6% (LARR, July 29, p. 3)

(continued)

Continued

November 9, 2003 Berger 34% Colom 26% Ríos Montt 19%	NO Berger 38% Colom 18% Ríos Montt 11% (LAWR, Oct. 21, p. 13).	NO Berger 44% Colom 17% Ríos Montt 3% (LAWR, Aug. 19, p. 13).	C.N.
September 9, 2007 Colom 28% Pérez Molina 24% Giammattei 17%	NO Colom 41% Pérez Molina 28% Giammattei 10% (LARR, Aug., p. 10)	YES Colom 26%, Pérez Molina 15% Giammattei below 10% (LARR, June, p. 4)	NO Colom 43% Pérez Molina 18% Giammattei 5% (LARR, Feb., p. 13)
September 11, 2011 Pérez Molina 36% Baldizón 23% Suger 16%	NO Pérez Molina 49% Baldizón 18% Suger 11% (LAWR, Sept. 8, p. 3).	C.N.	C.N.

HONDURAS

November 26, 1989 Callejas 53% Flores 44%	N.D.	N.D.	N.D.
November 27, 1993 Reina 52% Ramos 41% Valladares (PINU) 3%	NO Reina 39% Ramos 28% Valladares 10% (LAWR, Nov. 25, p. 551)	YES Reina 44% Ramos 41% (Latin America Database; docview 286663499)	N.D.
November 30, 1997 Flores 53% Melgar 42%	NO Flores 47% Melgar 30% (LAWR, Nov. 4, p. 521)	YES Flores 48% Melgar 31% (Latin America Database; docview 388383108)	N.D.
November 25, 2001 Maduro 52% Piñeda 44%	YES Maduro 50% Piñeda 38% (Source: See below)	YES Maduro 47% Piñeda 35% (Source: See below)	YES Maduro 46% Piñeda 35% (Source: See below)
November 27, 2005 Zelaya 49.9% Lobo 46%	NO Lobo had a "16-point lead" (LARR, November, p. 9)	YES Zelaya 35% Lobo 35% (LARR, October, p. 7)	NO Zelaya 37% Lobo 24% (Source: See below)

(continued)

Continued

November 29, 2009	NO	NO	NO
Lobo 57%	(October 2009)	(August 2009)	Lobo 42%
Santos 38%	Lobo 37%	Lobo 28%	Santos 37%
	Santos 21%	Santos 14%	(CID-Gallup,
	Reyes 6%	Reyes 12%	Angus Reid
	(CID-Gallup,	(onsultores en	Global Monitor,
	Casamérica,	Investigación de	July 6)
	October 27)	Mercados y Opinión	
		Pública, October 7).	

MEXICO

July 3, 2000	NO	NO	NO
Fox 43%	Labastida 42%	Labastida 45%	Labastida 43%
Labastida 37%	Fox 40%	Fox 42%	Fox 27%
Cárdenas 17%	Cárdenas 16%	Cárdenas 12%	Cárdenas 8%
See Lawson (2004: 9)	(LARR, June 6,	(LARR, June 6, p. 3)	(LAWR, Dec. 7 1999,
for additional polls.	p. 3)		p. 569)
July 3, 2006	YES	YES	NO
Calderón 36%	AMLO 32%	Calderón 38%	AMLO 34%
AMLO 35%	Calderón 30%	AMLO 35%	Calderón 21%
Madrazo 22%	Madrazo 23%	Madrazo 23%	Madrazo 18%
	(Lawson,	(LAWR, May 2, p. 4)	(LAWR, Dec. 6,
	2009: 9–10)		2005, p. 11)
July 1, 2012	NO	NO	NO
Peña Nieto 38%	Peña Nieto 42%	Peña Nieto 39%	Peña Nieto 47%
AMLO 32%	AMLO 28%	Vázquez Mota 19%	Vázquez Mota 19%
Vázquez Mota 25%	Vázquez Mota 26%	AMLO 18%	AMLO 15.5%
	(LAWR, June 21,	(LAWR, April 26,	(LARR, Dec. 2011,
	p. 3)	p. 10)	p. 3)

NICARAGUA

February 25, 1990	NO	NO	NO
Chamorro 55%	Ortega 53%	"Ortega victory"	"Ortega victory"
Ortega 41%	Chamorro 21%	(Anderson,	(Anderson,
	(LAWR, Feb. 8, p. 9)	1992: 93–119)	1992: 93–119)
October 20, 1996	YES	NO	YES
Alemán 51%	Alemán 41%	Alemán 36%	Alemán 36%
Ortega 38%	Ortega 35%	Ortega 30%	Ortega 26%
	(Butler, Dye, and	(Butler, Dye, and	(Butler, Dye, and
	Spence with	Spence with	Spence with
	Vickers, 1996:10)	Vickers, 1996:10)	Vickers, 1996:10)

(continued)

Continued

November 4, 2001 **Bolaños 56%** **Ortega 42%**	NO Ortega 40% Bolaños 39% (LARR, October 30, p. 2)	NO Ortega 37% Bolaños 35% (Source: See below)	NO Ortega 38% Bolaños 31% (LARR, June 12, p. 2)
November 5, 2006 **Ortega 38%** **Montealegre 29%** **Rizo 27%** **Jarquín 6%**	NO Ortega 35% Montealegre 19% Rizo 18% Jarquin 13% (LAWR, Oct. 24, p. 14)	NO Ortega 32% Montealegre 25% Jarquín 20% Rizo 14% (LAWR, Aug. 29, p. 12)	NO Montealegre 22% Lewites 18% (succeeded by Jarquín) Ortega 16% Rizo 13% (LARR, April, p. 2)
November 6, 2011 **Ortega 62%** **Gadea 31%** **Alemán 6%**	NO Ortega 46% Gadea 34% Alemán 10% (LAWR, Oct. 13, p. 14)	NO Ortega 42% Gadea 34% Alemán 10% (LAWR, Aug. 25, p. 15)	NO Ortega 36% Alemán 23% Gadea 17% (*Latin News Daily*, Feb. 23, Special Election Report 2011 ISSN 17414474)

PANAMA

May 8, 1994 **Pérez B. 33%** **Moscoso 29%** **Blades 17%** **Carles 16%**	NO Pérez B. 33% Carles 16% "in second place" Moscoso not in double digits (LARR, April 7, p. 3)	NO Pérez B. 26% Carles 12% Moscoso not cited (LARR, March 3, p. 3)	NO Blades 12% Perez B. 9% Moscoso 4% (LAWR, Sept. 23, 1993, p. 444).
May 2, 1999 **Moscoso 45%** **Torrijos 38%** **Vallarino 17%**	NO Torrijos 43% Moscoso 35% Vallarino 16% "Panama: Election Preview" (*Oxford Analytica Daily Brief Service*, April 1, 1999, p. 1)	NO Torrijos 45% Moscoso 32% Vallarino 17% "Panama: Election Preview" (*Oxford Analytica Daily Brief Service*, April 1, 1999, p. 1).	NO Torrijos 35% Moscoso 27% Vallarino 19% (LARR, Feb. 23, p. 3)

(continued)

Continued

May 2, 2004	NO	YES	YES
Torrijos 47%	Torrijos 44%	Torrijos 42%	Torrijos 43%
Endara 31%	Endara 25%	Endara 34%	Endara 28%
Alemán 16%	Alemán 23%	Alemán 8%	Alemán 10%
Martinelli 5%	Martinelli 22%	(LARR, Feb. 17, p. 13)	(LAWR, Sept. 23, 2003, p. 13)
	(LAWR, April 20, p. 15)		
May 3, 2009	NO	YES	NO
Martinelli 60%	Martinelli 48%	Martinelli 55%	Martinelli 36%
Herrera 38%	Herrera 36%	Herrera 32%	Herrera 31%
	(LAWR, April 23, p. 15)	(LAWR, Feb. 5, p. 13)	(LAWR, Dec. 4, 2008, p. 14)

PARAGUAY

May 9, 1993	NO	NO	N.C.
Wasmosy 40%	Caballero Vargas 33%	Caballero Vargas 35%	
Laíno 33%	Wasmosy 25%	Laíno 29%	
Caballero Vargas 24%	Laíno 20%	Possible Colorado candidates in 3rd and 4th place	
	(LAWR, April 29, p. 185)	(LAWR, March 18, p. 120)	
May 10, 1998	NO	YES	N.C.
Cubas (for Oviedo) 54%	Laíno 53%	Oviedo (expected to be the Colorados' candidate) 44%	
Laíno 44%	Cubas (for Oviedo) 47%	Laíno 36%	
	(LAWR, April 21, p. 169; figures approximate)	(LAWR, March 31, p. 153)	
April 27, 2003	NO	NO	NO
Duarte 38%	Duarte 33%	Duarte 28%	Franco was in the lead.
Franco 25%	Franco 22%	Franco 20%	(LAWR, April 8, p. 162)
Fadul 22%	Fadul 20%	Fadul 17%	
Sánchez (UNACE) 14%	UNACE 5%	UNACE 6%	
	(LARR, April 15, p. 2)	(LAWR, March 18, p. 127)	

(continued)

Continued

April 20, 2008	NO	YES	N.C.
Lugo 41%	Lugo 39%	Lugo 31%	
Ovelar 31%	Oviedo 22%	Oviedo 25%	
Oviedo 22%	Ovelar 21%	Ovelar 24%	
	(LAWR, March 27, p. 8)	(LAWR, February 21, p. 11)	

PERU

April 8, 1990	NO	NO	NO
Vargas Llosa 33%	Vargas Llosa 44%	Vargas Llosa 53%	Vargas Llosa 44%
Fujimori 29%	Alva Castro 13%	Barrantes 15%	Barrantes 26%
Alva Castro 23%	Barrantes 13%	Alva Castro 8%	Alva Castro 7%
Barrantes 5%	(LAWR, March 15, p. 3)	Fujimori not included (LAWR, Feb. 15, p. 11)	(*Ojo*, June 11, 1989, p. 2)
April 9, 1995	NO	NO	C.N.
Fujimori 64%	Fujimori 46%	Fujimori 49%	
Pérez de Cuéllar 22%	Pérez de Cuéllar 19% (LAWR, March 23, p. 124)	Pérez de Cuéllar 22% (LAWR, Feb. 2, p. 41)	
April 8, 2001	NO	NO	C.N.
Toledo 36.5%	Toledo 36%	Toledo 33%	
García 26%	Flores 25%	García 12%	
Flores 24%	García 15%	Flores 12%	
	(Carrión, 2001: 111)	(Carrión, 2001: 111)	
April 9, 2006	NO	NO	NO
Humala 32%	Humala 32%	Flores 27%	Flores 28%
García 24%	Flores 28%	Humala 24%	Fujimori 20%
Flores 24%	García 21%	García 14%	García 16%
	(LAWR, March 21, p. 4).	(LAWR Jan. 24, p. 5)	(LAWR, Oct. 11, 2005, p. 4)
April 10, 2011	NO	NO	NO
Humala 32%	Toledo 23%	Toledo 27%	Castañeda about 24%
Fujimori 24%	Fujimori 19%	Fujimori 22%	Toledo 12%
PPK 18.5%	Humala 19%	Castañeda 19%	(LAWR, Nov. 4, 2010, p. 7).
Toledo 16%	PPK 15%	Humala 10%	
Castañeda 9.8%	Castañeda 14% (Meléndez, 2013: 541).	PPK 5% (Meléndez, 2013: 541).	

Appendix 4

URUGUAY (Primaries were usually held in May or June, so six months before the election the candidates were not yet decided.)

November 26, 1989 Blancos 39% Colorados 30% Frente Amplio 15%	YES Blancos 33% Colorados 23% Frente Amplio 15% (LAWR, Nov. 9, p. 5)	YES Colorados 36% Blancos 35% Frente Amplio 15% (LARR, Sept. 7, p. 7)	N.D.
November 27, 1994 Colorados 32% Blancos 31% FA-EP 31%	NO Blancos 29% Colorados 28% FA-EP 24% (LARR, Nov. 24, p. 6)	YES Colorados 30% Blancos 23% FA-EP 24% (LARR, Oct. 20, p. 3)	YES Colorados "10 points ahead of Blancos." Blancos "7 points ahead of FA-EP." (LARR, June 2, p. 3)
October 31, 1999 Vázquez 40% Batlle 33% Lacalle 22%	YES Vázquez 36% Batlle 28% Lacalle 21% (LAWR, Oct. 19, p. 483)	NO Batlle 37% Vázquez 19% Lacalle 14% (LARR, Aug. 3, p. 8)	YES EP-FA 33% Blancos 28% Colorados 27% (LARR, April 20, p. 7)
October 31, 2004 Vázquez 52% Larrañaga 35% Stirling 11%	YES Vázquez 50% Larrañaga 32% Stirling 14% (LARR, Oct. 26, p. 1)	YES Vázquez 51% Larrañaga 34% Stirling 7% (LAWR, July 20, p. 6)	YES Vázquez 48% Blancos plus Colorados 42% (LAWR, May 11, p. 8)
October 25, 2009 Mujica 49% Lacalle 30% Bordaberry 18%	YES Mujica 43% Lacalle 31% Bordaberry 11% (LAWR, Oct. 8, p. 6)	YES Mujica 43% Lacalle 34% Bordaberry 12% (LAWR, July 2, p. 8)	NO FA 43% Blancos 35% Colorados 7% (LARR, June, p. 9)

VENEZUELA

December 4, 1988 Pérez 53% Fernández 40%	YES Pérez 13-point lead over Fernández (LAWR, Nov. 3, p. 8)	YES Pérez 47% Fernández 31% (LAWR, Oct. 13, p. 3)	YES Pérez "with 12% to 15% lead over Fernández" (LARR, June 23, p. 7)

(continued)

Continued

December 5, 1993 **Caldera 32%** **Fermín 24%** **Alvarez Paz 23%** **Velásquez 22%**	NO Caldera 31% Alvarez Paz 22% Velásquez 22% (Fermín below these 3 candidates) (LAWR, Dec. 9, p. 574)	NO Caldera 32% Alvarez Paz 22% Velásquez 17% Fermín 8% (LAWR, Oct. 7, p. 460)	NO Caldera 32% Alvarez Paz 32% Velásquez 17% Fermín 9% (LAWR, July 29, p. 346)
December 6, 1998 **Chávez 56%** **Salas Römer 40%** **Sáez 3%**	NO Chávez 42% Salas R. 33% Ucero 14% Sáez 7% (LAWR, Nov. 24, p. 542)	NO Chávez 42% Salas R. 31% Sáez 8% Ucero 8% (LARR, Oct. 6, p. 3)	NO Chávez 40% Salas R. 20% Sáez 16% (LARR, July 28, p. 6)
July 30, 2000 **Chávez 60%** **Arias 38%** (Election was postponed from late May.)	YES Chávez 54% Arias 33% (LARR, May 16, p. 2)	YES Chávez 50% Arias 39% (LARR, April 4, p. 3)	C.N.
December 3, 2006 **Chávez 63%** **Rosales 37%**	YES Chávez 45% Rosales 27% (LAWR, Nov. 14, p. 6)	NO Chávez 58% Rosales 17% (LAWR, Sep. 19, p. 4)	NO Chávez 62% Rosales 20% (LAWR, Aug 22, p. 3)
October 7, 2012 **Chávez 55%** **Capriles 44%**	YES Chávez 49% Capriles 39% (LAWR, Oct. 4, p. 1)	YES Chávez 47% Capriles 30% (LARR, July, p. 4)	NO Chávez 43% Capriles 26% (LAWR, May, p. 11)

Additional sources

Argentina 2011:

http://www.diarioregistrado.com/Politica-nota-49658-Otra-encuesta-da-como-ganadora-a-Cr.html#D

Chile 1993:

http://www.icso.cl/images/Paperss/eleccion93.pdf

Costa Rica 1994:
http://biblio.juridicas.unam.mx/libros/4/1990/5.pdf

Honduras 2001:
http://www.cepr.net/index.php/blogs/the-americas-blog/are-honduran-election-polls-reliable

Honduras 2005:
http://www.cepr.net/index.php/blogs/the-americas-blog/are-honduran-election-polls-reliable
http://omaredgardorivera.blogspot.com/2005/05/partido-liberal-ganara-las-prximas.html
http://www.observatorioelectoral.org/informes/op/?country=honduras&file=010824
http://www.observatorioelectoral.org/informes/op/?country=honduras&file=011120

Nicaragua 2001:
http://pdba.georgetown.edu/Elecdata/Nica/nica01.html
http://www.observatorioelectoral.org/informes/op/?country=nicaragua
http://www.observatorioelectoral.org/informes/op/?country=nicaragua&file=010915

Pre-Election Opinion Polls about Voters' Preferences for Presidential or Prime Ministerial Candidates in Europe, 2000–2012

EUROPE 2000–2012 (Candidates for president or prime minister, selected countries)

Country	Number of Elections	Correct within 5.0 points at 0 to 2 months before the election (ideally, 1 month)	Correct within 10.0 points at 2 to 4 months (ideally, 3 months)	Correct within 10.0 points at 5-9 months (ideally, 6 months)
France	3	3 of 3	3 of 3	2 of 3
Spain	4	3 of 4	4 of 4	4 of 4
Portugal	3	1 of 3	1 of 3	1 of 3
United Kingdom	3	1 of 3	3 of 3	3 of 3
United States	4	4 of 4	4 of 4	4 of 4
TOTAL	17	12 of 17 (71%)	15 of 17 (88%)	14 of 17 (82%)

Sources: See directly below. Data are courtesy of Julian Waller, Ph.D. candidate, George Washington University.

France

1. "Nossondagespubliés," *CSA*, 2014, Accessed August 2, 2014, http://www.csa.eu/fr/s26/nos-sondages-publies.aspx
2. "Études et points de vue," *TNS Sofres*, 2014, Accessed August 2, 2014, http://www.tns-sofres.com/etudes-et-points-de-vue
3. "Le baromètre de l'actionpolitiqueIpsos / Le Point," *IPSOS France*, 2014, Accessed August 2, 2014, http://www.ipsos.fr/barometre-politique/index.php
4. "BANQUE DES SONDAGES," *IPSOS France*, 2014, Accessed August 2, 2014, http://www.ipsos.fr/sondages

Portugal

5. Wert, Jose Ignacio. "Public Opinion Polling in Spain and Portugal," *Fulbright International Conference Paper*, February 2002, Accessed August 5, 2014, http://www.ics.ul.pt/ceapp/english/conferences/fulbright/10JIWert.pdf
6. "Intenções de votonasEleições de 23-00-1011 para Presidente da República," *Eurosondagem*, 2011, Accessed August 5, 2014, http://www.eurosondagem.pt/Presidenciais%202011.htm
7. "Sondages," *EntidadeReguladora para a Comunicação Social*, 2014, Accessed August 5, 2014, http://www.erc.pt/pt/sondagens
8. "EleiçõesPresidenciais 2006," *GrupoMarktest*, 2014, Accessed August 8, 2014, http://www.marktest.com/wap/a/p/sel~sondagens/id~c4.aspx

Spain

a. [Spain] "Índices de la OpiniónPública," *SIMPLE LÓGICA*, 2014, Accessed August 15, 2014, http://www.simplelogica.com/iop/indices-opinion-publica.asp
b. [Spain] "EleccionesGenerales," *Celeste-Tel*, 2014, Accessed August 15, 2014, http://www.celeste-tel.es/elecciones-generales.html
c. [Spain] "Elecciones," *Metroscopia*, 2014, Accessed August 15, 2014, http://www.metroscopia.org/datos-recientes/tag/metroscopia-dinamico/Elecciones
d. [Spain] "Búsqueda de Estudios," *Centro de InvestigacionesSociológicas*, 2014, Accessed August 15, 2014, http://www.analisis.cis.es/cisdb.jsp

United Kingdom

a. [UK] "Voting intentions (Westminster)—all companies' polls 1997–2001," *Ipsos-MORI*, 2014, Accessed August 21, 2014, http://www.ipsos-mori.com/researchpublications/researcharchive/poll.aspx?oItemId=105&view=wide
b. [UK] "Voting Intentions (Westminster)—all companies' polls 2001–2005," *Ipsos-MORI*, 2014, Accessed August 21, 2014, http://www.ipsos-mori.com/researchpublications/researcharchive/poll.aspx?oItemId=2446&view=wide
c. [UK] "Voting intentions (Westminster)—all companies' polls 2005–2010," *Ipsos-MORI*, 2014, Accessed August 21, 2014, http://www.ipsos-mori.com/researchpublications/researcharchive/poll.aspx?oItemId=106&view=wide

United States
a. "White House 2000: Trial Heat Trend, August-November," *PollingReport.com*, 2014, Accessed August 9, 2014, http://www.pollingreport.com/wh2genT.htm
b. "National 2-Way Trial Heat Summary 2004," *PollingReport.com*, 2014, Accessed August 9, 2014, http://www.pollingreport.com/wh04two.htm
c. "Presidential Trial Heat Summary 2008," *PollingReport.com*, 2014, Accessed August 9, 2014, http://www.pollingreport.com/wh08gen.htm
d. "Presidential Trial Heat Summary 2012," *PollingReport.com*, 2014, Accessed August 9, 2014, http://www.pollingreport.com/wh12gen.htm

Appendix 5

OLD-TIMER PRESIDENTIAL CANDIDATES IN LATIN AMERICA, 1978–2012

Following Corrales (2008), to be included in the table, a candidate has to win more than 10.0% of the vote in at least one election. (The reasons are candidate viability and information availability.) Also following Corrales (2008), fraudulent elections are included. However, the sets of countries are slightly different; I include only the countries colonized by Spain or Portugal (not Haiti, Jamaica, or Suriname) and, for reasons cited in Chapter 2, I exclude Bolivia. For classifications as an incumbent, ex-president, and ex-candidate, elections prior to the third wave are included.

Old-Timer Presidential Candidates in Latin America, 1978–2012

N.A.=Not Applicable.

Country and Its Number of Elections	Incumbent Candidates	Ex-President Candidates	Candidates with an Ex-President's Last Name	The number of candidates running three times or more, including at least once during the third wave, and the number of unique presidential candidates with more than 10.0%
Argentina, 7 elections, 1983–2011	(Allowed as of 1994) Carlos Menem 1995; Cristina Fernández de Kirchner, 2011	Italo Lúder, 1983; Carlos Menem 1995; Adolfo Rodríguez Saá, 2003; Eduardo Duhalde, 2011	Cristina Fernández de Kirchner, 2007, 2011; Ricardo Alfonsín, 2011	2 of 16 candidates: Elisa Carrió, 2003, 2007, 2011; Adolfo Rodríguez Saá, 2003, 2007, 2011
Brazil, 6 elections, 1989–2010	(Allowed as of 1997) Fernando Henrique Cardoso, 1998; "Lula" da Silva, 2006	None	None	1 of 12 candidates: "Lula" da Silva, 1989, 1994, 1998, 2002
Chile, 5 elections, 1989–2009	N.A.	Eduardo Frei, 2009	Eduardo Frei, 1993, 2009; Arturo Alessandri, 1993	0 of 12 candidates
Colombia, 9 elections, 1978–2010	(Allowed as of 2005) Alvaro Uribe, 2006	(Re-election was not allowed between 1991 and 2005) Alfonso López Michelsen, 1982	Alvaro Gómez Hurtado, 1986 & 1990; Juan Manuel Santos, 2010; Carlos Gaviria, 2006; Andrés Pastrana, 1998	4 of 17 candidates: Belisario Betancur, 1970, 1978, 1982; Alvaro Gómez Hurtado, 1974, 1986, 1990; Horacio Serpa 1998, 2002, 2006; Noemí Sanín, 1998, 2002, 2010

Country, elections, period	Re-election rules	Presidents re-elected	Candidates re-running
Costa Rica, 9 elections, 1978–2010	N.A.	(Re-election was not allowed until 2003) Oscar Arias, 2006	Rafael Angel Calderón, 1982, 1986, 1990; José María Figueres, 1994; Rolando Araya Monge, 2002	3 of 14 candidates: Rafael Angel Calderón, 1982, 1986, 1990; Ottón Solís, 2002, 2006, 2010; Otto Guevara, 2002, 2006, 2010
Dominican Republic, 10 elections, 1978–2012	Indefinite immediate re-election was allowed until 1994. Immediate re-election was not allowed between 1994 and 2002. Joaquín Balaguer, 1978, 1990, 1994, 2000; Hipólito Mejía, 2004; Leonel Fernández, 2008	Joaquín Balaguer, 3 1982, 1986; Juan Bosch, 1978, 1982, 1986, 1990, 1994; Leonel Fernández, 2004; Hipólito Mejía, 2012	Jacinto Peynado, 1996	4 of 12 candidates: Juan Bosch, 1978, 1982, 1986, 1990, 1994; Joaquín Balaguer, 1978, 1982, 1986, 1990, 1994, 2000; José F. Peña Gómez, 1990, 1994, 1996; Hipólito Mejía, 2000, 2004, 2012
Ecuador, 9 elections, 1979–2009	(Allowed as of 2008) Rafael Correa, 2009	Rodrigo Borja, 1998 and 2002; Lucio Gutiérrez, 2009	León Roldós, 1992, 2002, 2006; Gilmar Gutiérrez, 2006; Jacobo Bucarám, 2002	5 of 19 candidates: Abdalá Bucaram, 1988, 1992, 1996; Rodrigo Borja 1978, 1984, 1988,1998, 2002; Sixto Durán, 1978, 1988, 1992; Alvaro Noboa, 1998, 2002, 2006, 2009; León Roldós, 1992, 2002, 2006

(*continued*)

Continued

El Salvador, 4 elections, 1994–2009	N.A.	None	None	0 of 9 candidates
Guatemala, 7 elections, 1985–2011	N.A.	N.A. However, in 2003 Efraín Ríos Montt was allowed to run on the grounds that the rule could not be applied retroactively.	None	1 of 15 candidates: Alvaro Colom, 1999, 2003, 2007
Honduras, 8 elections, 1981–2009	N.A.	N.A.	Ricardo Zuñiga, 1981; Norma Melgar, 1997	0 of 13 candidates
Mexico, 3 elections, 2000–2012	N.A.	N.A.	Cuauhtémoc Cárdenas, 2000	1 of 8 candidates: Cuauthémoc Cárdenas, 1988, 1994, 2000
Nicaragua, 5 elections, 1990–2011	(Allowed before 1995 and after 2009) Daniel Ortega, 1990 and 2011	Daniel Ortega 1996, 2001, and 2006; Arnoldo Alemán, 2011	Violeta Barrios de Chamorro, 1990	1 of 7 candidates: Daniel Ortega, 1990, 1996, 2001, 2006, 2011
Panama, 4 elections, 1994–2009	N.A.	Guillermo Endara, 2004 and 2009	Mireyra Moscoso, 1994 and 1999; Martín Torrijos, 1994 and 2004	1 of 10 candidates: Guillermo Endara, 1989, 2004, 2009

Paraguay, 4 elections, 1993–2008	N.A.	N.A.	Guillermo Caballero Vargas, 2 of 11 candidates: Domingo Laíno, 1989, 1993, 1998; Lino Oviedo, 2008, and with stand-ins in 1998 and 2003
Peru, 8 elections, 1980–2011	N.A. (except for the 1995 and 2000 elections) Alberto Fujimori, 1995, 2000	Fernando Belaúnde, 1980; Alan García, 2001, 2006; Alejandro Toledo, 2011	Keiko Fujimori, 2011	4 of 16 candidates: Fernando Belaúnde, 1956, 1962, 1963, 1980; Alberto Fujimori, 1990, 1995, 2000; Alan García, 1985, 2001, 2006; Alejandro Toledo, 1995, 2000, 2001, 2011
Uruguay, 6 elections, 1984–2009	N.A.	Jorge Pacheco, 1989; Julio Sanguinetti 1994; Luis Alberto Lacalle, 1999 and 2009	Pedro Bordaberry, 2009; Jorge Batlle, 1989, 1994, 1999	4 of 16 candidates: Jorge Batlle, 1966, 1971, 1989, 1994, 1999; Jorge Pacheco, 1984, 1989, 1994; Tabaré Vázquez 1994, 1999, 2004; Líber Serengi, 1971, 1989, and with a stand-in 1984
Venezuela, 8 elections, 1978–2012	(Allowed as of 1998) Hugo Chávez, 2000, 2006, and 2012	Carlos Andrés Pérez, 1988; Rafael Caldera, 1983, 1993	None	3 of 14 candidates: Rafael Caldera, 1947, 1958, 1963, 1968 (won), 1983, 1993; Andrés Velásquez, 1983, 1988, 1993; Hugo Chávez, 1998, 2000, 2006, 2012

(*continued*)

Continued

Total number of elections in all countries: 112	Total number of elections in which the incumbent was allowed to compete: 22. Total number of elections in which an elected incumbent was allowed to compete and did compete: 20.	Total number of elections in which ex-presidents were allowed to compete: 84 (includes 1 election in Guatemala). Number of elections in which ex-presidents won 10.0%: 34. (For a total of 37 candidates; more than one ex-president competed in Argentina in 2003 and the Dominican Republic in 1982 & 1986.) Number of elections won by ex-presidents: 8.	Total number of elections with an ex-president's last name: 30	Total 37 candidates running three times or more of 221 unique candidates

Note: N.A. = Not applicable. The question of the incumbent's candidacy was not applicable when immediate re-election was prohibited and the question of ex-presidents' candidacies was not applicable when any re-election was prohibited.

Appendix 6

ELECTIONS WON WITH LESS THAN 50% OF THE VOTE, 1978–2012: WHAT WAS THE LIKELY RESULT OF A RUNOFF?

	Elections under Plurality (N = 24)	*Elections under Runoff* (N = 42)	*All Elections* (N = 66)
Result Was Uncertain	8 (33%)		

This appendix provides the country-by-country assessment on which Table 3.3 is based. These assessments are based in turn on the information in Chapters 4-7.

N.A. (Not Applicable): In the first column, N.A. is noted if the election was won with more than 50.0%. In the second column, N.A. is noted if the first-round winner did not tally between 40.0% and 49.9%.

Elections with Plurality

Election	If the election was won with less than 50%, what were the first-round winner's and the runner-up's tallies? Would a runoff victory for the first-round winner have been virtually certain or uncertain; or, was a reversal likely or virtually certain?	If the first-round winner tallied between 40.0% and 49.9% with a 10-point lead, would his or her win in a runoff have been virtually certain or uncertain; or, was a reversal likely or virtually certain?

Argentina

1983	N.A.	N.A.
1989	49.3% to 37%. Win uncertain.	Win uncertain.

Colombia

1978	49.5% to 46.6%. Win uncertain.	N.A.
1982	47% to 41%. Reversal virtually certain.	N.A.
1986	N.A.	N.A.
1990	48% to 24%. Win virtually certain.	Win virtually certain.

Dominican Republic

1978	N.A.	N.A.
1982	47% to 39%. Win virtually certain.	N.A.
1986	42% to 39%. Reversal virtually certain.	N.A.
1990	35.5% to 33.8%. Reversal virtually certain.	N.A.

Honduras

Eight elections between 1981 and 2009	N.A. except in the 2005 election: 49.9% to 46%. Win virtually certain.	N.A. in any of the 8.

Mexico

2000	43% to 37%. Win virtually certain.	N.A.
2006	36% to 35%. Win uncertain.	N.A.
2012	38% to 32%. Win virtually certain.	N.A.

Nicaragua

1990	N.A.	N.A.
2001	N.A.	N.A.
2006	38% to 29%. Reversal virtually certain.	N.A.
2011	N.A.	N.A.

Panama

1994	33% to 29%. Win uncertain.	N.A.
1999	45% to 38%. Win virtually certain.	N.A.
2004	47% to 31%. Win uncertain.	Win uncertain.
2009	N.A.	N.A.

Paraguay

1993	40% to 32%. Reversal likely.	Reversal likely.
1998	N.A.	N.A.
2003	37% to 25%. Reversal likely.	N.A.
2008	40.9% to 30.6%. Win uncertain.	Win uncertain.

Peru

1980	45% to 27%. Win virtually certain.	Win virtually certain.

Uruguay

1984	42% to 34%. Reversal likely.	N.A.
1989	39% to 30%. Win virtually certain.	N.A.
1994	32% to 31%. Win uncertain.	N.A.

Venezuela

1978	47% to 43%. Win uncertain.	N.A.
1983	N.A.	N.A.
1988	N.A.	N.A.
1993	30.5% to 24%. Win virtually certain.	N.A.
1998	N.A.	N.A.
2000	N.A.	N.A.
2006	N.A.	N.A.
2012	N.A.	N.A.

Elections with Runoff

Election	If the election was won with less than 50%, what were the first-round winner's and the runner-up's tallies? Was [or would have been] a runoff victory for the first-round winner virtually certain or uncertain; or, was a reversal likely or virtually certain?	If the first-round winner tallied between 40.0% and 49.9% with a 10-point lead, was [or would have been] his or her win in a runoff virtually certain or uncertain; or, was a reversal likely or virtually certain?

Argentina

1995	49.9% to 29%. Win uncertain.	Win uncertain.
1999	48% to 39%. Win uncertain.	N.A.
2003	24.5% to 22%. Reversal virtually certain.	N.A.
2007	45% to 23%. Win virtually certain.	Win virtually certain.
2011	N.A.	N.A.

Brazil

1989	31% to 17%. Win uncertain.	N.A.
1994	N.A.	N.A.
1998	N.A.	N.A.
2002	46% to 23%. Win virtually certain.	Win virtually certain.
2006	47% to 42%. Win uncertain.	N.A.
2010	47% to 33%. Win uncertain.	Win uncertain.

Chile

1989	N.A.	N.A.
1993	N.A.	N.A.
1999–2000	47.96% to 47.52%. Win uncertain.	N.A.
2005–2006	46% to 25%. Win uncertain.	Win uncertain.
2009–2010	44% to 30%. Win uncertain.	Win uncertain.

Colombia

1994	45.3% to 45.0%. Win uncertain.	N.A.
1998	34.4% to 34.0%. Win uncertain.	N.A.
2002	N.A.	N.A.
2006	N.A.	N.A.
2010	47% to 22%. Win virtually certain.	Win virtually certain.

Costa Rica

1978–1994, 5 elections	N.A.	N.A.
1998	47% to 45%. Win uncertain.	N.A.
2002	39% to 31%. Win uncertain.	N.A.
2006	41% to 40%. Win uncertain.	N.A.
2010	47% to 25%. Win virtually certain.	Win virtually certain.

Dominican Republic

1996	46% to 39%. Win uncertain.	N.A.
2000	49.9% to 25%. Win virtually certain.	Win virtually certain.
2004	N.A.	N.A.
2008	N.A.	N.A.
2012	N.A.	N.A.

Ecuador

1978–1979	28% to 24%. Win uncertain.	N.A.
1984	29% to 28%. Win uncertain.	N.A.
1988	24.5% to 18%. Win uncertain.	N.A.
1992	32% to 25%. Win virtually certain.	N.A.
1996	27% to 26%. Win uncertain.	N.A.
1998	35% to 27%. Win uncertain.	N.A.
2002	21% to 17%. Win uncertain.	N.A.
2006	27% to 23%. Win uncertain.	N.A.
2009	N.A.	N.A.

El Salvador

1994	49% to 26%. Win virtually certain.	Win virtually certain.
1999	N.A.	N.A.
2004	N.A.	N.A.
2009	N.A.	N.A.

Guatemala

1985	39% to 20%. Win uncertain.	N.A.
1990–91	26% to 24%. Win uncertain.	N.A.
1995–96	37% to 22%. Win virtually certain.	N.A.
1999	48% to 30%. Win virtually certain.	Win virtually certain.
2003	34% to 26%. Win uncertain.	N.A.
2007	28% to 24%. Win uncertain.	N.A.
2011	36% to 23%. Win uncertain.	N.A.

Nicaragua

1996	N.A.	N.A.

Peru

1985	N.A.*	N.A.
1990	33% to 29%. Reversal virtually certain.	N.A.
1995	N.A.	N.A.
2001	37% to 26%. Win uncertain.	N.A.
2006	31% to 24%. Win uncertain.	N.A.
2011	32% to 24%. Win uncertain.	N.A.

*As a percentage of all votes, not just valid votes.

Uruguay

1999	40% to 33%. Reversal virtually certain.	N.A.
2004	N.A.	N.A.
2009	49% to 30%. Win uncertain.	Win uncertain.

Appendix 7

NEW PARTIES AS SIGNIFICANT CONTENDERS IN PRESIDENTIAL ELECTIONS, 1978–2012

The rules for the classification of "significant contender" and "new party" are not fully established. For example, Levitsky, Loxton, and Van Dyck (2016: 6) set a very high threshold of at least 10% in five consecutive national legislative elections, plus other conditions, with the result of only eleven new parties in Latin America since 1979.

In general, I follow Mainwaring, Bejarano, and Leongómez (2006: 35–36) and Mainwaring (2016: 11, 63–64). However, I set higher thresholds and focus on presidential elections. I classify a "new party" as a "significant contender" when a party that has not tallied 15% of the presidential vote in any previous third-wave election or in the election just prior to the first third-wave election achieves 15%.

As Mainwaring (2016: 63–64) suggests, some judgments are difficult to make. One difficult judgment is whether or not a "new" party is actually an "old" party that has merely changed its name. If a "new" party is joined in a coalition for an election (or the first round of the election) by presidents or former presidents of an "old" party, I consider it "new" only if the party of the president or former president is the junior partner in a coalition with the "new" party. Also, parties led by former presidents or incumbent presidents or leaders who have won a subnational election for a party but have simply changed the party's name are not considered "new."

In the lists that follow, when the Spanish name of the party or the party's acronym is virtually the only one ever used even in English, the Spanish name or acronym is provided.

New Parties in Elections under Plurality

Total Number of Elections: 45	Number of Elections in Which a New Party won 15.0% or more: 14
Argentina, 2 elections	None
Colombia, 4 elections	National Salvation Movement, 1990
Dominican Republic, 4 elections	Party of Dominican Liberation, 1986
Honduras, 8 elections	None
Mexico, 3 elections	None
Nicaragua, 4 elections	Nicaraguan Liberal Alliance, 2006
Panama, 4 elections	Papa Egoró Movement, 1994; Christian Democratic Party, 1999; Solidarity Party, 2004; Democratic Change, 2009
Paraguay, 4 elections	National Encounter, 1993; Beloved Fatherland, 2003; Patriotic Alliance for Change, 2009
Peru, 1 election	None
Uruguay, 3 elections	None
Venezuela, 8 elections	Radical Cause, 1993; Fifth Republic Movement, 1998; A New Era, 2006; Democratic Unity Roundtable, 2012

Appendix 7 261

New Parties in Elections under Runoff

Total Number of Elections: 65	Number of Elections in Which a New Party won 15.0% or more: 31
Argentina, 5 elections	FREPASO, 1995; Civic Coalition, 2007; Socialist Party, 2011
Brazil, 6 elections	Party of National Reconstruction and the Workers' Party, 1989; Party of Brazilian Social Democracy, 1994; Brazilian Socialist Party, 2002; Green Party, 2006
Chile, 5 elections	Union of the Center-Center, 1989; National Renovation, 2005–2006; New Majority for Chile, 2009–2010
Colombia, 15 elections	Sí Colombia, 1998; Primero Colombia, 2002; Democratic Alternative Pole, 2006; Green Party, 2010
Costa Rica, 9 elections	Anti-Corruption Party, 2002; Libertarian Movement, 2010
Dominican Republic, 5 elections	None
Ecuador, 9 elections	Democratic Left, 1984; Pachakutik Plurinational Unity Movement/New Country, 1996; Patriotic Society Party, 2002; Alianza PAIS, 2006
El Salvador, 4 elections	The FMLN (leading a coalition), 1994
Guatemala, 7 elections	Party of National Advancement, 1990–1991; National Unity for Hope, 2003; Patriotic Party, 2007; Líder and Compromiso, Renovación, y Orden, 2011
Nicaragua, 1 election	None
Peru, 6 elections	United Left, 1985; Change '90, 1990; Union for Peru, 1995; Perú Possible, 2001; Peruvian Nationalist Party (albeit registered under an old party's name), 2006; Alliance for the Great Change, 2011
Uruguay, 3 elections	None

NOTES

Chapter 1

1. Following conventional scholarly definition, "Latin America" includes the countries that were colonized by Spain and Portugal.
2. Paraguay adopted runoff in its 1992 constitution but did not establish regulations for it and continued to use plurality. See http://aristeguinoticias.com/1904/mundo/paraguay-va-a-las-urnas-texto-de-daniel-zovatto/.
3. Author's calculation using www.electionguide.org and, if necessary, national constitutions. (Note that, by 2016, Freedom House classified neither Nicaragua nor Venezuela as "electoral democracies.") Classifications by region follow Freedom House. The figure for sub-Saharan Africa includes several countries that have a territorial distribution requirement.
4. Alejandro Moreno, "Avizoran cambios en el sistema electoral, [They evaluate changes in the electoral system]" *Reforma*, April 14, 2007, p. 6. The 2007 survey was in Mexico's Chamber of Deputies. "Don't know" and other responses were omitted from the calculation.
5. See "Propone Fox segunda vuelta [Fox proposes runoff]," *Reforma*, June 30, 2006, p. 15, and Rodríguez (2009). The former presidential candidate Andrés Manuel López Obrador criticized the rule at the "Private Breakfast with Andrés Manuel López Obrador" (Woodrow Wilson International Center for Scholars, October 11, 2011).
6. The 2006 Nicaraguan presidential candidate José Rizo called the reduction of Nicaragua's threshold from 45% to 35% "a serious mistake" (*Latin America Weekly Report* [LAWR], November 21, 2006, p. 14). Former Venezuelan presidential candidates criticizing plurality are Teodoro Petkoff (author's interview, Washington, DC, January 29, 2007); the COPEI's Eduardo Fernández (author's interview, Caracas, December 5, 2006), and A New Time's Manuel Rosales. For Rosales's view, see "Rosales propone ideas para reforma constitucional," *El Universal*, December 6, 2006, pp. 1–7. Also, Miriam Kornblith of the National Endowment for Democracy reported in an interview with the author on May 22, 2007, in Washington, DC, that, prior to Hugo Chávez's victory in 1998, he had favored a runoff. A Paraguayan former president criticizing plurality is Nicanor Duarte; see *Latin America Regional Report* (LARR), March 30 2004, p. 15. In 2012, the president of Paraguay's PRLA, Blas Llano, advocated runoff; see http://www.paraguay.com/nacionales/guino-a-aplicacion-del-ballotage-84322.
7. *Latin America Weekly Report* (LAWR), March 31, 1994, p. 134; *Latin America Weekly Report* (LAWR), October 3, 1996, p. 453.
8. A runoff was proposed in the legislature in 2013 but was not approved. See "Descartada la segunda vuelta electoral [Second electoral round discarded]," *La Prensa*, March 15, 2014, at www.laprensa.hn/honduras/tegucigalpa/585060-96. Also, comments to this effect by Kevin

Casas-Zamora at the seminar "Prospects for the November Elections in Honduras," The National Democratic Institute, September 24, 2013, Washington, DC.
9. Unfortunately, there is no cross-national measurement of problems of fraud. As Chapter 2 discusses, only two elections during this period were determined not to meet standards of freedom and fairness by the Organization of American States.
10. Author's interview, Professor Carlos Romero, Universidad Central de Venezuela, November 29, 2006, in Caracas.
11. Public-opinion analyst Marta Lagos, cited in Barrionuevo (2009: A5).
12. Author's interview, Senator Fernando Flores of the Partido por la Democracia, October 18, 2006, in Valparaiso, Chile.
13. The term "electoral sweet spot" was recently coined by Carey and Hix (2011).
14. Author's interview, Fernando Tuesta, Universidad Católica del Perú (by telephone), June 14, 2006.
15. Author's interview, Luis Rubio, President, CIDAC, in Mexico City, June 28, 2006.

Chapter 2

1. For example, at the Workshop entitled "Democracy in Latin America: Advances, Setbacks, and Impasses" at the meeting of the Latin American Studies Association on May 23–26, 2016 in New York City, V-Dem indices were used by the participants, including Evelyne Huber and Scott Mainwaring, more than any other.
2. Also, amid Mexico's disputed 2006 election, political analysts emphasized 40% as an important threshold for legitimacy. These analysts included Manuel Camacho Solís (at the time advisor to Andrés Manuel López Obrador), speaking at the Inter-American Dialogue, July 26, 2006, Washington, DC, and, in author's interviews, Professor Ilán Bitzberg (El Colegio de México), June 29, 2006, in Mexico City and Professor Eric Magar (Instituto Tecnológico Autónomo de México, ITAM), June 30, 3006, in Mexico City.

Chapter 3

1. Author's interview, Professor Luis Salamanca, Universidad Central de Venezuela, in Caracas, December 5, 2006.
2. For those elections not included in Payne, Zovatto G., and M. Díaz (2007: Appendix 3), the effective number was provided for Brazil in Mainwaring (1997: 74); for Chile in Valenzuela (1994: 178); for Costa Rica, courtesy of Fabrice Lehoucq; and for Ecuador, courtesy of Martin Needler, based on data in Maier (1969: 82). The calculation for El Salvador's 1982 Constituent Assembly election is my own from Nohlen (2005, Vol. 1: 281), for Guatemala's 1984 Constituent Assembly election my own from Nohlen (2005, Vol. 1: 331), and for Peru's 1978 Constituent Assembly election my own from Nohlen (2005, Vol. 2: 462).
3. Diamond (1996: 80–81), Huntington (1968: 42), Mainwaring and Shugart (1997b), and Weiner and LaPalombara (1966: 408). Gradually, the number of parties considered "too many" has increased; in the 1960s, more than two parties was usually considered "too many," but more recently the threshold has been four or more; see, for example, Mainwaring and Shugart (1997b: 466).
4. They also raise the possibility of a 40% threshold or a minimum gap between the first-place finisher and the runner-up.
5. Author's interview, Luis Rubio, President, CIDAC, in Mexico City, June 28, 2006.
6. However, Toledo competed in both Peru's 1995 and 2000 elections and led Peru's opposition after the 2000 election and, by my count, did have two years of experience.
7. Scholarly criticism of presidentialism has been rebutted. See Mainwaring and Shugart (1997b), Cheibub (2007), and Pérez-Liñán (2007: 203–213).
8. This possibility was originally suggested by Duverger himself; see Clark and Golder (2006: 706).
9. ConsultAndes, *Monthly Political Analysis*, June 2007, p. 2.

10. "The Politician as Thinker: Fernando Henrique Cardoso Dissects Brazil's Problems," *The Economist*, November 7, 2015, p. 32.
11. Information about disputes was drawn from the *Latin American Weekly Report* and *Latin American Regional Report*. See the final section of this chapter for a discussion of these sources.
12. Author's interview, Ambassador Guillermo Gonzáles, Tegucigalpa, October 29, 2013.
13. "Segunda vuelta en Bogotá [Second round in Bogota]?" *Semana*, April 9, 2017, p. 36.
14. Author's interviews with scholars and citizens in Chile, October 12–19, 2006.
15. Author's interview, Paula Alonso, Associate Professor of History, George Washington University, January 13, 2014, in Washington DC.
16. Author's interview, Senator Jaime Gazmuri of the Socialist Party, October 18, 2006, in Valparaíso. Similar statements were made also in author's interviews with former Senator Edgardo Boeninger of the Christian Democratic Party in Santiago, October 16, 2006, and by Juan Ignacio García (Director, Servicio Electoral de Chile) in Santiago, October 13, 2006.
17. On the classification of the Peronist Party, the PRI, and the Colorado Party as cartel parties, see Levitsky (2001). For the Peronist Party, see also Jones and Hwang (2005: 115). The two parties in Colombia, Honduras, Uruguay, and Venezuela have frequently been described as duopolies. For Colombia, see Hoskin (1988: 47–61) and Pearce (1990: 183–199); for Honduras, see McDonald and Ruhl (1989: 112–122) and Taylor-Robinson (2001: 594); for Uruguay, Luna (2006:15) and Weinstein (1975: 50–84); for Venezuela, Levine (1994: 170) and Coppedge (1994b: 41–51). For statements about the importance of patronage to these parties, see Chapters 4, 5, and 6.
18. My text about the PLD in Chapter 5 indicates the questions about its classification.
19. Author's interview, scholar and political analyst Nicolás Lynch, May 23, 2006, in Lima.
20. See http://www.nsd.uib./no/european_election_database/index.html. The author thanks Julian Waller, PhD candidate at George Washington University, for his research on this issue. We did not include countries that were semi-presidential or whose presidents were largely figureheads.
21. ConsultAndes (2011d: 8). See also ConsultAndes (2010: 1–3) with respect to García's discouragement of APRA's nomination of another presidential candidate in 2011.
22. See http://www.nsd.uib./no/european_election_database/index.html. The author thanks Julian Waller, PhD candidate at George Washington University, for his research on this issue. We did not include countries that were semi-presidential or whose presidents were largely figureheads.
23. Author's interview, scholar and political analyst Nicolás Lynch, May 23, 2006, in Lima, Peru.
24. See, for example, Fleischer (2014: 3).
25. Quoted by Weymouth (2012: B5).
26. "Voceros del Apra y humalismo descalifican a encuestadores [Spokespersons for APRA and Humalismo criticize survey companies]," *El Comercio*, September 19, 2010, p. A16.
27. Statement by 2016 Popular Action presidential candidate Alfredo Barnechea in an interview, "Nosotros creemos que vamos a competir en la segunda vuelta contra Keiko Fujimori [We believe that we will compete in the runoff against Keiko Fujimori]," *La República*, December 27, 2015, p. 4.
28. For Mexico, author's interview, Chappell Lawson (Massachusetts Institute of Technology), in Mexico City, July 2, 2006. For Peru, Alfredo Torres, president, Ipsos Apoyo Opinión y Mercado, speaking on Peru's television news program Cuarto Poder, May 29, 2011.
29. "Blind Data," *The Economist*, October 4, 2014, p. 42.

Chapter 4

1. Prior to 1978, in the 1958–1973 presidential elections, voter turnout was even higher, above 90%; see Crisp and Levine (1998: 34).
2. Author's interviews, COPEI's Eduardo Fernández, in Caracas, December 5, 2006; MAS's Teodoro Petkoff, in Washington, DC, January 29, 2007. For the view of A New Time's Manuel Rosales, see "Rosales propone ideas para reforma constitucional [Rosales proposes ideas for constitutional reform]," *El Universal*, December 6, 2006, 1–7. Also, Miriam Kornblith of the

National Endowment for Democracy reported in an author's interview on May 22, 2007, in Washington, DC, that, prior to Hugo Chávez's victory in 1998, he had favored a runoff.
3. These scholars include, in author's interviews, Professor Carlos Romero, Universidad Central de Venezuela, in Caracas, November 29, 2006, and Professor Luis Salamanca, Universidad Central de Venezuela, in Caracas, December 5, 2006.
4. Author's interviews with Professor Michael Coppedge, University of Notre Dame, September 1, 2006, in Philadelphia, Pennsylvania; Professor Steve Ellner, Universidad de Oriente, Venezuela, April 15, 2008, Washington, DC; Eduardo Fernández, former COPEI leader and President, Centro Internacional de Formación Aristides Calvani, in Caracas, December 5, 2006; José Antonio Gil Yepes, Datanalisís, in Caracas, November 27, 2006; Teodoro Petkoff, January 29, 2007, in Washington, DC; Professor Carlos Romero, Universidad Central de Venezuela, November 29, 2006, in Caracas; and Professor Luis Salamanca, Universidad Central de Venezuela, in Caracas, December 5, 2006.
5. Quoted by Farah (1992: A10).
6. Brooke (1993: A3). See also Dietz and Myers (2007: 71).
7. Among the political analysts believing that Velásquez had done better than fourth place were Hellinger (2003: 36) and, in author's interviews, José Antonio Gil Yepes, Datanalisis, in Caracas, November 27, 2006; Professor Luis Salamanca, Universidad Central de Venezuela, December 5, 2006, in Caracas; and Professor Carlos Romero, Universidad Central de Venezuela, November 29, 2006, in Caracas.
8. Author's interview, Eduardo Fernández, President, Centro Internacional de Formación Aristides Calvani, in Caracas, December 5, 2006.
9. Ambassador Patrick D. Duddy, speaking at "Political Transition in Venezuela: Next Steps and the Implications for U.S. Policy," at the Woodrow Wilson International Center for Scholars, February 25, 2013, Washington DC.
10. See also "Dealing with Daniel," *The Economist*, November 11, 2006, p. 15.
11. "Apoyan segunda vuelta y creen que beneficiaria a Morena y PAN [They support the second round and believe it would benefit Morena and the PAN]," reporting the results of surveys by Parametria in 2009 and 2017 and available at parametria.com.mx; the data were kindly forwarded to the author by Kevin J. Middlebrook, July 27, 2017.
12. Denise Dresser, presentation at the conference "Whither Mexican Democracy?" at the Woodrow Wilson International Center for Scholars, September 15, 2006, in Washington, DC.
13. Author's interviews with Raúl Benítez, Universidad Nacional Autónoma de México, July 4, 2006, in Mexico City; Ilán Bizberg, El Colegio de México, June 29, 2006, in Mexico City; Fabrice Lehoucq, Centro de Investigación y Docencia Económicas (CIDE), June 26, 2006, in Mexico City; Nora Lustig, George Washington University, September 13, 2007, in Washington, DC.; and Gabriel Szekely, El Colegio de México, June 27, 2006, in Mexico City.
14. Author's interviews with Federico Estévez, Instituto Tecnológico Autónomo de México (ITAM), June 30, 2006, in Mexico City; Joy Langston, Centro de Investigación y Docencia Económicas (CIDE), July 9, 2006, in Mexico City; and Jacqueline Preschard, Universidad Nacional Autónoma de México, March 16, 2006, in San Juan, Puerto Rico.
15. Author's interview, Duncan Wood, Director of the Mexico Institute, Woodrow Wilson International Center for Scholars, May 15, 2015, in Washington, DC. See also "Mexico's presidential election: Fresh Face, Same Old Party," *The Economist*, June 23, 2012, p. 41. On earlier ambivalence in the PAN and PRD, see Shugart (2007: 200).
16. "Happy Birthday, Señor Fox," *The Economist*, July 8, 2000, p. 32. See also Greene (2002: 779) and Berman (2000: 37).
17. Comments by Senator Adolfo Aguilar Zinser, "Luncheon Discussion," July 19, 2000, at the Brookings Institution, in Washington, DC. See also Magaloni and Poiré (2004: 281).
18. Dillon (2000: A9). Also, on the PRI's continuing power over media, see *Latin America Weekly Report* (LAWR), May 2, 2000, p. 199.

19. Author's interviews with Alejandro Poiré, Instituto Tecnológico Autónomo de México (ITAM), November 11, 2006, in Cambridge, Massachusetts, and Eric Magar, Instituto Tecnológico Autónomo de México (ITAM), in Mexico City, June 30, 2006.
20. Author's interviews with Rafael Aranda, Avantel, in Mexico City, July 4, 2006, and Ilán Bizberg, El Colegio de México, in Mexico City, June 29, 2006.
21. Author's interviews with Benito Nacif, Centro de Investigación y Docencia Económicas (CIDE), June 29, 2006, in Mexico City, and Alejandro Moreno, Instituto Tecnológico Autónomo de México (ITAM), in Mexico City, June 28, 2006.
22. Also, author's interview, Kevin J. Middlebrook, University of London, in Toronto, Canada, October 10, 2010; comments by John Bailey, Georgetown University, at the conference "Security, Drugs, and Democracy in Latin America," at the George Washington University, February 28, 2011; and "Mexico's presidential election: Fresh Face, Same Old Party," *The Economist*, June 23, 2012, p. 39. This view was not unanimous, however.
23. See, for example, "Murder in Mexico: The Great Mystery," *The Economist*, April 30, 2016, pp. 32–33.
24. Quoted in Miroff (2014: A8).
25. Quoted by O'Connor (2012: A16).
26. Quoted by O'Connor (2012: A16).
27. Especially in 2009, the precise figures were controversial. There was agreement, however, that the voter registry was inflated and that this inflation was one reason for low turnout.
28. These scholars and officials include Julieta Castellanos, Rector, Universidad Nacional Autónoma de Honduras, in her presentation "The Implications of Honduras' Elections," hosted by the Inter-American Dialogue and the Center for Inter-American Policy and Research, Washington, DC, November 27, 2013; also, in author's interviews, Alvaro Calix, Universidad Nacional Autónoma de Honduras, in Tegucigalpa, October 29, 2013; Jorge Milla-Reyes, Honduran Ambassador to the United States, in Washington, DC, January 25, 2016; Antonio Ortez, former Liberal Party legislator, in Tegucigalpa, October 30, 2013; Adán Palacios, former Honduran election official, in Tegucigalpa, October 30, 2013; Ernesto Paz, former foreign affairs minister and former professor, Universidad Nacional Autónoma de Honduras, in Tegucigalpa, October 30, 2013.
29. Author's interview, Antonio Ortez, former Liberal Party legislator, in Tegucigalpa, October 30, 2013.
30. Author's interview, Leo Valladares, former Director of the Honduran Human Rights Commission, in Tegucigalpa, October 28, 2013.
31. Castellanos, Rector, Universidad Nacional Autónoma de Honduras (2013); Adán Palacios, former election official, cited in Phillips and Malkin (2013: A5), and various author's interviews, including Antonio Ortez, former Liberal Party legislator, in Tegucigalpa, October 30, 2013.
32. Castellanos, Rector, Universidad Nacional Autónoma de Honduras (2013).
33. Author's interviews, Jorge Ceballos, Program Officer for Central America, International Republican Institute, in Tegucigalpa, October 29, 2013; Alvaro Calix, Professor, Universidad Nacional Autónoma de Honduras, in Tegucigalpa, October 29, 2013; and Antonio Ortez, former Liberal Party legislator, in Tegucigalpa, October 30, 2013.
34. The most compelling statement of this view was in author's interview, Juliette Handal de Castillo (Libre vice-presidential candidate), in Tegucigalpa, October 30, 2013.
35. "The Democracy Dividend," *The Economist*, December 7, 2006, pp. 45–46.
36. Exact figures vary by source. This figure is from Riquelme (1994: 51).
37. On the points in this paragraph, see Riquelme (1994: 24–26).
38. Fernando Lugo, in an address at the George Washington University, hosted by the George Washington University and the Washington Office on Latin America, Washington, DC, June 18, 2007.
39. "The Next Leftist on the Block," *The Economist*, August 9, 2008, p. 35, and Lugo (2009: 151).

Chapter 5

1. Turnout rates were similarly high in Chile, but registration was not required in Chile and, accordingly, if our indicator were turnout as a percentage of the population, Uruguay's rate would be the highest in the region.
2. "The Mystery behind Mujica's Mask," *The Economist*, October 24, 2009, p. 44.
3. Professor Jonathan Hartlyn, University of North Carolina at Chapel Hill, comments on a draft of this manuscript, February 6, 2014.
4. Professor Jonathan Hartlyn, University of North Carolina at Chapel Hill, comments on a draft of this manuscript, February 6, 2014. He points out that the Carter Center was invited to observe the election only at a very late date and, accordingly, was restricted to comments only about events after it had arrived in the Dominican Republic.
5. "Running Dry," *The Economist*, February 16, 1991, p. 34.
6. See also "A Rum Do," *The Economist*, November 24, 2012, p. 40.
7. Scott Mainwaring, "Democracy in Latin America," presentation at the Woodrow Wilson International Center for Scholars, March 22, 2013. For similar assessments, see Pereira and Melo (2012: 158) and Power (2010: 220–223).
8. Lula, speaking at the Conference on Latin American and Caribbean Debt, Havana, August 1985, cited in *Dollars and Sense* 111 (November 1985): cover page. See also Hunter (2010: 110–112) and Keck (1992: 159).
9. Author's interview, David Fleischer, Professor, University of Brasilia, June 10, 2009, in Rio de Janeiro; Leslie Bethell, speaking at the conference "Populism of the Twenty-First Century," Woodrow Wilson International Center for Scholars, October 8, 2009.
10. Former President Ricardo Lagos, speaking at the Inter-American Dialogue, January 24, 2012, in Washington, DC. Also, in author's interviews, Edgardo Boeninger, former senator and head of Michelle Bachelet's electoral commission, October 16, 2006, in Santiago and Genaro Arriagada, former minister of the presidency, October 14, 2006, in Santiago.
11. Author's interview, María de los Angeles, Professor, Univesidad Diego Portales and Executive Director, Fundación Chile 21, October 12, 2006, in Santiago, Chile.
12. Also, author's interviews, Dr. Claudio Fuentes, FLACSO, October 13, 2006, in Santiago; Professor Eugenio Guzmán, Universidad Adolfo Ibañez, October 16, 2006, in Santiago.
13. Under the 1980 constitution, terms for the lower house were to be four years and terms for the upper house eight years (with half the senators renewed in one election and half in the next) and were concurrent with a presidential term of eight years. These legislative term lengths continued but, as indicated in the text, the length of the presidential term changed several times.
14. Also, author's interview with Edgardo Boeninger, former senator and head of Michelle Bachelet's electoral-reform commission, in Santiago, October 16, 2006.
15. "Lagos no tiene garantizados los votos de la izquierda en la segunda vuelta [Lagos is not guaranteed the votes of the left in the runoff]," *La Vanguardia*, December 14, 1999 (via Factiva).
16. "Left Beats Fraud in Salvador Poll," *The Guardian*, March 22, 1994 (via Factiva).
17. E-mail communication from Geoff Thale, Program Director, Washington Office on Latin America, August 1, 2013. These problems were also observed by the author during her participation in an election-monitoring delegation in El Salvador in 1994.
18. Author's interview, Héctor Silva Avalos, Research Fellow, Center for Latin American and Latino Studies, American University, Washington, DC, October 1, 2013.
19. Author's interviews, Héctor Silva Avalos, Research Fellow, Center for Latin American and Latino Studies, American University, Washington, DC, October 1, 2013; Héctor Silva, Mayor of San Salvador, in a presentation at the Inter-American Dialogue, May 12, 1997; and Barry (1991: 17–18).
20. Vickers and Spence (1994: 10) and Héctor Silva Avalos, presentation at the Seminar "The Challenges of Sustaining Peace: An Examination of El Salvador's Peace Process and Its Consequences Today," George Washington University, Washington, DC, September 19, 2012.

21. "Left Beats Fraud in Salvador Poll," *The Guardian*, March 22, 1994 (via Factiva).
22. Beeson (2009). Also, Rubén I. Zamora, former candidate for the Salvadoran presidency, "15 Years After the Peace Agreement: Problems of Peace-Building in El Salvador," Presentation at the Woodrow Wilson International Center for Scholars, November 1, 2006, Washington, DC; Roberto Rubio, Executive Director, FUNDE (the National Foundation for Development) in El Salvador, presentation at the Washington Office on Latin America, January 15, 2009, Washington, DC, and many other sources.
23. PELA, "El Salvador: unas elecciones presidenciales marcadas por el conflicto y la polarización ideológica [El Salvador: Presidential Elections Marked by Conflict and Ideological Polarization]," No. 57 (January 2014), p. 2.

Chapter 6

1. Author's interview, former President Vinicio Cerezo, in Antigua, Guatemala, November 1, 2013. He cited in particular the advantage of open discussions among presidential candidates after the first round.
2. Author's interview, Edelberto Torres-Rivas, in Guatemala City, November 3, 2013.
3. The standard deviation was 2.40 for Colom in PELA's 2002 survey. It is rare that a standard deviation exceeds 2.0 in PELA surveys. In the case of Colom in 2002, he was classified at the "extreme right" or "right" by more than 20% of the respondents—very anomalous classifications for a candidate who had been the presidential nominee of a coalition of former guerrilla groups. By contrast, in 2004 the standard deviation for Colom was 1.70, within the conventional range.
4. http://www.cidob.org/es/documentación.bigrafias_lideres_políticos/amerca_central_y_caribe/guatemala/alvaro_colom_caballeros. Accessed July 1, 2014.
5. For GANA, see LARR, October 2007, p. 3; for the FRG, see LARR, November 2007, p. 2; for Suger, see PlazaPublíca.com.gt/content/Pequeñas-cosas-que-no-cuadran. Accessed November 13, 2013.
6. Cynicism emerged in part from endemic vote-buying. On vote-buying in Colombia, see www.freedomhouse/org/report/freedomintheworld/1998/Colombia and www.freedomhouse/org/report/freedomintheworld/2011/Colombia.
7. Pedro Vanegas, "Hacia una reforma necesaria?" [Towards a necessary reform?] *Revista Zero*, at http://190.7.110.123/pdf/5_revistaZero/ZERO%2025.PedroVanegas.pdf. Vanegas applies the concept of legitimacy.
8. This possibility is raised in "La metamorphosis," *Semana*, July 27, 1998, at www.semana.com/nacion/articulo/la-metamorfosis/36571-3.
9. Richani (2013: 172) and "El Voto Tirofijo," at http://www.semana.com/nacion/articulo/el-voto-de-tirofijo/36608-3.
10. Author's interview, Adam Isacson, Senior Associate for Regional Security Policy, Washington Office on Latin America, October 2, 2013, in Washington, DC.
11. Author's interview, Adam Isacson, Senior Associate for Regional Security Policy, Washington Office on Latin America, October 2, 2013, in Washington, DC.
12. "Por qué ganó Santos y por qué perdió Mockus, [Why did Santos win and Mockus lose]" *La Semana*, June 20, 2010, at www.semana.com/politica/articulo/por-que-gano-santos-que-perdio-mockus/118245-3. Accessed July 2, 2014.
13. Grupo de Opinión Pública de la Universidad de Lima, Barómetro, Estudio 463, Lima Metropolitana y Callao, September 10–11, 2005, item 32.
14. "El Horno de las Urnas, [The Making of the Balloting]" *Caretas*, March 31, 1994, pp. 12–13, 81.
15. Cited in *El Comercio*, April 11, 2011, p. A14.
16. For political analysts, see ConsultAndes (2009: 4); for the public, Grupo de Opinión Pública de la Universidad de Lima, Barómetro, Estudio 277, Provincia de Lima y Región Callao, August 15–16, 2009, item 21.

17. Schmidt is reporting survey data identical to PELA's, but gathered by a Peruvian firm among citizens, not legislators. PELA surveys are not available until the 1995 election.
18. Luis Pásara, writing in *Caretas*, February 25, 1991, p. 53, cited by Kenney (2004: 145).
19. Former agriculture minister Carlos Amat y Leon, cited in *La República*, May 3, 1992, and quoted in Daeschner (1993: 278).
20. Presentation by former President Osvaldo Hurtado, Inter-American Dialogue, April 6, 2005, Washington, DC.
21. "Going for Silver," *The Economist*, May 18, 1996, p. 42; LAWR, May 30, 1996, p. 229.
22. "Going for Silver," *The Economist*, May 18, 1996, p. 42.
23. "Ecuador's Post-Modern Coup," *The Economist*, February 15, 1997, p. 40.
24. "Mixed Blessings," *The Economist*, February 26, 2002, p. 35.

Chapter 7

1. A runoff would have been held in 1999 if the threshold were 40% plus a ten-point lead, but in Argentina 45% was sufficient also.
2. Author's interview with former vice-president Kevin Casas-Zamora, October 16, 2013, in Washington, DC.
3. President Óscar Arias, speaking at "Challenges for Latin America in the 21st Century," at the Carnegie Endowment-Council of the Americas, Washington, DC, December 4, 2006. Arias responded to a question about the rule and said that he was happy with it and believed the 40% threshold was better than 50%. Also, author's interview with former vice-president Kevin Casas-Zamora, October 16, 2013, in Washington, DC; and, Rodríguez Echeverría (2006: 163).
4. Sergio Berensztein, Professor, University Torcuato de Tella, Argentina, at the 19th Annual CAF Conference (Corporación Andino de Fomento and the Inter-American Dialogue), Washington, DC, September 9, 2015.
5. "Bello" [Michael Reid] in "The Persistence of Peronism," *The Economist*, October 17, 2015, p. 42.
6. My figures are from McGuire (1995: 241) and are the numbers most commonly provided. The figures in Nohlen (2005: 112) are slightly different.
7. Author's interview, Paula Alonso, Professor of History, George Washington University, January 13, 2014, in Washington, DC.
8. "A Good Day for Argentine Democracy," *The Economist*, November 1, 1997, p. 33.
9. "De la Rua's Surprise for Argentina," *The Economist*, February 19, 2000, p. 37.
10. Unfortunately, De la Rúa was not included in PELA surveys.
11. "Not So Super Powers," *The Economist*, August 12, 2006, p. 29; Reid (2007: 132).
12. See also "A Big Surprise," *The Economist*, October 31, 2015, p. 33.

Chapter 8

1. Information about the concurrence or non-concurrence of executive and presidential elections is ascertained from Nohlen (2005) and the other sources cited in Chapter 2.
2. Also, author's interview, Henry Pease, Catholic University of Peru (and 1990 presidential candidate), May 23, 2006, in Lima.
3. Acevedo, Ausejo, Rojas, and Sulmont (2011: 86–94), including such recommendations by Tanaka, Tuesta, and Pease, and numerous author's interviews.
4. See, for example, on the Peruvian case, "OPNPE y JNE piden debater ya la reforma electoral [The ONPE and the JNE Ask That The Electoral Reform Be Debated]," *La República*, July 27, 2015, p. 9.
5. www.news.gallup.com/219320/seven-dissatisfied-governed.aspx. Accessed December 8, 2017.

6. The Americas Barometer by the Latin America Public Opinion Project (LAPOP) at www.LapopSurveys.
7. www.fairvote.org/research-and-analysis/congressional-elections/dubious-democracy/dubious-democracy-1982-2010. Other assessments vary slightly.
8. Goldberg, Michelle. 2016. "Tyranny of the Minority." *The New York Times*, September 26, A25.
9. "Gerrymandering: Boundary Police," *The Economist*, June 24, 2017, p. 24.
10. "Powering Down," *The Economist*, November 8, 2014, p. 25; Keisling (2010: A5).
11. Eliza Collins, "Poll: Clinton, Trump Most Unfavorable Candidates Ever," at www.usatoday.com/story/news/politicss/onpolitics/2016/08/31/polls-clinton-trump-most-unpopular. Accessed October 21, 2016.
12. Joseph Carroll, "Seven out of 10 Americans Accept Bush as Legitimate President," at www.gallup.com/2001poll/46871/seven-americans-accept-bush-legitimate.president.aspx. Accessed September 5, 2015.
13. www.cnn.com/2016/11/10/politics-gary-johnson-jill-stein-spoiler.index.html. Accessed December 8, 2017.
14. See, for example, a 2013 Gallup poll, available at www.gallup.com/159881/amercains-call-term-limits-end-electoral-college.aspx. Accessed September 12, 2015.
15. Jeffrey M. Jones, "Americans' Desire for a Third Party Persists This Election Year," at www.gallup.com/poll/195920/americas-desire-third-party-persist.election.year.aspx. Accessed July 18, 2017.
16. To date, scholarly studies are limited. See, however, Nogourney (2013: A1 and A12) and Wilson (2013: A5).
17. See, for example, Dean (2016) and the editorials "A Weak Election Exposed" and "Election Upgrades," in *The Washington Post*, April 7, 2012, p. A12, and November 13, 2014, p. A18 (among numerous similar editorials).
18. Mayor Gavin Newsom, quoted in Heather Knight, "Ranked-Choice Voting Sets Stage for New Tactics," Accessed July 16, 2017, at http://www.sfgate.com/cgi-bin/article.cfi?f=/c/a/2010/11/16/BAVLIGCDQK.DTL&type=printable.
19. Author's interview, Professor Fabrice Lehoucq, CIDE, Mexico City, June 26, 2006.

BIBLIOGRAPHY

Abente Brun, Diego. 2005. "Uruguay and Paraguay: An Arduous Transition." In *Latin America: Its Problems and Its Promise*, ed. Jan K. Black, 4th ed., 556–579. Boulder, CO: Westview Press.

Abente Brun, Diego. 2007. "The Quality of Democracy in Small South American Countries: The Case of Paraguay." National Endowment for Democracy Working Paper #344. November.

Abente Brun, Diego. 2009. "Paraguay: The Unraveling of One-Party Rule." *Journal of Democracy* 20(1): 143–156.

Acemoglu, Daron, and James A. Robinson. 2006. *Economic Origins of Dictatorship and Democracy*. New York: Cambridge University Press.

Acevedo, Jorge, Flavio Ausejo, Josefa Rojas, and David Sulmont. 2011. "El sistema electoral en el Perú." In *La Democracia y sus Instituciones en Debate [Democracy and Its Institutions in Debate]*, eds. Henry Pease García and Giofianni Peirano Torriani, 69–96. Lima: Fondo Editorial Pontificia Universidad Católica del Perú.

Ahmed, Amel. 2013. *Democracy and the Politics of Electoral System Choice*. New York: Cambridge University Press.

Aizenman, Nureth Celina. 2006. "Old U.S. Adversary Poised for Comeback." *Washington Post*, November 5, A20.

Albarracín, Juan, and Juan Pablo Milanese. 2012. "The Impact of the Colombian Electoral Reform on Congressional and Sub-national Elections." Paper presented at the 30th International Congress of the Latin American Studies Association, San Francisco, CA, May 23–26.

Alcántara, Manuel. 2012. "Elections in Latin America 1999–2011: A Comparative Analysis." Helen Kellogg Institute Working Paper #386. Helen Kellogg Institute for International Studies.

Alemán, Eduardo, and Sebastián M. Saiegh. 2007. "Legislative Preferences, Political Parties, and Coalition Unity in Chile." *Comparative Politics* 39(3): 253–272.

Alexander, Gerard. 2004. "France: Reform-Mongering between Majority Runoff and Proportionality." In *Handbook of Electoral System Choice*, ed. Josep M. Colomer, 209–221. New York: Palgrave Macmillan.

Allison, Michael E. 2006. "The Transition from Armed Opposition to Electoral Opposition in Central America." *Latin American Politics and Society* 48(4): 137–161.

Altman, David. 2010. "The 2009 Elections in Uruguay." *Electoral Studies* 29(3): 533–536.

Altman, David, and Rosanna Castiglioni. 2006. "The 2004 Uruguayan Elections: A Political Earthquake Foretold." *Electoral Studies* 25: 147–191.

Amparo Casar, María. 2010. "Executive-Legislative Relations: Continuity or Change?." In *Mexico's Democratic Challenges: Politics, Government, and Society*, eds. Andrew Selee and Jacqueline Peschard, 117–134. Stanford, CA: Stanford University Press.

Anderson, Christopher J., André Blais, Shaun Bowler, Todd Donovan, and Ola Listhaug. 2005. *Losers' Consent: Elections and Democratic Legitimacy*. Oxford: Oxford University Press.

Anderson, Leslie. 2009. "The Problem of Single-Party Predominance in an Unconsolidated Democracy: The Example of Argentina." *Perspectives on Politics* 7(4): 767–784.

Anderson, Leslie, and Lawrence C. Dodd. 2002. "Nicaragua Votes: The Elections of 2001." *Journal of Democracy* 13(3): 80–94.

Anderson, Thomas P. 1998. *Politics in Central America: Guatemala, El Salvador, Honduras, and Nicaragua*. New York: Praeger Publishers.

Arceneaux, Craig. 2013. *Democratic Latin America*. Upper Saddle River, NJ: Pearson.

Artiga-González, Álvaro. 2004. "Guatemala." In *DV: La Elección Presidencial Mediante Doble Vuelta en Latinoamérica* [Runoff: Presidential Election Under Runoff in Latin America], ed. Rafael Martínez, 305–322. Barcelona: Insitut de Ciències Polítiques i Socials.

Azpuru, Dinorah. 2010. The Salience of Ideology: Fifteen Years of Presidential Elections in El Salvador. *Latin American Politics and Society* 52(2): 103–138.

Azpuru, Dinorah, and Ligia Blanco. 2008. "Guatemala 2007: Un Año de Contrastes para la Democracia [Guatemala 2007: A Year of Contrasts for Democracy]." *Revista de Ciencia Política* 28(1): 217–244.

Bagley, Bruce Michael. 1990. "Understanding Colombian Democracy." *Journal of Inter-American Studies and World Affairs* 32(2): 143–155.

Baiocchi, Gianpaolo, and Sofia Checa. 2008. "The New and the Old in Brazil's PT." In *Leftovers: Tales of the Latin American Left*, eds. Jorge G. Castañeda and Marco A. Morales, 105–128. New York: Routledge.

Barnes, William A. 1997. "Elections in Incomplete Democracies: The Myth and the Reality of Polarization, and the Puzzle of Voter Turnout, in Nicaragua and El Salvador." Paper presented at the 20th International Congress of the Latin American Studies Association, Guadalajara, Mexico, April 17–19.

Barrionuevo, Alexei. 2009. "Conservative Wins in the First Round of Elections in Chile." *New York Times*, December 13, A5.

Barry, Tom. 1991. *El Salvador: A Country Guide*. Albuquerque, NM: Inter-Hemispheric Education Resource Center.

Barry, Tom. 1992. *Inside Guatemala*. Albuquerque, NM: Inter-Hemispheric Education Resource Center.

Basombrío, Carlos. 2011. *Análisis de los Resultados Electorales* [Analysis of the Electoral Results]. Lima: Ipsos Apoyo

Beeson, Bart. 2009. "El Salvador's Revolution by Majority." *Foreign Policy* (Web Exclusive). Available at http://foreignpolicy.com/2009/03/11/el-salvadors-revolution-by-majority/

Bejarano, Ana María. 2011. *Precarious Democracies: Understanding Regime Stability and Change in Colombia and Venezuela*. Notre Dame, IN: University of Notre Dame Press.

Bejarano, Ana María. 2012. "Commentary: Two Decades of Negotiation in Colombia—Contrasting Results and Missed Opportunities." In *In the Wake of War*, ed. Cynthia J. Arnson, 207–214. Stanford: Stanford University Press.

Benjamin, Elizabeth. 2009. *Former Tupamaro Revolutionary José Mujica's Presidency Will Likely Follow the Incumbent's Successful Policies*. Council on Hemispheric Affairs. December 18.

Berman, Paul. 2000. "Mexico's Third Way." *New York Times Magazine*, July 2, 34–39.

Binder, Sarah. 2014. *Polarized We Govern?* Washington, DC: Brookings Institution Strengthening American Democracy Series, May 27.

Boas, Taylor C. 2007. "Varieties of Electioneering: Empathetic Personalism in Chile's Presidential Election Campaigns." Paper presented at the 27th International Congress of the Latin American Studies Association, Montreal, Canada, September 5–8.

Booth, John A., and Mitchell A. Seligson. 2009. *The Legitimacy Puzzle in Latin America: Political Support and Democracy in Eight Nations*. New York: Cambridge University Press.

Booth, John A., Christine J. Wade, and Thomas W. Walker. 2010. *Understanding Central America: Global Forces, Rebellion, and Change*, 5th ed. Boulder, CO: Westview Press.

Booth, John A., Christine J. Wade, and Thomas W. Walker. 2015. *Understanding Central America: Global Forces, Rebellion, and Change*, 6th ed. Boulder, CO: Westview Press.

Bormann, Nils-Christian, and Matt Golder. 2013. "Democratic Electoral Systems Around the World, 1946–2011." *Electoral Studies* 32(2): 360–369.

Brinks, Daniel, and Michael Coppedge. 2006. "Diffusion Is No Illusion." *Comparative Political Studies* 39(4): 463–489.

Brooke, James. 1993. "Venezuela Victor: Will Vows Be Kept?" *New York Times*, December 7, A3.

Brown Araúz, Harry. 2013. "Panamá: El crecimiento económico a expensas de la política [Panama: economic growth at the expense of politics]." *Revista Ciencia Política* 33: 287–301.

Bruhn, Kathleen. 2004. "The Making of the Mexican President, 2000: Parties, Candidates, and Campaign Strategy." In *Mexico's Pivotal Democratic Election: Candidates, Voters, and the Presidential Campaign of 2000*, eds. Jorge I. Domínguez and Chappell Lawson, 123–156. Stanford, CA: Stanford University Press.

Bruhn, Kathleen. 2012. "To Hell with Your Corrupt Institutions." In *Populism in Europe and the Americas*, eds. Cas Mudde and Cristóbal Rovira Kaltwasser, 88–112. New York: Cambridge University Press.

Bullock, Charles S., III, and Loch K. Johnson. 1992. *Runoff Elections in the United States*. Chapel Hill: University of North Carolina Press.

Buquet, Daniel, and Rafael Piñeiro. 2013. "Elecciones Uruguayas 2009–2010: La Consolidación de un Nuevo Sistema de Partidos [Uruguay's 2009–2010 Elections: The Consolidation of a New Party System]." In *Elecciones y Política en América Latina 2009–2011* [Elections and politics in Latin America 2009–2011], eds. Manuel Alcántara Sáez and María Luara Tagina, 197–234. México: Instituto Federal Electoral.

Burnett, Craig M., and Vladimir Kogan. 2015. "Ballot (and voter) 'exhaustion' under Instant Runoff Voting: An Examination of Four Ranked-Choice Elections," *Electoral Studies* 37: 41–49.

Butler, Judy, David R. Dye, and Jack Spence with George Vickers. 1996. *Democracy and Its Discontents: Nicaraguans Face the Election*. Cambridge, MA: Hemisphere Initiatives.

Buxton, Julia. 2000. "Realignment of the Party System in Venezuela?" Paper presented at the 22nd International Congress of the Latin American Studies Association, Miami, FL, March 16–18.

Buxton, Julia. 2003. "Economic Policy and the Rise of Hugo Chávez." In *Venezuelan Politics in the Chávez Era: Class, Polarization, and Conflict*, eds. Steve Ellner and Daniel Hellinger, 113–130. Boulder, CO: Lynne Rienner Publishing.

Cabrera, Ernesto. 1996. "Multiparty Politics in Argentina? Electoral Rules and Changing Patterns." *Electoral Studies* 15(4): 477–495.

Calvo, Ernesto, and María Victoria Murillo. 2005. "A New Iron Law of Argentine Politics? Partisanship, Clientelism, and Governability in Contemporary Argentina." In *Argentine Democracy: The Politics of Institutional Weakness*, eds. Steven Levitsky and María Victoria Murillo, 207–228. University Park: Pennsylvania State University Press.

Calvo, Ernesto, and María Victoria Murillo. 2012. "Argentina: The Persistence of Peronism." *Journal of Democracy* 23(2): 148–161.

Cameron, Maxwell A. 1994. *Democracy and Authoritarianism in Peru: Political Coalitions and Social Change*. New York: St. Martin's Press.

Cameron, Maxwell A. 1998. "Latin American Autogolpes: Dangerous Undertows in the Third Wave of Democratization." *Third World Quarterly* 19(2): 219–239.

Canchari Obregón, Guido. 2010. *Elecciones en América Latina (1978–2010): Doble vuelta o mayoría relativa?* [Elections in Latin America (1978–2010): Runoff or Plurality?] Lima: Universidad Nacional Mayor de San Marcos y Instituto Nacional Demócrata para Asuntos Internacionales (NDI).

Cannon, Barry. 2014. "As Clear as MUD: The Opposition in Bolivarian Venezuela." *Latin American Politics and Society* 56(4): 49–70.

Carey, John M. 2003. "Presidentialism and Representative Institutions." In *Constructing Democratic Governance in Latin America*, eds. Jorge I. Dominguez and Michael Shifter, 2nd ed., 11–42. Baltimore, MD: Johns Hopkins University Press.

Carey, John M., and Simon Hix. 2011. "The Electoral Sweet Spot: Low-Magnitude Proportional Electoral Systems." *American Journal of Political Science* 55(2): 383–397.

Carlin, Ryan E., Matthew M. Singer, and Elizabeth J. Zechmeister. 2015. "Introduction to the Latin American Voter." In *The Latin American Voter: Pursuing Representation and Accountability in Challenging Contexts*, eds. Ryan E. Carlin, Matthew M. Singer, and Elizabeth J. Zechmeister, 1–30. Ann Arbor: University of Michigan Press.

Carreras, Miguel. 2012. "The Rise of Political Outsiders in Latin America, 1980–2010: An Institutionalist Perspective." *Comparative Political Studies* 45(12): 1451–1482.

Carreras, Miguel. 2014. "Outsiders and Executive-Legislative Conflict in Latin America." *Latin American Politics and Society* 56(3): 70–92.

Carrión, Julio. 1998. "Partisan Decline and Presidential Popularity: The Politics and Economics of Representation in Peru." In *Deepening Democracy in Latin America*, eds. Kurt von Mettenheim and James Malloy, 55–70. Pittsburgh, PA: University of Pittsburgh Press.

Carrión, Julio. 2001. "Las elecciones peruanas de 2001: desmantelando la herencia autoritaria [Peru's 2001 elections: dismantling the authoritarian legacy]." *Reflexión Política* 3(6): 106–118.

Cason, Jeffrey. 2000. "Electoral Reform and Stability in Uruguay." *Journal of Democracy* 11(2): 85–96.

Cassa, Roberto. 1997. "Negotiated Elections: The Old Boss Steps to the Side." *NACLA Report on the Americas* 30(5): 20–26.

Castañeda, Jorge, and Marco Morales. 2007. "The Mexican Standoff: Looking to the Future." *Journal of Democracy* 18(1): 103–112.

Castellanos, Julieta. 2013. *The Implications of Honduras' Elections*. Presented at the joint seminar of the Inter-American Dialogue and the Center for Inter-American Policy and Research. Washington, DC, November 27.

Cerna Villagra, Patricia, and Juan Marío Solís Delgadillo. 2012. "La crisis institucional paraguaya de 2012 a la luz de las élites parlamentarias [Paraguay's 2012 institutional crisis in the views of parliamentary elites]." *Elites Parlamentarias Latinoamericanas (PELA)* 42 (October).

Chasquetti, Daniel. 2001. "Elecciones Presidenciales Mayoritarias en América Latina [Majoritarian presidential elections in Latin America]." *América Latina Hoy* 29: 31–51.

Cheibub, José Antonio. 2007. *Presidentialism, Parliamentarianism, and Democracy*. New York: Cambridge University Press.

Chen, Linda. 2014. "Argentina in the Twenty-First Century." In *Latin American Politics and Development*, eds. Howard J. Wiarda and Harvey F. Kline, 8th ed., 75–96. Boulder, CO: Westview.

Clark, William R., and Matt Golder. 2006. "Rehabilitating Duverger's Theory: Testing the Mechanical and Strategic Modifying Effects of Electoral Laws." *Comparative Political Studies* 39(6): 670–708.

Clement, Scott. 2016. "One-third of Clinton Supporters Say Trump Election Is Not Legitimate, Poll Finds." *The Washington Post*, November 13, 2016.

Close, David, and Salvador Martí i Puig. 2012. "The Sandinistas and Nicaragua since 1979." In *The Sandinistas and Nicaragua since 1979*, eds. David Close, Salvador Martí i Puig, and Shelley A. McConnell, 1–20. Boulder, CO: Lynne Rienner.

Colburn, Forrest D. 2009. "The Turnover in El Salvador." *Journal of Democracy* 20(3): 143–152.

Colburn, Forrest D., and Arturo Cruz S. 2012. "Personalism and Populism in Nicaragua." *Journal of Democracy* 23(2): 104–118.

Colburn, Forrest D., and Arturo Cruz S. 2014. "El Salvador's Beleaguered Democracy." *Journal of Democracy* 25(3): 149–158.

Colomer, Josep M. 2001. *Political Institutions: Democracy and Social Choice*. New York: Oxford University Press.

Colomer, Josep M. 2004. "The Americas: General Overview." In *Handbook of Electoral System Choice*, ed. Josep M. Colomer, 81–109. New York: Palgrave Macmillan.

Colomer, Josep M. 2005. "It's Parties that Choose Electoral Systems (or, Duverger's Laws Upside Down)." *Political Studies* 53: 1–21.

Colomer, Josep M. 2007. "Non-Median and Condorcet-Loser Presidents in Latin America: A Factor of Instability." Paper presented at the annual meeting of the American Political Science Association, Chicago, IL, August 30–September 2.

Conaghan, Catherine M. 1987. "Los Vargazos and the Crisis of Ecuadorean Democracy." *LASA Forum* 18(1): 1–4.
Conaghan, Catherine M. 1995. "Politicians against Parties: Discord and Disconnection in Ecuador's Party System." In *Building Democratic Institutions: Party Systems in Latin America*, eds. Scott P. Mainwaring and Timothy R. Scully, 434–458. Stanford, CA: Stanford University Press.
Conaghan, Catherine M. 2005. *Fujimori's Peru: Deception in the Public Sphere*. Pittsburgh, PA: University of Pittsburgh Press.
Conaghan, Catherine M., and Rosario Espinal. 1990. "Unlikely Transitions to Uncertain Regimes? Democracy without Compromise in the Dominican Republic and Ecuador." *Journal of Latin American Studies* 22(3): 553–574.
Congressional Research Service. 2008. *Guatemala: 2007 Elections and Issues for Congress*. CRS Report for Congress, Washington, DC, January 9.
ConsultAndes. 2009. *Weekly Key Indicators*. Lima: ConsultAndes. December 7.
ConsultAndes. 2010. *Weekly Key Indicators*. Lima: ConsultAndes. November 8.
ConsultAndes. 2011a. *Weekly Key Indicators*. Lima: ConsultAndes. April 4.
ConsultAndes. 2011b. *Sector Report—April 2011: Peru's Unexpected Runoff Election*. Lima: ConsultAndes.
ConsultAndes. 2011c. *Monthly Political Analysis*. Lima: ConsultAndes. April.
ConsultAndes. 2011d. *Monthly Political Analysis*. Lima: ConsultAndes. October.
Constable, Pamela. 1990a. "Exit Polls Have Fujimori Winning Peruvian Election." *Boston Globe*, June 11.
Constable, Pamela. 1990b. "On Victory's Heels, a Headache." *Boston Globe*, June 12.
Coppedge, Michael. 1994a. *Strong Parties and Lame Ducks: Presidential Partyarchy and Factionalism in Venezuela*. Stanford, CA: Stanford University Press.
Coppedge, Michael. 1994b. "Prospects for Democratic Governability in Venezuela." *Journal of Inter-American Studies and World Affairs* 36(2): 39–64.
Coppedge, Michael. 1997. "A Classification of Latin American Political Parties." Working Paper Series 244, November. The Helen Kellogg Institute for International Studies, University of Notre Dame.
Coppedge, Michael. 2000. "Presidential Runoffs Do Not Fragment Legislative Party Systems." Paper presented at the Annual Meeting of the American Political Science Association. Washington, DC, August 31–September 3.
Coppedge, Michael, and John Gerring. 2011. "Conceptualizing and Measuring Democracy: A New Approach." *Perspectives on Politics* 9(2): 247–268.
Córdova Macías, Ricardo, and Carlos G. Ramos. 2012. "The Peace Process and the Construction of Democracy in El Salvador: Progress, Deficiencies, and Challenges." In *In the Wake of War: Democratization and Internal Armed Conflict in Latin America*, ed. Cynthia J. Arnson, 79–106. Washington, DC, and Stanford, CA: Woodrow Wilson Center Press and Stanford University Press.
Corella, Roberto. 1999. "La campaña electoral 1997–1998 en Costa Rica: Entre el desinterés y la apatía [The 1997–1998 Electoral Campaign in Costa Rica: Between Disinterest and Apathy]." In *Campañas Electorales y Medios de Comunicación en América Latina* [Electoral campaigns and the media in Latin America], eds. Frank Priess and Fernando Tuesta Soldevilla, Vol. 1., 291–380. Buenos Aires, Argentina: Konrad Adenauer-Stiftugn A.C. CIEDLA.
Corkill, David. 1985. "Democratic Politics in Ecuador, 1979–1984." *Bulletin of Latin American Research* 4(2): 63–74.
Corrales, Javier. 2002. *Presidents without Parties: The Politics of Economic Reform in Argentina and Venezuela in the 1990s*. University Park: Pennsylvania State University Press.
Corrales, Javier. 2008. "Latin America's Neocaudillismo: Ex-Presidents and Newcomers Running for President—and Winning." *Latin American Politics and Society* 50(3): 1–35.
Corrales, Javier, and Michael Penfold. 2007. "Venezuela: Crowding Out the Opposition." *Journal of Democracy* 18(2): 99–113.

Cotler, Julio. 1978. *Clases, estado y nación en el Perú.* [Classes, state, and nation in Peru] Lima: Instituto de Estudios Peruanos.

Cotler, Julio. 1995. "Political Parties and the Problems of Democratic Consolidation in Peru." In *Building Democratic Institutions: Party Systems in Latin America*, eds. Scott Mainwaring and Timothy R. Scully, 354–398. Stanford, CA: Stanford University Press.

Crisp, Brian F. 2000. *Democratic Institutional Design: The Powers and Incentives of Venezuelan Politicians and Interest Groups.* Paper presented at the 22nd International Congress of the Latin American Studies Association, Miami, FL, March 16–18.

Crisp, Brian F., and Daniel H. Levine. 1998. "Democratizing the Democracy? Crisis and Reform in Venezuela." *Journal of Inter-American Studies and World Affairs* 40(2): 27–62.

Cueto, Francisco. 2004. "République Dominicana." In *Doble Vuelta: La Elección Presidencial Mediante Doble Vuelta en LatinoAmérica* [Runoff: presidential elections through runoff in Latin America], ed. Rafael Martinez, 425–456. Barcelona: Institut de Ciències Polítiques i Socials.

Cunha Filho, Clayton M., André Luiz Coelho, and Fidel I. Pérez Flores. 2013. "A Right-to-Left Policy Switch? An Analysis of the Honduran Case under Manuel Zelaya." *International Political Science Review* 34(5): 519–542.

Daeschner, Jeff. 1993. *The War of the End of Democracy.* Lima: Peru Reporting.

Dargent Bocanegra, Eduardo. 2016. "Peru: A Close Win for Continuity." *Journal of Democracy* 27(4): 145–158.

Dargent, Eduardo, and Paula Muñoz. 2016. *Demócratas Precarios: Elites y debilidad democrática en el Perú y América Latina.* [Precarious democrats: elites and democratic fragility in Peru and Latin America] Lima: Instituto de Estudios Peruanos.

Dean, Howard. 2016. "How to Get Beyond Two Parties." *New York Times*, October 8, A19.

DeShazo, Peter. 2006. "The Triumph of the 'Pact' in Nicaragua." *CSIS Hemisphere Focus* 14(8): 1–3.

De Souza, Amaury. 2011. "The Politics of Personality in Brazil." *Journal of Democracy* 22(2): 75–88.

Dettrey, Bryan J., and Leslie A. Schwindt-Bayer. 2009. "Voter Turnout in Presidential Democracies." *Comparative Political Studies* 42(10): 1317–1338.

Diamond, Larry. 1996. "Democracy in Latin America: Degrees, Illusions, and Directions for Consolidation." In *Beyond Sovereignty: Collectively Defending Democracy*, ed. Tom Farer, 52–106. Baltimore, MD: Johns Hopkins University Press.

Diamond, Larry. 2006. *Book Launch: Electoral Systems and Democracy: What Have We Learned?* Paper for the National Endowment for Democracy. Washington, DC, October 25. Online: www.ned.org/events/past/events06.html.

Diamond, Larry. 2011. "Reformers." *Washington Post*, February 6, Sunday Outlook Section, B5.

Dietz, Henry, and David J. Myers. 2007. "From Thaw to Deluge: Party System Collapse in Venezuela and Peru." *Latin American Politics and Society* 49(2): 59–86.

Dillon, Sam. 2000. "Mexican Party Reported to Quash Polls Predicting Its Defeat." *New York Times*, July 17, A9.

Domínguez, Jorge I. 2003. "Taking Stock of the 1990s." In *Constructing Democratic Governance in Latin America*, eds. Jorge I. Domínguez and Michael Shifter, 2nd ed., 351–381. Baltimore, MD: Johns Hopkins University Press.

Drake, Paul W., and Peter Winn. 2000. "The Presidential Election of 1999/2000 and Chile's Transition to Democracy." *LASA Forum* 31(1): 5–9.

Dugas, John C. 2012. "Colombia." In *Politics of Latin America: The Power Game*, eds. Harry E. Vanden and Gary F. Prevost, 4th ed., 305–332. New York: Oxford University Press.

Dye, David R. with Jack Spence and George Vickers. 2000. *Patchwork Democracy: Nicaraguan Politics Ten Years after the Fall.* Cambridge, MA: Hemisphere Initiatives.

Dye, David R. with Shelley McConnell. 2002. *Final Report on Observing the 2001 Nicaraguan Elections.* Atlanta, GA: The Carter Center. April.

Ebel, Roland. 1990. "Guatemala: The Politics of Unstable Stability." In *Latin American Politics and Development*, eds. Howard J. Wiarda and Harvey Kline, 3rd ed., 498–518. Boulder, CO: Westview Press.

Ebel, Roland. 1996. "Guatemala: Politics in a Central American City State." In *Latin American Politics and Development*, eds. Howard J. Wiarda and Harvey Kline, 4th ed., 453–474. Boulder, CO: Westview Press.

Edwards, Margaret E. 2015. "Understanding Presidential Failure in South America." *Latin American Politics and Society* 57(2): 111–131.

Eguiguren, Francisco P. 1990. *Los Retos de una Democracia Insuficiente* [The challenges of an insufficient democracy]. Lima: Comisión Andina de Juristas and Fundación Friedrich Naumann.

Eisenstadt, Todd A. 2004. *Courting Democracy in Mexico: Party Strategies and Electoral Institutions.* New York: Cambridge University Press.

Ellner, Steve. 1988. *Venezuela's Movimiento al Socialismo: From Guerrilla Defeat to Innovative Politics.* Durham, NC: Duke University Press.

Ellner, Steve. 2008. *Rethinking Venezuelan Politics: Class, Conflict, and the Chávez Phenomenon.* Boulder, CO: Lynne Rienner Publishing.

Engstrom, Richard L., and Richard N. Engstrom. 2008. "The Majority Vote Rule and Runoff Primaries in the United States." *Electoral Studies* 27(3):407–416.

Escobar, Gabriel. 1997. "Ecuador Counts Losses to Allegedly Epic Corruption." *Washington Post*, February 16, A33.

Espíndola, Roberto. 2001. "No Change in Uruguay: The 1999 Presidential and Parliamentary Elections." *Electoral Studies* 20(4): 643–659.

Farah, Douglas. 1992. "Poor Lament Coup Failure in Venezuela." *Washington Post*, February 9, A10.

Felix, David. 1990. "Latin America's Debt Crisis." *World Policy Journal* 7(4): 733–771.

Fleischer, David. 1998. "Brazilian Political Parties and Party System, 1945–1997." Washington, DC: The Institute of Brazilian Issues Working Paper, January.

Fleischer, David. 2011. "Attempts at Political Reform in Brazil: A Never-Ending Story." *Brazil under Rousseff Task Force*, Center for Hemispheric Policy, University of Miami, November 29.

Fleischer, David. 2014. *Brazil Focus Weekly Report.* Brasilia: David Fleischer, October 11–17.

Fleischer, David. 2017. "Brazil's Experience with Second Round Runoff Elections and Reelection since the 1988 Constitution." Paper presented at the 35th International Congress of the Latin American Studies Association, Lima, Peru, April 29–May 1.

Flores-Macías, Gustavo. 2013. "Mexico's 2012 Elections: The Return of the PRI." *Journal of Democracy* 24(1): 128–141.

Fontaine, Arturo Talavera. 2000. "Chile's Elections: The New Face of the Right." *Journal of Democracy* 11(2): 70–77.

Freedom House. 1992. *Freedom in the World 1991–1992.* New York: Freedom House.

Freidenberg, Flavia. 2004. "Ecuador." In *Doble Vuelta: La Elección Presidencial Mediante Doble Vuelta en Latinoamérica*, ed. Rafael Martínez, 229–276. Barcelona: Insitut de Ciències Polítiques i Socials.

French, Howard R. 1990. "One Last Round for 2 Old Dominican Rivals." *New York Times*, May 8, A5.

Fukuyama, Francis, Björn Dressel, and Boo-Seung Chang. 2005. "Challenges and Change in East Asia: Facing the Perils of Presidentialism." *Journal of Democracy* 16(2): 102–116.

Gamboa, Ricardo, and Carolina Segovia. 2006. "Las Elecciones Presidenciales y Parlamentarias en Chile, Diciembre 2005–Enero 2006 [The Presidential and parliamentary elections in Chile, December 2005–January 2006]." *Revista de Ciencia Política* 26(1): 84–113.

García, Miguel. 2010. *Political Violence and Electoral Democracy in Colombia: Participation and Voting Behavior in Violent Contexts.* PhD Dissertation, University of Pittsburgh.

García Belaúnde, Domingo. 1986. *Una democracia en transición: Las elecciones peruanas de 1985* [A democracy in transition: Peru's 1985 elections]. Lima: Centrointeramericano Asesoría y Promoción Electoral y Instituto Interamericano de Derechos Humanos.

Garretón, Manuel Antonio. 2000. "Chile's Elections: Change and Continuity." *Journal of Democracy* 11(2): 78–84.

Gerson, Michael. 2016. "The Triumph of Cynicism." *Washington Post*, July 8, A21.

Gilley, Bruce. 2008. "Legitimacy and Institutional Change: The Case of China." *Comparative Political Studies* 41(3): 259–284.

Goertzel, Ted. G.1999. *Fernando Henrique Cardoso: Reinventing Democracy in Brazil.* Boulder, CO: Lynne Rienner Publishers.

Gómez-Bruera, Hernán. 2013. *Lula, the Workers' Party and the Governability Dilemma in Brazil.* New York: Routledge.

González, Francisco E. 2009. "Mexico's Drug Wars Get Brutal." *Current History* 108(715): 72–76.

González, Luis E. 1995. "Continuity and Change in the Uruguayan Party System." In *Building Democratic Institutions: Party Systems in Latin America,* eds. Scott Mainwaring and Timothy R. Scully, 138–163. Stanford, CA: Stanford University Press.

González, Secundino. 2013. "Las elecciones guatemaltecas de 2011: más de lo mismo [Guatemala's 2011 elections: more of the same]." In *Elecciones y Política en América Latina 2009–2011,* eds. Manuel Alcántara Sáez and María Laura Tagina, 603–629. Mexico City: Instituto Federal Electoral.

Graham, Carol.1993. "Government and Politics." In *Peru: A Country Study,* ed. Rex A. Hudson, 4th ed., 205–258. Washington, DC: Library of Congress.

Grayson, George W. 2000. *Mexico's President Vicente Fox Quesada.* Foreign Policy Research Institute, July 7. Online: www.fpri.org.

Grayson, George W. 2007. *Mexican Messiah: Andrés Manuel López Obrador.* University Park: Pennsylvania State University Press.

Grayson, George W. 2009. *The PRI Makes a Comeback in Mexico.* Foreign Policy Research Institute. July 9. Online: www.fpri.org.

Greene, Kenneth F. 2002. "Opposition Party Strategy and Spatial Competition in Dominant Party Regimes: A Theory and the Case of Mexico." *Comparative Political Studies* 35(7): 755–783.

Greene, Kenneth F. 2007a. *Why Dominant Parties Lose: Mexico's Democratization in Comparative Perspective.* New York: Cambridge University Press.

Greene, Kenneth F. 2007b. "El votante mediano y la regla de mayoría relativa para elegir presidente en México [The median voter and the plurality rule for the election of the president in Mexico]." *Política y gobierno* 14(1): 203–213.

Gutiérrez Sanín, Francisco. 2006. "Checks and Imbalances: Problems with Congress in Colombia and Ecuador, 1978–2003." In *State and Society in Conflict: Comparative Perspectives on Andean Crises,* eds. Paul W. Drake and Eric Hershberg, 257–287. Pittsburgh, PA: University of Pittsburgh Press.

Haber, Stephen, Herbert S. Klein, Noel Maurer, and Kevin J. Middlebrook. 2008. *Mexico since 1980.* New York: Cambridge University Press.

Hagopian, Frances. 1990. "Democracy by Undemocratic Means? Elites, Political Pacts, and Regime Transition in Brazil." *Comparative Political Studies* 23(2): 147–170.

Hakim, Peter. 2000. "Ecuador's Desperation." *Christian Science Monitor,* January 27.

Haluani, Makram. 1987. *The Politics of Resignation: Whatever Happened to the Venezuelan Revolutionaries?* Paper presented at the 28th Annual Convention of the International Studies Association, Washington, DC, April 14–18.

Hampson, Fen Osler. 1996. *Nurturing Peace: Why Peace Settlements Succeed or Fail.* Washington, DC: United States Institute of Peace Press.

Handelman, Howard. 1980. *Peru: The March to Civilian Rule.* Hanover, New Hampshire: American Universities Field Staff Reports No. 2 (South America).

Hartlyn, Jonathan. 1990. "The Dominican Republic's Disputed Elections." *Journal of Democracy* 1(4): 92–103.

Hartlyn, Jonathan. 1994a. *Crisis-Ridden Elections and Authoritarian Regression: Presidentialism and Electoral Oversight in the Dominican Republic, 1978–1994.* Paper presented at the Annual Meeting of the American Political Science Association. New York, September 1–4.

Hartlyn, Jonathan. 1994b. "Los problemas de una segunda ronda electoral [The problems of a second electoral round]." *Revista Rumbo* 37 (October 5–11): 46–49.

Hartlyn, Jonathan. 1998. *The Struggle for Democratic Politics in the Dominican Republic.* Chapel Hill: University of North Carolina Press.

Hartlyn, Jonathan, and John Dugas. 1999. "Colombia: The Politics of Violence and Democratic Transformation." In *Democracy in Developing Countries: Latin America*, eds. Larry Diamond, Jonathan Hartlyn, Juan J. Linz, and Seymour Martin Lipset, 2nd ed., 249–307. Boulder, CO: Lynne Rienner Publishing.

Hartlyn, Jonathan, and Rosario Espinal. 2009. "The Presidential Election in the Dominican Republic, May 2008." *Electoral Studies* 28: 333–336.

Hebblethwaite, Margaret. 2003. "Elections Bring 'Same Old Thing'—For Now." *National Catholic Reporter*, May 9, p. 5.

Herman, Donald L. 1985. "Colombian and Venezuelan Democracy: A Model." Paper presented at the 12th International Congress of the Latin American Studies Association, Albuquerque, New Mexico, April 18–20.

Hernandez, Ramona. 2012. "Dominicans, in Three Continents, Go to the Polls." *NACLA Report on the Americas* 45(4): 65–66.

Hicken, Allen, and Erik Martínez Kuhonta. 2011. "Shadows from the Past: Party System Institutionalization in Asia." *Comparative Political Studies* 44(5): 572–597.

Holland, Alisha C. 2013. "Right on Crime? Conservative Party Politics and Mano Dura Policies in El Salvador." *Latin American Research Review* 48(1): 44–67.

Hoskin, Gary. 1988. "Colombian Political Parties and Electoral Behavior during the Post-National Front Period." In *Democracy in Latin America: Colombia and Venezuela*, ed. Donald L. Herman, 47–62. New York: Praeger.

Hough, Jerry F. 2006. "A Closer Look at a Close Vote in Mexico." *Washington Post*, July 21.

Hunter, Wendy. 2010. *The Transformation of the Workers' Party in Brazil, 1989–2009*. New York: Cambridge University Press.

Huntington, Samuel P. 1968. *Political Order in Changing Societies*. New Haven, CT: Yale University Press.

Inter-American Dialogue. 2016. *The Economy vs. Democracy in Ortega's Nicaragua*. Washington, DC: Inter-American Dialogue.

International IDEA (Institute for Democracy and Electoral Assistance). 2014. *Electoral System Design Database*. At http://www.idea.int/esd/. Accessed June 20, 2014.

Ipsos. 2009. *Estudio de Opinión Pública* [Study of public opinion]. Santiago. IPSOS. October.

Isaacs, Anita. 1991. "Problems of Democratic Consolidation in Ecuador." *Bulletin of Latin American Research* 10(2): 221–238.

Isaacs, Anita. 2010. "Guatemala on the Brink." *Journal of Democracy* 21(2): 108–122.

Jeter, Jon. 2003. "Menem May Quit Race in Argentina." *Washington Post*, May 14, A16.

John, Sarah, and Andrew Douglas. 2017. "Candidate Civility and Voter Engagement in Seven Cities with Ranked Choice Voting." *National Civic Review* (Spring): 25–29.

Jones, Mark P. 1995. *Electoral Laws and the Survival of Presidential Democracies*. Notre Dame, IN: University of Notre Dame Press.

Jones, Mark P. 1999. "Electoral Laws and the Effective Number of Candidates in Presidential Elections." *Journal of Politics* 61(1): 171–184.

Jones, Mark P., and Wonjae Hwang. 2005. "Provincial Party Bosses: Keystone of the Argentine Congress." In *Argentine Democracy: The Politics of Institutional Weakness*, eds. Steven Levitsky and María Victoria Murillo, 115–138. University Park: Pennsylvania State University Press.

Katz, Joseph, and Kevin Quealy. 2016. "Feel Free to Ignore Polls for a Few Weeks." *New York Times*, July 23, A3.

Katz, Richard S., and Peter Mair. 2009. "The Cartel Party Thesis: A Restatement." *Perspectives on Politics* 7(4):753–766.

Kazin, Michael. 2017. "Some Presidents Will Never Be Popular." *Washington Post*, July 23, B2.

Keck, Margaret E. 1992. *The Workers' Party and Democratization in Brazil*. New Haven, CT: Yale University Press.

Keisling, Phil. 2010. "To Reduce Partisanship, Get Rid of Partisans." *New York Times*, March 22, A5.

Kenney, Charles D. 1998. "The Second Round of the Majority Runoff Debate: Classification, Evidence, and Analysis." Paper presented at the 21st International Congress of the Latin American Studies Association, Chicago, IL, September 24–26.

Kenney, Charles D. 2003. "The Death and Rebirth of a Party System: Peru 1978–2001." *Comparative Political Studies* 36(10): 1210–1239.

Kenney, Charles D. 2004. *Fujimori's Coup and the Breakdown of Democracy in Latin America*. Notre Dame, IN: University of Notre Dame Press.

Kingstone, Peter R. 1999. *Crafting Coalitions for Reform: Business Preferences, Political Institutions, and Neoliberal Reform in Brazil*. University Park: University of Pennsylvania Press.

Kitschelt, Herbert, Kirk A. Hawkins, Juan Pablo Luna, Guillermo Rosas, and Elizabeth J. Zechmeister. 2010. *Latin American Party Systems*. New York: Cambridge University Press.

Kline, Harvey F. 1988. "The Colombian State in Crisis: Continuity and Change." In *Democracy in Latin America: Colombia and Venezuela*, ed. Donald L. Herman, 87–108. New York: Praeger.

Laakso, Murkku, and Rein Taagepera. 1979. "Effective Number of Parties: A Measure with Application to West Europe." *Comparative Political Studies* 12(1): 3–27.

Lacey, Marc. 2006. "Ex-Firebrand Ortega on the Comeback Trail." *New York Times*, September 30, A5.

Lacey, Marc. 2007a. "Businessman Beats Ex-General in Guatemala Voting." *New York Times*, November 5, A11.

Lacey, Marc. 2007b. "Healing Hearts and, Possibly, Divisions in Guatemala." *New York Times*, November 6, A11.

Lanzaro, Jorge. 2011. "Uruguay: A Social Democratic Government in Latin America." In *The Resurgence of the Latin American Left*, eds. Steven Levitsky and Kenneth Roberts, 348–374. Baltimore, MD: The Johns Hopkins University Press.

Lawson, Chappell. 2004. "Introduction." In *Mexico's Pivotal Democratic Election: Candidates, Voters, and the Presidential Campaign of 2000*, eds. Jorge I. Domínguez and Chappell Lawson, 1–24. Stanford, CA: Stanford University Press.

Lawson, Chappell. 2009. "Introduction: The Mexican 2006 Election in Context." In *Consolidating Mexico's Democracy: The 2006 Presidential Campaign in Comparative Perspective*, eds. Jorge I. Domínguez, Chappell Lawson, and Alejandro Moreno, 1–27. Baltimore, MD: Johns Hopkins University Press.

Lehoucq, Fabrice. 2004. "Costa Rica: Modifying Majoritarianism with 40 per cent Threshold." In *Handbook of Electoral System Choice*, ed. Josep M. Colomer, 133–44. New York: Palgrave Macmillan.

Lehoucq, Fabrice. 2005. "Costa Rica: Paradise in Doubt." *Journal of Democracy* 16(3): 140–154.

Lehoucq, Fabrice. 2012. *The Politics of Modern Central America: Civil War, Democratization, and Underdevelopment*. New York: Cambridge University Press.

Leiras, Marcelo. 2007. *Todos los caballos del rey: La integración de los partidos políticos y el gobierno democrático de la Argentina, 1995–2003* [All the king's horses: the integration of the political parties and the democratic government of Argentina, 1995–2003]. Buenos Aires: Prometeo Libros.

Leis, Raúl. 2009. "Panamá: caja negra electoral [Panama: electoral black box]." *Nueva Sociedad* 222: 19–29.

Levine, Daniel H. 1994. "Goodbye to Venezuelan Exceptionalism." *Journal of Inter-American Studies and World Affairs* 36(4): 145–182.

Levitsky, Steven. 2001. "Inside the Black Box: Recent Studies of Latin American Party Organizations." *Studies in Comparative International Development* 36(2): 92–110.

Levitsky, Steven. 2003. *Transforming Labor-Based Parties in Latin America: Argentine Peronism in Comparative Perspective*. New York: Cambridge University Press.

Levitsky, Steven. 2005. "Argentina: Democratic Survival." In *The Third Wave of Democratization in Latin America: Advances and Setbacks*, eds. Frances Hagopian and Scott P. Mainwaring, 63–89. New York: Cambridge University Press.

Levitsky, Steven. 2011. "Peru's 2011 Elections: A Surprising Left Turn." *Journal of Democracy* 22(4): 84–94.

Levitsky, Steven. 2013. "Peru: The Challenges of a Democracy without Parties." In *Constructing Democratic Governance in Latin America*, eds. Jorge I. Domínguez and Michael Shifter, 4th ed., 282–315. Baltimore, MD: Johns Hopkins University Press.

Levitsky, Steven, and María Victoria Murillo. 2005. "Building Castles in the Sand? The Politics of Institutional Weakness in Argentina." In *Argentine Democracy: The Politics of Institutional Weakness*, eds. Steven Levitsky and María Victoria Murillo, 21–44. University Park: Pennsylvania State University Press.

Levitsky, Steven, James Loxton, and Brandon Van Dyck. 2017. "Introduction: Challenges of Party-Building in Latin America." In *Challenges of Party-Building in Latin America*, eds. Steven Levitsky, James Loxton, Brandon Van Dyck, and Jorge I. Domínguez, 1–48. New York: Cambridge University Press.

Levy, Daniel C., and Kathleen Bruhn. 2006. *Mexico: The Struggle for Democratic Development*. 2nd ed. Berkeley: University of California Press.

Lindberg, Staffan I., Michael Coppedge, John Gerring, and Jan Teorell. 2014. "V-Dem: A New Way to Measure Democracy." *Journal of Democracy* 25(3): 159–169.

Linz, Juan J. 1990a. "The Virtues of Parliamentarianism." *Journal of Democracy* 1(1): 50–69.

Linz, Juan J. 1990b."The Perils of Presidentialism." *Journal of Democracy* 1(4): 84–91.

Linz, Juan J. 1994. "Presidential or Parliamentary Democracy: Does It Make a Difference?" In *The Failure of Presidential Democracy*, eds. Juan J. Linz and Arturo Valenzuela, 3–89. Baltimore, MD: Johns Hopkins University Press.

López-Maya, Margarita, and Luis E. Lander. 2008. "Venezuela: las elecciones presidenciales de 2006: Hacia el socialismo del siglo XXI." [Venezuela: The 2006 presidential elections: towards socialism of the twenty-first century?]" In *Elecciones y Política en América Latina* [Elections and politics in Latin America], eds. Manuel Alcántara Sáez and Fátima García Díez, 329–352. Mexico City, México: Instituto Electoral de Estado de México.

Loxton, James. 2015. "Authoritarian Successor Parties." *Journal of Democracy* 26(3): 157–170.

Lugo, Fernando. 2009. "What has happened in Paraguay?" *Diplomacy, Strategy, and Politics Review* 9: 149–158.

Luna, Juan Pablo. 2006. "Frente Amplio and the Crafting of a Social-Democratic Alternative in Uruguay." Paper presented at the Woodrow Wilson International Center for Scholars conference on the New Latin American Left. Washington, DC: November.

Luna, Juan Pablo. 2007. "Frente Amplio and the Crafting of a Social Democratic Alternative in Uruguay." *Latin American Politics and Society* 49(4): 1–27.

Luna, Juan Pablo. 2014. *Segmented Representation: Political Party Strategies in Unequal Democracies*. New York: Oxford University Press.

Luna, Juan Pablo, and David Altman. 2011. "Uprooted but Stable: Chilean Parties and the Concept of Institutionalization." *Latin American Politics and Society* 53(2): 1–28.

Luna, Juan Pablo, and Cristóbal Rovira Kaltwasser. 2014. "Introduction." In *The Resilience of the Latin American Right*, eds. Juan Pablo Luna and Cristóbal Rovira Kaltwasser, 1–24. Baltimore: Johns Hopkins University Press.

Lupu, Noam. 2012. "The 2011 General Elections in Peru." *Electoral Studies* 31(3): 621–624.

Lupu, Noam. 2014. "Brand Dilution and the Breakdown of Political Parties in Latin America." *World Politics* 66(4): 561–602.

Lupu, Noam. 2016. "Mass-Elite Congruence and Representation in Argentina." In *Malaise in Representation in Latin American Countries: Chile, Argentina, Uruguay*, eds. Alfredo Joignant, Maurcio Morales, and Claudio Fuentes, 281–302. New York: Palgrave Macmillan.

Machado, Aline. 2009. "Minimum Winning Electoral Coalitions under Presidentialism? Reality or Fiction? The Case of Brazil." *Latin American Politics and Society* 51(3): 87–110.

Madrid, Raúl L. 2011. "Ethnic Proximity and Ethnic Voting in Peru." *Journal of Latin American Studies* 43: 267–297.

Magaloni, Beatriz. 2006. *Voting for Autocracy: Hegemonic Party Survival and Its Demise in Mexico.* New York: Cambridge University Press.

Magaloni, Beatriz, and Alejandro Poiré. 2004. "Strategic Coordination in the 2000 Mexican Presidential Race." In *Mexico's Pivotal Democratic Election: Candidates, Voters, and the Presidential Campaign of 2000*, eds. Jorge I. Domínguez and Chappell Lawson, 264–282. Stanford, CA: Stanford University Press.

Maier, G. 1969. *The Ecuadorean Presidential Election of June 2, 1968: An Analysis.* Washington, DC: Institute for the Comparative Study of Political Systems.

Mainwaring, Scott. 1993. "Presidentialism, Multipartism, and Democracy: The Difficult Combination." *Comparative Political Studies* 26(2): 198–228.

Mainwaring, Scott. 1995. "Brazil: Weak Parties, Feckless Democracy." In *Building Democratic Institutions: Party Systems in Latin America*, eds. Scott Mainwaring and Timothy R. Scully, 354–398. Stanford, CA: Stanford University Press.

Mainwaring, Scott. 1997. "Multipartism, Robust Federalism, and Presidentialism in Brazil." In *Presidentialism and Democracy in Latin America*, eds. Scott Mainwaring and Matthew Soberg Shugart, 55–109. New York: Cambridge University Press.

Mainwaring, Scott. 2013. *Democracy in Latin America: Analysis and Policy Implications.* Presentation at the Woodrow Wilson International Center for Scholars, March 22.

Mainwaring, Scott. 2016. "Party Institutionalization in Contemporary Latin America." Paper presented at the 34th International Congress of the Latin American Studies Association, New York, NY, May 27–30.

Mainwaring, Scott, Ana María Bejarano, and Eduardo Pizarro Leongómez. 2006. *The Crisis of Democratic Representation in the Andes.* Stanford, CA: Stanford University Press.

Mainwaring, Scott, Daniel Brinks, and Aníbal Pérez-Liñán. 2001. "Classifying Political Regimes in Latin America, 1945–1999." *Studies in Comparative International Development* 36(1): 37–65.

Mainwaring, Scott P., and Aníbal Pérez-Liñán. 2013. *Democracies and Dictatorships in Latin America: Emergence, Survival, and Fall.* New York: Cambridge University Press.

Mainwaring, Scott P., and Timothy R. Scully. 1995. *Building Democratic Institutions: Party Systems in Latin America.* Stanford, CA: Stanford University Press.

Mainwaring, Scott, and Timothy R. Scully, eds. 2003. *Christian Democracy in Latin America: Electoral Competition and Regime Conflicts.* Stanford, CA: Stanford University Press.

Mainwaring, Scott P., and Matthew S. Shugart. 1997a. "Conclusion." In *Presidentialism and Democracy in Latin America*, 394–439. New York: Cambridge University Press.

Mainwaring, Scott P., and Matthew S. Shugart. 1997b. "Juan Linz, Presidentialism and Democracy: A Critical Appraisal." *Comparative Politics* 29(4): 449–472.

Mainwaring, Scott, Mariano Torcal, and Nicolás M. Somma. 2015. "The Left and the Mobilization of Class Voting in Latin America." In *The Latin American Voter: Pursuing Representation and Accountability in Challenging Contexts*, eds. Ryan E. Carlin, Matthew M. Singer, and Elizabeth J. Zechmeister, 69–98. Ann Arbor: University of Michigan Press.

María-Bidó, Angel. 2007. *44 Años de Elecciones Democráticas en la República Dominicana 1962–2006* [44 Years of democratic elections in the Dominican Republic 1962–2006.]. Santo Domingo, Dominican Republic: Impresos Vargas.

Marsteintredet, Leiv, Mariana Llanos, and Detlef Note. 2013. "Paraguay and the Politics of Impeachment." *Journal of Democracy* 24(4): 110–123.

Martínez, Rafael. 2004. "Conclusiones." In *Doble Vuelta: La Elección Presidencial Mediante Doble Vuelta en Latinoamérica* [Runoff: presidential election through runoff in Latin America], ed. Rafael Martinez, 539–562. Barcelona: Institut de Ciències Politiques i Socials.

Martz, John D. 1983. "Populist Leadership and the Party Caudillo: Ecuador and the CFP, 1962–1981." *Studies in Comparative International Development* 17(3): 21–50.

Martz, John D. 1985. "Conservatism and Reformism: The Ecuadorean Elections of 1984." Paper presented at the Annual Meeting of the Southwestern Political Science Association, Houston, TX, March 20–23.

Martz, John D. 1987. *Politics and Petroleum in Ecuador.* New Brunswick, NJ: Transaction.

Martz, John. D. 1991. "Party Elites and Leadership in Colombia and Venezuela." *Journal of Latin American Studies* 24(1): 87–121.
Mayorga, René Antonio. 1997. "Bolivia: Electoral Reform in Latin America." In *The International IDEA Handbook of Electoral System Design*, eds. Andrew Reynolds and Ben Reilly, 79–81. Stockholm: IDEA.
McClintock, Cynthia. 1993. "Peru's Fujimori: A Caudillo Derails Democracy." *Current History* 92(March): 112–119.
McClintock, Cynthia. 2006. "Electoral Authoritarian Versus Partially Democratic Regimes: The Case of the Fujimori Government and the 2000 Elections." In *The Fujimori Legacy: The Rise of Electoral Authoritarianism in Peru*, ed. Julio Carrión, 242–267. University Park: The Pennsylvania State University Press.
McClintock, Cynthia. 2008. "Preferencias por una Segunda Vuelta o Una Sola Votación: Los Resultados de una Encuesta en Chile, Mexico, Paraguay, Peru, y Venezuela [Preferences for runoff or plurality: the results of a survey in Chile, Mexico, Paraguay, Peru, and Venezuela].
McClintock, Cynthia, and James H. Lebovic. 2006. "Correlates of Levels of Democracy in Latin America during the 1990s." *Latin American Politics and Society* 48(2): 29–59.
McConnell, Shelley A. 2012. "The Uncertain Evolution of the Electoral System." In *The Sandinistas and Nicaragua since 1979*, eds. David Close, Salvador Martí i Puig, and Shelley A. McConnell, 121–160. Boulder, CO: Lynne Rienner Publishing.
McCoy, Jennifer L., and William C. Smith. 1995. "Democratic Disequilibrium in Venezuela." *Journal of Inter-American Studies and World Affairs* 37(2): 113–180.
McDonald, Ronald H. 1996. "Uruguay: Redefining Normalcy." In *Latin American Politics and Development*, 4th ed., eds. Howard J. Wiarda and Harvey F. Kline, 271–285. Boulder, CO: Westview.
McDonald, Ronald H., and Mark J. Ruhl. 1989. *Party Politics and Elections in Latin America*. Boulder, CO: Westview Press.
McGuire, James W. 1995. "Political Parties and Democracy in Argentina." In *Building Democratic Institutions: Party Systems in Latin America*, eds. Scott Mainwaring and Timothy Scully, 200–248. Stanford, CA: Stanford University Press.
McKewen, Darren. 1989. *Transition from Stroessner: The 1989 Paraguayan Elections* (Report). CSIS Latin American Elections Studies Series, Center for Strategic and International Studies, May 18, p. 1.
McLean, Philip. 2002. "Who Is Alvaro Uribe and How Did He Get Elected?" Center for Strategic and International Studies, *Hemisphere Focus* X(9), July 12.
McLean, Stephanie C. 2006. *Electoral Legitimacy in the United States: Effects on Political Efficacy, Trust, and Participation*. PhD Dissertation, University of Pittsburgh.
Meilán, Xabier. 2014. "Dominican Republic's 2012 Presidential Election." *Electoral Studies* 33(1): 347–352.
Mejía Acosta, Andrés. 1997. *Ecuador: The Search for Democratic Governance*. Online: www.aceproject.org/main/english/es/esy_ec.htm.
Mejía Acosta, Andrés. 2009. *Informal Coalitions and Policymaking in Latin America: Ecuador in Comparative Perspective*. New York: Routledge.
Meléndez, Carlos. 2013. "Perú: las elecciones de 2011. Populistas e integrados. Las divisiones políticas en un sistema 'partido' Peru: the 2011 elections: the populists and the mainstream. The political divisions in a 'party' system]." In *Elecciones y Política en América Latina 2009–2011* [Elections and politics in Latin America 2009-2011], eds. Manuel Alcántara Sáez and María Laura Tagina, 523–562. Mexico City: Instituto Federal Electoral.
Meyer, Maureen. 2009. *Election Season in El Salvador*. Washington, DC: Washington Office on Latin America.
Mieres, Pablo. 2004. "Uruguay." In *DV: La Elección Presidencial Mediante Doble Vuelta en LatinoAmérica* [Runoff: presidential election through runoff in Latin America], ed. Rafael Martínez, 457–480. Barcelona: Institut de Ciències Polítiques i Socials (ICPS).
Miroff, Nick. 2014. "Mexican Leader Praised Abroad, Booed at Home." *Washington Post*, April 14, A8.

Molina, José E., and Carmen Pérez. 2004. "Radical Change at the Ballot Box: Causes and Consequences of Electoral Behavior in Venezuela's 2000 Elections." *Latin American Politics and Society* 46(1): 103–134.

Morales Quiroga, Maurcio. 2008. "La primera presidenta de Chile: Qué explicó el triunfo de Michelle Bachelet en las elecciones de 2005–2006? [The first woman president of Chille: what explained the triumph of Michelle Bachelet in the 2005–2006 elections]" *Latin American Research Review* 43(1): 7–32.

Morgan, Jana. 2011. *Bankrupt Representation and Party System Collapse*. University Park: Pennsylvania State University Press.

Morgan, Jana, Jonathan Hartlyn, and Rosario Espinal. 2008. "Party System Institutionalization in the Dominican Republic: Ideology Ethnicity, and Migration." Paper presented at the Annual Meeting of the American Political Science Association, Boston, MA, August 28–31.

Morris, Kenneth E. 2010. *Unfinished Revolution: Daniel Ortega and Nicaragua's Struggle for Liberation*. Chicago, IL: Lawrence Hill Books.

Mossige, Dag. 2013. *Mexico's Left: The Paradox of the PRD*. Boulder, CO: First Forum Press (a division of Lynne Rienner).

Munck, Gerardo L. 2011. "Measuring Democracy: Framing a Needed Debate." *APSA-Comparative Democratization* 9(1): 1–11.

Munck, Gerardo L., and Jay Verkuilen. 2002. "Conceptualizing and Measuring Democracy: Evaluating Alternative Indices." *Comparative Political Studies* 35(1): 5–34.

Muñoz, Paula. 2014. "An Informational Theory of Campaign Clientelism: The Case of Peru." *Comparative Politics* 47(1): 79–98.

Murillo, María Victoria, Virginia Oliveros, and Milan Vaishnav. 2008. "Voting for the Left or Governing on the Left?" Unpublished manuscript, Department of Political Science, Columbia University, October.

Murillo, María Victoria, Virginia Oliveros, and Milan Vaishnav. 2010. "Electoral Revolution or Democratic Alternation?" *Latin American Research Review* 45(3): 87–114.

Murillo, María Victoria, Virginia Oliveros, and Milan Vaishnav. 2011. "Economic Constraints and Presidential Agency." In *The Resurgence of the Latin American Left*, eds. Steven Levitsky and Kenneth M. Roberts, 52–70. Baltimore, MD: Johns Hopkins University Press.

Mustapic, Ana María. 2002. "Argentina: La Crisis de Representación y los Partidos Políticos [Argentina: the crisis of representation of the political parties]." *América Latina Hoy* 32: 163–183.

Myers, David J. 2004. "The Normalization of Punto Fijo Democracy." In *The Unraveling of Representative Democracy in Venezuela*, eds. Jennifer L. McCoy and David J. Myers, 11–32. Baltimore, MD: Johns Hopkins University Press.

Myers, David J. 2008. "Venezuela: Delegative Democracy or Electoral Autocracy?" In *Constructing Democratic Governance in Latin America*, eds. Jorge I. Domínguez and Michael Shifter, 3rd ed., 285–321. Baltimore, MD: Johns Hopkins University Press.

Myers, David J., and Robert E. O'Connor. 1998. "Support for Coups in Democratic Political Culture: A Venezuelan Exploration." *Comparative Politics* 30(2): 193–212.

Mylonas, Harris, and Nasos Roussias. 2008. "When Do Votes Count? Regime Type, Electoral Conduct, and Political Competition in Africa." *Comparative Political Studies* 41(11): 1466–1491.

National Democratic Institute for International Affairs (NDI). 2010. *2009 Honduran General Elections Final Report: International Election Assessment Mission*. Washington, DC: NDI, January 27.

Navia, Patricio. 2006. *Rafael Correa: entre la supervivencia y la refundación*. Online: http://www.infolatam.com/analisis.php?id=2212.

Negretto, Gabriel L. 2004. "Argentina: Compromising on a Qualified Plurality System." In *Handbook of Electoral System Choice*, ed. Josep M. Colomer, 110–120. New York: Palgrave Macmillan.

Negretto, Gabriel L. 2006. "Minority Presidents and Democratic Performance in Latin America." *Latin American Politics and Society* 48(3): 63–92.

Negretto, Gabriel L. 2007. "Propuesta para una reforma electoral en México [Proposal for an electoral reform in Mexico]." *Política y Gobierno* XIV(1): 215–227.
Negretto, Gabriel L. 2013. *Making Constitutions: Presidents, Parties, and Institutional Choice in Latin America*. New York: Cambridge University Press.
Neuman, William. 2012. "Chávez Wins a Third Term in Venezuela amid Historically High Turnout." *New York Times*, October 8, A9.
Nickson, Andrew. 2009. "The General Election in Paraguay, April 2008." *Electoral Studies* 28: 145–149.
Nicolau, Jairo M. 2004. "Brazil: Democratizing with Majority Runoff." In *Handbook of Electoral System Choice*, ed. Josep M. Colomer, 121–132. New York: Palgrave Macmillan.
Nohlen, Dieter, ed. 2005. *Elections in the Americas: A Data Handbook*. Vols. 1 & 2. New York: Oxford University Press.
Nogourney, Adam. 2013. "California Sees Gridlock Ease in Governing." *New York Times*, October 19, A1, A12.
Noriega, Roger F. 2006. "Back by Unpopular Demand: Nicaragua's Daniel Ortega." *Washington Post*, October 9. Special to washingtonpost.com's Think Tank Town.
Norris, Pippa. 2004. *Electoral Engineering: Voting Rules and Political Behavior*. New York: Cambridge University Press.
Novaro, Marcos. 2004. "Argentina." In *DV: La Elección Presidencial Mediante Doble Vuelta en Latinoamérica* [Runoff: presidential election through runoff in Latin America], ed. Rafael Martínez, 25–58. Barcelona: Institut de Ciències Polítiques i Sociales.
O'Connor, Anne-Marie. 2012. "Mexican Voters Dismiss the New López Obrador." *Washington Post*, May 27, A16.
Ondetti, Gabriel. 2008. *Land, Protest, and Politics: The Landless Movement and the Struggle for Agrarian Reform in Brazil*. University Park: Pennsylvania State University Press.
Ortega, Francisco. 2007. "El *Comandante* Returns." *Berkeley Review of Latin American Studies* (Spring): 18–19.
Pachano, Simón. 2006. "Ecuador: The Provincialization of Representation." In *The Crisis of Democratic Representation in the Andes*, eds. Scott Mainwaring, Ana María Bejarano, and Eduardo Pizarro Leongómez, 100–131. Stanford, CA: Stanford University Press.
Palacios, Marco. 2006. *Between Legitimacy and Violence: A History of Colombia, 1875–2002*. Durham, NC: Duke University Press.
Palacios, Marco. 2012. "A Historical Perspective on Counterinsurgency and the 'War on Drugs' in Colombia. In *In the Wake of War*, ed. Cynthia J. Arnson, 175–206. Stanford, CA: Stanford University Press.
Pallister, Kevin. 2013. "Why No Mayan Party? Indigenous Movements and National Politics in Guatemala." *Latin American Politics and Society* 55(3): 117–138.
Parlapiano, Alicia, and Adam Pearce. 2016. "Only 9% of Americans Chose Trump and Clinton as the Nominees." *New York Times*, August 2, A16.
Payne, Arnold. 1968. *The Peruvian Coup d'Etat of 1962: The Overthrow of Manuel Prado*. Washington, DC: Institute for the Comparative Study of Political Systems.
Payne, Mark J., Daniel Zovatto G., and Mercedes Mateo Díaz. 2007. *Democracies in Development: Politics and Reform in Latin America*. Washington, DC: Inter-American Development Bank.
Paz, Miguel. 2005. "Guillermo Teillier y la Eliminación del Binomialismo: A Michelle Bachelet le sale baratísimo nuestra propuesta [Guillermo Teiller and the elimination of the binomial rule: our proposal will cost Michelle Bachelet very little]." *La Nación*, 18 December. Online: http://www.archivochile.com/Debate/debate_izqch/debatich0061.pdf.
Pearce, Jenny. 1990. *Colombia: Inside the Labyrinth*. London: Latin America Bureau.
Peirce, Neal R., and Lawrence D. Longley. 1981. *The People's President: The Electoral College in American History and the Direct Vote Alternative*. New Haven: Yale University Press.
PELA (Parliamentary Elites of Latin America, Elites Parlamentarias de América Latina. Universidad de Salamanca. Online: http://americo.usal.es.oir.

Pereira, Carlos, and Marcus André Melo. 2012. "The Surprising Success of Multiparty Presidentialism." *Journal of Democracy* 23(3): 156–170.
Pérez Baltodano, Andrés. 2012. "Political Culture." In *The Sandinistas and Nicaragua since 1979*, eds. David Close, Salvador Martí i Puig, and Shelley A. McConnell, 121–160. Boulder, CO: Lynne Rienner Publishing.
Pérez-Liñán, Aníbal. 2006. "Evaluating Presidential Runoff Elections." *Electoral Studies* 25(1): 129–146.
Pérez-Liñán, Aníbal. 2007. *Presidential Impeachment and the New Political Instability in Latin America*. New York: Cambridge University Press.
Pérez-Liñán, Aníbal, German Lodola, Andrea Castagnola, Yen-Pin Su, John Polga-Hecimovich, Juan Negri, and Alicia Quebral. 2011. *Latin American Political Processes: Scandals, Protests, and Institutional Conflicts, 1980–2007*. Codebook available at the Department of Political Science, University of Pittsburgh.
Pérez-Liñán, Aníbal, and Scott Mainwaring. 2013. "Regime Legacies and Levels of Democracy: Evidence from Latin America." *Comparative Politics* 45(4):379–397.
Philip, George. 2000. *The Strange Death of the Venezuelan Party System*. Unpublished manuscript, London School of Economics, London, England.
Phillips, Nicholas, and Elisabeth Malkin. 2013. "Close Vote Raises Tensions in Honduras." *New York Times*, November 25, A5.
Pizarro, Eduardo, and Ana María Bejarano. 2007. "Political Reform After 1991: What Still Needs to Be Reformed?" In *Peace, Democracy, and Human Rights in Colombia*, eds. Christopher Welna and Gustavo Gallón, 219–267. Notre Dame, IN: University of Notre Dame Press.
Plattner, Marc. 2009. "From Liberalism to Liberal Democracy." In *Democracy: A Reader*, eds. Larry Diamond and Marc F. Plattner, 58–72. Baltimore, MD: Johns Hopkins University Press.
Posada-Carbó, Eduardo. 2006. "Colombia Hews to the Path of Change." *Journal of Democracy* 17(4): 80–94.
Posada-Carbó, Eduardo. 2013. "Colombia: Democratic Governance amidst an Armed Conflict." In *Constructing Democratic Governance in Latin America*, eds. Jorge I. Domínguez and Michael Shifter, 4th ed., 233–254. Baltimore, MD: Johns Hopkins University Press.
Power, Timothy J. 2009. "Compulsory for Whom? Mandatory Voting and Electoral Participation in Brazil, 1986–2006." *Journal of Politics in Latin America* 1(1): 100.
Power, Timothy J. 2010. "Brazilian Democracy as a Late Bloomer." Special Issue, *Latin American Research Review* July(45): 218.
Quintero-López, Rafael. 2005. *Electores Contra Partidos en Un Sistema Político de Mandos* [Voters against parties in a political system of bosses]. Quito: Editorial Abyayala.
Quiroz, Alfonso. 2008. *Corrupt Circles: A History of Unbound Graft in Peru*. Washington, DC: Woodrow Wilson Center Press.
Reel, Monte. 2006. "Election Could Be Landmark for Chile." *Washington Post*, January 15, A20.
Reid, Michael. 2007. *Forgotten Continent: The Battle for Latin America's Soul*. New Haven, CT: Yale University Press.
Richani, Nazih. 2013. *Systems of Violence: The Political Economy of War and Peace in Colombia*, 2nd ed. Albany: State University of New York.
Riker, William H. 1992. "The Entry of Game Theory into Political Science." In *Toward a History of Game Theory*, ed. E. Roy Weintraub, 207–224. Durham: Duke University Press.
Riquelme, Marcial. 1994. *Negotiating Democratic Corridors in Paraguay. The Report of the Latin American Studies Association Delegation to Observe the 1993 Paraguayan Elections*. Pittsburgh, PA: Latin American Studies Association.
Rivas, David. 2004. "Costa Rica." In *DV: La Elección Presidencial Mediante Doble Vuelta en Latinoamérica* [Runoff: presidential election through runoff in Latin America], ed. Rafael Martínez, 199–228. Barcelona: Institut de Ciències Polítiques i Sociales.
Rock, David. 1985. *Argentina 1516–1982: From Spanish Colonization to the Falklands War*. Berkeley: University of California Press.

Rodríguez Echeverría, Miguel Angel. 2006. "Getting Costa Rica Right." *Journal of Democracy* 17(2): 161–164.

Rodríguez Olga R. 2009. "Mexico's Calderón Proposes Major Political Reform." *Associated Press*, December 15. Online: http://www.google.com/hostednews/ap/article/ALegM5ist0_G31JPy4bAgkC4MgXW_9evwD9CIVS102.

Rodríguez Raga, Juan Carlos. 2006. "Voto Preferente y Cohesión Partidista: Entre el Voto Personal y el Voto de Partido [The preferential vote and party cohesion: between the personal vote and the party vote]." In *La Reforma Política de 2003: La salvación de los partidos politicos colombianos?* [The 2003 political reform: the salvation of Colombia's political parties] eds. Gary Hoskin and Miguel García Sánchez, 447–476. Bogotá: CESO (Centro de Estudios Socioculturales e Internacionales), Universidad de los Andes.

Rohter, Larry. 2003. "Menem, Polls Slipping, Quits Argentine Race." *New York Times*, May 15, A7.

Rohter, Larry. 2005. "Top Aide to Brazil's Leader Quits after Scandal Charge." *New York Times*, June 18, A3.

Rohter, Larry. 2006. "In Brazil, Former Ally May Spoil Race for the President." *New York Times*, September 7, A3.

Roig-Franzia, Manuel. 2007. "In Guatemala, Colom Yields Surprise Win." *Washington Post*, November 5, A11.

Romero, Simon. 2006. "Link to Chávez May Have Hurt Ecuadorean Candidate." *New York Times*, October 17, A3.

Roncagliolo, Rafael. 2011. "Of Parties and Party Systems." In *Fractured Politics: Peruvian Democracy Past and Present*, ed. John Crabtree, 67–88. London: Institute for the Study of the Americas, University of London.

Ropp, Steve C. 2007. "Panama: New Politics for a New Millennium?" In *Latin American Politics and Development*, eds. Howard Wiarda and Harvey F. Kline, 6th ed., 550–564. Boulder, CO: Westview Press.

Rosales, Manuel. 2006. "Rosales propone ideas para reforma constitucional [Rosales proposes ideas for constitutional reform]." *El Universal*, December 6.

Ruhl, Mark J. 1997. "Doubting Democracy in Honduras." *Current History* 96(607): 81–86.

Ruhl, Mark J. 2007. "Honduras: Problems of Democratic Consolidation." In *Latin American Politics and Development*, eds. Howard J. Wiarda and Harvey F. Kline, 6th ed., 519–533. Boulder, CO: Westview Press.

Ruhl, Mark J. 2010. "Honduras Unravels." *Journal of Democracy* 21(2): 92–107.

Ruiz Rodríguez, Leticia M. 2004. "Chile." In *DV: La Elección Presidencial Mediante Doble Vuelta en LatinoAmérica* [Runoff: presidential election through runoff in Latin America], ed. Rafael Martínez, 139–168. Barcelona: Institut de Ciències Polítiques i Socials.

Sagás, Ernesto. 1997. "The 1996 Presidential Elections in the Dominican Republic." *Electoral Studies* 16(1): 103–107.

Sagás, Ernesto. 2001. "The 2000 Presidential Election in the Dominican Republic." *Electoral Studies* 20(3): 495–501.

Sagás, Ernesto. 2006. "Las elecciones legislativas y municipales de 2006 en le República Dominicana [The 2006 legislative and municipal elections in the Dominican Republic]." *Revista de Ciencia Política* 26(1): 152–157.

Samuels, David J., and Matthew S. Shugart. 2010. *Presidents, Parties, and Prime Ministers: How the Separation of Powers Affects Party Organization and Behavior*. New York: Cambridge University Press.

Sanborn, Cynthia. 1988. "El Futuro Diferente? The Legacy of the 1970s for Peruvian Populism in the '80s." Paper presented at the 14th International Congress of the Latin American Studies Association, New Orleans, LA, March 17–19.

Sánchez, Francisco. 2004. "Perú." In *DV: La Elección Presidencial Mediante Doble Vuelta en LatinoAmérica* [Runoff: presidential election through runoff in Latin America], ed. Rafael Martínez, 391–424. Barcelona: Institut de Ciències Polítiques i Socials.

Sanders, Thomas G. 1984. *Peru between Democracy and the Sendero Luminoso.* Universities Field Staff International Reports No. 21 (South America).

Sanders, Thomas G. 1986. *Prospects for Political Change in Paraguay.* Universities Field Staff International Reports No. 37.

Sarria, Nidya. 2009. *Nicaragua under Daniel Ortega's Second Presidency: Daniel-Style Politics as Usual?* Council on Hemispheric Affairs. Online: http://www.coha.org/2009/07.

Sartori, Giovanni. 2001. "The Party Effects of Electoral Systems." In *Political Parties and Democracy,* eds. Larry Diamond and Richard Gunther, 90–108. Baltimore, MD: Johns Hopkins University Press.

Schedler, Andreas. 2002. "The Nested Game of Democratization by Elections." *International Political Science Review* 23(1): 103–122.

Schmidt, Gregory D. 1996. "Fujimori's 1990 Upset Victory in Peru: Electoral Rules, Contingencies, and Adaptive Strategies." *Comparative Politics* 28(3): 321–354.

Schmidt, Gregory D. 1999. "Crónica de una Reelección [The story of a reelection]." In *El Juego Político: Fujimori, la oposición, y las reglas* [The political game: Fujimori, the opposition, and the rules], ed. Fernando Tuesta Soldevilla, 97–130. Lima: Fundación Friedrich Ebert Stiftung.

Schmidt, Gregory D. 2007. "Back to the Future? The 2006 Peruvian General Election." *Electoral Studies* 26(4): 813–819.

Schmidt, Gregory D. 2012. "AIDS or Cancer? The 2011 Peruvian Elections." *Electoral Studies* 31(3): 624–628.

Schodt, David W. 1987. *Ecuador: An Andean Enigma.* Boulder, CO: Westview Press.

Scully, Timothy R. 1995. "Reconstituting Party Politics in Chile." In *Building Democratic Institutions: Party Systems in Latin America,* eds. Scott Mainwaring and Timothy R. Scully, 100–137. Stanford, CA: Stanford University Press.

Seawright, Jason. 2012. *Party-System Collapse: The Roots of Crisis in Peru and Venezuela.* Stanford, CA: Stanford University Press.

Seligson, Mitchell A. 2002. "Trouble in Paradise? The Erosion of System Support in Costa Rica, 1978–1999." *Latin American Research Review* 37(1): 160–185.

Seligson, Mitchell A. 2005. "Guatemala: Democracy on Ice." In *The Third Wave of Democratization in Latin America,* eds. Frances Hagopian and Scott P. Mainwaring, 202–235. Cambridge, UK: Cambridge University Press.

Serrill, Michael S. 1996. "Improbable Comeback." *Time,* October 14, p. 27.

Shifter, Michael. 2011a. "Perú vive una paradoja, con altos niveles de crecimiento y descontento [Peru lives a paradox, with high levels of both growth and discontent]." *El País,* April 15.

Shifter, Michael. 2011b. "Peru's Democratic Test." *Washington Post,* May 23, A19.

Shifter, Michael. 2011c. "Latin America: A Surge to the Center." *Journal of Democracy* 22(1): 107–121.

Shugart, Matthew S. 2004. "The American Process of Selecting a President: A Comparative Perspective." *Presidential Studies Quarterly* 34(3): 632–655.

Shugart, Matthew S. 2007. "Mayoría relativa vs. Segunda vuelta: La elección presidencial mexicana de 2006 en perspectiva comparada [Plurality vs. runoff: Mexico's 2006 presidential election in comparative perspective]." *Política y Gobierno* XIV(1): 175–201.

Shugart, Matthew S., and John Carey. 1992. *Presidents and Assemblies: Constitutional Design and Electoral Dynamics.* New York: Cambridge University Press.

Shugart, Matthew S., and Rein Taagepera. 1994. "Plurality versus Majority Election of Presidents: A Proposal for a Double Complement Rule." *Comparative Political Studies* 27(3): 323–348.

Siavelis, Peter M. 2000. *The President and Congress in PostAuthoritarian Chile: Institutional Constraints to Democratic Consolidation.* University Park: Pennsylvania State University Press.

Siavelis, Peter M. 2005. "Electoral System, Coalitional Disintegration, and the Future of Chile's Concertación." *Latin American Research Review* 40(1): 56–82.

Siavelis, Peter M. 2008. "Chile: The End of the Unfinished Transition." In *Constructing Democratic Governance in Latin America,* eds. Jorge I. Domínguez and Michael Shifter, 3rd ed., 177–208. Baltimore, MD: Johns Hopkins University Press.

Sides, John. 2006. "The Origins of Campaign Agendas." *British Journal of Political Science* 36(3): 407–436.

Singer, Matthew W. 2016. "Elite Polarization and the Electoral Impact of Left-Right Placements: Evidence from Latin America." *Latin American Research Review* 51(2): 174–194.

Singer, Matthew W., and Carlos Fara. 2008. "The Presidential and Legislative Elections in Argentina, October 2007." *Electoral Studies* 27(4): 756–760.

Smith, Peter H. 2008. *Talons of the Eagle: Latin America, the United States, and the World*, 3rd ed. New York: Oxford University Press.

Snow, Peter G., and Luigi Manzetti. 1993. *Political Forces in Argentina*. 3rd ed. Westport, CT: Praeger.

Sondrol, Paul C. 2007. "Paraguay: Democracy Challenged." In *Latin American Politics and Development*, eds. Howard J. Wiarda and Harvey F. Kline, 6th ed., 325–344. Boulder, CO: Westview Press.

Soudriette, Richard W., and Andrew Ellis. 2006. "A Global Snapshot." In *Electoral Systems and Democracy*, eds. Larry Diamond and Marc F. Plattner, 16–26. Baltimore: MD: Johns Hopkins University Press.

Spence, Jack. 2004. *War and Peace in Central America: Comparing Transitions toward Democracy and Social Equity in Guatemala, El Salvador, and Nicaragua*. Brookline, MA: Hemisphere Initiatives, November.

Spence, Jack, David R. Dye, and George Vickers. 1994. *El Salvador: Elections of the Century*. Cambridge, MA: Hemisphere Initiatives, July.

Spence, Jack, Mike Lanchin, and Geoff Thale. 2001. *From Elections to Earthquakes: Reform and Participation in Post-War El Salvador*. Cambridge, MA: Hemisphere Initiatives, April.

Starr, Pamela K. 2012. "Mexico's Big, Inherited Challenges." *Current History* 111(742): 43–49.

Stokes, Susan C. 1996. "Peru: The Rupture of Democratic Rule." In *Constructing Democratic Governance: Latin America and the Caribbean in the 1990s*, eds. Jorge I. Domínguez and Abraham F. Lowenthal, 58–71. Baltimore, MD: Johns Hopkins University Press.

Stokes, Susan C. 1997. "Democratic Accountability and Policy Change: Economic Policy in Fujimori's Peru." *Comparative Politics* 29(2): 209–226.

Tagina, María Laura. 2013. "Elecciones 2009 y 2011 en Argentina: Ocaso y resurgimiento del gobierno de Cristina Kirchner [The 2009 and 2011 elections in Argentina: eclipse and resurgence of the government of Cristina Kirchner]." In *Elecciones y Política en América Latina 2009–2011* [Elections and politics in Latin America 2009–2011], eds. Manuel Alcántara and María Laura Tagina, 563–629. Mexico: Instituto Federal Electoral.

Tanaka, Martín. 1998. *Los Espejismos de la Democracia: El colapso del sistema de partidos en el Perú* [Democratic mirages: the collapse of the party system in Peru]. Lima: Instituto de Estudios Peruanos.

Tanaka, Martín. 2005. *Democracia sin partidos: Perú, 2000–2005: Los Problemas de Representación y las Propuestas de Reforma [Democracy without parties: Peru, 2000–2005: the problems of representation and the proposals for reform]*. Lima: Instituto de Estudios Peruanos.

Tanaka, Martín. 2011. "Peru's 2011 Elections: A Vote for Moderate Change." *Journal of Democracy* 22(4): 75–83.

Tanaka, Martín, and Sofía Vera. 2007. "Perú: Entre Los Sobresaltos Electorales y la Agenda Pendiente de la Exclusión [Peru: between electoral scares and the pending agenda of social exclusion]." *Revista de Ciencia Política*, Special Volume, 235–247.

Taylor, Steven L. 2009. *Voting amid Violence: Electoral Democracy in Colombia*. Boston, MA: Northeastern University Press.

Taylor-Robinson, Michelle M. 2001. "Old Parties and New Democracies: Do They Bring Out the Best in One Another?" *Party Politics* 7(5): 594.

Taylor-Robinson, Michelle M. 2006. "La Política Hondureña y las Elecciones de 2005 [Honduran politics and the elections of 2005]." *Revista de Ciencia Política* 26(1): 114–124.

Taylor-Robinson, Michelle M. 2010. *Do the Poor Count? Democratic Institutions and Accountability in a Context of Poverty*. University Park: Pennsylvania State University Press.

The Carter Center. 1997. *"The Observation of the 1996 Nicaraguan Elections."* Atlanta, GA: The Carter Center.

Thompson, José. 2010. "Ballotage in Latin America." *Electoral World* 3(8).

Tolbert, Caroline, and Peverill Squire. 2009. "Reforming the Presidential Nomination Process." *PS: Political Science and Politics* 42(1): 27–32.

Toledo, Alejandro. 2015. *The Shared Society: A Vision for the Global Future of Latin America*. Stanford, CA: Stanford University Press.

Torre, Juan Carlos. 2005. "Citizens Versus Political Class: The Crisis of Partisan Representation." In *Argentine Democracy: The Politics of Institutional Weakness*, eds. Steven Levitsky and María Victoria Murillo, 165–180. University Park, PA: Pennsylvania State University Press.

Torres-Rivas, Edelberto. 2012. "The Limits of Peace and Democracy in Guatemala." In *In the Wake of War*, ed. Cynthia J. Arnson, 107–138. Stanford, CA: Stanford University Press.

Torres-Rivas, Edelberto. 2013. *Revoluciones sin cambios revolucionarios: Ensayos sobre la crisis en Centroamérica* [Revolutions without revolutionary changes: essays on the crisis in Central America]. Guatemala City: F & G Editores.

Trudeau, Robert H. 1993. *Guatemalan Politics: The Popular Struggle for Democracy*. Boulder, CO: Lynne Rienner Publishers.

Trudeau, Robert H. 2000. "Guatemala: Democratic Rebirth?" In *Latin American Politics and Development*, eds. Howard J. Wiarda and Harvey Kline, 5th ed., 493–511. Boulder, CO: Westview Press.

Tuesta Soldevilla, Fernando. 2008. "Las Elecciones Presidenciales Perú 2006 [Peru's 2006 presidential elections]." In *Elecciones y Política en América Latina* [Elections and Politics in Latin America], eds. Manuel Alcántara Sáez and Fátima García Díaz, 123–144. Mexico City: Instituto Electoral del Estado de México.

Uharte Pozas, Luis Miguel. 2012. "El Proceso de Democratización Paraguayo: Avances y Resistencias [Paraguay's process of democratization: advances and resistances]." *América Latina Hoy* 60(1): 17–42.

Ulloa, Fernando C., and Eduardo Posada-Carbó. 1999. "The Colombian Presidential Elections of 1998." *Electoral Studies* 18(3): 411–450.

Ulloa, Fernando C., and Eduardo Posada-Carbó. 2003. "The Congressional and Presidential Elections in Colombia, 2002." *Electoral Studies* 22(4): 765–807.

Valenzuela, Arturo. 1993. "Latin America: Presidentialism in Crisis." *Journal of Democracy* 4(4): 7–9.

Valenzuela, Arturo. 1994. "Party Politics and the Crisis of Presidentialism in Chile." In *The Failure of Presidential Democracy*, eds. Juan J. Linz and Arturo Valenzuela, 91–150. Baltimore, MD: Johns Hopkins University Press.

Valenzuela, Arturo. 1997. "Paraguay: The Coup that Didn't Happen." *Journal of Democracy* 8(1): 49–52.

Valenzuela, Arturo. 2004. "Latin American Presidencies Interrupted." *Journal of Democracy* 15(4): 5–19.

Valenzuela, Arturo, and Lucia Dammert. 2006. "Problems of Success in Chile." *Journal of Democracy* 17(4): 65–79.

Van de Walle, Nicholas. 2006. "Tipping Games: When Do Opposition Parties Coalesce?" In *Electoral Authoritarianism: The Dynamics of Unfree Competition*, ed. Andreas Schedler, 77–94. Boulder, CO: Lynne Rienner Publishers.

Vargas Cullell, Jorge. 2007. "Costa Rica: fin de una era política [Costa Rica; end of a political era]." *Revista de Ciencia Política*. Volumen Especial: 113–128.

Vargas Llosa, Alvaro, and Santiago Aroca. 1995. *Riding the Tiger: Ramiro de Léon Carpio's Battle for Human Rights in Guatemala*. Miami, FL: Brickell Communications.

Vergara, Alberto. 2007. *Ni Amnésicos ni Irracionales: Las Elecciones Peruanas de 2006 en Perspectiva Histórica* [Neither Amnesiacs nor Irrationals: Peru's 2006 elections in historical perspective]. Lima: Solar Central de Proyectos EIRL.

Vickers, George, and Jack Spence. 1994. "Elections: The Right Consolidates Power." *NACLA Report on the Americas* XXVII(1): 6–11.

Villagrán de León, Francisco. 1993. "Thwarting the Guatemalan Coup." *Journal of Democracy* 4(4): 117–124.

Wang, Ching-Hsing. 2012. "The Effects of Party Fractionalization and Party Polarization on Democracy." *Party Politics* 5(5): 687–699.

Weiner, Myron, and Joseph LaPalombara. 1966. "Conclusion: The Impact of Parties on Political Development." In *Political Parties and Political Development*, eds. Joseph LaPalombara and Myron Weiner, 399–438. Princeton, NJ: Princeton University Press.

Weinstein, Martin. 1975. *Uruguay: The Politics of Failure*. Westport, CT: Greenwood Press.

Weyland, Kurt. 1993. "The Rise and Fall of President Collor and Its Impact on Brazilian Democracy." *Journal of Inter-American Studies and World Affairs* 35(1): 1–37.

Weyland, Kurt. 2002. *The Politics of Market Reform in Fragile Democracies: Argentina, Brazil, Peru, and Venezuela*. Princeton, NJ: Princeton University Press.

Weymouth, Lally. 2012. "Interview with Mexican Presidential Candidate Andrés Manuel López Obrador." *Washington Post*, May 18, B5.

Wilson, Bruce M. 1999. "Leftist Parties, Neoliberal Policies, and Reelection Strategies." *Comparative Political Studies* 22(6): 752–779.

Wilson, Bruce M. 2003. "The Elections in Costa Rica, February and April 2002." *Electoral Studies* 22(3): 509–516.

Wilson, Bruce M. 2007. "The General Election in Costa Rica, February 2006." *Electoral Studies* 26(3): 712–716.

Wilson, Reid. 2013. "To Cure Rampant Partisanship, Empower Voters in the Middle." *Washington Post*, October 19, A5.

Wood, Elisabeth J. 2000. "Civil War and the Transformation of Elite Representation in El Salvador." In *Conservative Parties, the Right, and Democracy in Latin America*, ed. Kevin J. Middlebrook, 223–254. Baltimore, MD: Johns Hopkins University Press.

World Bank. 2011. *World Development Indicators 2011*. Washington, DC: The World Bank.

World Bank. 2013. *Database of Political Institutions 2012* (updated Jan. 2013). Online: http://go.worldbank.org/EAGGLRZ40.

Wright, Stephen G., and William H. Riker. 1989. "Plurality and Runoff Systems and Numbers of Candidates." *Public Choice* 60(2): 155–175.

Wynia, Gary W. 1986. *Argentina: Illusions and Realities*. New York: Holmes and Meier.

Zechmeister, Elizabeth J., and Margarita Corral. 2013. "Individual and Context Constraints on Ideological Labels in Latin America." *Comparative Political Studies* 46(6): 675–701.

Zucco, Cesar, and Timothy J. Power. 2013. "Bolsa Família and the Shift in Lula's Electoral Base, 2002–2006: A Reply to Bohn." *Latin American Research Review* 48(3): 3–24.

INDEX

Figures, tables, and notes are indicated by f, t, and n respectively.

Abente Brun, Diego, 95
Acción Popular (Popular Action, AP, Peru), 157–159
Acción Democrática (Democratic Action, AD, Venezuela), 55, 67–70, 72–74, 195
Acemoglu, Daron, 4
Acosta, Andrés Mejía, 42
AD (Acción Democrática, Democratic Action, Venezuela), 55, 67–70, 72–74, 195
AD/M-19 (Alianza Democrática/Movimiento 19 de Abril, Democratic Alliance/Movement of April 19th, Colombia), 152
Aguayo, Sergio, 86
Ahmed, Amel, 4
ALBA (Alianza Bolivariana para las Américas, Bolivarian Alliance for the Americas), 91, 93
Alckmin, Geraldo, 123
Alemán, Arnoldo, 76–77
Alfaro Ucero, Luis, 72
Alfonsín, Raúl, 183, 185
Alianza Bolivariana para las Américas, Bolivarian Alliance for the Americas (ALBA), 91, 93
Alianza del Centro (Alliance of the Center, Argentina), 186
Alianza Democrática/Movimiento 19 de Abril (Democratic Alliance/Movement of April 19th, AD/M-19, Colombia), 152
Alianza por el Cambio (Alliance for Change, Panama), 104
Alianza Liberal (Liberal Alliance, Nicaragua), 76
Alianza Pais (Ecuador), 199
Alianza Patriótica para el Cambio (Patriotic Alliance for Change, APC, Paraguay), 98
Alianza Popular Revolucionario Americana, or American Popular Revolutionary Alliance, Peru (APRA), 38, 50, 51, 58, 156–161
Alianza por el Cambio (Alliance for Change, Mexico), 82

Alianza por el Trabajo, la Educación, y la Justicia (Alliance for Jobs, Justice, and Education, Argentina), 188
Alianza Repúblicana Nacionalista (Nationalist Republican Alliance, ARENA, El Salvador), 51, 132–136, 137, 177, 198
Allende, Salvador, 1, 41, 124, 126–128, 137, 198
Alliance for Change, Mexico (Alianza por el Cambio), 82
Alliance for Change, Panama (Alianza por el Cambio), 104
Alliance for Jobs, Justice, and Education, Argentina (Alianza por el Trabajo, la Educación, y la Justicia), 188
Alliance of the Center, Argentina (Alianza del Centro), 186
Allison, Michael, 87
Allocation of public goods, 201
Almagro, Luis, 165
Álvarez, Carlos, 188
Alvear, Soledad, 129
American Bar Association, 204
AMLO. *See* López Obrador, Andrés Manuel
Anderson, Leslie, 184
Anderson, Thomas P., 88
Angeloz, Eduardo, 186
AntiCorruption Party, PAC, Honduras (Partido AntiCorrupción), 93
AP (Acción Popular, Popular Action, Peru), 157–159
APC (Alianza Patriótica para el Cambio, Patriotic Alliance for Change, Paraguay), 98
APRA (Alianza Popular Revolucionario Americana, American Popular Revolutionary Alliance, Peru), 38, 50, 51, 58, 156–161
Araya, Johnny, 182
Araya, Rolando, 180

Index

ARENA (Alianza Repúblicana Nacionalista, Nationalist Republican Alliance, El Salvador), 51, 132–136, 137, 177, 198
Argaña, Luis María, 96
Argentina, 11, 182–191
  1963 election, 42, 185
  1973 election, 185
  1983 election under plurality, 183, 185
  1989 election under plurality, 183, 186
  1995 election, 176, 183, 186–188, 191
  1999 election, 176, 183, 188–189, 191
  2003 election, 183, 189, 191
  2007 and 2011 elections, 176, 189–190
  2015 election, 190–191, 199
  barriers to entry in, 183, 191
  corruption in, 187
  debt crisis and economic conditions in, 182, 189–190
  democracy level in, 182
  elections won with less than 50% of the vote (1978–2012), likely result of runoff, 254t, 256t
  free and fair elections in, year of commencing in, 17, 185
  Freedom House and V-Dem scores, 182, 189–190, 196–197
  human-rights violations in, 185
  legislative majorities of president's party in, 216t, 219t
  legislative threshold of vote in, 201
  midterm elections, reduce frequency of, 200
  military coups in, 41, 185
  new parties in, 260–261t
  number of parties in, 32, 176, 183, 199
  old-timer presidential candidates in, 248t
  PELA surveys, 185, 189, 190
  as plurality country, 1, 14, 183, 184–185, 186, 196
  political parties in, 50, 176, 184–185
  pre-election opinion polls, accuracy of, 190, 227t, 228–229t
  as runoff country with reduced threshold, 183, 196
  shorter term for presidency in, 184
  term limits in, 57, 184
  threshold for runoff in, 15, 175–176, 191
Arias, Arnulfo, 101
Arias, Óscar, 178, 180–182, 270n3 (Ch. 7)
Arias Cárdenas, Francisco, 73
Arnulfista Party (Panama), 50, 51, 101, 104
Artiga-González, Álvaro, 142
Arzú, Álvaro, 142, 145
Asian elections, legitimacy issues for elected presidents in, 42
Astori, Danilo, 111
Authentic Radical Liberal Party, PLRA, Paraguay (Partido Liberal Radical Auténtico), 94–98

Authoritarian legacies, 5, 47–51, 52–53t, 193, 194, 202
Autogolpes (self-coups)
  Guatemala, 39, 140, 141, 145, 198
  Peru, 39, 140, 156, 160–161, 198
Aylwin, Patricio, 127
Azcona, José, 90

Bachelet, Michelle, 128–130, 137, 197
Balaguer, Joaquín, 57, 112, 114–116, 137, 196
Baldizón, Manuel, 147–148
Barco, Virgilio, 151
Barrantes, Alfonso, 158, 159
Barriers to entry, 3–4, 10–11, 29–30, 47, 193, 194, 197. *See also* New parties; Pre-election opinion polls, accuracy of
Batlle, Jorge, 58, 110, 111
Bejarano, Ana María, 259
Belaúnde, Fernando, 157–158
Beloved Fatherland Movement, Paraguay (Movimiento Patria Querida), 97
Berensztein, Sergio, 183
Berger, Oscar, 142, 146
Besa, Alessandri, 127
Betancur, Belisario, 151
Binner, Hermes, 190
Blades, Rubén, 35, 102
Blanco Party (Blancos, Uruguay), 54, 55, 108–110, 112
Bolaños, Enrique, 78
Bolivia, 14–15, 175, 201
Bolsa Família, 122
Boo-Seung Chang, 42
Booth, John A., 40
Bordaberry, Juan María, 109, 112
Bordón, José Octavio, 187, 191
Borja, Rodrigo, 168–170, 172, 197
Bormann, Nils-Christian, 22
Bosch, Juan, 50, 58, 113, 115
Brazil, 117–124
  1945–1964 elections, 41
  1985 election, 17, 118
  1989 election, 118–120, 199
  1994 and 1998 elections, 120–121
  2002 elections, 121–122
  2006, 2010, 2014 elections, 122–124
  cartel parties in, 197
  Condorcet winners in, 119, 120
  corruption in, 120, 123–124
  currency change in, 121
  debt crisis and economic conditions in, 117, 118
  democracy level in, 106, 107, 117, 137
  elections won with less than 50% of the vote (1978–2012), likely result of runoff, 256t
  free and fair elections in, year of commencing in, 17

Freedom House and V-Dem scores, 12, 106, 117, 124, 196
  leftist shift in, 124
  legislative elections concurrent with presidential elections in, 200
  legislative majorities of president's party in, 220t
  legislative threshold of vote in, 201
  military coup (1955), 41
  moderate left president elected in, 107
  new parties in, 138, 261t
  number of parties in, 32, 107, 118, 198, 200
  old-timer presidential candidates in, 248t
  outsider candidates in, 119
  PELA surveys, 107, 124
  as plurality country, 1, 20
  pre-election opinion polls, accuracy of, 227t, 229t
  as runoff country, 118, 124, 137, 196
  shift from Hare Quota to D'Hondt formula for calculation of seats in, 201
  term limits in, 57
  voter turnout in, 36, 106
Brizola, Leonel, 119–120
Broad Front, Costa Rica (Frente Amplio), 182
Broad Front, FA, Uruguay (Frente Amplio), 63, 109–111, 136–137
Bruhn, Kathleen, 18
Bucaram, Abdalá ("El Loco"), 166, 168–171, 174, 197
Bucaram, Assad, 167, 169
Buchanan, Patrick, 203
Büchi, Hernán, 127
Bullock, Charles, 204
Bush, George W., 203

Caballero Vargas, Guillermo, 96
Cáceres, Andrés, 163
CAFTA (Central American Free Trade Agreement), 91, 181
Caldera, Rafael, 58, 67, 68, 70–71, 195
Calderón, Felipe, 2, 83–84, 195
Calderón Sol, Armando, 133
Calderón, Rafael Angel, 181
Callejas, Rafael, 90
Cambiemos (Let's Change, Argentina), 191
Cambio 90 (Change 90, Peru), 159–161
Cambio 90/Nueva Mayoría (Change 90/New Majority, Peru), 161–162
Cambio Democrático (Democratic Change, CD, Panama), 103
Campa, Roberto, 84
Campaign-finance rules
  Costa Rica, 178, 201
  Dominican Republic, 201
  Mexico, 83
Campíns, Luis Herrera, 69

Campos, Eduardo, 123
Capriles Radonski, Henrique, 74
Cárdenas, Cuauthémoc, 58, 81–82
Cardoso, Fernando Henrique, 38–39, 120–121
Carey, John, 3, 30, 31
Carles, Rubén, 102
Carpio, Jorge, 143–145, 197
Carreras, Miguel, 35
Carrió, Elisa, 189–190
Cartel parties, 5–6, 51–55, 265n17
  Brazil, 197
  Dominican Republic, 116, 197, 198, 199
  endurance of, 199
  Honduras, 54, 66, 87, 89
  Mexico, 66, 81, 105, 195
  Nicaragua, 66
  Panama, 101
  Paraguay, 105, 196
  in plurality countries, 66, 69
  polls' advantage of, 61
  strategies to defeat, 59, 194
  Uruguay, 54
  Venezuela, 66, 69
Carter Center, 268n4
Cartes, Horacio, 100
Casas-Zamora, Kevin, 178
Cason, Jeffrey, 108
Castagnola, Andrea, 14
Castañeda, Jorge, 80, 82, 85
Castañeda, Luis, 164
Castro de Zelaya, Xiomara, 93
Catholic Church, 50, 68, 77, 81, 82, 97, 108, 126, 185
Caudillismo, 5, 77, 87
  neo-caudillismo, 56
  perpetuation of old-timers, 55–58
  (see also Old-timer presidential candidates)
Cavallo, Domingo, 188
CD (Cambio Democrático, Democratic Change, Panama), 103
CDU (Centro Democrático Unido, United Democratic Center, El Salvador), 135
Center-left parties, 45, 50, 71, 82, 88, 100–101, 110–111, 142, 168–172, 179, 197
Central American Free Trade Agreement (CAFTA), 91, 181
Cerezo, Vinicio, 141, 143–144, 174, 197
CFP (Concentración de Fuerzas Populares, Concentration of Popular Forces, Ecuador), 167
Chamorro, Violeta Barrios de, 35, 76
Change 90, Peru (Cambio 90), 159–161
Change 90/New Majority, Peru (Cambio 90/Nueva Mayoría), 161–162
Chasquetti, Daniel, 15

Chávez, Hugo, 8, 10, 20, 35, 67, 69–70, 72–74, 92, 104–105, 133, 155, 172, 173, 195, 263n6
  as model for other politicians, 98, 111–112, 135
Chávez Mena, Fidel, 134
Cheibub, José Antonio, 44
Chile, 124–130
  1989 and 1993 elections, 127
  1999–2000 election, 124, 127
  2005–2006 election, 124, 128, 137
  2009–2010 election, 129–130, 137, 199
  2013 election, 130, 137
  authoritarianism in, 125
  binomial rule in, 125
  Condorcet winners in, 130
  corruption in, 128
  democracy's history in, 1, 41, 106, 137
  duopoly in, 130
  economic conditions in, 124
  elections won with less than 50% of the vote (1978–2012), likely result of runoff, 256t
  free and fair elections in, year of commencing in, 17
  Freedom House and V-Dem scores, 106, 124, 196
  ideological moderation in, 124, 198
  inclusion created by new parties in, 5
  incumbent blocked from re-election in, 56
  legislative elections concurrent with presidential elections in, 125, 200
  legislative majorities of president's party in, 220t
  mandatory voting in, 21, 125, 148
  military coup (1973), 41, 124
  moderate left president elected in, 107
  new parties in, 138, 261t
  number of parties in, 32, 107, 198, 200
  old-timer presidential candidates in, 248t
  outsider candidates in, 35, 127
  PELA surveys, 107, 126, 127, 129
  as plurality country, 1, 20
  political coalitions in, 125–126, 198
  pre-election opinion polls, accuracy of, 60, 61, 227t, 230t
  as runoff country, 2, 137, 196, 209, 210t
  shortening of presidential term in, 125
  threshold for runoff favored in, 175
  voter turnout in, 21, 36, 106, 268n1
Chinchilla, Laura, 182
Christian Democratic parties, 50, 167. *See also* COPEI (Venezuela)
Christian Democratic Party, PDC, Chile (Partido Demócrata Cristiano), 126–128
Christian Democratic Party, PDC, El Salvador (Partido Demócrata Cristiano), 132, 134, 135
Christian Democratic Party of Honduras, PDC (Partido Demócrata Cristiano de Honduras), 88

Citizen Action Party, PAC, Costa Rica (Partido Acción Ciudadana), 63, 179–180, 182, 191, 197
Clientelism. *See* Cartel parties
  Colombia, 150
  Paraguay, 95
Clinton, Hillary, 203
Coalición Cívica (Civic Coalition, Argentina), 190
Coalition of Parties for Democracy, Chile (Concertación de Partidos por la Democracia), 126–130, 137
Colburn, Forrest, 136
Cold War
  Christian Democratic parties in, 50
  Marxist parties in, 8, 50–51
  polarization in Latin American countries in, 4, 51
  political violence in Latin American during, 139
Collor de Mello, Fernando, 119–121
Colom, Álvaro, 9, 142, 146–148, 174, 197, 269n3
Colombia, 11, 148–156
  1978–1990 elections, 151–152
  1994 election, 152–153
  1998 election, 139, 153
  2002 and 2006 elections, 154–155, 174
  2010 election, 155
  2014 election, 139, 155–156, 174
  authoritarian action committed by political parties in, 51, 52t
  civil war in, 150
  clientelism in, 150
  Condorcet winners in, 139, 140
  democracy levels in, 139, 148
  economic conditions in, 150
  election fraud and corruption in, 153, 269n6
  elections won with less than 50% of the vote (1978–2012), likely result of runoff, 254t, 257t
  executive-legislative gridlock in, 139
  executive–legislative gridlock in, 139
  free and fair elections in, year of commencing in, 17
  Freedom House and V-Dem scores, 12, 139, 148, 156, 196–197
  history of parties in, 50, 51
  legislative election non-concurrent in, 200
  legislative majorities of president's party in, 216t, 221t
  legislative threshold of vote in, 200–201
  legitimacy crisis in, 149
  new parties in, 260–261t
  number of parties in, 32, 33, 139, 149–150, 198
  old-timer presidential candidates in, 248t
  outsider candidates in, 35, 149, 154
  peace negotiations with FARC in, 153–155
  PELA surveys, 153, 154

as plurality country (1978–1990),
  151–152, 196
 political violence and assassinations in, 139,
  148–149, 151–152, 154, 174
 pre-election opinion polls, accuracy of, 61, 227,
  230–231t
 as runoff country (runoff adopted 1991), 25,
  139–140, 149, 152, 174, 196
 two long-standing parties and emergence of
  duopoly in, 50, 150–151, 154, 196
 voluntary voting in, 13, 148
 voter turnout in, 36, 139, 148–149
Colombia First (Primero Colombia), 154
Colomer, Josep, 15, 30, 39, 44–45
Colorado Party (Colorados, Uruguay), 51, 54, 55,
  66, 108–110, 112
Colorado Party (Paraguay), 94–98, 105, 194,
  196, 199
Comité de Organización Política Electoral
  Independiente (Christian Democrats,
  Venezuela). See COPEI (Venezuela)
Communist Party (El Salvador), 135
Communist Party (Venezuela), 68, 69
Communist Party of Chile, PC (Partido
  Comunista de Chile), 125, 126, 129,
  130, 198
Compulsory voting, 13, 21, 86, 148, 177
CONAIE (Confederación de Nacionalidades
  Indígenas del Ecuador, Confederation
  of Indigenous Nationalities of Ecuador),
  167, 171
Concentración de Fuerzas Populares
  (Concentration of Popular Forces, CFP,
  Ecuador), 167
Concertación de Partidos por la Democracia
  (Coalition of Parties for Democracy, Chile),
  126–130, 137
Condorcet winners, 6, 43, 198–199
 Brazil, 119, 120
 Chile, 130
 Colombia, 139, 140
 defined, 6
 Ecuador, 140, 166, 170, 172, 174
 Guatemala, 142
 Peru, 164
 ranked-choice voting and, 206
Confederación de Nacionalidades Indígenas del
  Ecuador, Confederation of Indigenous
  Nationalities of Ecuador (CONAIE),
  167, 171
Conservative Party, renamed Social Conservative
  Party, Colombia (Partido Conservador),
  149, 150, 151–153, 196
Convergencia (Venezuela), 70, 71
COPEI (Venezuela), 50, 55, 67–70, 72–74,
  194, 195
Coppedge, Michael, 13, 31, 45, 67, 70, 179

Cordero, Febrés, 169
Corrales, Javier, 17, 18, 35, 55–56, 212, 247
Corrales, José Miguel, 180
Correa, Rafael, 35, 45, 140, 166, 173–174,
  175–176, 197
Corruption
 Argentina, 187
 Brazil, 120, 123–124
 Chile, 128
 Colombia, 153, 269n6
 Costa Rica, 180–181
 damage to democracy from, 174
 Dominican Republic, 115, 137
 Ecuador, 170–171
 electoral support despite, 59
 Guatemala, 148
 Honduras, 89
 Mexico, 81, 83–84, 86
 Nicaragua, 77, 78
 Panama, 104
 Paraguay, 95–96
 parties running on anti-corruption themes, 63
 Peru, 160, 161–162
 in plurality countries, 104
 survey companies controlling polls and, 61
 Venezuela, 68, 70, 71, 73
 voters' concerns over, 5
Costa Rica, 11, 177–182
 1978–1994 elections, 179–180
 1988 and 2002 elections, 178, 180–181
 1998 election, 178
 2002 election, 199
 2006 and 2010 elections, 176, 178, 181–182
 2014 election, 182
 barriers to entry in, 178
 campaign-finance rules in, 178, 201
 candidates running multiple times and
  losing in, 58
 corruption in, 180–181
 duopoly in, 178–179
 economic conditions in, 178–179
 elections won with less than 50% of the vote
  (1978–2012), likely result of runoff, 257t
 favorable democratic record in, 2, 33, 176,
  177–178
 free and fair elections in, year of
  commencing in, 17
 Freedom House and V-Dem scores, 177, 196
 incumbent blocked from re-election in, 56, 179
 legislative elections concurrent with
  presidential elections in, 200
 legislative majorities of president's party
  in, 222t
 mandatory voting in, 177
 new parties in, 261t
 number of parties in, 33, 176, 179, 198, 199
 old-timer presidential candidates in, 249t

Costa Rica (*Cont.*)
  PELA surveys, 180, 181
  PLN and PUSC dominance in, 179–182
  as plurality country until mid-1990s, 15
  pre-election opinion polls, accuracy of, 227*t*, 231–232*t*
  as runoff country, 2, 178, 196
  threshold for runoff in, 15, 175–176, 178, 191
  voter turnout in, 36, 177, 180
Cotler, Julio, 160
Covas, Mário, 120
Cristiani, Alfredo, 133, 134
Cubas, Raúl, 96–97
Cueto, Francisco, 112–113
Cunha Filho, Clayton M., 92

Dargent, Eduardo, 165
D'Aubuisson, Roberto, 132–133
DCG (Democracia Cristiana Guatemalteca, Guatemalan Christian Democrats), 143–145
Debt crisis, 5, 8
De La Cruz De Lemos, Vladimir, 180
De la Rúa, Fernando, 188
de León Carpio, Ramiro, 145, 147
Democracia Cristiana Guatemalteca (Guatemalan Christian Democrats, DCG), 143–145
Democracia Popular (Popular Democracy, Ecuador), 167, 170–171
Democracy
  adaptation of, 192
  constitutional changes and, 192
  democratic breakdown due to executive-legislative gridlock, 36, 38
  indices of, 12–13
  liberal democracy, 13
  number of political parties viewed as danger to, 32–33, 192
  in plurality countries, 65
  in runoff countries, 194
  trends in levels of, under plurality vs. runoff, 19–21, 20–21*f*
  voter turnout as indicator for, 13
  year of transition to, for creation of dataset, 17–19
Democracy level. *See* Freedom House and V-Dem scores
  Argentina, 182
  Brazil, 106, 107, 117, 137
  Colombia, 139, 148
  Costa Rica, 2, 33, 176, 177–178
  Dominican Republic, 106, 107, 137
  Ecuador, 139, 140, 165
  El Salvador, 106, 130–131
  Guatemala, 139, 141
  Honduras, 86, 195–196
  Mexico, 10, 65–66, 80, 85, 195
  Nicaragua, 10, 65, 75, 77, 80, 195

  Panama, 100–101, 194
  Paraguay, 93, 196
  Peru, 139, 156
  Uruguay, 106, 107, 136
  Venezuela, 10, 65, 66–67, 70
Democratic Action, AD, Venezuela (Acción Democrática), 55, 67–70, 72–74, 195
Democratic Alliance/Movement of April 19th, AD/M-19, Colombia (Alianza Democrática/Movimiento 19 de Abril), 152
Democratic Change, CD, Panama (Cambio Democrático), 103
Democratic Front, FREDEMO, Peru (Frente Democrático), 159–161
Democratic Independent Union, UDI, Chile (Unión Demócrata Independiente), 62, 126, 128
Democratic Left, ID, Ecuador (Izquierda Democrática), 167, 172
Democratic Liberty Renewed, Líder, Guatemala (Libertad Democrática Renovada), 147
Democratic Party (U.S.), 203
Democratic Republican Union, URD, Venezuela (Unión Republicana Democrática), 68
Democratic Revolutionary Party, PRD, Panama (Partido Revolucionario Democrático), 100–101, 103, 196
Diamond, Larry, 59
"Dirty War," 185
Domínguez, Jorge I., 3
Dominican Republic, 11, 112–117
  1978 election, 57
  1986 election, 40, 137, 196
  1990 election, 34, 40, 137, 196
  1994 election, 18–19, 40, 115, 137
  1996 election, 106, 112, 115–116, 137
  2000–2016 elections, 116–117
  2004 election, 57, 116
  2012 election, 116–117
  campaign-finance rules in, 201
  cartel parties in, 116, 197, 198, 199
  democracy level in, 106, 107, 137
  economic conditions in, 117
  election fraud and corruption in, 115, 137
  elections won with less than 50% of the vote (1978–2012), likely result of runoff, 254*t*, 257*t*
  free and fair elections in, year of commencing in, 17
  Freedom House and V-Dem scores, 106, 112, 116, 196–197
  legislative election non-concurrent in, 200
  legislative majorities of president's party in, 216*t*, 222*t*
  moderate left president elected in, 107
  new parties in, 138, 260–261*t*
  number of parties in, 32, 107, 137, 198

Index 301

old-timer presidential candidates in, 249t
PELA surveys, 107, 116, 117
as plurality country, 20, 112, 113–115, 137, 196
pre-election opinion polls, accuracy of, 227t, 232–233t
racism and anti-Haitian nationalism in, 116
as runoff country, 106, 115–117, 137, 196
term limits in, 116
voter turnout in, 36, 106
wasteful government spending in, 117
Dominican Revolutionary Party, PRD (Partido Revolucionario Dominicano), 50, 113–117
Double simultaneous vote (DSV) rule, 108–109
Dressel, Björn, 42
Dresser, Denise, 80, 86
DSV (Double simultaneous vote) rule, 108–109
Duarte, Napoleón, 132
Duarte Frutos, Nicanor, 97–98, 263n6
Dugas, John, 149
Duhalde, Eduardo, 188
Duopolies, 50, 55, 66, 67, 68, 87, 194, 265n17
　Chile, 130
　Colombia, 50, 150–151, 154, 196
　Costa Rica, 178–179
　Honduras, 50, 87–89, 93, 105, 194, 195–196
　Panama without, 101
　Uruguay, 196
　Venezuela, 104, 194, 195
Durán, Sixto, 168–170
Duverger, Maurice, 30

Economic conditions
　Argentina, 182, 189–190
　Brazil, 117, 118
　Chile, 124
　Colombia, 150
　Costa Rica, 178–179
　Dominican Republic, 117
　Ecuador, 5, 166, 167, 171
　El Salvador, 131, 136
　Guatemala, 141, 144, 145
　Honduras, 87, 90, 92
　Mexico, 5
　Nicaragua, 76, 78, 104
　Panama, 100–101, 104
　Paraguay, 93, 94, 97
　Peru, 156, 158, 159, 163
　Uruguay, 108, 109, 111
　Venezuela, 5, 68–69, 71, 73, 104
Ecuador, 11, 165–174
　1956 election, 166
　1960 election, 166
　1968 election, 42, 166
　1978–1979 election, 166, 168
　1984 election, 168–169
　1988 election, 166, 169
　1992 election, 169–170

1996 election, 170–171, 199
1998 election, 171
2002 election, 166, 172, 175, 199
2006 election, 166, 173, 175
2009 and 2013 elections, 173–174, 175
2017 election, 176, 177, 199
Condorcet winners in, 140, 166, 170, 172, 174
consecutive terms permissible for presidents in, 167
corruption in, 170–171
debt crisis and economic conditions in, 5, 166, 167, 171
democracy levels in, 139, 140, 165
elections won with less than 50% of the vote (1978–2012), likely result of runoff, 257t
executive-legislative conflict in, 166
free and fair elections in, year of commencing in, 17
Freedom House and V-Dem scores, 165–167, 173, 175, 196
Gutiérrez ouster (2004), 172–173
ideological moderation in, 166
indigenous vs. nonindigenous parties in, 167
legislative elections concurrent with presidential elections in, 200
legislative majorities of president's party in, 223t
Mahuad's ouster (2000), 171–172
military coup (1968), 41
new parties in, 175, 261t
number of parties in, 6, 32, 166–167, 174, 175, 198, 199
oil prices in, 27, 167, 171
old-timer presidential candidates in, 249t
outsider candidates in, 35, 170, 172, 173
PELA surveys, 170, 171, 172, 173
as plurality country, 1
pre-election opinion polls, accuracy of, 61, 227t, 234–235t
qualified runoffs in, 174, 175
as runoff country, 166–167, 174, 196
shift from Hare Quota to D'Hondt formula for calculation of seats in, 201
threshold in, 15, 175, 191, 199
voter turnout in, 36, 139, 165
Eguiguren, Francisco, 42
Ehlers, Freddy, 35, 170
Eisenstadt, Todd A., 18
Ejército Revolucionario del Pueblo (Revolutionary Army of the People, ERP, El Salvador), 134
Election fraud. *See* Corruption
Electoral rules. *See* Presidential-election rule
　authoritarian legacies, 5, 47–51 (*see also* Authoritarian legacies)
　cartel parties, 5, 51–55 (*see also* Cartel parties)
　ideological moderation and, 8–10, 44–47
　　(*see also* Ideological moderation)

Electoral rules (*Cont.*)
    legislative minorities, risk of, 36–39, 198
    need for reform, 202–203
    new parties, rise of, 32, 61–64
        (*see also* New parties)
    number of parties, 34–35
        (*see also* Number of political parties)
    openness of political arena and, 4–7
    outsider candidates and, 34–35, 34t
        (*see also* Outsider candidates)
    perpetuation of old-timer presidential candidates, 5–6, 55–58 (*see also* Old-timer presidential candidates)
    presidential legitimacy and, 7–8, 39–44
        (*see also* Legitimacy)
    proposals for reform, 204–206
    voter fatigue, 36
"Electoral sweet spot," 7, 11, 199, 264n13
Ellner, Steve, 67
El Salvador, 11, 130–136
    1994 election, 133–134
    1999 and 2004 elections, 134–135
    2009 election, 135–136
    2014 election, 106, 136, 177, 199
    authoritarian action committed by political parties in, 51, 52t, 198
    caudillismo in, 58
    civil war's effects in, 132, 137, 198
    Cold-War polarization in, 51
    democracy level, improvement in, 106, 130–131
    economic conditions in, 131, 136
    elections won with less than 50% of the vote (1978–2012), likely result of runoff, 258t
    free and fair elections in, year of commencing in, 17–18
    Freedom House and V-Dem scores, 106, 130–131, 196
    ideological moderation in, 198
    incumbent blocked from re-election in, 56
    legislative election non-concurrent in, 200
    legislative majorities of president's party in, 223t
    legitimacy deficit in, 199
    moderate party in, 9
    new parties in, 261t
    number of parties in, 32, 107, 137, 198, 199
    old-timer presidential candidates in, 58, 250t
    outsider candidates in, 35, 135
    PELA surveys, 131, 132, 135
    as plurality country, 20
    polarization in, 131, 137
    political parties in, 132–133, 176
    pre-election opinion polls, accuracy of, 227t, 235–236t
    as runoff country, 132, 137, 196
    voter turnout in, 21, 36, 106, 131
Encuentro Nacional (National Encounter, Paraguay), 95–96

Encuentro Progresista (Progressive Encounter, EP, Uruguay), 110
Endorsement power of party not in runoff election, 4, 30
Engstrom, Richard L. and Richard N., 205
Enríquez-Ominami, Marco, 130, 137, 197
Entrenched parties. *See* Cartel parties
EP (Encuentro Progresista, Progressive Encounter, Uruguay), 110
EP-FA-NM coalition (Uruguay), 111
ERP (Ejército Revolucionario del Pueblo, Revolutionary Army of the People, El Salvador), 134
Errázuriz, Francisco Javier, 35, 127
Europe
    accuracy of pre-election opinion polls (2000–2012), 59, 60t, 244–245t
    candidates running three times and losing three times in, 58
    old-timer presidential candidates in Latin America vs. Europe (1978–2006), 56, 57t
    term limits on presidents in, 58
Executive-legislative conflict, 3, 14, 36, 140
    Colombia, 139
    in countries with large numbers of political parties, 6, 174
    in countries with legislative minorities, 36–39, 37t
    Ecuador, 166
    Guatemala, 139, 142
    Mexico, 81
    Peru, 140

FA (Frente Amplio, Broad Front, Uruguay), 63, 109–111, 136–137
Fadul, Pedro, 35
Falklands-Malvinas war, 185
Farabundo Martí National Liberation Front, FMLN, El Salvador (Frente Farabundo Martí de Liberación Nacional), 9, 51, 132–136, 177, 197, 198
FARC (Fuerzas Armadas Revolucionarias de Colombia, Revolutionary Armed Forces of Colombia), 149, 151, 153–155
Fascist parties, 50
Febrés Cordero, León, 166, 168–169
Fernández, Eduardo, 67, 71
Fernández, Leonel, 9–10, 115–116, 137, 197
Fernández de Kirchner, Cristina, 189–190
Ferreira, Wilson, 109
Fifth Republic Movement, MVR, Venezuela (Movimiento Quinta República), 72
Figueres, José María, 180
Filizzola, Carlos, 96
Fleischer, David, 41
Flores, Francisco, 134, 137, 198
Flores, Lourdes, 162–163

Flores-Macías, Gustavo, 85
FMLN (Farabundo Martí National Liberation Front, El Salvador), 9, 51, 132–136, 177, 197, 198
Force 2011, Peru (Fuerza 2011), 164
Fox, Vicente, 2, 82–83
France
   candidates running three times and losing three times in, 58
   legislative election scheduled after presidential election in, 200
   pre-election opinion polls, accuracy of (2000–2012), 60
   runoff elections adopted in, 2, 41
   term limits on presidents in, 58
Franco, Itamar, 120
Franco, Julio César, 97–98
Fraud, 4, 264n9. *See also* Corruption
   leftist leaders complaining of election fraud, 9
   post-election disputes involving, 40
FREDEMO (Frente Democrático, Democratic Front, Peru), 159–161
Free and fair elections, 17–19, 40
Freedom House and V-Dem scores, 2, 10, 12–14, 19, 20f, 22–23, 24t, 26t, 33, 65, 66, 196
   Argentina, 182, 189–190, 196–197
   Brazil, 12, 106, 117, 124, 196
   Chile, 106, 124, 196
   classification of countries, 2, 263n3
   Colombia, 12, 139, 148, 156, 196–197
   Costa Rica, 177, 196
   Dominican Republic, 106, 112, 116, 196–197
   Ecuador, 165–167, 173, 175, 196
   El Salvador, 106, 130–131, 196
   Guatemala, 139, 141, 196–197
   Honduras, 86, 194
   Mexico, 12, 80, 85, 194
   Nicaragua, 74–75, 194
   number of political parties and, 33f
   Panama, 100
   Paraguay, 93, 97, 100, 194
   Peru, 156, 196
   runoff vs. plurality and, 194
   Uruguay, 106, 107, 112, 196
   Venezuela, 66–67, 194
Freidenberg, Flavia, 42
Frei Ruiz-Tagle, Eduardo, 58, 127, 129–130
Frente Amplio (Broad Front, Costa Rica), 182
Frente Amplio (Broad Front, FA, Uruguay), 63, 109–111, 136–137
Frente Democrático (Democratic Front, FREDEMO, Peru), 159–161
Frente Farabundo Martí de Liberación Nacional (Farabundo Martí National Liberation Front, FMLN, El Salvador), 9, 51, 132–136, 177, 197, 198
Frente para la Victoria (Front for Victory, Argentina), 189–191
Frente para un País Solidario (Front for a Country in Solidarity, FREPASO, Argentina), 183, 186–188
Frente Republicano Guatemalteco (Guatemalan Republican Front, FRG, Guatemala), 144–146
Frente Sandinista de Liberación Nacional (Sandinista National Liberation Front, FSLN, Nicaragua), 51, 55, 75–80, 194, 195, 199
FREPASO (Frente para un País Solidario, Front for a Country in Solidarity, Argentina), 183, 186–188
FRG (Frente Republicano Guatemalteco, Guatemalan Republican Front, Guatemala), 144–146
Front for a Country in Solidarity, FREPASO, Argentina (Frente para un País Solidario), 183, 186–188
Front for Victory, Argentina (Frente para la Victoria), 189–191
FSLN (Frente Sandinista de Liberación Nacional, Sandinista National Liberation Front, Nicaragua), 51, 55, 75–80, 194, 195, 199
Fuerza 2011 (Force 2011, Peru), 164
Fuerzas Armadas Revolucionarias de Colombia, Revolutionary Armed Forces of Colombia (FARC), 149, 151, 153–155
Fujimori, Alberto, 14, 20, 35, 38, 39, 140, 156, 158–162, 174, 196, 197, 199
Fujimori, Keiko, 164–165, 177
Fukuyama, Francis, 42
Funes, Mauricio, 9, 35, 45, 47, 135, 137, 198

Gadea, Fabio, 80
Gaitán, Jorge, 150
Galán, Luis Carlos, 151–152
GANA (Gran Alianza Nacional, Grand National Alliance, Guatemala), 143, 146
Gana Perú (Win Peru), 63, 163
García, Alan, 38, 58, 61, 156–158, 162–163
Garzón, Luis Eduardo, 154
Gaviria, Carlos, 154–155, 174
Gaviria, César, 152
Germany's Christian Democratic party, 50
Gerring, John, 13
Gilley, Bruce, 40
Globo network (Brazil), 119
Golder, Matt, 22
Gordillo, Elba Esther, 84
Gore, Al, 203
Goulart, João, 120
Gran Alianza Nacional (Grand National Alliance, GANA, Guatemala), 143, 146

Gran Alianza para el Cambio (Great Alliance for Change, Colombia), 153
Grayson, George W., 80
Great Alliance for Change, Colombia (Gran Alianza para el Cambio), 153
Greene, Kenneth, 55, 59
Green Party (Brazil), 197
Green Party (Colombia), 63, 149, 155–156, 197
Green Party (U.S.), 203
Guardado, Facundo, 35, 135
Guatemala, 11, 141–148
   1985 election, 143–144
   1990–1991 elections, 139, 144–145
   1993 election, 144–145
   1995–1996, 1999, and 2003 elections, 145–146
   2007 election, 146–147
   2011 election, 147–148
   autogolpes (self-coups) in, 39, 140, 141, 145, 198
   Condorcet winners in, 142
   corruption in, 148
   debt crisis and economic conditions in, 141, 144, 145
   democracy levels in, 139, 141
   elections won with less than 50% of the vote (1978–2012), likely result of runoff, 258*t*
   executive–legislative conflict in, 139, 142
   free and fair elections in, year of commencing in, 17
   Freedom House and V-Dem scores, 139, 141, 196–197
   human rights violations in, 148
   ideological cleavages and civil war in, 142–143
   legislative elections concurrent with presidential elections in, 200
   legislative majorities of president's party in, 224*t*
   Marxist guerrilla groups in, 141
   new parties in, 261*t*
   number of parties in, 32, 139, 141, 142–143, 198
   old-timer presidential candidates in, 250*t*
   outsider candidates in, 148
   PELA surveys, 146, 147
   political violence in, 139, 141, 174
   pre-election opinion polls, accuracy of, 227*t*, 236–237*t*
   as runoff country, 141–142, 145, 174, 196
   term limits in, 56
   voluntary voting in, 13, 141
   voter turnout in, 21, 36, 139, 141
Guatemalan Christian Democrats, DCG (Democracia Cristiana Guatemalteca), 143–145
Guatemalan National Revolutionary Union, URNG (Unidad Revolucionaria Nacional Guatemalteca), 141, 143, 146, 174
Guatemalan Republican Front, FRG, Guatemala (Frente Republicano Guatemalteco), 144–146
Guevara, Otto, 58, 181–182
Gutiérrez, Lucio, 10, 35, 166, 171–173, 197
Guzmán, Abimael, 161
Guzmán, Julio, 165
Gómez Hurtado, Álvaro, 151

Hampson, Fen Osler, 18
Handal, Schafik, 135–136
Hartlyn, Jonathan, 3
Haya de la Torre, Víctor Raúl, 42, 51, 157
Herman, Donald, 151
Herrera, Balbina, 103–104
Homeland for All, PPT, Venezuela (Patria Para Todos), 72
Honduras, 11, 86–93
   1963–1981 military rule, 87
   1981–2005 elections, 89–91, 90*t*
   2009 coup, 88
   2013 election, 34, 40, 66, 105, 196
   cartel parties in, 54, 66, 87, 89
   caudillismo in, 58
   civil war in, 90
   democracy's decline in, 86, 195–196
   disaffection of the public in, 91
   economic conditions in, 87, 90, 92
   election fraud in, 89
   elections won with less than 50% of the vote (1978–2012), likely result of runoff, 254*t*
   free and fair elections in, year of commencing in, 17
   Freedom House and V-Dem scores, 86, 194
   human rights violations in, 90
   leftist parties in, 9, 87
   leftist shift starting in 2008 in, 87, 91–93
   legislative elections concurrent with presidential elections in, 200
   legislative majorities of president's party in, 217*t*
   new parties in, 88, 260*t*
   old-timer presidential candidates in, 250*t*
   parties and emergence of duopoly in, 50, 87–89, 93, 105, 194, 195–196
   parties' classification as left or right in, 45, 88
   PELA surveys, 87, 88, 90, 93
   as plurality country, 2, 9, 20, 87, 104, 194
   pre-election opinion polls, accuracy of, 227*t*, 237–238*t*
   runoff considered as option in, 3, 87
   term limits in, 56
   voter turnout in, 21, 65, 86, 194
Hough, Jerry F., 80
Humala, Ollanta, 9, 35, 38, 140, 157, 162–164, 174, 197
Humanist Party (Chile), 127, 129

Human-rights violations
  Argentina, 185
  Guatemala, 148
  Honduras, 90
Humphrey, Hubert, 204
Hurricane Mitch (1998), 77, 90
Hurtado, Álvaro Gómez, 58
Hurtado, Osvaldo, 168

ID (Izquierda Democrática, Democratic Left, Ecuador), 167, 172
Ideological moderation, 4, 8–10
  Chile, 124, 198
  Ecuador, 166
  El Salvador, 198
  more research needed on, 193
  Peru, 157
  reduced threshold and, 176
  requirement of 50%-plus-one vote for victory and, 197
  runoff elections and, 3, 8, 44–47, 157, 166, 193
Ideological shifts
  dangers of, 44
  from plurality to runoff (see Runoff elections)
  of presidents, 9 (see also specific president's name)
Illia, Arturo, 42, 183, 185
IMF (International Monetary Fund), 5, 71, 171–172
INDEC (National Institute of Statistics and Censuses, Argentina), 190
Innovation and Unity Party, PINU, Honduras (Partido de Innovación y Unidad), 88
Institutional Revolutionary Party (Partido Revolucionario Institucional, Mexico). See PRI
Institutional Revolutionary Party, Mexico (Partido Revolucionario Institucional). See PRI
International Monetary Fund (IMF), 5, 71, 171–172
IS (Izquierda Socialista, Socialist Left, Peru), 159
IU (Izquierda Unida, United Left, Peru), 158, 159
Izquierda Democrática (Democratic Left, ID, Ecuador), 167, 172
Izquierda Socialista (Socialist Left, IS, Peru), 159
Izquierda Unida (United Left, IU, Peru), 158, 159

Jackson, Sherman Thomas, 180
Jaramillo, Bernardo, 152
Johnson, Loch, 204
Jones, Mark, 3, 15, 29, 31
Juntos Podemos Más (Together We Can Do More, Chile), 129
Justice First, Venezuela (Primero Justicia), 74

Kaltwasser, Cristóbal Rovira, 44
Katz, Joseph, 60–61
Katz, Richard, 51

Kazin, Michael, 7
Kenney, Charles, 15, 160
Kirchner, Néstor, 189
Kubitschek, Juscelino, 41
Kuczynski, Pedro Pablo, 39, 164–165, 177

Laakso, Murkku, 22, 27
Labastida, Francisco, 82
Lacalle, Luis Alberto, 109, 111, 112
La Causa Radical (La Causa R, The Radical Cause, Venezuela), 70–71, 72
Lagos, Marta, 5
Lagos, Ricardo, 111, 124, 127–128, 137, 197
Laíno, Domingo, 58, 95, 96
La Nueva Mayoría para Chile (A New Majority for Chile), 130
Lasso, Guillermo, 173
Latin American Political Report (LAPR), 27–28
Latin American Regional Report (LARR), 27–28, 35
Latin American Weekly Report (LAWR), 27–28, 35, 135
Lavín, Joaquín, 127, 129
Lawson, Chappell, 18
Leftist parties. See Center-left parties
  emerging as significant contenders, 197
  plurality countries, extreme left presidents in, 66, 105
  plurality vs. runoff elections, candidates in, 46t, 47
  runoff elections and, 4, 8–10, 193
Legislatures. See Executive-legislative conflict
  concurrent election with plurality presidential election, 200
  concurrent election with runoff presidential election, 200
  election strategies for, 200–201
  legislative majorities of president's party, 215–216, 216–225t
  legislative minorities and likelihood of executive-legislative conflict, 36–39, 37t, 198
  number of parties in, 200–201
  proportional representation in, 32, 201
  shift from Hare Quota to D'Hondt formula for calculation of seats, 201
  surveys among Latin American legislators, 2, 36, 40, 209–211, 210–211t
  threshold for party in legislative elections, 200
Legitimacy
  defined, 7, 40
  dual legitimacy in countries that popularly elect both executive and legislature, 36
  electoral rules and, 7–8
  more research needed on, 193
  runoff elections and, 3, 7–8, 39–44, 132, 174, 197, 209, 210t
  runoff with reduced threshold and, 15, 175–177

Legitimacy deficit, 7–8, 43, 66, 70, 106, 177, 193, 195, 197, 199
  Colombia, 149, 153
  El Salvador, 199
  Guatemala, 144
  Mexico, 8, 195
  Panama without, 103
  Paraguay, 8
  Peru, 156
  Venezuela, 8, 66, 70, 195
Lehoucq, Fabrice, 178
Leongómez, Eduardo Pizarro, 259
Let's Change, Argentina (Cambiemos), 191
Levine, Daniel, 70
Levitsky, Steven, 54, 55, 259
Levy, Daniel C., 18
León-Gómez, Carlos Pizarro, 152
Liberal Alliance, Nicaragua (Alianza Liberal), 76
Liberal Constitutionalist Party, PLC, Nicaragua (Partido Liberal Constitucionalista), 76–80
Liberal Front, PFL, Brazil (Partido da Frente Liberal), 118
Liberal Party (Colombia), 149, 150, 151–154, 196
Liberal Party (Honduras), 45, 54, 55, 87–93, 105, 194, 195–196
Liberal Party (Nicaragua), 48, 51, 75, 104, 195
Liberal Party (Paraguay), 94–95
Libertad Democrática Renovada (Democratic Liberty Renewed, Líder, Guatemala), 147
Libertad y Refundación, Libre (Liberty and Refoundation, Free, Honduras), 92–93
Libertarian Movement, Costa Rica (Movimiento Libertario), 181–182
Libertarian Party (U.S.), 203
Liberty and Refoundation, Free, Honduras (Libertad y Refundación, Libre), 92–93
Liberty Movement, Peru (Movimiento Libertad), 159
Lindberg, Staffan I., 13
Linz, Juan, 3, 29
Lobo, Porfirio, 92
Lodola, German, 14
López Obrador, Andrés Manuel (AMLO), 2, 10, 61, 81, 83–86, 105, 195, 263n5
Loxton, James, 259
Luder, Italo, 185
Lugo, Fernando, 10, 35, 54, 94, 97–100, 195, 196
Luiz Coelho, André, 92
Lula da Silva, Luiz Inácio, 9, 58, 98, 118–123, 135, 137, 197
  as model for other politicians, 111–112, 146, 164
Luna, Juan Pablo, 44
Lupu, Noam, 190
Lusinchi, Jaime, 69
López Michelsen, Alfonso, 151

Macri, Mauricio, 191

Macron, Emmanuel, 200
Maduro, Ricardo, 90–91
Mahuad, Jamil, 171
Mainwaring, Scott, 3, 21, 30, 31, 45, 259
Mair, Peter, 51
Majluta, Jacobo, 114
Majority runoff countries, 16t, 199. *See also* Brazil; Chile; Colombia; Dominican Republic; El Salvador; Guatemala; Peru; Uruguay
Mandatory voting. *See* Compulsory voting
Martinelli, Ricardo, 35, 103–104
Martínez, Rafael, 39–40
Marxist parties, 4, 8, 50–51, 126, 146, 151, 158, 202
MAS (Movimiento al Socialismo, Movement toward Socialism, Venezuela), 69
MAS (Movimiento de Acción Solidaria, Solidarity Action Movement, Guatemala), 143
Massa, Sergio, 191
Massaccesi, Horacio, 187
Mateo Díaz, Mercedes, 13–14, 17, 18, 22
Mayorga, René, 14
McCoy, Jennifer, 70
McKewen, Darren, 18
Media, electoral use of, 61
Medina, Danilo, 116–117
Meijide, Graciela Fernández, 187
Mejía, Hipólito, 57, 116
Menchú, Rigoberta, 147
Menem, Carlos Saúl, 183–184, 186–189, 191, 197
Mexico, 11, 80–86
  1988 election, 54
  2000 election, 82–83
  2006 election, 34, 40, 65–66, 81, 83–85, 105, 195
  2012 election, 34, 85–86
  campaign-finance rules in, 83
  cartel parties in, 66, 81, 105, 195
  criticism of plurality elections in, 2
  debt crisis in, 5
  democracy's decline in, 10, 65–66, 80, 85, 195
  election fraud and corruption in, 81, 83–84, 86
  elections won with less than 50% of the vote (1978–2012), likely result of runoff, 254t
  executive–legislative gridlock in, 81
  Federal Electoral Institute (IFE), 84, 86
  free and fair elections in, year of commencing in, 17
  Freedom House and V-Dem scores, 12, 80, 85, 194
  legislative majorities of president's party in, 217t
  legislative threshold of vote in, 201
  legitimacy deficit in, 8, 195
  major political parties in, 81–82
  midterm legislative elections in, 200
  new parties in, 260t
  oil industry in, 82

old-timer presidential candidates in, 250t
PELA surveys, 81–82
as plurality country, 2, 65, 81, 104, 194
pre-election opinion polls, accuracy of, 83, 85–86, 227t, 238t
runoff considered as option in, 2, 80, 83–84, 209, 210t
term limits in, 56
threshold for runoff favored in, 175
transition year to democracy in, 18
violence of drug war in, 85
voter turnout in, 80, 194
Micheletti, Roberto, 91–92
Minority presidents, 38–39, 41
Mockus, Antanas, 5, 155
Moderation. *See* Ideological moderation
Modernization theory, 22
MOLIRENA (Movimiento Liberal Republicano Nacionalista, Nationalist Republican Liberal Movement, Panama), 102, 104
Moraes, Heloísa Helena de, 118, 123, 137
Morales, Evo, 175
Morales, Jimmy, 148
Morales, Marco, 80
Moreno, Lenín, 176, 177
Morris, Kenneth, 15
Moscoso, Mireyra, 103
Movement of April 19th, M-19, Colombia (Movimiento 19 de Abril), 149, 151, 152, 174
Movement of National Salvation, Colombia (Movimiento de Salvación Nacional), 152
Movement toward Socialism, MAS, Venezuela (Movimiento al Socialismo), 69
Movimiento 19 de Abril (Movement of April 19th, M-19, Colombia), 149, 151, 152, 174
Movimiento al Socialismo (Movement toward Socialism, MAS, Venezuela), 69
Movimiento de Acción Solidaria (Solidarity Action Movement, MAS, Guatemala), 143
Movimiento de Salvación Nacional (Movement of National Salvation, Colombia), 152
Movimiento de Unidad Plurinacional Pachakutik/ Nuevo País (Pachakutik Plurinational Unity Movement/New Country, MUPP-NP, Ecuador), 167, 170, 171
Movimiento Liberal Republicano Nacionalista (Nationalist Republican Liberal Movement, MOLIRENA, Panama), 102, 104
Movimiento Libertad (Liberty Movement, Peru), 159
Movimiento Libertario (Libertarian Movement, Costa Rica), 181–182
Movimiento Papa Egoró (Papa Egoró Movement, Panama), 102
Movimiento Patria Querida (Beloved Fatherland Movement, Paraguay), 97

Movimiento Quinta República (Fifth Republic Movement, MVR, Venezuela), 72
Movimiento Renovador Sandinista (Sandinista Renovation Movement, MRS, Nicaragua), 77
MRS (Movimiento Renovador Sandinista, Sandinista Renovation Movement, Nicaragua), 77
Mujica, José, 111–112, 197
Muñoz, Paula, 165
Muñoz Ledo, Porfirio, 82
MUPP-NP (Movimiento de Unidad Plurinacional Pachakutik/Nuevo País, Pachakutik Plurinational Unity Movement/New Country, Ecuador), 167, 170, 171
Murillo, María Victoria, 44, 45, 169, 170, 179
MVR (Movimiento Quinta República, Fifth Republic Movement, Venezuela), 72

Nader, Ralph, 203
Nasralla, Salvador, 93
National Action Party, PAN, Mexico (Partido Acción Nacional), 50, 80–86, 105, 195
National Encounter, Paraguay (Encuentro Nacional), 95–96
National Front (Colombia), 150
National Institute of Statistics and Censuses, Argentina (INDEC), 190
Nationalist Republican Alliance, ARENA, El Salvador (Alianza Repúblicana Nacionalista), 51, 132–136, 137, 177, 198
Nationalist Republican Liberal Movement, MOLIRENA, Panama (Movimiento Liberal Republicano Nacionalista), 102, 104
National Liberation Party, PLN, Costa Rica (Partido Liberación Nacional), 55, 178–182
National Opposition Union, UNO, Nicaragua (Unión Nacional Opositora), 75–76
National Party (Honduras), 45, 51, 54, 55, 87–91, 105, 194, 195–196
National Party (Partido Nacional, Chile), 126
National Party (Uruguay). *See* Blanco Party (Uruguay)
National Renovation, RN, Chile (Renovación Nacional), 126, 129
National Resistance, RN, El Salvador (Resistencia Nacional), 134
National Union of the Center, UCN, Guatemala (Unión del Centro Nacional), 143
National Unity, UN, Peru (Unidad Nacional), 162
National Unity for Hope, UNE, Guatemala (Unidad Nacional de la Esperanza), 146, 148, 197
Navarro Wolff, Antonio, 152, 154
Nebot, Jaime, 169, 170
Negretto, Gabriel, 2, 27, 30, 31, 80
Negri, Juan, 14

Neo-caudillismo, 56
Neoliberalism, 5, 71, 112, 173
Neves, Aécio, 123
Neves, Tancredo, 118
New Alliance Party, PANAL, Mexico (Partido Nueva Alianza), 84
New Majority, Chile (Nueva Mayoría), 126, 197
New Majority, NM, Uruguay (Nueva Mayoría), 111
A New Majority for Chile (La Nueva Mayoría para Chile), 130
New parties
  advantages of, 5
  allocation of public goods and, 201
  Argentina, 260–261t
  Brazil, 138, 261t
  Chile, 138, 261t
  Colombia, 260–261t
  Costa Rica, 261t
  destabilizing effects of, 4, 193–194, 198–199
  Dominican Republic, 138, 260–261t
  Ecuador, 175, 261t
  El Salvador, 261t
  factors in rise of, 32, 61–64
  Guatemala, 261t
  Honduras, 88, 260t
  in legislatures, 4
  Mexico, 260t
  Nicaragua, 260–261t
  Panama, 260t
  Paraguay, 260t
  as personalistic parties (*see* Personalistic parties)
  Peru, 260–261t
  in plurality vs. runoff elections, 61–62, 61t
  political exclusion of, 66, 67
  runoff elections as opportunities for, 4–7
  as significant contenders in presidential elections (1978–2012), 4, 259, 260–261t
  Uruguay, 260–261t
  Venezuela, 260t
New Space, Uruguay (Nuevo Espacio), 110–111
Nicaragua, 11, 74–80
  1990 election, 57, 75–76
  1996 election, 66, 76–77
  2001 election, 78
  2006 election, 34, 65, 75, 78–79
  2011 election, 79–80
  authoritarian action committed by political parties in, 51, 52t, 77
  cartel parties in, 66
  Cold-War polarization in, 51
  criticism of plurality elections in, 2, 263n6
  debt crisis in, 76
  democracy's decline in, 10, 65, 75, 77, 80, 195
  economic conditions in, 76, 78, 104
  election fraud and corruption in, 77, 78
  elections won with less than 50% of the vote (1978–2012), likely result of runoff, 255t, 258t
  free and fair elections in, year of commencing in, 17
  Freedom House and V-Dem scores, 74–75, 194
  leading party founded in 1830s in, 48
  legislative elections concurrent with presidential elections in, 200
  legislative majorities of president's party in, 217t, 224t
  legislative threshold of vote in, 201
  new parties in, 260–261t
  old-timer presidential candidates in, 250t
  outsider candidates in, 35
  "the pact" between Alemán and Ortega (1999), 77–78, 195
  PELA surveys, 76, 78
  as plurality country, 65, 104, 194
  pre-election opinion polls, accuracy of, 227t, 238–239t
  as qualified plurality country, 2, 15, 16t, 20, 27, 80, 195
  runoff with threshold in, 15, 175, 195
  voluntary voting in, 13
Nicolau, Jairo, 41
Nixon, Richard, 204
NM (Nueva Mayoría, New Majority, Uruguay), 111
Noboa, Álvaro, 58, 171–173, 197
Noboa, Gustavo, 172
Nohlen, Dieter, 27
Noriega, Manuel Antonio, 101, 104
Nueva Mayoría (New Majority, Chile), 126, 197
Nueva Mayoría (New Majority, NM, Uruguay), 111
Nuevo Espacio (New Space, Uruguay), 110–111
Number of political parties, 27, 32, 107, 137, 198, 199
  Argentina, 32, 176, 183, 199
  Brazil, 32, 107, 118, 198, 200
  causing political problems, 6, 198–199, 264n3
  Chile, 32, 107, 198, 200
  Colombia, 32, 33, 139, 149–150, 198
  Costa Rica, 33, 176, 179, 198, 199
  Dominican Republic, 32, 107, 137, 198
  Ecuador, 6, 32, 166–167, 174, 175, 198, 199
  effective number of political parties (ENPP), 22, 23, 24–26t, 33, 33f
  factors contributing to larger number, 32
  Guatemala, 32, 139, 141, 142–143, 198
  more research needed on effects of, 199
  Panama, 100, 196
  Peru, 32, 157, 174, 198
  remedies for proliferation of parties, 199–201
  in runoff vs. plurality countries, 31–32, 31f, 193, 194, 198

Uruguay, 32, 107, 108, 137, 198
Venezuela, 33

OAS (Organization of American States), 18, 40, 115
Obama, Barack, 135
Obregón, Guido Canchari, 41
Old-timer presidential candidates
  defined, 56
  excluding newcomers, 192
  Latin America, 247, 247–252*t*
  Latin America vs. Europe, 56, 57*t*
  perpetuation of, 5–6, 55–58
Oliveros, Virginia, 44, 45, 169, 170, 179
Ominami, Marco Enríquez, 5
Ordaz, Luis Piñerúa, 69
Organization of American States, 18, 40, 115
Orlando Hernández, Juan, 93
Ortega, Daniel, 10, 15–16, 57, 58, 65, 75–80, 104–105, 195
Outsider candidates, 3, 27, 34–35, 34*t*, 212, 212–214*t*
  Brazil, 119
  Chile, 35
  Colombia, 35, 149, 154
  Ecuador, 35, 170, 172, 173
  El Salvador, 35, 135
  Guatemala, 148
  Nicaragua, 35
  Panama, 35, 102, 104
  Paraguay, 35, 94, 100
  Peru, 35, 157–160, 162
  Venezuela, 35
Oviedo, Lino, 94, 96, 98

PAC (Partido Acción Ciudadana, Citizen Action Party, Costa Rica), 63, 179–180, 182, 191, 197
PAC (Partido AntiCorrupción, AntiCorruption Party, Honduras), 93
Pachakutik Plurinational Unity Movement/New Country, MUPP-NP, Ecuador (Movimiento de Unidad Plurinacional Pachakutik/Nuevo País), 167, 170, 171
Pacheco, Abel, 180–181
Palacio, Alfredo, 173
PAN (Partido Acción Nacional, National Action Party, Mexico), 50, 80–86, 105, 195
PAN (Partido de Avanzada Nacional, Party of National Advancement, Guatemala), 143, 145
PANAL (Partido Nueva Alianza, New Alliance Party, Mexico), 84
Panama, 11, 100–104
  1989 election, 17
  1994 election, 34, 66, 102, 196
  1999 and 2004 elections, 103, 196
  2009 election, 103–104
  authoritarian action committed by political parties in, 51, 52*t*
  cartel parties in, 101
  corruption in, 104
  economic conditions in, 100–101, 104
  elections won with less than 50% of the vote (1978–2012), likely result of runoff, 255*t*
  favorable democratic trajectory in, 100–101, 194
  free and fair elections in, year of commencing in, 17
  Freedom House and V-Dem scores, 100
  historical context for political parties in, 101–102, 196
  incumbent blocked from re-election in, 56
  legislative elections concurrent with presidential elections in, 200
  legislative majorities of president's party in, 217*t*
  new parties in, 260*t*
  no duopoly in, 101
  no leftist party in, 100, 104, 196
  no legitimacy deficit in, 103
  number of parties in, 100, 196
  old-timer presidential candidates in, 250*t*
  outsider candidates in, 35, 102, 104
  PELA surveys, 100, 101, 104
  as plurality country, 2, 9, 65, 100, 194, 196
  pre-election opinion polls, accuracy of, 227*t*, 239–240*t*
  runoff considered as option in, 2–3, 196
Panameñista Party, PP, Panama (Partido Panameñista). *See* Arnulfista Party (Panama)
Papa Egoró Movement, Panama (Movimiento Papa Egoró), 102
Paraguay, 11, 93–100
  1989 election, 18
  1993 election, 34, 66, 95–96, 195
  1998 election, 96–97
  2003 election, 66, 97
  2008 election, 34, 54, 66, 97–100, 195, 196
  authoritarian action committed by political parties in, 51, 53*t*
  cartel parties in, 105, 196
  clientelism in, 95
  coup attempts in, 96, 99
  criticism of plurality elections in, 2, 263n6
  democracy level in, 93, 196
  disaffection of the public in, 105
  economic conditions in, 93, 94, 97
  election fraud and corruption in, 95–96
  elections won with less than 50% of the vote (1978–2012), likely result of runoff, 255*t*
  free and fair elections in, year of commencing in, 17
  Freedom House and V-Dem scores, 93, 97, 100, 194

Paraguay (Cont.)
  history of parties in, 48–51
  leftist parties in, 9
  legislative elections concurrent with presidential elections in, 200
  legislative majorities of president's party in, 218t
  legitimacy deficit in, 8
  new parties in, 260t
  old-timer presidential candidates in, 251t
  outsider candidates in, 35, 94, 100
  PELA surveys, 94, 95
  as plurality country, 2, 9, 65, 94, 104, 194, 263n2
  political parties in, 95
  pre-election opinion polls, accuracy of, 61, 227t, 240–241t
  runoff considered as option in, 94, 209, 210t
  term limits in, 56
  threshold for runoff favored in, 175
  voter turnout in, 194
Pardo Leal, Jaime, 151–152
Parliamentary regimes, 36–37
Partido Acción Ciudadana (Citizen Action Party, PAC, Costa Rica), 63, 179–180, 182, 191, 197
Partido Acción Nacional (National Action Party, PAN, Mexico), 50, 80–86, 105, 195
Partido Alternativa Socialdemócrata y Campesina (Social Democratic and Peasant Alternative Party, PASC, Mexico), 84
Partido AntiCorrupción (AntiCorruption Party, PAC, Honduras), 93
Partido Arnulfista. See Arnulfista Party (Panama)
Partido Colorado. See Colorado Party
Partido Comunista de Chile (Communist Party of Chile, PC), 125, 126, 129, 130, 198
Partido Conservador (Conservative Party, renamed Social Conservative Party, Colombia), 149, 150, 151–153, 196
Partido da Frente Liberal (Liberal Front, PFL, Brazil), 118
Partido da Social Democracia Brasileira (Party of Brazilian Social Democracy, PSDB, Brazil), 118, 120–123
Partido de Avanzada Nacional (Party of National Advancement, PAN, Guatemala), 143, 145
Partido de Conciliación Nacional (Party of National Conciliation, PCN, El Salvador), 132, 134
Partido de Innovación y Unidad (Innovation and Unity Party, PINU, Honduras), 88
Partido de la Liberación Dominicana (Party of Dominican Liberation, PLD), 9–10, 55, 62, 63, 113–117, 137
Partido de la Revolución Democrática (Party of the Democratic Revolution, PRD, Mexico), 81–86, 195
Partido Demócrata Cristiano (Christian Democratic Party, PDC, El Salvador), 132, 134, 135
Partido Demócrata Cristiano de Honduras (Christian Democratic Party of Honduras, PDC), 88
Partido Democrático Social (Social Democratic Party, PDS, Brazil), 118–119
Partido Demócrata Cristiano (Christian Democratic Party, PDC, Chile), 126–128
Partido de Renovação Nacional (Party of National Reconstruction, PRN, Brazil), 119
Partido do Movimento Democrático Brasileiro (Party of the Brazilian Democratic Movement, PMDB, Brazil), 119
Partido dos Trabalhadores (Workers' Party, PT, Brazil), 62–63, 118, 119, 122–123, 137, 164, 197
Partido Liberación Nacional (National Liberation Party, PLN, Costa Rica), 55, 178–182
Partido Liberal. See Liberal Party
Partido Liberal Constitucionalista (Liberal Constitutionalist Party, PLC, Nicaragua), 76–80
Partido Liberal de Honduras (Liberal Party, PLH). See Liberal Party (Honduras)
Partido Liberal Radical Auténtico (Authentic Radical Liberal Party, PLRA, Paraguay), 94–98
Partido Nacional. See National Party
Partido Nacional (National Party, Uruguay). See Blanco Party (Uruguay)
Partido Nueva Alianza (New Alliance Party, PANAL, Mexico), 84
Partido Panameñista (Panameñista Party, PP, Panama). See Arnulfista Party (Panama)
Partido Patriota (Patriotic Party, PP, Guatemala), 146, 147
Partido Popular Cristiano (Popular Christian Party, PPC, Peru), 158, 159
Partido por el Gobierno del Pueblo (Party for the Government of the People, PGP, Uruguay), 110
Partido por la Democracia (Party for Democracy, PPD, Chile), 126
Partido Reformista (Dominican Republic), 113
Partido Reformista Social Cristiano (Reformist Christian Social Party, PRSC, Dominican Republic), 113–116
Partido Revolucionario Democrático (Democratic Revolutionary Party, PRD, Panama), 100–101, 103, 196
Partido Revolucionario Dominicano (Dominican Revolutionary Party, PRD), 50, 113–117
Partido Revolucionario Institucional (Institutional Revolutionary Party, Mexico). See PRI
Partido Roldosista Ecuatoriano (Roldosista Party of Ecuador, PRE), 169, 172

Index

Partido Social Cristiano (Social Christian Party, PSC, Ecuador), 167–170
Partido Socialismo e Liberdade (Party of Socialism and Liberty, PSOL, Brazil), 123
Partido Socialista (Socialist Party, PS, Chile), 126, 198
Partido Socialista Brasiliero (Socialist Party of Brazil, PSB), 123
Partido Socialista Unido de Venezuela (United Socialist Party of Venezuela, PSUV), 74, 194, 199
Partido Sociedad Patriótica 21 de enero (Patriotic Society Party January 21, PSP, Ecuador), 172
Partido Unidad Social Cristiana (Social Christian Unity Party, PUSC, Costa Rica), 55, 178–182
Partido Unificación Democrática de Honduras (Party of Democratic Unification, PUD, Honduras), 87
Partido Verde (PV, Colombia). *See* Green Party (Colombia)
Party for Democracy, PPD, Chile (Partido por la Democracia), 126
Party for the Government of the People, PGP, Uruguay (Partido por el Gobierno del Pueblo), 110
Party of Brazilian Social Democracy, PSDB, Brazil (Partido da Social Democracia Brasileira), 118, 120–123
Party of Democratic Unification, PUD, Honduras (Partido Unificación Democrática de Honduras), 87
Party of Dominican Liberation, PLD (Partido de la Liberación Dominicana), 9–10, 55, 62, 63, 113–117, 137
Party of National Advancement, PAN, Guatemala (Partido de Avanzada Nacional), 143, 145
Party of National Conciliation, PCN, El Salvador (Partido de Conciliación Nacional), 132, 134
Party of National Reconstruction, PRN, Brazil (Partido de Renovação Nacional), 119
Party of Socialism and Liberty, PSOL, Brazil (Partido Socialismo e Liberdade), 123
Party of the Brazilian Democratic Movement, PMDB, Brazil (Partido do Movimiento Democrático Brasileiro), 119
Party of the Democratic Revolution, PRD, Mexico (Partido de la Revolución Democrática), 81–86, 195
Party of the U (Colombia), 155
PASC (Partido Alternativa Socialdemócrata y Campesina, Social Democratic and Peasant Alternative Party, Mexico), 84
Pastrana, Andrés, 152–154
Patria Para Todos (Homeland for All, PPT, Venezuela), 72
Patriotic Alliance for Change, APC, Paraguay (Alianza Patriótica para el Cambio), 98
Patriotic Party, PP, Guatemala (Partido Patriota), 146, 147
Patriotic Society Party January 21, PSP, Ecuador (Partido Sociedad Patriótica 21 de enero), 172
Patriotic Union, UP, Colombia (Unión Patriótica), 151–152
Patronage, 54–55, 68, 87, 94. *See also* Clientelism
Payne, Mark J., 13–14, 17, 18, 22
Paz, Rodrigo, 170
Paz y Paz, Claudia, 147
PC (Partido Comunista de Chile, Communist Party of Chile), 125, 126, 129, 130, 198
PCN (Partido de Conciliación Nacional, Party of National Conciliation, El Salvador), 132, 134
PDA (Polo Democrático Alternativo, Democratic Alternative Pole, Colombia), 149, 154, 155, 174, 197
PDC (Partido Demócrata Cristiano de Honduras, Christian Democratic Party of Honduras), 88
PDC (Partido Demócrata Cristiano, Christian Democratic Party, El Salvador), 132, 134, 135
PDC (Partido Demócrata Cristiano, Christian Democratic Party, Chile), 126–128
PDS (Partido Democrático Social, Social Democratic Party, Brazil), 118–119
Pease García, Henry, 156
PELA surveys, 9, 45, 51, 269n3, 269n17
  Argentina, 185, 189, 190
  Brazil, 107, 124
  Chile, 107, 126, 127, 129
  Colombia, 153, 154
  Costa Rica, 180, 181
  Dominican Republic, 107, 116, 117
  Ecuador, 170, 171, 172, 173
  El Salvador, 131, 132, 135
  Guatemala, 146, 147
  Honduras, 87, 88, 90, 93
  Mexico, 81–82
  Nicaragua, 76, 78
  Panama, 100, 101, 104
  Paraguay, 94, 95
  Peru, 159, 162, 163, 164
  Uruguay, 107, 109–111
  Venezuela, 70, 73
Peña Gómez, José Francisco, 114–116
Peña Nieto, Enrique, 85
Pérez, Carlos Andrés, 67, 69–70
Pérez Balladares, Ernesto, 102
Pérez de Cuellar, Javier, 161
Pérez Flores, Fidel I., 92
Pérez-Liñán, Aníbal, 3, 14, 17, 18, 21, 29, 42–43, 45
Pérez Molina, Otto, 142, 146–148

Perón, Isabel, 185
Perón, Juan, 32, 50, 185
Peronist Party (Argentina), 50, 51, 55, 176, 183–190, 191, 194, 199
Personalistic parties and campaigns, 6, 142, 159
Peru, 11, 156–165
  1962 election, 42
  1963 election, 158
  1980 election, 157–158
  1985 election, 58, 157, 158
  1990 and 1992 election, 156, 158–161
  1995 election, 161–162
  2000 election, 19, 40
  2001, 2006, and 2011 elections, 58, 156, 162–165, 199
  2006 election, 38, 157, 174
  2016 election, 156, 165, 177, 199
  autogolpes (self-coups) in, 39, 140, 156, 160–161, 198
  Condorcet winners in, 164
  coup following 1962 plurality election in, 1
  democracy levels in, 139, 156
  economic conditions in, 156, 158, 159, 163
  election fraud and corruption in, 160, 161–162
  elections won with less than 50% of the vote (1978–2012), likely result of runoff, 255t, 258t
  ethnic cacerismo in, 163
  executive–legislative conflict in, 140
  free and fair elections in, year of commencing in, 17
  Freedom House and V-Dem scores, 156, 196
  ideological moderation in, 157
  incumbent blocked from re-election in, 56, 157, 162
  legislative elections concurrent with presidential elections in, 200
  legislative majorities of president's party in, 218t, 224t
  legislative threshold of vote in, 201
  military coup (1962), 41
  new parties in, 260–261t
  number of parties in, 32, 157, 174, 198
  old-timer presidential candidates in, 251t
  ouster of Fujimori in, 20, 162
  outsider candidates in, 35, 157–160, 162
  PELA surveys, 159, 162, 163, 164
  political parties in, 157–158
  pre-election opinion polls, accuracy of, 227t, 241t
  qualified-plurality elections in, 157
  as runoff country, 2, 156–157, 174, 196, 209, 210t
  threshold for runoff favored in, 175
  voter turnout in, 36, 139, 156
Perú Posible (Peru Possible, PP), 162
Petkoff, Teodoro, 67, 71
Petro, Gustavo, 154

Petrobras (Brazil oil company), 124
PetroCaribe, 91
Pew Research Center poll on U.S. presidential election system, 203
Peynado, Jacinto, 115
PFL (Partido da Frente Liberal, Liberal Front, Brazil), 118
PGP (Partido por el Gobierno del Pueblo, Party for the Government of the People, Uruguay), 110
Piñera, Sebastián, 128–130, 137
Pinilla, Gustavo Rojas, 150
Pinochet, Augusto José Ramón, 124, 126, 128, 198
PINU (Partido de Innovación y Unidad, Innovation and Unity Party, Honduras), 88
PLC (Partido Liberal Constitucionalista, Liberal Constitutionalist Party, Nicaragua), 76–80
PLD (Partido de la Liberación Dominicana, Party of Dominican Liberation), 9–10, 55, 62, 63, 113–117, 137
PLN (Partido Liberación Nacional, National Liberation Party, Costa Rica), 55, 178–182
PLRA (Partido Liberal Radical Auténtico, Authentic Radical Liberal Party, Paraguay), 94–98
Plurality elections, 1–2, 11
  arguments in favor of, 3, 29–39, 198, 211, 211t
  criticism of, 2, 3
  defined, 1
  fraud suspected in, 4, 264n9
  global trends in use of, 2
  as inferior system for democracies, 193–196, 206–207
  Latin American countries using, 2, 16t (*see also* Honduras; Mexico; Panama; Paraguay; Venezuela)
  leading parties becoming entrenched and, 62–63, 62t
  leftist party candidates in, 46t, 47
  legislative majorities of president's party in, 216–219t
  new parties and, 4, 260t
  number of political parties and, 31, 31f, 34
  outsider candidates and, 34–35, 34t, 212, 212–213t (*see also* Outsider candidates)
  rightist party candidates in, 47, 48t
  shift to runoff system, 196
  strategic coordination required by opposition parties in, 4, 6, 59, 194
  voter fatigue and, 36
  voter turnout in, 194
  years of plurality, effect of, 23, 26t
PMDB (Partido do Movimiento Democrático Brasileiro, Party of the Brazilian Democratic Movement, Brazil), 119
Polarization in Latin American countries, 4, 51, 195
Polga-Hecimovich, John, 14

Political violence
  Colombia, 139, 148–149, 151–152, 154, 174
  Guatemala, 139, 141, 174
  Mexico, 85
Polo Democrático Alternativo (Democratic Alternative Pole, PDA, Colombia), 149, 154, 155, 174, 197
Popular Action, AP, Peru (Acción Popular), 157–159
Popular Christian Party, PPC, Peru (Partido Popular Cristiano), 158, 159
Popular Democracy, Ecuador (Democracia Popular), 167, 170–171
Portillo, Alfonso, 142, 145
Posada-Carbó, Eduardo, 150
Power, Timothy J., 13
PP (Panameñista Party, Partido Panameñista). See Arnulfista Party (Panama)
PP (Partido Patriota, Patriotic Party, Guatemala), 146, 147
PPC (Partido Popular Cristiano, Popular Christian Party, Peru), 158, 159
PPD (Partido por la Democracia, Party for Democracy, Chile), 126
PPT (Patria Para Todos, Homeland for All, Venezuela), 72
PRD (Partido de la Revolución Democrática, Party of the Democratic Revolution, Mexico), 81–86, 195
PRD (Partido Revolucionario Democrático, Democratic Revolutionary Party, Panama), 100–101, 103, 196
PRD (Partido Revolucionario Dominicano, Dominican Revolutionary Party), 50, 113–117
PRE (Partido Roldosista Ecuatoriano, Roldosista Party of Ecuador), 169, 172
Pre-election opinion polls, accuracy of, 4, 6, 8, 27, 59–61, 192
  Argentina, 190, 227t, 228–229t
  Brazil, 227t, 229t
  Chile, 60, 61, 227t, 230t
  Colombia, 61, 227, 230–231t
  Costa Rica, 227t, 231–232t
  Dominican Republic, 227t, 232–233t
  Ecuador, 61, 227t, 234–235t
  El Salvador, 227t, 235–236t
  Europe, 59, 60t, 244–245t
  Guatemala, 227t, 236–237t
  Honduras, 227t, 237–238t
  Latin America, 59, 60t, 226, 227–244t
  Mexico, 83, 85–86, 227t, 238t
  Nicaragua, 227t, 238–239t
  Paraguay, 61, 227t, 240–241t
  Peru, 227t, 241t
  United States, 60–61, 60t, 203
  Uruguay, 60, 227t, 242t
  Venezuela, 227t, 242–243t

Presidential-election rule, 2, 14–17, 16t, 23, 24–25t
Presidential legitimacy. See Legitimacy
PRI (Partido Revolucionario Institucional, Institutional Revolutionary Party, Mexico), 18, 51, 54, 55, 59, 66, 80–86, 105, 194, 195, 199
Primero Colombia (Colombia First), 154
Primero Justicia (Justice First, Venezuela), 74
PRN (Partido de Renovação Nacional, Party of National Reconstruction, Brazil), 119
Progressive Encounter, EP, Uruguay (Encuentro Progresista), 110
Proyecto Elites Parlamentarias de América Latina (Parliamentary Elites of Latin American Project). See PELA surveys
PRSC (Partido Reformista Social Cristiano, Reformist Christian Social Party, Dominican Republic), 113–116
PS (Partido Socialista, Socialist Party, Chile), 126, 198
PSB (Partido Socialista Brasiliero, Socialist Party of Brazil), 123
PSC (Partido Social Cristiano, Social Christian Party, Ecuador), 167–170
PSDB (Partido da Social Democracia Brasileira, Party of Brazilian Social Democracy, Brazil), 118, 120–123
PSOL (Partido Socialismo e Liberdade, Party of Socialism and Liberty, Brazil), 123
PSP (Partido Sociedad Patriótica 21 de enero, Patriotic Society Party January 21, Ecuador), 172
PSUV (Partido Socialista Unido de Venezuela, United Socialist Party of Venezuela), 74, 194, 199
PT (Partido dos Trabalhadores, Workers' Party, Brazil), 62–63, 118, 119, 122–123, 137, 164, 197
PUD (Partido Unificación Democrática de Honduras, Party of Democratic Unification, Honduras), 87
PUSC (Partido Unidad Social Cristiana, Social Christian Unity Party, Costa Rica), 55, 178–182
PV (Partido Verde, Colombia). See Green Party (Colombia)

Quadros, Jânio, 41
Qualified plurality, 2
  defined, 15
  Latin American countries using, 16t (see also Nicaragua)
Qualified runoffs
  defined, 15
  Latin American countries using, 16t, 174 (see also Argentina; Bolivia; Costa Rica; Ecuador)

Quealy, Kevin, 61
Quebral, Alicia, 14
Quijano, Norman, 136

Radical Cause, Venezuela (La Causa Radical), 70–71, 72
Radical Party, UCR, Argentina (Unión Cívica Radical), 183–190
Ranked-choice voting, 7, 192, 205–206
Reformist Christian Social Party, PRSC, Dominican Republic (Partido Reformista Social Cristiano), 113–116
Reid, Michael, 150, 184
Reina, Carlos Roberto, 90
Renovación Nacional (National Renovation, RN, Chile), 126, 129
Republican Party (U.S.), 203
Research design and quantitative analysis, 10, 12–28
  effective number of political parties (ENPP), 22, 23, 24–26*t*
  free and fair elections in dataset, 17–19
  GDP growth and, 23, 24–26*t*
  institutional factors, 22
  level of democracy as dependent variable, 12–14
  presidential-election rule as independent variable, 2, 14–17, 16*t*, 24–25*t*
  socioeconomic factors, 21–22, 24*t*
  sources for other cited data and information, 27–28
  statistical analysis and results, 21–27
  surveys among Latin American legislators, 2, 209–211, 210–211*t*
  trends in levels of democracy, 19–21
  voter turnout, 23, 25*t*
Resistencia Nacional (National Resistance, RN, El Salvador), 134
Reyes, Carlos Humberto, 92
Rightist parties
  plurality vs. runoff elections, candidates in, 47, 48*t*
  runoff elections and, 8
Ríos Montt, Eraín, 141–147
Riquelme, Marcial, 18
Rizo, José, 263n6
RN (Renovación Nacional, National Renovation, Chile), 126, 129
RN (Resistencia Nacional, National Resistance, El Salvador), 134
Robinson, James A., 4
Rodríguez, Abraham, 134
Rodríguez, Andrés, 95
Rodríguez Echeverría, Miguel Angel, 178, 180–181
Rojas Pinilla, Gustavo, 150
Roldosista Party of Ecuador, PRE (Partido Roldosista Ecuatoriano), 169, 172

Roldós, Jaime, 9, 168, 197
Roldós, Leon, 172
Romero, Carlos, 67
Romero, Oscar, 132
Ropp, Steve C., 101
Rosales, Manuel, 67, 73, 263n6
Rousseff, Dilma, 123–124
Ruhl, J. Mark, 88, 92
Ruiz Rodríguez, Leticia, 41
Runoff elections, 10, 11, 106–107
  alliances formed for, 37–39
  arguments in favor of, 3, 39–47, 207, 210, 210*t*
  criticisms of, 3, 34, 198
  defined, 2
  for elections won with less than 50% of the vote (1978–2012), likely result of runoff, 8, 253–258*t*
  first-round winner as loser in, 197
  first-round winner as victor in, 42–43, 43*t*, 177
  global trends in use of, 2
  ideological moderation and, 3, 8, 44–47
  Latin American countries using majority runoff system, 2, 16*t*, 196 (*see also* Brazil; Chile; Colombia; Dominican Republic; El Salvador; Guatemala; Peru; Uruguay)
  leading parties, stability in, 62–63, 63*t*
  leftist party candidates in, 46*t*, 47
  legislative majorities of president's party in, 219–225*t*
  legitimacy of winner in, 3, 7–8, 39–44, 193
  majority runoff countries, 16*t*, 199
  new parties and, 4–7, 261*t*
  number of political parties in, 31–32, 31*f*, 193, 207
  outsider candidates and, 34–35, 34*t*, 212, 213–214*t* (*see also* Outsider candidates)
  qualified runoff countries, 16*t*, 175
  with a reduced threshold, 15, 175, 199
  reversal of first-round winner in, 8, 43, 43*t*, 177
  rightist party candidates in, 47, 48*t*
  as superior system for democracies, 3, 29–64, 193–194, 196–199, 206
  voter fatigue and, 36
  voter strategy in first round prior to, 30
  years of runoff, effect of, 23

Saca, Elías Antonio ("Tony"), 35, 135–136, 137, 198
Sáez, Irene, 72
Salamanca, Luis, 67
Salas Römer, Henrique, 72
Samper, Ernesto, 152–153
Sanborn, Cynthia, 158
Sánchez, Francisco, 160
Sánchez Cerén, Salvador, 132, 136, 177, 197, 198
Sandinista National Liberation Front, FSLN, Nicaragua (Frente Sandinista de Liberación Nacional), 51, 55, 75–80, 194, 195, 199

Sandinista Renovation Movement, MRS, Nicaragua (Movimiento Renovador Sandinista), 77
Sandoval, Mario, 143–144
Sanguinetti, Julio María, 109
Sanín, Noemí, 153
Santos, Elvin, 92
Santos, Juan Manuel, 150, 155–156
Sarney, José, 118
Sarria, Nidya, 16
Schmidt, Gregory D., 164, 269n17
Scioli, Daniel, 191, 197
Self-coups. See Autogolpes
Seligson, Mitchell A., 40, 141, 142
Semana (Colombian newsweekly), 41
Sendero Luminoso. See Shining Path guerrillas
Seregni, Líber, 58, 109
Serpa, Horacio, 153–154
Serrano, Jorge, 35, 39, 139, 141–145, 174, 197
Shining Path (Sendero Luminoso) guerrillas (Peru), 158–161, 164
Shugart, Matthew S., 3, 30, 31
Silva, Héctor, 134–135
Silva, Marina, 5, 118, 123, 137, 155
Similox, Vitalino, 146
Smith, William, 70
Social Christian Party, PSC, Ecuador (Partido Social Cristiano), 167–170
Social Christian Unity Party, PUSC, Costa Rica (Partido Unidad Social Cristiana), 55, 178–182
Social Conservative Party (Partido Conservador, formerly Conservative Party, Colombia), 149, 150, 151–153, 196
Social Democratic and Peasant Alternative Party, PASC, Mexico (Partido Alternativa Socialdemócrata y Campesina), 84
Social Democratic Party, PDS, Brazil (Partido Democrático Social), 118–119
Socialist Left, IS, Peru (Izquierda Socialista), 159
Socialist Party, PS, Chile (Partido Socialista), 126, 198
Socialist Party of Brazil, PSB (Partido Socialista Brasiliero), 123
Social protest and legitimacy of election outcome, 40
Solidarity Action Movement, MAS, Guatemala (Movimiento de Acción Solidaria), 143
Solís, Ottón, 5, 58, 180–183, 197
Somoza governments and family dynasty, 48, 75, 76
Sondrol, Paul, 18
Stokes, Susan, 161
Stroessner, Alfredo, 18, 95, 96
Strongmen. See Caudillismo
Su, Yen-Pin, 14
Suazo, Roberto, 90

Suger, Eduardo, 147

Taagepera, Rein, 22, 27
Tanaka, Martín, 3, 30, 156, 160, 175
Taylor-Robinson, Michelle, 54, 87, 88
Teorell, Jan, 13
Term limits
　Argentina, 57, 184
　Brazil, 57
　Chile, 56
　Costa Rica, 56, 179
　Dominican Republic, 116
　Ecuador, 167
　El Salvador, 56
　Guatemala, 56
　Honduras, 56
　Mexico, 56
　Panama, 56
　Paraguay, 56
　Peru, 56, 157, 162
　Uruguay, 56
Third democratic wave
　alternatives to plurality elections and, 1–2
　authoritarian right and, 8
　debt crisis and, 5
　democratic breakdown in, 36
　elections won with 41% or less in, 34
　leftist leaders and, 4
　number of parties and, 33
　parties winning first election in, 48–50, 49t
　party stability since founding in, 62
　in plurality countries, 65
　virtuous circle in, 3–4, 193, 206
Threshold for party in legislative elections, 200
Threshold for runoff, 15, 175
　legitimacy, 40% threshold for, 175, 264n2 (Ch. 2)
　reduced threshold, risks of, 191
　reduced threshold as remedy to proliferation of parties, 199
Together We Can Do More, Chile (Juntos Podemos Más), 129
Toledo, Alejandro, 35, 38, 40, 162–164, 264n6
Torres, Sandra, 148
Torres-Rivas, Edelberto, 141
Torrijos, Omar, 101, 103
Trudeau, Robert H., 144
Trujillo, Rafael Leónidas, 113
Trump, Donald, 203
Tuesta, Fernando, 156
Tupamaros (Uruguay), 109
Turbay Ayala, Julio César, 151

UCeDé (Unión del Centro Democrático, Union of the Democratic Center, Argentina), 186
UCN (Unión del Centro Nacional, National Union of the Center, Guatemala), 143

UCR (Unión Cívica Radical (Radical Party, Argentina), 183–190
UDI (Unión Demócrata Independiente, Democratic Independent Union, Chile), 62, 126, 128
UN (Unidad Nacional, National Unity, Peru), 162
UNACE (Unión Nacional de Colorados Éticos, National Union of Ethical Colorados, Paraguay), 97–99
UNE (Unidad Nacional de la Esperanza, National Unity for Hope, Guatemala), 146, 148, 197
Unidad Nacional (National Unity, UN, Peru), 162
Unidad Nacional de la Esperanza (National Unity for Hope, UNE, Guatemala), 146, 148, 197
Unidad Revolucionaria Nacional Guatemalteca (Guatemalan National Revolutionary Union, URNG), 141, 143, 146, 174
Unión del Centro Democrático (Union of the Democratic Center, UCeDé, Argentina), 186
Unión del Centro Nacional (National Union of the Center, UCN, Guatemala), 143
Unión Demócrata Independiente (Democratic Independent Union, UDI, Chile), 62, 126, 128
Union for Peru, UPP, Peru (Unión por el Perú), 161
Unión Nacional de Colorados Éticos, National Union of Ethical Colorados, Paraguay (UNACE), 97–99
Unión Nacional Opositora (National Opposition Union, UNO, Nicaragua), 75–76
Union of the Center-Center, Chile (Unión de Centro-Centro), 127
Union of the Democratic Center, UCeDé, Argentina (Unión del Centro Democrático), 186
Unión Patriótica (Patriotic Union, UP, Colombia), 151–152
Unión Republicana Democrática (Democratic Republican Union, URD, Venezuela), 68
United Left, IU, Peru (Izquierda Unida), 158, 159
United Nations Truth Commission, 141
United Socialist Party of Venezuela, PSUV (Partido Socialista Unido de Venezuela), 74, 194, 199
United States
  2016 election, 203
  anachronistic electoral rules in, 192, 201
  citizen dissatisfaction government of, 202
  Electoral-College reform, 204
  gerrymandering in, 202
  legitimacy deficit in, 203
  old-timer advantage in, 203
  polarization of political parties in, 202
  popular vote vs. Electoral College, 11, 201–203
  pre-election opinion polls, accuracy of (2000–2012), 60–61, 60t
  presidents who lose popular vote, legitimacy of, 7, 203
  primary voter turnout in, 202
  proposals to change from present system of presidential elections in, 201, 204–206
  ranked-choice voting as option for, 205–206
  runoff approach, proposals of, 204
  third-party spoilers in, 203
  top-two primary, state adoption of, 205
Unión Cívica Radical (Radical Party, UCR, Argentina), 183–190
Unión de Centro-Centro (Union of the Center-Center, Chile), 127
Unión Demócrata Independiente (Democratic Independent Union, UDI, Chile), 62
Unión por el Perú (Union for Peru, UPP, Peru), 161
UNO (Unión Nacional Opositora, National Opposition Union, Nicaragua), 75–76
UP (Unión Patriótica, Patriotic Union, Colombia), 151–152
UPP (Unión por el Perú, Union for Peru, Peru), 161
URD (Unión Republicana Democrática, Democratic Republican Union, Venezuela), 68
Uribe, Álvaro, 149, 154–155
URNG (Unidad Revolucionaria Nacional Guatemalteca, Guatemalan National Revolutionary Union), 141, 143, 146, 174
Uruguay, 11, 107–112
  1971 election, 109
  1984–1994 plurality elections, 108–110
  1989 election, 34
  1994 election, 34
  1999 election, 106, 110, 136
  2004 election of moderate left, 111
  2009 runoff election and legitimacy advantage, 111–112
  2014 election, 112
  candidates running multiple times and losing in, 58
  cartel parties in, 54
  democracy level in, 106, 107, 136
  double simultaneous vote (DSV) rule in, 108–109
  duopoly in, 196
  economic conditions in, 108, 109, 111
  elections won with less than 50% of the vote (1978–2012), likely result of runoff, 255t, 258t
  free and fair elections in, year of commencing in, 17
  Freedom House and V-Dem scores, 106, 107, 112, 196
  incumbent blocked from re-election in, 56
  legislative elections concurrent with presidential elections in, 200
  legislative majorities of president's party in, 218t, 225t
  military rule in, 109

moderate left president elected in, 107, 111
new parties in, 260–261t
number of parties in, 32, 107, 108, 137, 198
old-timer presidential candidates in, 251t
PELA surveys, 107, 109–111
as plurality country, 1, 20, 108–110, 196
political parties in, 50, 108–110
pre-election opinion polls, accuracy of, 60, 227t, 242t
as runoff country, 106, 108, 196
Tupamaro guerrillas in, 110, 111
voter turnout in, 36, 106, 107, 268n1

Vaishnav, Milan, 44, 45, 169, 170, 179
Valenzuela, Arturo, 3, 29, 31, 37
Vallarino, Alberto, 35, 103
Van Dyck, Brandon, 259
Varela, Juan Carlos, 104
Vargas, Guillermo Caballero, 35
Vargas, Getúlio, 41
Vargas Llosa, Mario, 35, 158–160, 164, 197
Varieties of Democracy (V-Dem) scores. *See* Freedom House and V-Dem scores
Vázquez, Tabaré, 9, 109–112, 137, 197
Vázquez Mota, Josefina, 85
Velasco Ibarra, José María, 167
Velásquez, Andrés, 58, 70, 266n7
Venezuela, 11, 66–74
    1968 election, 58
    1978–1988 Punto Fijo democracy, 68–70
    1983 election, 58
    1993 election, 34, 58, 65, 66, 70–71, 195
    1998 election, 20, 67, 72, 195
    2000 election, 73
    2006 election, 73
    2012 election, 73–74
    Carmona Decree, 73, 74
    cartel parties in, 66, 69
    corruption in, 70, 71, 73
    coup attempts, 69–70, 73
    criticism of plurality elections in, 2, 195, 263n6
    debt crisis and lost decade in, 5, 69
    democracy's decline in, 10, 65, 66–67, 70
    duopoly, end of, 104, 194, 195
    economic conditions in, 68–69, 71, 73, 104
    elections won with less than 50% of the vote (1978–2012), likely result of runoff, 255t
    free and fair elections in, year of commencing in, 17
    Freedom House and V-Dem scores, 66–67, 194
    leftist parties in, 9, 68–69
    legislative majorities of president's party in, 219t
    legitimacy deficit in, 8, 66, 70, 195
    new parties in, 260t
    number of parties in, 33
    oil prices in, 27, 68, 73
    old-timer presidential candidates in, 251t
    outsider candidates in, 35
    Pact of Punto Fijo (1958), 68
    PELA surveys, 70, 73
    as plurality country, 2, 9, 65, 104, 194
    pre-election opinion polls, accuracy of, 227t, 242–243t
    runoff considered as option in, 67, 71, 74, 210t
    voluntary voting in, 13
    voter turnout in, 21, 73, 194
Vicious circle, 9, 104, 195
Villalba, Jóvito, 68
Villalobos, Joaquín, 134
Villalta, José María, 182
Villanueva, Armando, 158
Virtuous circle, 3–4, 193, 206
Volonté, Alberto, 109–110
Voluntary voting, 13, 148
Voter fatigue, 36
Voter turnout, 10, 13–14, 21, 21f, 23, 25t, 36. *See also* Compulsory voting
    Brazil, 36, 106
    Chile, 21, 36, 106, 268n1
    Colombia, 36, 139, 148–149
    Costa Rica, 36, 177, 180
    Dominican Republic, 36, 106
    Ecuador, 36, 139, 165
    El Salvador, 21, 36, 106, 131
    Guatemala, 21, 36, 139, 141
    Honduras, 21, 65, 86, 194
    legitimacy of election outcome and, 40
    Mexico, 80, 194
    Paraguay, 194
    Peru, 36, 139, 156
    in plurality countries, 65
    Uruguay, 36, 106, 107, 268n1
    Venezuela, 21, 73, 194

Wallace, George, 204
Wasmosy, Juan Carlos, 96, 195
Win Peru (Gana Perú), 63, 163
Wolff, Antonio Navarro, 35
Workers' Party (Partido dos Trabalhadores, PT, Brazil), 62–63, 118, 119, 122–123, 137, 164, 197
World Bank, 45
Wynia, Gary W., 42

Yepes, José Antonio Gil, 67
Yo Soy 132 (anti–Peña Nieto movement, Mexico), 85

Zamora, Rubén, 133–134
Zelaya, Manuel, 10, 86, 87, 91–93, 105, 195–196
Zovatto G., Daniel, 13–14, 17, 18, 22
Zuluaga, Óscar Iván, 155–156, 197